The Arab Spring

This volume provides a wealth of in-depth, country-specific analyses of the Arab Spring, in addition to works that examine the larger theoretical framework and socio-political implications of events. Unlike other analyses, often from the perspective of Western scholarship from the outside looking in, the articles here are drawn primarily from within the Arab world and are authored mainly by Arab experts and scholars with intimate, first-hand knowledge and direct experience of their subject matter and the particular countries on which they focus. The studies and readings included here deal with the countries affected directly by the Arab Spring in addition to ones that focus on meta-trends in the Arab world: the unprecedented mass movements and attendant phenomena, from the mass mobilizations of social media to the effectiveness of non-violent resistance. The volume provides a wealth of insider information as well as valuable analytical tools and models for understanding the Arab Spring.

This book was published as a special issue of *Contemporary Arab Affairs*.

Khair El-Din Haseeb is the founding Director of the Centre of Arab Unity Studies in Beirut and currently the Chairman of its Board of Trustees and Executive Committee. He has played a highly active and influential role in Arab nationalist concerns and initiatives since the 1970s. From 1976 to 1984, he served as Chief of the Natural Resources Science and Technology Division of the United Nations' Economic Commission of Western Asia. Previous to that he was Professor of Economics at the University of Baghdad and he served as Governor and Chairman of the Board of the Central Bank of Iraq from 1963 to 1965. He is the author of numerous books and articles in both Arabic and English including *The Future of the Arab Nation* (Routledge, 1991), *Arab-Iranian Relations* (British Academic Press, 1998) and *The Arabs and Africa* (Croom Helm, 1985).

The Arab Spring

Critical Analyses

Edited by
Khair El-Din Haseeb

Routledge
Taylor & Francis Group
LONDON AND NEW YORK

مركز دراسات الوحدة العربية
CENTRE FOR ARAB UNITY STUDIES

First published 2013
by Routledge
2 Park Square, Milton Park, Abingdon, Oxfordshire OX14 4RN

Simultaneously published in the USA and Canada
by Routledge
711 Third Avenue, New York, NY 10017

First issued in paperback 2014

Routledge is an imprint of the Taylor & Francis Group, an informa business

This book is a reproduction of articles from various issues in Contemporary Arab Affairs. The Publisher requests to those authors who may be citing this book to state, also, the bibliographical details of the special issue on which the book was based.

British Library Cataloguing in Publication Data

A catalogue record for this book is available from the British Library

ISBN 13: 978-0-415-81036-4 (hbk)
ISBN 13: 978-0-415-72309-1 (pbk)

Typeset in Times New Roman
by Cenveo Publisher Services

Publisher's Note
The publisher would like to make readers aware that the chapters in this book may be referred to as articles as they are identical to the articles published in the special issue. The publisher accepts responsibility for any inconsistencies that may have arisen in the course of preparing this volume for print.

Contents

Citation Information vii

1. Introduction 1
   Khair El-Din Haseeb

2. The Arab Spring Revisited 4
   Khair El-Din Haseeb

3. The Arab revolutions; the emergence of a new political subjectivity 17
   Sari Hanafi

4. The socio-economic factors behind the Arab revolutions 33
   Georges Corm

5. The 'Arab Spring': breaking the chains of authoritarianism and postponed democracy 50
   Mohammed Noureddine Affaya

6. War of Creative Destruction: the central tendency in the globalized Arab revolutions (a study in the formation of the future) 71
   Fatḥī al-ʿAfīfī

7. The revolutions of the Arab Spring: are democracy, development and modernity at the gates? 92
   Michael Sakbani

8. On the Arab 'Democratic Spring': lessons derived 113
   Khair El-Din Haseeb

9. Post-Gadhafi Libya: Interactive Dynamics and the Political Future 123
   Youssef M. Sawani

10. Libya … hopes and fears 153
    Khair El-Din Haseeb

11. Syria … the road to where? 159
    Michel Kilo

12. Morocco and democratic transition: a reading of the constitutional amendments – their contexts and results 173
    Abdelilah Belkeziz

13. Political Islam in Morocco: negotiating the Kingdom's liberal space 200
Emanuela Delmasso and Francesco Cavatorta

14. Copts in Egypt and their demands: between inclusion and exclusion 217
Mai Mogib

15. 'Suleiman: Mubarak decided to step down #egypt #jan25 OH MY GOD': examining the use of social media in the 2011 Egyptian revolution 238
Genevieve Barrons

16. Egypt's Muslim Brotherhood and the January 25 Revolution: new political party, new circumstances 252
Mona Farag

17. Repercussions of the Arab movements for democracy on the Saudi street 268
Mohammed Iben Sunitan

18. Repercussions of the Arab movements for democracy in Bahrain 276
Ali Mohammed Fakhro

19. Palestinian youth and the Arab Spring. Learning to think critically: a case study 282
Nadia Nasser-Najjab

20. The 'end of pan-Arabism' revisited: reflections on the Arab Spring 295
Youssef Mohamed Sawani

Index 311

Citation Information

The following chapters were originally published in *Contemporary Arab Affairs*. When citing this material, please use the original page numbering for each article, as follows:

Chapter 2
The Arab Spring Revisited
Khair El-Din Haseeb
Contemporary Arab Affairs, volume 5, issue 2 (April 2012) pp. 185–197

Chapter 3
The Arab revolutions; the emergence of a new political subjectivity
Sari Hanafi
Contemporary Arab Affairs, volume 5, issue 2 (April 2012) pp. 198–213

Chapter 4
The socio-economic factors behind the Arab revolutions
Georges Corm
Contemporary Arab Affairs, volume 5, issue 3 (July-September 2012) pp. 355–371

Chapter 5
The 'Arab Spring': breaking the chains of authoritarianism and postponed democracy
Mohammed Noureddine Affaya
Contemporary Arab Affairs, volume 4, issue 4 (October 2011) pp. 463–483

Chapter 6
War of Creative Destruction: the central tendency in the globalized Arab revolutions (a study in the formation of the future)
Fatḥī al-ʿAfīfī
Contemporary Arab Affairs, volume 5, issue 3 (July-September 2012) pp. 427–447

Chapter 7
The revolutions of the Arab Spring: are democracy, development and modernity at the gates?
Michael Sakbani
Contemporary Arab Affairs, volume 4, issue 2 (April-June 2011) pp. 127–147

Chapter 8
On the Arab 'Democratic Spring': lessons derived
Khair El-Din Haseeb
Contemporary Arab Affairs, volume 4, issue 2 (April-June 2011) pp. 113–122

Chapter 10
Libya...hopes and fears
Khair El-Din Haseeb
Contemporary Arab Affairs, volume 4, issue 4 (October 2011) pp. 425–430

Chapter 11
Syria ... the road to where?
Michel Kilo
Contemporary Arab Affairs, volume 4, issue 4 (October 2011) pp. 431–444

Chapter 12
Morocco and democratic transition: a reading of the constitutional amendments – their contexts and results
Abdelilah Belkeziz
Contemporary Arab Affairs, volume 5, issue 1 (January-March 2012) pp. 27–53

Chapter 13
Political Islam in Morocco: negotiating the Kingdom's liberal space
Emanuela Delmasso and Francesco Cavatorta
Contemporary Arab Affairs, volume 4, issue 4 (October 2011) pp. 484–500

Chapter 15
Suleiman: Mubarak decided to step down #egypt #jan25 OH MY GOD': examining the use of social media in the 2011 Egyptian revolution
Genevieve Barrons
Contemporary Arab Affairs, volume 5, issue 1 (January-March 2012) pp. 54–67

Chapter 16
Egypt's Muslim Brotherhood and the January 25 Revolution: new political party, new circumstances
Mona Farag
Contemporary Arab Affairs, volume 5, issue 2 (April 2012) pp. 214–229

Chapter 17
Repercussions of the Arab movements for democracy on the Saudi street
Mohammed Iben Sunitan
Contemporary Arab Affairs, volume 4, issue 4 (October 2011) pp. 501–509

Chapter 18
Repercussions of the Arab movements for democracy in Bahrain
Ali Mohammed Fakhro
Contemporary Arab Affairs, volume 4, issue 4 (October 2011) pp. 518–523

Chapter 19
Palestinian youth and the Arab Spring. Learning to think critically: a case study
Nadia Nasser-Najjab
Contemporary Arab Affairs, volume 5, issue 2 (April 2012) pp. 279–291

Chapter 20
The 'end of pan-Arabism' revisited: reflections on the Arab Spring
Youssef Mohamed Sawani
Contemporary Arab Affairs, volume 5, issue 3 (July-September 2012) pp. 382–397

Introduction

Khair El-Din Haseeb

This book, through a collection of articles, tries to shed light on a number of relevant questions about what happened during the last two years in certain Arab countries. Questions such as: Why we call it Arab Spring and not Revolutions? Why did it happen when it did and not before that, although the reasons for such uprisings existed long before it happened? Why it happened in certain Arab countries and not others, although the same justifications existed in those 'others? To what extent foreign powers were aware and instrumental in all or any of them? What was the role of the Arab and foreign media in instigating such uprisings? These and other less important questions are what these papers try to answer, not only to help in understanding what happened, but also to expect what might happen elsewhere in other Arab countries.

To start with, we called these events and grouped them as 'Arab Spring' and not 'Arab Revolutions' because a Revolution implies major political, social, economic and cultural changes, much more comprehensive and drastic than what happened so far in Tunisia, Egypt, Libya and Yemen, regardless of the intentions of those who carried out those uprisings. The term 'Spring', we believe, is more relevant, since it usually involves a number of contradictory events: Sunny and rainy days; quietness and thunderstorms, as well as other contradictory phenomena. This is what is happening so far in these Arab countries regardless of the intentions of the people who initiated and carried out these uprisings. Some managed to change the political system, which is great in itself, but not enough to call them Revolutions. Some of them might or can develop later into a Revolution, but not yet, so we might call some of them 'Possible or Attempted Revolution' or 'Uprisings' or 'Rebellion'.

As to the question of whether the reasons and justifications for such uprisings existed before, and if so, then why they did not happen before, this is a relevant and important question to address. The justifications for such uprisings existed before in many Arab countries, but it was the 'Barrier of Fear' which prevented people to move en masse to the street to take their future into their own hands. The miracle happened in Tunisia, when Abu Azizi set fire to himself defending his dignity, that ignited the uprising and drove people to the street regardless of police attempts to put it down. Tunisians managed to quell and destroy 'The Barrier of Fear' that quickly enhanced people in Egypt, Yemen, Libya, Bahrain, Oman, Syria and Jordan, so far, to do the same.

The question then arises of why some of these uprisings succeeded in toppling dictatorial regimes, and why others did not fully succeed yet or partially succeeded in doing so? It is a relevant though confusing question which needs to be addressed. There are four factors as prerequisites which need to be available, if these uprisings were to succeed in toppling regimes as a first step. These are: breaking the barrier of fear; a homogeneous population; non-violent resistance and uprisings; and the neutrality at least of the armed forces if not siding with the uprisings. These four factors were available in Tunisia and Egypt, but not Libya where the Atlantic Alliance intervened, with the help of a Security Council Resolution, on the side of the uprising and was instrumental in overcoming and defeating Qadhafi forces, and which resulted in different outcomes than those in Tunisia and Egypt. In Yemen, the neutrality of the army was not available and the uprising ended in a compromise solution. In Syria, with the exception of breaking the barrier of fear, the rest of the four factors were and are still not available and so the uprising is still dwindling. So was the case in Bahrain, Oman and Jordan so far.

As to the role of 'foreign powers', if any, in instigating these uprisings in Tunisia and Egypt, one can fairly say that initially they had no such role in at least Tunisia and Egypt, although they tried later on, after the initial success of these two uprisings to set foot in them with different degrees of success so far. However, the role of foreign powers (particularly the Atlantic Alliance) was crucial in bringing down the regime in Libya. In Yemen the political intervention of the United States and Saudi Arabia, in addition to the negative role of most of the Yemeni army, forced the uprising there to accept a compromise solution and enabled president Ali Abdullah Salih to get away safely with all his crimes.

So the role of foreign powers in the uprisings differed; while they initially had no role in the cases of Tunisia and Egypt and thus the point is proved that drastic political changes in the region can sometimes be accomplished without, and sometimes in spite of, their will. However, the intervention of the foreign powers was nonetheless crucial in the case of Libya by bringing down the Qadhafi regime. The involvements of international powers in the support of the uprisings in Syria were there from the very beginning, although at different sides and the western powers could not, so far, force a regime change there.

In the case of Bahrain, the stand of the USA and other Western powers was more or less neutral, which enabled Saudi Arabia to intervene militarily on the regime's side and tilt the balance of the uprising, so far, in the regime's favour. So one can fairly say that the attitude of the Western Powers towards the Arab Spring was inconsistent and sometimes indecisive.

The roles and attitudes of many Arab regimes towards these uprisings were different and sometimes contradictory, in spite of the fact that the charter of the Arab League prohibits the interference of member countries in the internal affairs of each other. While Qatar was forceful, at least at the media level, in favour of the uprisings in Tunisia and Egypt, Qatar also provided arms and money to the uprising in Libya. Saudi Arabia and other Arab Gulf countries were quiet in these cases, with some opposing signs to the uprisings in them. Saudi Arabia provided ex-president Ibn Ali a safe refuge in it, and tried hard, but unsuccessfully, to save ex-president Mubarak of Egypt from indictment. However Arab Gulf countries, particularly Qatar and Saudi Arabia, took a completely different stand in the case of the uprising in Syria, as they are providing Syria's armed opposition with arms and money. They also kept quiet towards the uprisings in Bahrain, Oman and Jordan. As to the attitude of Algeria, she kept quiet towards uprisings elsewhere. Therefore, as was stated earlier, the stands of the different Arab countries varied considerably towards uprisings elsewhere in the Arab World and their stands were sometimes contradictory to the charter of the Arab League.

As to the role of the media in the success or failure of these uprisings, one cannot underestimate its role, but one can fairly say that it was not always instrumental in the success of uprisings, as is clearly the case in Syria, and the two main Arab television stations, Al Jazeera (under Qatar's influence) and Al-Arabiyah (under Saudi's influence) were inconsistent towards Arab Springs, and were sometimes inventing news rather than reporting them! As a result of that, they lost a lot of their credibility. The media bias was also evident in many of the Western media, though to a much lesser degree than the Arab media and was done in a more sophisticated way.

As to the future and what might happen in other Arab countries in the short and medium terms, that will depend on not only the extent of success of the uprisings of Egypt. Tunisia, Libya and Yemen, in crossing their transitional period successfully and achieving their main objectives, but also to what extent the regimes in those other Arab countries, who did not witness yet such uprisings, will adjust their political systems and introduce serious political and social reforms. At the present, they do not seem to be in that state of mind; on the contrary they seem to be counting on the failure of the new regimes where the uprisings took place rather than introducing the necessary and overdue political reforms needed in their countries. Time and history will have the answer for those rulers who are trying to move against history.

The Arab Spring Revisited*

Khair El-Din Haseeb

Editor-in-Chief, Contemporary Arab Affairs

In a March 2011 Editorial published in this journal (Haseeb 2011), I attempted to elucidate the primary lessons that might be drawn from the dramatic Arab social movements and changes transpiring at the time. Now, there would seem to be a need to revisit these events analytically in order to tender an explanation for the different developments and outcomes of the Arab Spring and to posit a hypothesis as to why some movements succeed in toppling regimes, as in Tunisia and Egypt, but not in others, notably Syria. My intention is also to explore the extent to which the model for settlement in Yemen might be applicable – with some variation or modification – elsewhere in the Arab region where uprisings have taken place or where they might conceivably occur in the future.

This analysis revolves around the coincidence of four component factors or catalysts for the uprisings, which *in conjunction* successfully brought about regime changes and major transformations in at least two Arab countries, and which could also serve as analytical criteria for assessing the potential for further civilian uprisings, as well as predictors for outcomes. I will endeavour to examine these in the context of the uprisings and revolutions, as well as the aftermaths of these, in a number of countries, including Tunisia, Egypt, Yemen, Libya, Syria and Bahrain – adding a few words about other Arab states and general reactions to the Arab Spring, which is still continuing.

Before defining the four factors or conditions that may be taken as objective analytical criteria for assessing the prospects of change, including the toppling of despots and dictatorial Arab regimes, it should be mentioned that, in terms of this analysis, they 'function' as a *set*, wherein the confluence and co-incidence of all four tends to correlate strongly with the potential of collective social action for change, whereas the absence of any one of these factors mitigates against such. First, there must initially be a breaking of the 'barrier of fear', where fear had previously constrained populations and had effectively dissuaded them from entertaining the possibility of revolt, despite ample grounds, grievances and justifications for doing so. Second, a revolt should be *non-violent* in nature, since it cannot rival the might of the regime anyway and resort to violence by the opposition will afford the regime in question legal justifications for utilizing whatever violent means necessary to suppress or quash the uprisings. Third, there should exist a sufficient threshold of social cohesion and shared sentiment for national unity among the people opposing a given regime, so that religious, confessional, sectarian or ethnic divisions – if they persist or prevail – do not fracture the population

*This Editorial was penned and completed before 5 March 2012.

and undermine the resistance. Fourth, and *crucially*, is the question of the stance of the 'army' or armed forces towards a civilian revolt. If the military is supportive or at least neutral, there is a much greater chance for success than if the army sides with the regime and inflicts heavy losses, an eventuality which consequently throws the outcomes of uprisings into doubt. Applying these four factors and criteria can facilitate one's understanding of the disparate outcomes of the Arab Spring, wherein there were some highly positive results, as in the cases of Tunisia and Egypt, but also many setbacks, as transpired in Libya, Syria, Yemen, Bahrain and Oman.

Tunisia: a model with four out of four factors

In Tunisia the four component factors were present. The produce peddler Muhammad Bouazizi's act of desperation – his self-immolation – galvanized Tunisians, impelled them to break the 'barrier of fear' and quite literally served as the 'spark' for the revolt. Demographically, Tunisia is highly homogeneous, where virtually all are Muslims belonging to the Mālkī *madhab*, and where the middle class is thought to constitute approximately 50% of the population. Participation in the revolution was broadly representative, including the educated, the trade unions and the youth. The uprisings began as non-violent ones and continued as such, despite some provocations. The Tunisian army, which is small and poorly equipped, remained neutral throughout the uprisings. Thus, the co-occurrence of the four aforementioned factors, it can be argued, conjoined to facilitate and bring about the ouster of the regime of former President Zayn al-'Abidin bin 'Ali and his flight to political asylum in Saudi Arabia.

In addition to their role in the success of the uprisings in Tunisia, the availability of the four component factors also facilitated transition in the subsequent post-revolution stage. Free and democratic elections for a Constitutional Assembly were carried out on 23 October 2011, a coalition government was formed and a temporary interim president was elected. A draft constitution is to be written by the assembly and will be submitted to a plebiscite along with a new election to elect a new parliament, both to take place within a year. Law and order was restored to a large extent; and the revolution is keeping its promises with regard to human rights and democratic practices to a great extent. As in the case of its revolution, Tunisia seems once again to be providing a model for the post-uprising transitional phase towards genuine democracy. The primary challenge in the post-revolution phase is in the economic sphere, where the combination of problems faced demands long-term solutions, as well as Arab and international economic and financial support, which is slow in coming.

Egypt: four out of four factors on a larger and more complex scale

In Egypt, it was the example of the Tunisian uprisings that emboldened Egyptians to break their own 'barrier of fear'. Religious and sectarian differences have never been pronounced or a serious matter of contention in modern Egypt, and therefore Muslim and Christian Egyptians alike joined the uprisings in Tahrir Square from the outset. Likewise, the protests were peaceful in spite of antagonism by the security forces. Unlike those forces loyal to President Hosni Mubarak, the Egyptian army initially remained neutral – refusing to put down the demonstrations by force – before subsequently siding with the revolt of the people. The confluence of these factors – as in the case of Tunisia, but albeit on a significantly greater scale of magnitude – served to topple the former President's regime in a mere seventeen days. The changes and their importance in Egypt, sometimes referred to in Arabic as *umm al-dunyā* (literally, 'mother of the world') are even more remarkable given the size of the country's population, the largest in the Arab world. If the Tunisian model suggested that the co-incidence of the four factors constituted a powerful force for change, the Egyptian model suggested this on a truly vast scale.

In the Egyptian transitional period, free elections for the national People's Assembly (*majlis al-shaʿb*) and the Consultative Council (*majlis al-shūrā*) took place, which are set to elect in the near future a 100 member council to draft a new constitution. A call for presidential candidates was announced in the expectation that elections for a new Egyptian president will take place in May 2012; and the Supreme Council of the Armed Forces (SCAF) is expected to hand over authority to the new president and the two houses of the national parliament.

The transitional period has not been smooth throughout – and this is, again, logical given the sheer size of the country; but temporary setbacks and obstacles seem to have been overcome. It is expected that the revolution may be on the verge of seeing a successful end to the particular challenges of this phase. There are, however, at least three major challenges that will confront the incumbent Egyptian government to be formed at the end of the transitional period in June 2012: (1) the challenge of extremist *salafist* Muslims organized in the al-Nūr Party, which secured 20% of the seats in elections for the People's Assembly; (2) the fate of the Egypt–Israel Treaty; and (3) the economic problem. Naturally, it remains to be seen to what extent the new regime will succeed in tackling these problems or what particular strategies it might adopt to these ends. Similarly, a key question is to what extent the new government will succeed in curtailing or ending the role of the Egyptian army in politics or in re-evaluating and redressing the matter of the economic privileges and various perks its officers acquired and enjoyed during Mubarak's tenure.

Yemen: three factors out of four and a Faustian bargain?

In Yemen, the masses successfully broke the barrier of fear in protests beginning initially in January 2011; and the uprisings involved a number of major cities; although a limited segment of the population in the capital of Sana'a backed President 'Ali 'Abdullah Saleh intermittently. The demonstrations, which included a number of theme-Fridays such as the 'Friday of Anger' on 18 February in Taiz, Sana'a and Aden, as well as the 'Friday of No Return' on 11 March 2011, were generally non-violent, despite resort by the regime to the use of force, and the death of three protestors on the latter occasion. The situation erupted on 18 March in Sana'a when government forces fired on protestors, reportedly killing 52 people. This incident prompted some members of the armed forces to join the ranks of the opposition. By and large, however, the army – commanded as it was by Saleh, his sons and relatives – remained stolidly loyal to the regime, with the exception of one division, which defected.

The Gulf Cooperation Council (GCC) attempted to broker a deal with Saleh for a peaceful transition, which the president rejected on 23 May, leading to the defection of long-time supporter Sheikh Ṣādiq al-Aḥmar. On 3 June, Saleh was severely injured in an explosion at the presidential compound and taken to Saudi Arabia for medical treatment. Although he ultimately returned, Saleh agreed to a GCC deal on 23 January 2012 to hand over power to his Deputy Vice President ʿAbd Rabbuh Manṣūr al-Hādī on condition of immunity against prosecution or trial for himself, his family and all those who had worked for his government during his 33 years in power – as was in fact secured through a law passed by the Yemeni Cabinet over the objections of wide sectors of the Yemeni public. On 21 February 2012, after purportedly 'winning' nearly 100% of the vote as the *sole* candidate, al-Hādī was sworn in as President for a period of two years, after which presidential elections will be held. Consequently, the case of Yemen is distinct and regime change, if it can be called that, was not clear cut. Additionally, only three of the four factors highlighted here were operative, and the absence of support for the uprisings by the army factored decisively in preventing the uprisings from toppling the regime. Also significant were the stances of Saudi Arabia and the United States vis-à-vis the uprisings. Neither power was interested in an outright victory for the opposition; positions which shed light on the nature of the stalemate that ultimately forced the leading opposition group al-Liqāʾ al-Mushtarak to accept the GCC settlement proposal.

Libya: bloodletting with only one out of four factors

In Libya, unlike Tunisia and Egypt, the Arab Spring produced a very different set of sanguinary results. With the exception of a small Amazigh minority that belongs to the Ibāḍī *madhab*, Libya is predominantly Sunni Muslim with the population belonging to the Mālkī *madhab*, as in Tunisia; yet, it is *not* a homogenous society from the standpoint of divisions along tribal and regional lines, even if historically tribal alliances have mitigated some of these to a certain extent. In February 2011, Libyans 'broke the barrier of fear', but initially the uprising was essentially confined to Benghazi, only later spreading to other major cities. Furthermore, a sizeable support base for Col Muammar Qadhafi endured in Tripoli as well as among particular tribal groups (such as the Warfallah, Tarhūna, al-Aṣābʿah, and al-Ṣīʿān) affiliated or loyal to his regime, along with his own tribe (al-Qadhādhifah) in the region of Sirt, meaning that the factor of relative national consensus and cohesion was lacking, at least in the early phases.

Additionally, in contradistinction to the situations in Tunisia and Egypt, the Libyan uprising turned violent – due partially to the fact that Qadhafi had armed elements sympathetic to him among the Libyan population as a facet of his 'strategy' (in so far as he had one) to counter the revolt. Also, there was a marked imbalance between the fighting capabilities of the forces of the opposition and those of Qadhafi's regime, and the armed forces proved – in the final analysis – to be divided. Many regular army units, in contrast to the elite Qadhafi battalions, remained out of the fray. Numerous soldiers did not report for duty; there were some deserters and high-profile defections such as that of ʿAbd al-Fattāḥ Yūnis, and as time progressed army battalions gradually began joining the side of the opposition. Significantly, the regular Libyan air force remained passive with pilots refusing to go into action against the revolt; and all of this obliged Qadhafi to rely on foreign pilots and his special, fanatically loyal, squads. Nevertheless, and in any case, sufficient numbers were fielded in fierce fighting so that it cannot be maintained that 'the army', or more properly here, that the armed forces *as a whole* maintained a neutral or supportive stance in a sense that would qualify or fulfil the condition of the fourth factor under consideration in this editorial.[1]

It was the interdiction of NATO air forces, military advisors and logistical support that swung the balance decisively in favour of the uprisings and led to the toppling of Qadhafi's regime. United Nations Security Council Resolution 1973 of 17 March, prompted by an appeal from the GCC on 7 March, and a similar one by the Arab League on 12 March in turn prompted by the Coalition for the Protection of the

Libyan People (initiated by Qatar, the United Arab Emirates (UAE) and Jordan), simply opened the way. Intensive military operations and airstrikes carried a high human cost that ultimately included the cruel torture and summary execution of Qadhafi himself on 19 October, along with his son Muʿtaṣim and respected Revolutionary Command Council Member Abū Bakr Yūnis Jābir, who had no official powers. Therefore, the essential absence of the four factors in aggregate that catalyzed the successful transitions in Tunisia and Egypt were not forthcoming in Libya (where only the barrier of fear was broken), and their absence is also reflected in the present chaotic situation on the ground there.[2]

The National Transitional Council or *al-majlis al-waṭanī al-intiqālī* (NTC) of Libya, established by the opposition to Qadhafi, which has constituted a *de facto* government and that announced a Constitutional Declaration in August 2011, retains only a fragile hold over the situation in the country. While the Cabinet chosen by the NTC runs day-to-day affairs, it retains full responsibility for the security situation. A new National Assembly is to be elected in June 2012, which will, in turn, draft a new constitution. The different forces that participated in the revolution that brought down Qadhafi's regime, to say nothing of the foreign powers involved, were a diverse collection in terms of both their experience and objectives. Thus, the matter of controlling them or subjecting them to a central authority is not a simple or straightforward proposition. What arguably should ease the transitional period and facilitate the administration of it in Libya is the availability of foreign exchange surpluses, equivalent to between US $140 billion and US$160 billion. In any case, the future rests on the question of whether or not a significant threshold of national cohesion can be achieved to permit unity, or whether tribal allegiances as well as religious currents (such as the *salafist*) and ethnic minorities like the Tuareg and Amazigh, will – in aggregate – prove too divisive to the new and fragile project of state. Just as the question of the army has factored in the outcomes of the revolutions, so it will in Libya in the transitional period, where it remains to be seen whether or not the various armed militias can be successfully integrated into a new national army.

Bahrain: a Gulf sectarian test bed, two factors out of four and momentary stasis

In Bahrain, a majority of essentially second-class citizens, comprised of underprivileged and under-represented Shīʿah, took to the streets and occupied the Pearl Roundabout, against the minority Sunni regime, over long-standing grievances. Sunni participation in the demonstrations was minimal, and after protestors effectively cut off the small island-country's downtown financial centre and entrepôt and subsequently approached al-Rifāʿ neighbourhood, home to the palaces of the ruling Āl Khalīfah family, security forces opened fire. Initially, protestors had limited their demands to calling for political reforms, including a transition to constitutional monarchy; however, the bloody scenes, broadcast live on television, impelled many among them to shift to the more radical slogan of 'bringing down the regime' (*isqāṭ al-niẓām*), used to great effect elsewhere during the Arab Spring. While Bahraini demonstrators did successfully break the 'barrier of fear', there was not complete participation in the protests nor consensus over the precise nature and extent of the demands. Significantly, when the situation was threatening to spiral out of control, Saudi Arabia facilitated the deployment of the Peninsula Shield Force into Bahrain on 16 March to protect the royal family; a move which introduced a new and distinctive dimension to the situation, of an army not comprised of Bahrainis, and one which sided decisively with the ruling regime. Crown Prince Salmān bin Ḥamad bin ʿĪsā Āl Khalīfah put forward a call for a national dialogue, and while the initial wave of protests abated, there has continued to be sporadic unrest. So far, therefore, the Bahraini uprising has failed to produce tangible changes of noteworthy significance and perhaps not surprisingly again the conjunction of four factors crucial to success in Tunisia and Egypt did not occur.[3] Lastly, it does bear mentioning that Bahrain, which is relatively small and in possession of only meagre oil reserves and revenues, was also subject to a timely injection of cash by Saudi Arabia and the UAE – a grant payable over ten years (which also included payments to Yemen) reported to be in the range of US$20 billion – that apparently was intended to go some way towards placating the masses (Fakhro 2011, p. 515).

Recently in Bahrain an independent reconciliation committee, chaired by former Minister of Health and Education ʻAli Fakhro and comprising over 100 Bahrainis, was formed to mediate between the monarchy and the opposition. Thus far, nothing has come of this mediation; and recent developments in Saudi Arabia that have brought Prince Nayyif, current Minister of the Interior, forward as an heir to the throne are likely to complicate the situation and make any compromise solution in Bahrain more difficult, so far as can be seen. Yet, the longer resolution of the situation is delayed, the more costly it is likely to be. While a variant of the Yemeni solution, oriented towards constitutional monarchy, might be within reach at the present, it is unlikely that such will prove sufficient in the future, given, in particular, political developments in Saudi Arabia. So long as social and political grievances as well as economic disparities persist in this small island nation with a pronounced sectarian dimension, the prevailing stasis will remain unstable.

Syria: one out of four factors, and the most dangerous 'game'

Syria presents a distinct case, wherein, for reasons distinct from those that pertained in Libya, the requisite component factors for a successful non-violent uprising were not forthcoming. Syrian protests began in March, after the 'barrier of fear' had been broken in Tunisia and Egypt and the regimes in both countries had been brought down successfully. While peaceful at the outset, in Syria the uprising, or multiple uprisings, became gradually and increasingly more violent along with the iron-fist tactics employed early by the regime. Significantly, the population is divided along religious, sectarian and ethnic lines; and those taking to the streets were not joined by a majority, with Damascus and Aleppo remaining acquiescent or loyal – for different reasons – to the regime of Bashar al-Assad. Opposition has been centred in Hama, once the target of a brutal February 1982 reprisal assault by former President Hafez Al-Assad against Islamist elements (including the Syrian Muslim Brotherhood) that had attacked government forces, as well as, this time around, in Homs and outlying areas, such as Deir al-Zour, Idlib, Zabadani and others. Additionally, there seems to be strong evidence that elements affiliated to al-Qāʿidah are active in the field as well as possibly foreign mercenaries in armed action against the regime. The Syrian army and security forces, which have not hesitated in using withering force against the opposition, have seen few defectors and remain steadfastly behind the president. Though neither side has been able decisively to gain the upper hand, the balance of forces seems to remain with Bashar al-Assad's regime. In any event, even though segments of the population did break the 'barrier of fear' and descend into the streets to confront soldiers, armoured BMPs (infantry-fighting vehicles) and tanks, non-violent means and the other requisite component factors for a successful uprising and transition – or at least one without extremely high human and material costs – are lacking in Syria, and their absence would seem to go a long way towards explaining the present standoff.[4]

The impasse in Syria at the time of writing is a stalemate prevailing between the regime and the opposition behind the uprisings and armed resistance, which is not united and lacks a unified programme for the future. States in the region and beyond – Turkey, the GCC countries (especially Qatar and Saudi Arabia), the United States and Western European states (such as France) – are supporting the Syrian uprisings morally and, in some cases, materially; while Iran, the Russian Federation and China are backing the regime, with lukewarm support also coming from Lebanon and Iraq. Regional and international attempts, with the backing of the Arab League and the UN General Assembly, to oust Bashar al-Assad or oblige him to step down have failed; and, unlike in the case of Libya, a military solution is neither a likely option nor applicable in Syria. The regime remains intransigent and has resorted to a strategy combining political reforms – or the promise of them – with a security crackdown to quash the uprisings. The political dimension entails a 'made to measure' presidential model for a new constitution put to a referendum – on 26 February – which was preceded by new election, political party and information laws. In theory, these political reforms have gone some way towards satisfying demands made in the uprising; however, they have been strictly unilateral and top-down, enacted without the direct input of or dialogue with the opposition. The political reforms adopted – at least theoretically – abolished the role of the Baath Party that has effectively dominated and even been synonymous with Syrian political life since 1963, and they introduced a multiparty system along with the promotion of some basic democratic rights. According to Syrian television, the new constitution was approved in the 26 February plebiscite, with, so it was claimed, 57% of the eligible population participating and 89% of these voting in favour, with 10% against. Predictably, the West – bent on removing Bashar al-Assad from office – denounced the move without serious consideration as to whether or not it might satisfy the demands of the opposition, with US Secretary of State Hillary Clinton terming it 'a cynical ploy' and German Foreign Minister Guido Westerwelle calling it a 'farce' and a 'sham vote' (Karam and Hubbard 2012). The question of the genuineness or seriousness of the reforms aside, it can safely be said that these would not have been offered by the Syrian regime at all had it not been for the uprisings.

Simultaneously, the regime has ruthlessly applied the security solution with an iron fist; and outside forces of opposition, including Qatar and Saudi Arabia, have begun calling for the arming of the Syrian uprising, which is already partially armed. Certain members of the opposition, such as Michel Kilo and others of the Coordination Forum (*hay'at al-tansīq*), have voiced concerns that resort to arms by the opposition only serves to undermine the moral and political positions it is meant to serve and that violence only plays into the hands of the regime, affording it an even greater pretext to crush the opposition as a whole with impunity. Despite the draconian measures already employed and the collapse of Baba Amr and Homs at the hands of the Syrian regime, there is still room for the regime to resort to even more drastic means. Furthermore, the actual situation inside Syria is not as it is being portrayed in mainstream international and Arab media. Syria has been dealt a number of severe blows through economic sanctions, first by the United States and the European Union and then by the Arab League headed by Sheikh Ḥamad bin Jāsim al-Thānī, which on 27 November 2011 put an end to virtually all Syrian trade within the Arab world, all of which came in response to an initial reluctance by the regime to allow in Arab observers, but to which it later acquiesced. The deleterious effects of sanctions on the Syrian economy have been mitigated to a small degree due to the porous borders with Iraq (and thence Iran) and Lebanon; however, in the case of the latter these have also afforded access to Gulf-funded gunrunners supplying arms to the opposition, as Syrian sources and at least one arrest by the Lebanese authorities have revealed.[5]

The situation in Syria is very unlikely to be resolved along the lines of either the Tunisian or the Egyptian model, whereas the precedent set in Yemen – albeit with some modifications – might be more applicable with the major caveat that there is no possibility of removing Bashar al-Assad from office, which must be taken into account. At this point, what would be most productive would be recourse to the mechanism of a third party, trusted by both the regime and the main national opposition forces. This formula will also require that regional and international forces back down from their unsuccessful support of the external Syrian opposition and the so-called Free Syrian Army, in which connection the degree to which they have actually helped the Syrian uprising has been minimal, and has enabled some elements to play into the hands – wittingly or unwittingly – of regional and international actors. Regardless of the outcomes of the Syrian uprisings, it is clear that the regime's image is tarnished and that whatever sort of Syria may emerge from the present crisis will have lost much of its standing and be unable to play as prominent or decisive international and regional roles as the country has done over the past 40 years.

Morocco, Oman and Jordan: different dynamics, deft manoeuvres, swift reforms and false starts?

Morocco: a friendly transition towards constitutional monarchy?

In Morocco, where an absolute monarchy existed, King Muhammad VI, in light of what occurred in Tunisia, Egypt and Libya as well as a peaceful mass outpouring of Moroccans into the streets, prudently took the initiative of setting up a committee of respected and trustworthy personages to propose constitutional amendments that would steer the country in the direction of a constitutional monarchy. The committee selected to draft amendments to the constitution proposed changes along these lines, which were put to a plebiscite and approved by an overwhelming majority. Subsequent reasonably fair elections saw the election of a prime minister from the party winning the largest number of seats and the formation of a coalition cabinet. Although the new constitutional formula is something of a curious amalgam that speaks to the many different sides of the relatively vibrant political life of Morocco since independence, it falls short of a constitutional monarchy, even if significant strides have been made in that direction. The king still retains significant powers as well as the somewhat nebulous and all-inclusive title of Amīr al-Mu'minīn ('Commander of the Faithful'), but in the end the quick and considered measures of Muhammad VI sufficiently placated the demands of Moroccans in general. In sum, the four factors considered here were essentially inapplicable in the case of Morocco, and the explanation, as has been suggested, may have to do with the particular political structure and milieu in this country.[6]

Oman: Qaboos still dodging challenges after all these years

In the Sultanate of Oman, Sultan Qaboos, who has managed to rule the country since deposing his father in a palace coup and acceding to the throne on 23 July 1970, has a long history of avoiding regime change. In 1973, for instance, he resorted to the military assistance and intervention of the Shah of Iran who sent Imperial Iranian troops and helicopters to assist in putting down the bloody and long-running Dhofar Rebellion, helped by the British SAS among others.[7] Although a peaceful uprising did take place in Oman in 2011, Sultan Qaboos seems to have read the signs presciently, and was able to pre-empt the sort of events occurring elsewhere through a number of deft manoeuvres. He conceded to the primary demands of the demonstrators, sacked certain members of the government and introduced a number of constitutional amendments, all of which served to quieten down the uprising, which has yet to flare up again.

Jordan: the Palestinian question and one of applicability

For its part, Jordan has witnessed sporadic uprisings on a recurring basis and enough to suggest that segments of the population have essentially broken the 'barrier of fear' or are prepared to do so. Jordan's population, however, is not homogenous given the large numbers of Palestinian Jordanians, as opposed to the indigenous Jordanians, the so-called East Bankers, often of Bedouin tribal heritage and generally fiercely loyal to the monarchy. The history of relations between the two groups has been checkered, especially after the Israeli occupation of the West Bank in 1967, and has sometimes witnessed the outbreak of full-blown warfare, such as that which occurred in the clashes between the Jordanian army and Palestinians during the events of 'Black September' in 1970. As Aḥmad 'Ubaydāt recently noted, however, even non-Palestinian Jordanians do not uniformly or unreservedly back King 'Abdullah if for no reason other than the seriousness of corruption and its various manifestations as in, for example, the selling off of Jordan's strategic assets to foreign interests at negligible prices. The question of Palestinian Jordanian 'citizenship' and, in fact, the proposal for a 'constitutional monarchy' were addressed by the 1952 Constitution and have long since been on the 'agenda'— at least in theory. Yet, at the level of implementation little has been done, in no small part due to the lack of a clearly defined mechanism.[8]

Jordanians, by and large, supported the uprisings of the Arab Spring from the outset with the eruption of the Tunisian revolt. Indeed, they overcame the barrier of fear and descended into the streets; and, those demonstrations that did occur were peaceful, but contrary to protestors in neighboring countries, Jordanians chanted: 'The people want the *reform* (*iṣlāḥ*) of the regime' as opposed to the 'overthrow' (*isqāṭ*) of it. Latterly, King Abdullah did move to introduce some constitutional amendments, although these were considerably less substantial than those ratified in Morocco, and it is unclear as to precisely how reforms are to be carried out. Predictably, the army—which is a world unto itself and the object of a huge, overinflated and unjustifiable military spending—has remained unwavering in its support for the regime. The uprisings in response to the Arab Spring saw the entrance of a new political force into the arena around the nucleus of a youth movement known by various names but ultimately coalescing into 'National Front for Reform' and comprising independent personalities as well as opposition parties from among Islamists, Arab-nationalists and the Left. As 'Ubaydāt contends, the integration and durability of this coalition are by no means certain. Moreover, the requisite degree of social- or national cohesion was either not forthcoming or at least not as evident as elsewhere, perhaps partly due to long-standing demographic dynamics, where in some sense, Jordan, in this context remains an extension of a 'Palestinian question'. In the absence of hard and fast empirical data, it can be said that there is a significant percentage of the population that still backs the monarchy, or for whom relatively modest political demands along with attention to fighting corruption would seem to suffice, which obviates against the adoption of more radical sorts of themes and demands revolving around the Arab Spring, which so far have diminished significance in Jordan. Lastly, it bears mentioning that Jordan's highly sensitive geo-political proximity to Israel might well indeed militate against the possibility of the United States (or Israel itself) permitting demonstrations to ever reach any sort of dangerous titration point in the unlikely event they were to achieve a critical mass.

Other Arab countries

Across the Arab world, there are a number of countries where it remains to be seen what the ultimate outcomes of the Arab Spring will be. These countries, such as Algeria, the Sudan, Mauritania, Saudi Arabia, Kuwait, the UAE and Lebanon, are still highly susceptible if not likely to be influenced by the demonstration effects of the Arab Spring in other Arab countries. Some, such as Saudi Arabia and Kuwait. have significant minority Shi'ite populations in contrast to others, such as Mauritania, which are, at least in terms of religious or sectarian affiliation, more homogenous. Nevertheless, the rapidity with which the uprisings spread and the fact that the outcomes – some of which were more positive than others – communicated to the Arab peoples at large that change is indeed possible from *within* and is within reach, all suggest that there is still more to come. Certain measures may deter uprisings, and would-be protestors may be placated through financial and minor political concessions, or increased subsidies, that serve as pressure release valves. Some may even be bought off in some of the wealthy Gulf countries. However, there are those who see that temporary fixes may signal only a lull in the storm and that it is only a matter of time before the Arab tsunami returns and sweeps over those islands that have remained as yet relatively untouched.

The question of the role of the media in the Arab Spring

It goes without saying that many revolutions of the modern period – such as the Indonesian or Iranian, for example – were accomplished without satellite or social media. Nevertheless, this Editorial would not be complete without broaching the question of the effect and significant role of the media in the Arab Spring and the relative success or failure of the uprisings, even if space here does not permit complete discussion. Both social media (such as Facebook and Twitter) and satellite news media (notably Al-Jazeera, and Al-ʿArabīyah to a lesser extent) played major roles in popular mobilization and, in the case of the former, in providing actual logistics. Foreign media, such as Iranian channels – particularly in the case of Bahrain – as well as Russian media were also active in the events; but it cannot be argued conclusively that satellite news media was *always* a decisive factor as, so far, Syria serves as a counterpoint to such a contention. The question of the precise strategic value or utility of the media in mobilization and fate of the uprisings aside, there is no doubt that the live coverage afforded by the internet and television, coupled with video footage from cell phones, served to communicate the various messages and themes of the revolutions to the global community and to draw a vast audience into the very heart of the uprisings.

The role of Arab, regional and international players in the Arab Spring

Lastly, some attention should be accorded to the positions and attitudes of Arab, regional and international players towards the Arab Spring. If anything, at the global level the Arab Spring revealed a set of highly conspicuous double standards; attitudes and stances predicated purely on some personal or vested interests; and what – for lack of a more euphemistic term – might simply be called hypocrisy. Overall, these reactions and positions were neither principled nor consistent. In the case of the Tunisian and Egyptian uprisings, Syria, Algeria, Morocco and the GCC countries – with the notable exception of Qatar – home to Al-Jazeera – kept quiet. Qatar was in full support of the revolutions and devoted exclusive and highly influential media coverage to them; yet, it was opposed to any possible spread or ramifications within its own borders. Many in the United States and Western Europe openly admitted that they as well as academics and institutions of critical studies and analysis were taken by surprise (Gause 2011); and Western governments were hesitant towards supporting the revolutions in either of the two countries, until it became clear that they would prove successful. All these countries, however, did not remain quiet in the aftermath of events in Tunisia and Egypt; and in the case of Libya, all the GCC countries and some Arab ones (with the exception of Syria, Algeria and Morocco) supported the overthrow of Qadhafi's regime. The Arab League, at the behest of the GCC, passed a resolution to ask the UN Security Council to intervene militarily and institute a no-fly zone, through NATO, to protect the Libyan population in what was instrumental in bringing down the regime. Through NATO, the United States and Europe participated militarily in deposing Qadhafi and pummelling forces loyal to him. At the outset of hostilities, Turkey was reluctant due to its economic interests and ties to Libya under Qadhafi, but it later sided with NATO.

In the case of Yemen, and in spite of the hardline tactics employed by 'Ali 'Abdullah Saleh's regime to suppress the revolution, the Arab League – in conspicuous contrast to its stand towards Libya – kept silent in a way paralleled by the Western powers. The GCC backed by the United States put forward a compromise initiative intended to provide Saleh with a face-saving exit as well as to avoid upsetting the balance of power abruptly and the very dangerous possibility in Yemen of an outright civil war. In the case of Bahrain, Oman and Jordan, the GCC countries remained fully supportive of the regimes in power; and the Arab League maintained silence, while the West paid a modicum of lip-service only to the events and violence in Bahrain, where Saudi Arabia, as mentioned, hastened to deploy the Peninsula Shield Force to preclude any serious threat to the monarchy. In the case of Syria, the GCC countries – particularly Qatar and Saudi Arabia – and the Arab League were heavily and directly involved in calling for and approving economic sanctions against the regime. The West and Turkey, despite a relative thaw in Turkish–Syrian bilateral relations in recent years, have railed against the al-Assad regime and done their utmost to unseat it, with Russia, China and Iran remaining steadfast behind the regime. It bears mentioning that the polarization that has taken place between international actors – with Russia, China and Iran at one pole and the West and most of the Arab states at the other, in the cases of Libya and Syria in particular – is a result of outside causal factors and not limited strictly to the Arab Spring.

To deal comprehensively with the question of the influence of positions taken by the United States and European powers as well as the UN on the Arab Spring would require a separate analytical framework outside the modest scope of this Editorial. These positions were, however, crucially effective at the level of encouraging various Arab opposition groups to advance their demands and slogans to include slogans such 'he [i.e., the president] must go' and others that impacted both heads of regimes attempting to cling to power and demonstrators themselves. This having been said, in terms of the factor of direct outside support it may be concluded that it was not always necessary for the success of revolutions – as in the cases of Egypt and Tunisia. An exception was the indispensible direct military role played by NATO in Libya following on UN Security Council Resolution 1973 that authorized the imposition of a no-fly zone and effectively permitted it to cripple Qadhafi's forces and unseat him. Though they have not resorted to military intervention, powerful international and Arab players (primarily the GCC) have been exerting tremendous pressure on the Syrian regime through an array of means, but not yet been able to effect the overthrow of al-Assad. This would seem to suggest that foreign support or the lack thereof is not a 'prerequisite' nor did or does it guarantee outcomes either way in the case of the uprisings of the Arab Spring. Thus, while there are different objective conditions on the ground in all countries, the role of outside, international and regional actors cannot absolutely be considered a decisive factor in the complete success or failure of the uprisings. As far as the future is concerned and the likely effect of this in the Gulf countries in particular, it should be noted that the unsung presence of US military bases militates – at least in principle – against the potential for radical political change.

In any case, what should be clear from this discussion is that the international community as well as many Arabs apply double standards at will. Arguably, they are neither principled nor consistent in their positions and stances towards the Arab Spring or with regard to mandating consistent and like responses for similar situations – there being marked disparities in both the rhetoric and the actions taken. Finally, it is also increasingly clear that the international scene is no longer subject to the hegemony of the United States or other Western powers and that the stand of other powers, particular Russia and China, suggest that the unipolar world system that emerged after the collapse of the former Soviet Union is becoming a thing of the past.

Conclusion

With little doubt, the Arab Spring as well as its present and future ramifications along with the possibility of its continuation will remain an object of fascination and study. It would be presumptuous for anyone to suggest that all its lessons have been learned or that some sort of absolute, conclusive and all-inclusive theoretical or analytical model has been produced. Neither the factor of outside Arab, foreign, regional and international intervention nor that of the media can be considered always or *invariably* to have been decisive, as the case of Syria demonstrates. What I have suggested here is that there *is* a set of four factors that when co-incident are *decisive*, and these are: breaking the 'barrier of fear'; non-violent resistance; sufficient national cohesion and popular sentiment; and the question of the stance of the armed forces vis-à-vis uprisings. The foregoing analyses support the hypothesis enunciated in the introduction to this Editorial, and it is hoped that such may shed light on the dynamics and possible future developments where uprisings occurred. I would contend that the four factors discussed and their confluence or lack thereof are useful as analytical tools and highly informative as criteria in both explaining the results and relative successes of the various Arab uprisings as well as in gauging prospects for the various transitional stages and any potential future uprisings.

Notes

1. These inside details with regard to the Libyan armed forces were kindly supplied by Dr Youssef M. Sawani, whose review of this Editorial I solicited in Beirut (29 February 2012).
2. For a detailed account of the Libyan uprisings and the key players on the scene, especially after the fall of Qadhafi, see Sawani (2012).
3. For a discussion of the uprisings in Bahrain, see Fakhro (2011).
4. For an account of the dynamics of the Syrian situation and the nature of the opposition to Bashar al-Assad's regime, see Kilo (2011).
5. Lebanese authorities issued arrest warrants for three Syrian nationals (Ammar Omar al-Adib, Muhammad Shaker Bashlah and Muhammad Hamad al-Kik) for involvement in illegal weapons dealing. Bashlah was arrested on the night of 31 October 2011 at Beirut international airport on his way to Riyadh on charges of smuggling arms into Syria. On 10 November 2011, Lebanon's General Security confirmed that al-Adeeb and Bashlah were transferred to al-Quba prison in Tripoli, northern Lebanon (*Daily Star* 2011a, 2011b, 2011c).
6. For a detailed discussion and full account of the Moroccan constitutional amendments in the context of the Arab Spring, see Belkeziz (2012).
7. See for instance: Jaʿabūb, Munā, Sālim, Saʿīd, 2010. *Qiyādah al-Mujtamaʿ Naḥw al-Taghyīr al-Tajribah āl-Tarbawīyah li Thawrat Ẓufār (1969–1992)* [Leading Society Towards Change: Educational Experience of the Revolution of Dhofar (1969–1992)]. Beirut: Centre for Arab Unity Studies.
8. From a paper entitled: "Tadāʿiyāt al-Thawrah fi al-Urdun" delivered by Aḥmad ʿUbaydāt at the 6–9 February 2012 Conference held in Tunisia: "Al-Thawrah wa al-Intiqāl al-Dīmuqrāṭī fī al-Waṭan al-ʿArabī: Naḥwa Khuṭat Ṭarīq"–"Revolution and Democratic Transition in the Arab World: Towards a Roadmap", sponsored by the Centre for Arab Unity Studies (Beirut) in association with the Swedish Institute. (Conference papers and proceedings are scheduled to be published in Arabic by the Centre for Arab Unity Studies in the summer of 2012.)

References

Belkeziz, Abdelilah, 2012. Morocco and democratic transition: a reading of the constitutional amendments – their context and results. *Contemporary Arab Affairs*, 5 (1), 27–53.

Daily Star, 2011a. Syrian arrested in Beirut on arms smuggling charges. *The Daily Star (Beirut)*, 31 October. Available from: http://www.dailystar.com.lb/News/Politics/2011/Oct-31/152672-syrian-arrested-in-beirut-on-arms-smuggling-charges.ashx#axzz1nvrw4OAG [Accessed 1 March 2012].

Daily Star, 2011b. Lebanon issues warrants for 3 Syrians involved in arms trade. *The Daily Star (Beirut)*, 3 November. Available from: http://www.dailystar.com.lb/News/Local-News/2011/Nov-03/153061-lebanon-issues-warrants-for-3-syrians-involved-in-arms-trade.ashx#axzz1nvrw4OAG [Accessed 1 March 2012].

Daily Star, 2011c. Lebanese security sends two Syrian prison detainees to Al-Quba. The Daily Star (Beirut), 10 November. Available from: http://www.nowlebanon.com/arabic/NewsArchiveDetails.aspx?ID=330777 [Accessed 1 March 2012].

Fakhro, AliMohammed, 2011. Repercussions of the Arab movements for democracy in Bahrain. *Contemporary Arab Affairs*, 4 (4), 518–523.

Gause, G. III, 2011. Why Middle East studies missed the Arab Spring. *Foreign Affairs*, July/August. Available from: http://www.foreignaffairs.com/articles/67932/f-gregory-gause-iii/why-middle-east-studies-missed-the-arab-spring/

Haseeb, Khair El-Din, 2011. On the Arab 'Democratic Spring' lessons derived. *Contemporary Arab Affairs*, 4 (2), 113–122.

Karam, Zeina and Hubbard, B., 2012. West dismisses Syria constitution vote as 'farce'. Associated Press, 26 February. Available from: http://www.msnbc.msn.com/id/46529956/ns/local_news-clarksburg_wv/t/west-dismisses-syria-constitution-vote-farce/ [Accessed 6/063 2012].

Kilo, M., 2011. Syria … the road to where? *Contemporary Arab Affairs*, 4 (4), 431–444.

Sawani, Youssef M., 2012. Post-Qadhafi Libya: interactive dynamics and the political future. *Contemporary Arab Affairs*, 5 (1), 1–26.

The Arab revolutions; the emergence of a new political subjectivity

Sari Hanafi

American University of Beirut, Beirut, Lebanon

Since late 2010, the Arab World has witnessed regime changes in Tunisia, Egypt and Libya; and revolts by Arab citizens are still underway in Syria, Bahrain and Yemen, along with reform initiatives at different levels. These processes cannot be accurately be described by Orientalist terms such as 'Arab Spring', 'Arab unrest' or the 'Facebook Revolution', where such categorizations fail to account for the radical transformation in politics and values that the Arab World is undergoing and the significance that resides in the confluence of social and democratic demands. The ultimate fate of these popular uprisings remains in the balance, but it is all too clear that they have produced the most dramatic changes in the region since the mid-twentieth century which marked the end of the colonial era. This article aims to elucidate the import of term 'the people' and to whom it applies in the popular slogan: 'The people want the overthrow of the regime' (*al-shaʿb yurīd isqāṭ al-niẓām*). It aims to identify the actors involved in the revolution, particularly the youth and participants among the labour movement. Through this analysis the study explores the new political subjectivity ushered in by these revolutions, in the specific form of *individuality*, or what is termed here *reflexive individualism*. This individualism, which is different from the neoliberal concept, is not a straightforward one predicated on anti-patriarchal authority, anti-tribe, anti-community or anti-political party sentiments. The political subjectivity of the individuals who have taken part is formed and shaped both within and across the shadowy edges of political institutions and their production of legitimacy and knowledge.

Introduction

> Now is the time of the furnaces, and only light should be seen. (Jose Marti, cited by Che Guevara 1967/1981)

Over the past year the Arab World has witnessed regime change in Tunisia, Egypt and Libya; Arab citizen revolts are underway in Syria, Bahrain and Yemen; and different levels of reform initiatives can be found in Morocco,[1] Algeria[2] and Jordan.[3] These processes cannot be captured by Orientalist terms such as 'Arab Spring',[4] 'Arab unrest' or 'the Facebook Revolution'. These labels do not account for the radical transformation in politics and values that the Arab World is undertaking. The 'Arab revolutions', as people in this region opt to call them, have already inspired protests in Israel, Mexico, Afghanistan and beyond. The fate of these popular uprisings remains in the balance, but it is all too clear that they have produced the most dramatic changes in the region since the mid-twentieth century, which marked the end of the colonial era.

The significance of these revolutions resides in the realization of social and democratic demands. One should read them as continuities in a long history of protest in the region rather than a total rupture. One should keep in mind, for example, that the Tunisian uprising had its beginnings in Gafsa, three years ago, in a protest over bread prices and unemployment. Also, in 2009, dissident bloggers and Facebook users in the Tunisian city of Jarjis demanded the release of political prisoners and called for freedom of expression. In the cases of both Tunisia and Egypt, the revolutions were aimed at achieving social and democratic reform, initiated by unemployed university graduates and workers who independently organized themselves into unions.[5]

In the name of justice, dignity and freedom (freedom to join political groups and parties, freedom of expression, and freedom of religious practice), protestors fought against unemployment and grew hostile towards neoliberal and neo-patrimonial regimes.

Beyond the structural conditions that drove the forces of these revolutions, they may also be interpreted in different ways in terms of their cultural power (Alexander 2011) and the power of symbols. The sheer theatre of the drama that unfolded in Tunisia caused a domino effect in other Arab countries, starting in Egypt. In this setting, the revolutionary youth are educated individuals – men and women, Muslims and Christians – who used all forms of contemporary technology, such as their mobile phones and laptop computers, as well as hand-made signs and banners, to convey their message and spread their demands. The carnivalesque performances (Bakhtin 1984), particularly those in al-Tahrir Square, Cairo, were replete with chants, music, comedic acts, humour and sarcasm. In these essentially indigenous revolutions (except for Libya's), no sign of US Agency for International Development (USAID) or other international agencies was found or requested for funding glossy placards and brochures or hosting workshops in five-star hotels. In complete contrast, official feasts were full of the supporters of the calcified regime who came with their horses and their camels, bricks, knives and sticks.

The intention in this article is to reveal the *people* in the popular slogan 'the people want the fall of the regime'. It aims to identify the actors involved in the revolution, namely the youth and the labour movement. By doing so, it will explore the new political subjectivity ushered in by these revolutions, in the specific form of individuality that will be labelled *reflexive individualism*. One cannot understand this subjectivity of the revolutionaries without addressing the complexity of the political–judicial structure (and the regime's constant use of the state of exception[6]) and the social structure (socio-economic and demographic factors) in this region that push actors to revolt. As Yasine al-Hafez once singled out social structures as a medium to explain the 1948 defeat (Bardawl 2011, p. 65), they will be used here to explain the uprisings.

This paper draws mainly upon 18 in-depth interviews conducted by the author during 2011 with activists who participated in the revolutions in Tunisia (two), Egypt (seven), Libya (one) and Syria (eight). In addition, it is informed by many informal meetings the author had with many activists.

The context: some facts

Although this paper is more focused on *how* the revolutions happened rather than *why*, it is important to highlight some socio-economic and demographic factors. The performance of the state in the Arab region has been flawed and volatile, especially as of 2007, since when a substantial drop in gross domestic product (GDP) growth and GDP per capita growth is evident (it dropped from around 3% to less than 0.3%). Furthermore, the region lags behind other regions such as East Asia (Dhillon and Yousef 2011, p. 15).

According to the Economist Intelligence Unit (2011, p. 13), many Arab countries (Jordan, Algeria and Saudi Arabia) have an unemployment rate in excess of 10%, and in Tunisia in particular it rose to 13%. Corruption in the Arab World is clearly very high: half of the countries are rated above 80 in the Corruption Perceptions Index (CPI).

Four characteristics are commonly identified with the Arab World. The first concerns the unemployment rate, which is much higher among the youth. The rate increased from 10% for the average population to over 20% for the young population in many Arab countries (20.1% for Syria, 28% for Egypt and 30% for Tunisia), reaching more than 40% for Algeria and the Palestinian territories (Dhillon and Yousef 2011, p. 22). This rate also registered increases among the highly qualified youth (especially in Jordan and Egypt), especially for the female population (Dhillon and Yousef 2011, pp. 22–25).

The second factor concerns the rampant inequality within Arab societies. According to Marcus Marktanner this inequality has risen markedly (Marktanner 2011): the difference between the Estimated Household Income Inequality (EHII) in the 1980s versus that in the 1990s for the Middle East North Africa (MENA) region was 3.8 (Tunisia = 10.0, Egypt = 3.2) – higher than the world average (3.2). One should not forget that the so-called 'Tunisian economic miracle', a paraphrase frequently used by the International Monetary Fund (IMF) and The World Bank, refers to the capital and northern coastal cities, but not the interior of Tunisia or the south. The deregulation of the property (real estate) market, the absence of social housing projects and the absence of protection for tenants who rent has a tremendous impact on the young generation. The increase in inequality has worsened since 2007 in the wake of what Marktanner (2011) called a 'Triple F crisis' (fuel, food and financial). Rising fuel and food prices rendered universal subsidy systems no longer financeable. Due to the ending of state food subsidies (pushed by the IMF) and the inelasticity of fuel and food prices and consumption, and the fact that poor households spend greater proportions of their income on food and fuel, real income inequality has accelerated in recent years far beyond the nominal one. The global financial crisis has, moreover, reduced receipts from remittances, affecting many vulnerable households (Marktanner 2011). In the words of Michael Burawoy,[7] we are in an era in which exploitation and societal exclusion (social, urban and economic) comprise the main phenomenon that strikes most societies and the sweeping impact of the exclusion has made the exclusion a sort of privilege, especially for a young generation.

The third factor is that the Arab region, specifically the Arab East, is considered an area particularly vulnerable to the negative impacts of climate change. This is even more significant given that the Arab East is also one of the most volatile regions in the world in terms of inter- and intrastate conflict and instability. The United Nations Development Programme (UNDP) (2009) *Arab Human Development Report* considers the relationship between resource pressures, environmental sustainability and human security in the Arab region as a matter of utmost importance.[8] Syria is also facing climate extremes in the form of successive droughts and migration from the north-east. Since 2007, Syria's north-east (particularly 150 villages in districts of

Hasakeh and Raqqa) has suffered from the worst drought to hit the country in five decades, combined with an increase in the temperature in March and April (Shayeb 2010, cited by Hanafi 2010c).

Finally, the Arab region is a conflict-ridden one that deters investors from risking their capital there. In addition, immense resources are often used for buying arms at the expense of healthcare and education.

While these economic indicators are dramatically negative, many socio-cultural factors are relatively positive. Courbage and Todd (2007/2011) pointed out three dynamics: the rapid increase in literacy,[9] particularly among women; a falling birth rate;[10] and a significant decline in the widespread custom of endogamy, or marriage between first cousins. Although there is a reported observation of a 'youth bulge' (an above-average proportion of young people aged between fifteen and 25 years in a society), this bulge will not be maintained by highly qualified young people whose fertility rate has fallen significantly.

Complexity of the authoritarian regime

According to the Economist Intelligence Unit (2011), the majority of Arab countries are governed by authoritarian regimes, and only three countries (Lebanon, the Palestinian territories and Iraq) have been classified as having hybrid or pluralist regimes. The Arab World notably avoided the waves of democratization that took place in Latin America, Southern and Eastern Europe, and parts of Sub-Saharan Africa and Asia in the 1970s, 1980s and 1990s (Economist Intelligence Unit 2011). Other organizations such as the Arab Reform Initiative (ARI) (for instance, ARI 2010) and Freedom House established similar indices using similar methodologies. These indices prove helpful in tracking the micro-transformations of the Arab World and in determining which state has undergone governance change and moved towards the rule of law. However, they fail to examine the impact of events on the following levels.

First level

The relationship between the legal and the political, i.e. how the *rule of law*, when it exists, does not hinder the *law of rules*. The presidents of Syria, Tunisia and Egypt acted as sovereigns making ultimate decisions over whether to enact a law or to suspend it, whether to 'take life or let live'. They violated their people's rights – arresting, torturing, murdering and ruining their countries economically. The 'state of exception' (see below) has been particularly felt in the peripheries, often outside the capital, in spaces of exception, where the state only served as a security apparatus or as a surveillance machine over foreign aid dispersal. There, in places such as Daraa, Banias and Homs in Syria, local identities emerged and uprisings started.

Arab revolutions have shown that a reform process based on changing laws and regulations without a real political restructuring is a hollow process. The state of emergency, as one of the forms of the state of exception, can be seen as more than a legal doctrine, and rather as a governmental structure (Reynolds 2011). In Syria, the revocation of the emergency law and abolition of its associated security courts in April 2011 have not reduced state repression. Giorgio Agamben offered a compelling argument for how this ruse works when he discerned that both the Italian Fascist and German Nazi regimes operated without cancelling their respective constitutions through a paradigm that has been defined as a 'dual state', whereby a further structure that was not legally formalized was added to the constitutional settings by virtue of a 'state of exception' (Agamben 2005). Dismantling the state security apparatus thus requires regime change and not only issuing a new set of laws, as demonstrated in the case of Syria.

Second level

These indices failed to uncover the complexity of the state apparatus. The authoritarian states have governed through their heavy 'right hand', to borrow this concept from Bourdieu (1999), using their security and repressive apparatus and exemplified by the alliance between bureaucrats and crony capitalists. Up to 2000, the population has 'borne' or tolerated this because the same state also has a 'left hand' which provides public goods to a large portion of the population, it being a remnant of the welfare state. Pierre Bourdieu's powerful metaphor breaks with the unitary vision of 'the state' as an organizational monolith and explains the internal divisions and struggles it harbours. The problem that faces many Arab societies is that the neoliberal and deregulatory system of the right hand no longer wants to pay for the left hand. These cutbacks in the 'welfare' state become without precedent with the acute economic crisis. For instance, it is shocking for those who have visited Libya to notice the extent to which this wealthy country has a poor infrastructure outside Tripoli and to witness the harsh level of poverty. The rentier economy was incapable of generating surplus to subsidize the deprived strata of the population (al-Madini 2011).

The Arab youth feel that they have become a *Homo sacer*, in the sense of Agamben (1998), which means that this was the revolt of 'bare lives', of defenceless hungry bodies that the regime has stripped of political identity and of the right to belong to such groups as the Islamic Renaissance Movement 'al-Nahda', the Tunisian Communist Labor Party, and the Muslim brotherhood.

State of exception

In a book that I edited in 2010 called *The State of Exception and Resistance in the Arab World* (Hanafi 2010b), the Tunisian sociologist Mohsen Bouazizi (Bouazizi 2010) wrote about the silent expressions of opposition among the Tunisian youth and how indifference and carelessness are deployed against the regime. But what Bouazizi did not see then is how Mohamed Bouazizi, who is from the same city as Mohsen – Sidi Bouzid – was alienated from the social structures to become, echoing Touraine's (1995) words, a subject: the driving force of a social movement.

Mohamed's body, like that of other young Tunisians, was a target for the oppressive regime and its disciplinary authority, which aimed to strip it of its political identity. Thus by committing protest-suicide, Mohamed created a pattern of resistance whose effectiveness was achieved at the moment of the body's self-immolation. We are at a moment similar to the time when the Palestinian resistance in the occupied territories challenged the sovereign authority that sought to turn them into humiliated subjects who could be killed without any recognition, i.e. death without value. Mohamed Bouazizi and his fellows, who died by committing suicide, became actors who deliberately sacrificed themselves, and by that act, inverted the relationship with the sovereign authority.

The Syrian revolution has gone through another dynamic. 'State of exception' and bio-politics cannot account for the topographies of cruelty of the Syrian regime. According to the Syrian Observatory of Human Rights,[11] the death of 4342 civilians in the nine months suggests a necro-politics, to echo Achille Mbembe (Mbembe 2003). This Syrian combination between a state of exception, bio-politics and necro-politics has created new conditions that blur the lines between resistance and pacific demonstration, sacrifice and redemption, violence and freedom.

Despite all the technological and imbedded power that Arab regimes have, they are not total institutions that control everything. After all, it is often the case that oppression is a sign of weakness rather than strength, as was seen when the 'mighty' regime of Zine El Abidine Ben Ali in Tunisia could not get the army to follow the oppressive rule of the police. The system also failed to silence the opposition, especially in the diaspora. This offers a ray of hope to all those struggling for democratization – to learn how to use the regimes' weaknesses to produce change in the order.

Actors of the social movements

While the *people* literally engaged in the Arab revolutions, two groups of actors played a critical role. The first group included the educated independent youth, combined with political parties and unions that give such movements the needed momentum, organization and mobilization. The second group was composed of labourers, some members of unions, some not.[12] Many analysts, deliberately or not, neglect the importance of the latter group and mythically present the youth as classless, middle classes[13] and/or non-ideological. In reality, these revolutions represent emerging social movements that combine the classical form based on social classes with a new form in which the struggle for civil rights prevails.

Youth: new political subjectivity and reflexive individualism

The individuals construct themselves in the space between social integration and disintegration, what Touraine (1995, p. 285) calls commitment and non-commitment, armed with the power of reflexivity. This individualism, which I refer to as *reflexive individualism* to distinguish it from the *neoliberal* one, is thus not a straightforward anti-patriarchal authority, anti-tribe, anti-community and anti-political party. It is a type of individualism that involves the constant negotiation of an actor with the existing social structure in order to realize a (partial) emancipation from it. This is an act of self-reference of an agent that recognizes forces of socialization but alters their place in the social structure and resists their disciplinary power.

The new political subjectivity of the youth (in addition to the labourers, as will be shown below, and the peasants in the case of Syria), embodied the nation, *al-watan.* The actors became a source of unification for all the civilians in opposition to the regime and all the people facing the regime, without raising narrower or particularistic claims. Carrying their national flag, the Syrian protestors chanted 'United, united, united, the Syrian people are united'; and the Palestinians called for the end of their division (Fatah versus Hamas and West Bank versus Gaza). Sectarian or religious slogans became morally inferior and unfit for grounding the new political subjectivity. As Challand (2011) pointed out, we are in a process of a radical re-imagining, in the sense of Cornelius Castoriadis, of uniting the effort of the nation and of self-organization, that is, opposing, from one side, the classical fragmentation and atomization of the non-governmental organizations' (NGOs) sphere, and from the other side, the violent political tradition of some political parties. If there is an ideology for this radical re-imagination it is that they used a non-violent mode of action that gives them inexhaustible sources.

This individuality used in the new political subjectivity is not a neo-liberal one that used to be promoted by NGOs and other formalized civil society organizations. These organizations are too comfortable to mobilize. However, what about the human rights associations and NGOs? Many donors and international organizations limited their view of civil society to the 'depoliticized' and professionalized associations, and believed they were the ones that would carry the winds of change. These associations played an auxiliary role to the syndicates and opposition parties. This role consisted of disseminating information about casualties and death tolls, urging international powers, at both official and unofficial levels, to take firm positions against authoritarian regimes. However, two features were missing. First, the fact that most of these organizations are non-membership organizations (except human rights organizations in Tunisia and Morocco) and they have a very feeble capacity to mobilize the public. Second, the synergy between the four pillars of civil society: syndicates, (oppositional) parties, independent press and NGOs, are missing. Donors that focused only on NGOs have fostered, among other factors, the emergence of a globalized elite (Hanafi and Tabar 2005) whose connection to the local society is very loose, and which has led to an inflation of NGOs, and to a weakening of the syndicates and parties that historically fed the NGOs with fresh talent. This globalized elite has embodied the figure of the *Homo economicus*, as Benoit Challand eloquently put it:

> [these organizations] are precisely geared at producing new subjectivities, of 'active' citizens educated in the dominant language of development, made of 'empowerment' and other projects geared at molding good citizens. These are in reality thought as rational *homineso economici*, taught to weigh the costs and benefits of each individual action, and who might be critical but still subject to the global neoliberal dominant order, consumers of global goods, and 'beneficiaries' of democracy assistance programs. The neoliberal agenda, premised on a methodological individualism, and other democratization or good governance programs often overlook, not to say actively deny, the defense of collective rights (such as workers' rights, right to self-determination) unless geared at supporting minorities (typically in terms of gender or religious minorities). (Challand 2011, p. 275)

This neoliberal individualism was promoted by (the late) capitalism that has sought to shift society from total state to total individual (Todorov 2011). A television reality show broadcast on one of the American channels, on 2 November 2011, featured a debate on ageing, mercy death and the costs for the social security budget of elderly ill people in their protracted last stage of life. When someone exposed a story of a man who had a prolonged coma, people from the audience started screaming 'let him die … let him die …'. This is what I call a neoliberal individualism or the notion of a total individual that is in dissonance with the collective identity embodied by the nation or family.

In contrast to this form of individualism, the political subjectivity of the Arab revolutionary is formed and shaped both within and across the shadowy edges of political institutions and their production of legitimacy and knowledge. For instance, some activists in al-Tahrir Square that I interviewed are members of the Muslim Brotherhood, but they also criticized its actions and how quickly it entered into a dialogue with the old regime. In the same vein, a Nasserist activist declared to me that she and her group in al-Tahrir Square did not reply to phone calls from the headquarters of their political party for fear that they would impose orders and slogans that they might not like.

Many studies have shown that there is a close link between patrilinear family structures and authoritarian political systems (Courbage and Todd 2007/2011). Without fully equating modernization to eventual democratization, the ongoing change in family structure may be a contributing factor in the Arab revolutions. Given the literacy, exogamy and decrease in fertility rates, the Arab societies were the reference point and context, as argued above, for the individual to become an important autonomous entity. The political subjectivity is expressed not only by toppling the regime, but also by changing the individual. Challand (2011) brings the example of cleaning al-Tahrir Square and the surrounding streets after the end of the protests as a sign of struggling against the past sense of collective inertia and the largely apathetic usage of the public sphere.

Cyberspace comes to empower this reflexive individualism. Each demonstrator became a 'journalist' carrying a mobile phone and filming state repression, thereby bypassing the official media. The success of the protestors in launching the revolution can be attributed to the fact that they use governmentality, the grammar of which is unknown to the state governmentality. For instance, the security apparatus that used to control national mass media, phone and, to an extent, the internet has not been able to control the social media that has been used through different proxies, bypassing the state filtering efforts. While this apparatus has controlled the public sphere, the public cyberspace, with the help of the Arab television channels and alternative media, has been a very important space for activism and mobilization.

Take the case of the high-risk political activism of S.F. interviewed in August 2011. S.F. is a 22-year-old Syrian student studying civil engineering. His family is middle class with his father employed as an engineer. He says:

> I have never been a member of any political party. [...] My family is literally an a-political one. [...] We have never been supporters of the regime nor against it. After one month of reflection, I decided to open an account on Facebook. I use a nickname and I become informed about the place and time of protests in Damascus. I was afraid to join protests on the street. Despite the fact I have never prayed, I went to the mosque and I joined the demonstration from there. I did it three times. I did not tell my family but one of my relatives saw me and informed my parents. My parents gently tried to persuade me not to go to demonstration. When I refused, my parents became so tough with me. I have a wealthy friend who lives alone. He accepted that I live with him for a few weeks. I left home. I kept calling them once every day to assure them that I was safe. Two weeks ago I was arrested on the street while demonstrating. The Syrian intelligence asked me how I knew about the place and the time of the demonstration. I told them from internet and Al Jazeera TV. They asked me to open my Facebook or twitter account. Thank God! I have it with a nickname. They beat me on and off for one day. I kept denying having a social media account. They asked me about my religiosity. I told them that I am not religious at all. Weirdly, they asked me if I am ready to drink alcohol. [...] I was released after three days.

When I asked S.F. about the motivations behind his activism, he replied:

> I want freedom for me and for my people. Tunisians and Egyptians are not better than us. We, Syrians, have provided intellectual debates for the whole Arab World. I cannot bear the idea that someone in power for 11 years and his dad before him for 30 years. In addition, the people around the regime are so corrupted. My engineer friends have told me many stories about how much they would pay to buy off [the authorities] every time they want to get a construction contract from the state. The regime keep talking about the 'new Syria', but we want new Syrian citizens.

When I asked him if political pluralism is established in Syria, would he adhere to a political party, he replied:

> I don't know. I hope I find a party which will bring social justice to people and generate employment for youth. I don't like conservative parties. I will not vote for religious people to become politicians.

The case of S.F. clearly illustrates the capacity of the individual to negotiate his actions with his family and his environment. His political subjectivity is expressed in the form of citizenship and the utopia (in Karl Mannheim's sense of word)[14] of being a new Syrian citizen. His motivation is not ideology, but his commitment showed real claims to freedom, social justice and secularism.

Two factors will influence tremendously the new political subjectivity based on reflexive individualism: the role of the external forces and the media.

Faced with this subjectivity and peaceful protests, foreign powers (especially the Western ones) tried to 'orient' the process and the future new elite formation. In spite of the importance of the international community in effecting the isolation of the ousted regimes, these revolutions are chiefly driven by very reflexive local actors. Suspicion comes from two groups. The first is composed of those who support these regimes that often highlight a Western plot to weaken the Arab World by these revolutions, stating especially the case of Syria and Libya as two regimes that have for long resisted Western imperialism. Faced with the Western intervention in Libya, the Arab nationalists and leftists have been divided over this intervention: between those who support it and those who consider it as a new colonial enterprise. However, in my opinion, we are witnessing a reflexivity in the form of a new dynamic of construction of otherness which is less essentialist and binary, i.e. West versus Islam and Islamic people, to a more nuanced and dynamic otherness. In the case of Syria, the debate is often expressed in terms of conspiracy: Syrian regime supporters coin the opposition as pro-American or anti-resistance; while the latter branded the former as sectarian and vehicles of an Iranian agenda. Rare are those who discuss the two positions, of those who believe in the possibility of reforming the Syrian regime and those who do not.

The second group comprises those who have underestimated the agency of the Arab revolutionaries. In his lecture at the American University of Beirut (AUB) on 1 April 2011, the philosopher and theologist Tareq Ramadan stated that Arab politicized bloggers and some of those who use Facebook and Twitter are trained by the US State Department, a claim that was not confirmed or backed by any evidence.

Concerning the mass media, its pluralism has enabled the new political subjectivity of individuals. The phenomenon of Al Jazeera contributed to the creation of an Arab public sphere, in a Habermasian sense, wherein dialogue, rational, critical, and deliberative debates emerge and evade control by the national regimes. For instance, El Oifi (2005a, p. 68) argues that while Al Jazeera seems to be part of the American recipe for media liberalism that is capable of producing political moderation, it indeed gave voices to individuals and groups to produce the most effective critique of American policy. While mass media, albeit less important, was a means to report the events, the national television stations were completely misinforming their publics. On the 26 January 2011, Egyptian television screened a cooking programme, as if in complete oblivion of what filled the streets. Alternative media (al-Khoury 2011), as well as channels such as Al Jazeera, Al Arabiya, BBC Arabic and France 24 transmitted images sent to them by activist mobiles, providing information and analysis. I should stress that Al Jazeera turned from the 'principle of non-interference' in internal Arab affairs to a stance of 'solidarity' with Arab public grievances.[15] This is why 'mediology', to borrow Debray's (1991) terminology, is a form of new ideology dictated not by intellectuals and philosophers, but by pluralistic actors who are shaping and influencing the new political subjectivity of the revolutionaries.

The importance of the labour movement

In Tunisia, Mohamed Bouazizi's self-immolation sparked an uprising that began as an unorganized and spontaneous event, but which was soon taken over by labour unions. Here again there are different degrees of reflexivity. The General Union of Tunisian Workers (UGTT) was masterful in dealing with the regime: in northern Tunisia, especially in the capital, Tunis, the leaders of the union were negotiating with the regime (low reflexivity) while their counterparts in the south were opposing it (high reflexivity). The Bar Association, with its large force of mobilization in contrast with NGOs, also played an important role in widening the age group of protesters from the youth to all ages, and in spreading it from the peripheries to the capital. It is also important to note the prominent role of lawyers, and even judges, in social movements across the Arab and Islamic world, most obviously Egypt and Pakistan.

As for Egypt, the revolution was sparked by the 6th April Movement that began as a youth group acting in solidarity with the labour strikes in al-Mahalla al-Kubra in 2008 (Abaza 2010). However, the role of labour movements dates back to much earlier than the youth movement. Paul Amar pointed out that:

> 2009 and 2010 were marked by mass national strikes, nation-wide sit-ins, and visible labour protests often in the same locations that spawned this 2011 uprising. Moreover, the rural areas have been rising up against the government's efforts to evict small farmers from their lands and opposed the regime's attempts to re-create the vast land-owner fiefdoms that defined the countryside during the Ottoman and British Colonial periods. [...] In 2008 and in December 2010 we saw the first independent public sector unions emerge. Only one month later, 2011 clusters of unions from most major industrial towns gathered to form an Independent Trade Union Federation. (Amar 2011)

The Egyptian revolution was triggered by the mobilization of the 6th April Movement and the Information Technology group, led by Khaled Said. Both groups used blogs, Facebook, Twitter and SMS to mobilize thousands of demonstrators on 25 January. With the help of the political opposition (with a very particular role of the Muslim Brotherhood) they reached millions of protestors in al-Tahrir Square in Cairo, Alexandria, Zakazik, Mansoura, etc. In addition to their role in all these cities, in Suez the workers' demonstrations led by independent unions initiated the protest there and were the first in the revolution to claim the overthrow of the Hosni Mubarak regime.

Reflexive Islamism

We are in a period of revolutions where political and civil rights supersede (but do not replace) the ideological. Arab regimes as well as some Arab and Western scholars and journalists thought that the 'Arab street' was chaotic, passionate and 'mobilizable' only by political Islam (for instance, Eickelman 2002).[16] The Yemeni, Syrian, Libyan, Tunisian and Egyptian cases show the importance of Islamic movements, yet the success of the first stage of the revolutions can only be attributed to the alliances with other oppositional groups (Bayat 2011, Hroub 2011). Undergoing internal transformations, the

Muslim Brotherhood (and to certain extent the Salafists) raised slogans that go beyond the simplistic: 'Islam is the solution' towards freedom and democracy and concrete claims – as in the cases of other oppositional parties. Thus, we are in an era of post-Islamism in the sense of a new form of *reflexive Islamism* whose leaders have declared constantly their desire for pluralism and respect for freedom of expression. This reflexivity allowed a revolutionary language and political symbols that have referred to democracy, social justice and dignity rather than religious slogans.

Several members of the Muslim Brotherhood and al-Nahda declared they were in favour neither of a secular state nor of a religious one. The use of the notion of *dawla madaneyya* (civil state) is again a self-referencing exercise which raises a problem that terms are not yet determined. In spite of this blurring of terminology and declarations of some Islamic leaders, there is no reason for many Westerner leaders to consider the newly stated position of the Muslim Brotherhood as a smokescreen for a long-term objective of establishing an Islamic state governed by the strict application of *sharia* (Islamic law) (see, for instance, Economist Intelligence Unit 2011).

As such, those who argue for the cultural specificity and exceptionalism of the region no longer have a valid argument. The consequences of exceptionalism are regarded as a digression from the real debate on societies, politics and culture in the Arab World (Kabbanji 2011). One question I have been debating with my students for the past two years on my course on transitional justice at AUB is whether freedom and democracy are universal aspirations or Western values not transferable as such to other societies. My students always brought up the case of the Arab World as the living proof that not all people, regardless of culture and religion, aspire to being free and living under the rule of law. For them, Muslim countries with their autocratic or theocratic regimes are just content to live that way, under the stick of dictatorship and/or *sharia*. What we have been witnessing in Tunisia and Egypt settles that![17] I fully agree with Slavoj Zizek that what is now required is a universalistic position of solidarity.[18] People's aspirations for democracy and freedom are universal objectives.

Conclusion

The Arab World is on the verge of a new history. Revolutions sometimes end up as something different from what their supporters proclaim at the beginning. The equation of people versus dictatorship is still the most important dynamic, but one should watch carefully the active role of the military and the conflicting views within the elite on these revolutions.

This article has argued that the revolution was driven mainly by very 'reflexive' youth and labourers and cannot be understood as Facebook-driven protest waves. There are behind the scenes of these waves; indeed, there are huge structural and economic forces and institutional realignments at work (Amar 2011). We are witnessing a twilight of American hegemony in the region. In spite of the importance of the Western countries in isolating the ousted regimes, these revolutions are chiefly driven by the local actors. However, US foreign policy seeks to influence the process. Its policy is not a realism- nor an idealism-based one, but should be read in the light of territoriality, expediency and utilitarianism.

In contrast with the Eastern and Central European revolutions, the reflexive individualism in the Arab revolutions makes it difficult to have a unified opposition leadership. There are no leaders among the self-appointed NGO leaders, nor among political party leaders, nor among tribal sheikhs. Rather, we are witnessing post-Leninist revolutions without leaders (Badie 2011) (à la the French Revolution), a sort of fragmentation without organization, although over time this has been improved in Yemen and Syria.

The effects of these revolutions are multiple and go beyond toppling the political regime to generate new values. Mohamed Bamyeh coined the term 'of the new patriotism' to describe how these revolutions are transforming the sense of Arab nationalism from 'a project that was assumed to require being represented by leaders or parties, to a popular practice, in which patriotism remains concrete and leaderless, expressed largely as a sense of convivial commonness' (Bamyeh 2011). The role of Al Jazeera television has undeniably been significant in generating a common Arab space and in fostering an Arab public sphere. By extrapolation, the Arab–Israeli conflict was not completely absent from the mind of the protestors. In interviews I conducted, protestors repeatedly used the word 'dignity'[19] and/or 'Arab dignity', something they had been denied by the ousted regimes. Both Egyptian and Tunisian regimes, being part of what is called the 'axis of moderation',[20] had a political discourse that was deeply at odds with popular feelings, which saw their regimes' moderation as a green light for Israel's colonial project and the siege of Gaza. I was surprised to see that even in a pro-government newspaper like *al-Ahram*, there was criticism of Mubarak for having received Benjamin Netanyahu on 4 January 2011, the day after Israel demolished four houses in East Jerusalem and after a bombing of Gaza in which three Palestinians were killed.

There are neighbourhood effects in which upheaval in one country causes a domino effect in others. However, this starting point for a process of democratization is full of minefields. People will no longer be convinced that the only choice is between the stability and security of a dictator and the danger of Islamic extremism. Mao Zedong's old motto is pertinent: 'There is great chaos under heaven – the situation is excellent.' For the immediate future, we should expect many difficult moments and a lot of negotiation with the military authority that has taken power in Egypt. Seen in this light, there are three issues at stake in the next phase.

The first issue is the extent to which opposition elites will unify around their basic claim in the face off with the military elite. In all countries undergoing turmoil, the army plays an important role, but its nature varies in each country (Sayigh 2011). The question to be posed now is: Would the army shift from being part of a regime to a formal institution obliged by constitutional provision and obligations to help in the formation and transition to a democratic state? So far armies in Yemen, Libya and Syria are embedded within the power structures, within ruling elites, whose commanders are part of the family of the rulers (Sayigh 2011). The armies in Egypt and Syria have established an alliance with the new emerging capitalists. In essence, however, the soldiers often reflect socio-economically the mass of the population. As in the case of Latin America, one of the main challenges to democratic state-building processes has been the enforcement of civilian control over the military. Varas (2011) highlights the importance of the professionalization and de-politicization of the army and shows in this regard many trajectories in different regions of Latin America.

The second issue is the extent to which ethnicity, tribalism and sectarianism will obstruct the political reform/revolutions. It is clear that wherever there are such divisions (Bahrain, Yemen, Syria and Libya), the revolution is yet undelivered. While this is a real issue, sometimes it is just a proclaimed one by the regime in order to disqualify the people's claims (the Syrian or Bahraini cases). The case of Lebanon is a very difficult one, where the primary allegiance of the population is to their sect and not to the state.

The third issue emerges after the overthrow of a certain regime, where old differences that had been set aside have come to the fore again – differences of class and ideology, all of which affect the vision of what a just society should be. The major question is the extent to which al-Nahda and the Muslim Brotherhood movements can deepen and consolidate their moderate stances which are based on respecting the principles of democracy and pluralism, as often expressed by their leaders Sheikh Rashid Ghannouchi and Mahmoud Hussein Ahman. It is now known that inside these movements there are many trends ranging from those that are close to a Turkish model and those that reflect conservative Salafists. Scholars such as Burgat (2010) and Tammam (2010) highlight that the former trend is much stronger than the latter, and this affords hope that the process of democratization will accompany personal freedom.

Notes

1. The new Moroccan constitution, replacing that of 1996, supposedly represents a further step in the direction of establishing a liberal-democratic system and does indeed contain provisions to that effect. For instance, there is now explicit recognition that Morocco is a 'parliamentary constitutional monarchy', that national identity is pluralistic and not simply Arab and Muslim, and that, crucially, the figure of the king is no longer 'sacred', but simply inviolable. In addition, parliament's powers have been increased (Dalmasso and Cavatorta 2011).
2. Pressure from protestors in Algeria led to the lifting of the state of emergency in February 2011 as part of a package of concessions by the government.
3. The reform consists of the following. (1) The establishment of a constitutional court to monitor the constitutionality of laws and regulations. (2) The establishment of an independent commission to oversee elections instead of the Ministry of Interior which has previously been in charge of the electoral process. All electoral contestations will be referred to the judiciary instead of parliament. (3) The enhancement of civil liberties, including the criminalization of any infringement on rights and public freedoms or on the sanctity of Jordanians' private life; the prohibition of torture in any form; and a declaration that all forms of communication between citizens shall be treated as secret and not subject to censorship, suspension or confiscation, except by judicial order. (4) The limitation of the government's ability to issue temporary laws during the absence of parliament, a practice that governments exercised at will in the past. (5) The limitation of the State Security Court's jurisdiction to cases of high treason, espionage and terrorism, with citizens being otherwise tried in civilian courts; this includes ministers who were previously tried by a parliamentary high tribunal. (6) The limitation of the government's ability to dissolve parliament without having to resign itself (Muasher 2011).
4. For a criticism of this term, see Khouri (2011).
5. I qualified these unions as 'autonomous' to contrast them with the official workers' unions which are often co-opted by the regime. In this regard, see Duboc (2011), Longuenesse (2007) and Clément (2007).
6. The Agambian concept of state of exception refers to the capacity of the sovereign to claim anytime the state of exception, i.e., governing by the suspension of law rather than by the force of law. For more analytical analysis of the use of the state of exception in the Arab World, see Hanafi (2010a).
7. At a speech given to the European Sociological Association Congress in Geneva, Switzerland, 23 September 2011.
8. Smith and Vivekananda (2007), from Alert International, drew up a list of states at risk based on the identification of two types of risk. First, the Arab states that face a high risk of armed conflict as an indirect consequence of climate change include Algeria, Djibouti, Eritrea, Iraq, the Occupied Territories, Jordan, Lebanon, Somalia, Somaliland, Sudan and Syria. Second, the Arab states that face the potential for political instability

as a knock-on consequence of climate change are Egypt, Libya, Mauritania, Morocco, Saudi Arabia, Western Sahara and Yemen.

9. Ninety per cent across the board, except in Morocco, where it is 81% (Barbin 2011).
10. Impressive declines in fertility have been recorded in the Arab region as a result of increased school enrolment among girls, stronger participation of women in the labour force and delayed marriage. The decline in fertility simultaneously affected two-thirds of Arab countries (Courbage and Todd 2007/2011). According to the 2008 revision, the unweighted average total fertility rate for the Arab countries declined from 6.2 live births per woman in 1980–1985 to 3.3 in 2005–2010, compared with 2.6 at world level, consequently reshaping the age structure of the population of the Arab region (United Nations Economic and Social Commission on Western Asia (ESCWA) 2012).
11. Since the revolution and up to 20 January 2012, the Strategic Research and Communication Center reported 4342 Syrians killed, 6159 missing, 15 000 protestors incarcerated and upwards of 12 577 Syrian refugees (Syrian Observatory of Human Rights 2012).
12. For a compelling description of the constituency of al-Tahrir Square, see Khairi (2011).
13. For a critical assessment of using the ambiguous term of social classes, see Kabbanji (2011).
14. Also very interesting is how many times Wael Ghonaim in his Facebook account used the word 'dream'. In the words of Jeffery Alexander: 'Ghonaim insisted to his fellow Egyptians that dreaming is a civil obligation' (Alexander 2011, p. 66).
15. The solidarity position (qualified by some as lacking professionalism and neutrality), however, is debatable, yet very instrumental in the Egyptian, Libyan and Syrian cases.
16. For a critique of the usage of the Arab Street, see El Oifi (2005b).
17. See also Badawi and Makdisi (2010), who show the falsity of the argument that religion explains the democracy deficit in the Arab World; and the criticism of Challand (2009) of the idea of a civil society deficit in Arab–Islamic areas.
18. Interview with him on Al Jazeera, 5 February 2011.
19. Dignity expressed by different evocable: *sharaf* ('honour', 'virtue') as in Wael Ghonaim's letter in his Facebook account, 'All of Egypt is demanding honor' (Alexander, 2011, p. 7).
20. The regimes of Augusto Pinochet of Chile as well as of the Shah of Iran, Mohammad Reza Pahlavi, used to be called moderate.

References

Abaza, Mona, 2010. On recent social protests in Egypt: a success story in spite of the absence of political parties. *In*: Sari Hanafi, ed. *The state of exception and resistance in the Arab world*. Beirut: Center for Arab Unity Studies, pp. 175–206. [in Arabic].

Agamben, G., 1998. *Homo sacer. Sovereign power and bare life*. Stanford, CA: Stanford University Press.

Agamben, G., 2005. *State of exception*. Chicago: University of Chicago Press.

Alexander, A., 2011. *Performative revolution in Egypt: an essay in cultural power*. London: Bloomsbury.

Amar, P., 2011. *Why Mubarak is out February 1, 2011*. Posted by bullybloggers in Current Affairs.

ARI, 2010. The state of reform in the Arab world 2009-2010 (annual report). Arab Reform Initiative. Available from: http://www.arab-reform.net/spip.php?article2990. [Accessed 5 July 2010].

Badie, D., 2011. La revanche des sociétés arabes. Interview with Bertrande Badie. *Le Monde*, 24 February.

Bakhtin, M., 1984. *Rabelais and his world*. Bloomington, IA: Indiana University Press.

Bamyeh, Mohammed A., 2011. Arab revolutions and the making of a new patriotism. *Orient*. Available from: http://redchannels.org/writings/RC001/pdf/Furnaces_RC001.pdf/.

Barbin, J.L.S., 2011. The Arab Spring and demography: the revolutionary power of youth. Available from: http://en.qantara.de/The-Revolutionary-Power-of-Youth/16590c16844i0p/index.html/.

Bardawl, Fadi, 2011. Ufūl al-Iktiʾāb: mulāḥaẓātān ḥawla al-thawrāt al-ʿarabīyah al-rāhinah [Two notes about the Arab revolutions]. *Majallat al-Dirāsāt al-Filasṭīnīyah*, 88, 63–68. [in Arabic].

Bayat, Asef, 2011. Egypt, and the post-Islamist Middle East. *Open Democracy*, 8 February. Available from: http://www.opendemocracy.net/asef-bayat/egypt-and-post-islamist-middle-east/.

Bouazizi, Mohsen, 2010. Sociology of the indifference: from indifference to the free aggression in Tunisia. *In*: Sari Hanafi, ed. *The state of exception and resistance in the Arab world*. Beirut: Center for Arab Unity Studies, 207–208. [in Arabic].

Bourdieu, P., 1999. *Acts of resistance: against the tyranny of the market*. New York, NY: New Press.

Burgat, F., 2010. Un Changement islamiste dans la continuité: Salafistes contre Frères musulmans. *Le Monde diplomatique*, June.

Challand, B., 2009. *Palestinian civil society: foreign donors and the power to promote and exclude*. London: Routledge.

Challand, B., 2011. The counter-power of civil society and the emergence of a new political imaginary in the Arab world. *Constellations*, 18 (3).

Che Guevara, 1967/1981. Message to the Tricontinental [April 1967]. *In: Resurrecting a revolutionary cinema. The hour of the furnaces*. 5 December 1981. Available from: http://redchannels.org/writings/RC001/pdf/Furnaces_RC001.pdf/.

Clément, F., 2007. Élections ouvrières: entre fraude et chasse aux 'Frères masqués. *In*: E. Klaus and C. Hassabo, eds. *Chroniques égyptiennes*. Cairo: Cedej, 59–86.

Courbage, Y. and Todd, E., 2007/2011. Le rendez-vous des civilisations [2007]. *In*: Y. Courbage and E. Todd, eds. *A convergence of civilizations: the transformation of Muslim societies*. New York, NY: Columbia University Press.

Dalmasso, E. and Cavatorta, F., 2011. *Jadaliyya*. Available from: http://www.jadaliyya.com/pages/index/2365/the-never-ending-story_protests-and-constitutions/.

Debray, R., 1991. *Cours de mediologiegenerale*. Paris: Gallimard.

Dhillon, Navtej and Yousef, Tarik, 2011. *Generation in waiting: the unfulfilled promise of young people in the Middle East*. Washington, DC: Brookings Institution Press.

Duboc, M., 2011. La contestation sociale en Égypte depuis 2004 – précarisation et mobilisation locale des ouvriers de l'industrie textile. *RevueTiers monde*, numbero hors series, 95–116.

Elbadawi, Ibrahim and Makdisi, Samir, eds, 2010. *Democracy in the Arab world: explaining the deficit*. Abingdon: Routledge.

Economist Intelligence Unit, 2011. *Spring tide or will the Arab risings yield democracy, dictatorship or disorder?* Report. Available from: http://pages.eiu.com/rs/eiu2/images/Arab_Spring_Tide_Whitepaper_Jun2011.pdf [Accessed 5 July 2011].

Eickelman, D.F., 2002. The Arab 'street' and the Middle East's democracy deficit. *Naval War College Review*, 40 (4), 39–48.

El Oifi, Mohammed, 2005a. Influence without power: Aljazeera and the Arab public sphere. *In*: M. Zayeni, ed. *The Al Jazeera phenomenon: critical perspectives on new Arab media*. Boulder, CO: Paradigm, 124–145.

El Oifi, Mohammed, 2005b. L'opinion publique arabe entre logiques étatiques et solidarités transnationales. *Raisons politiques*, 2005/3 (no. 19), 45–62.

Hanafi, Sari, 2010a. Framing Arab socio-political space: state governmentality, governance and non-institutional protestation. *Contemporary Arab Affairs*, 3 (2), 148–162.

Hanafi, Sari, ed., 2010b. *The state of exception and resistance in the Arab world*. Beirut: Center for Arab Unity Studies. [in Arabic].

Hanafi, Sari 2010c. Displacement due to environmental pressures and climate changes in the Arab countries. Unpublished report presented to UNDP, Beirut.

Hanafi, S. and Tabar, L. 2005. *Donors, international organizations, local NGOs. Emergence of the Palestinian globalized elite*. Ramallah: Muwatin.

Hroub, Khaled, 2011. Arab third way: beyond dictators and Islamists. *Open Democracy*, 9 February. Available from: http://www.opendemocracy.net/khaled-hroub/arab-third-way-beyond-dictators-and-islamists/.

Kabbanji, J., 2011. Why have the Tunisian and Egyptian revolutions surprised us? *Iḍāfāt: Arab Journal of Sociology*, 14, 9–31. [in Arabic].

Khairi, Amina, 2011. Tahrir Square gathered all groups of youth, *al-Hayat*, 7 February, 7.

Khouri, Rami, 2011. *Drop the Orientalist term 'Arab Spring'*. Available from: http://www.dailystar.com.lb/Opinion/Columnist/2011/Aug-17/Drop-the-Orientalist-term-Arab-Spring.ashx#ixzz1VGW806O8/.

Al-Khoury, Tania, 2011. Kulonashohoud 'ayan: rabii al-Arab bi al-sowarwa al-harb al-Ilekitroniyya [We are all witness: the Arab Spring in image and the cyberwar]. *Majallat al-dirast al-falastiniyya*, 88, 122–132. [in Arabic].
Longuenesse, E., 2007. *Professions et société au Proche-Orient. Déclin des élites et crise des classes moyennes*. Rennes: Presses Universitaires de Rennes.
Al-Madini, Tawfic, 2011. Rabii al-thawrat al-dimocratiyya al-Arabiyya [The Spring of the Arab revolutions]. *al-mustaqbal al-Arabi*. [in Arabic].
Marktanner, M., 2011. The economic causes of the Arab uprising. Paper presented at a workshop at the American University of Beirut (AUB), Beirut, Lebanon, 2011.
Mbembe, A., 2003. Necropolitics. *Public Culture*, 15 (1), 11–40.
Muasher, Marwan, 2011. *Jordan's proposed constitutional amendments – a first step in the right direction*. Beirut: The Carnegie Middle East Program.
Reynolds, J., 2011. Emergency, governmentality, and the Arab Spring. *Jadaliyya*, 14 August.
Sayigh, Yezid, 2011. The role of the army in the Arab uprisings. Paper presented at the Centre for Mediterranean, Middle East and Islamic Studies. Athens, Greece, 4 May 2011.
Shayeb, Riyad, 2010. Social impact of drought and principle of liberating prices in the north eastern region, Alnour. Available from: http://www.an-nour.com/index.php?option=com_content&task=view&id=10320&Itemid=34 Myriam (in Arabic).
Smith, D. and Vivenkananda, J., 2007. *A climate of conflict: the links between climate change, peace and war*. London: International Alert.
Syrian Observatory of Human Rights, 2012. Available from: http://www.syriahr.com/. [Accessed 5 January 2012].
Tammam, Hossam, 2010. *Salafazed Moslim Brotherhood*. Alexandria: Alexandria Library. [in Arabic].
Todorov, T., 2011. La tyrannie de l'individu. *Le Monde*, 28 March, 18.
Touraine, A., 1995. *Critique of modernity*. Oxford: Basil Blackwell.
United Nations Development Programme (UNDP), 2009. *Arab human development report*. Washington, DC: UNDP.
United Nations Economic and Social Commission on Western Asia (ESCWA), 2012. *Population in the Arab World declines*. Available from: http://www.alarabiya.net/articles/2010/07/27/115002.html.
Varas, A., 2011. *Democratic transitions and the Latin American military*. ARI Thematic Studies, Available from: http://www.arab-reform.net/IMG/pdf/Sector_Reforms_Augusto_Varas_Eng.pdf.

The socio-economic factors behind the Arab revolutions†

Georges Corm

Professor of Economics and former Lebanese Minister of Finance

Western and Arab media have understated the socio-economic factors behind the various mass uprisings in different Arab countries. Focus has been placed on demand for political freedom and the ousting of corrupted dictators. The demand for greater social justice and a different developmental model has been largely ignored in most cases. For Western media, it was only natural that values of *political* freedom which were part of the revolutionary slogans should be emphasized, on the consideration that such represents a virtuous Western influence that animated the Arab revolts against tyranny and the deprivation of human rights. For pan-Arab media largely owned and managed by Saudi wealth, joining the chorus of condemnations of corrupted dictators originating from the military establishment in various Arab republics was intended to make the monarchy be looked upon as a regime that cares for its people.

In fact, both Western and pan-Arab media avoided discussion in any depth of socio-economic issues that caused the uprisings of large masses of people for whom poverty and marginalization prevent them aspiring to priority or individual political liberties and freedoms. These masses who emerged in huge numbers to demonstrate together with other more well-to-do social strata of the population were first and foremost motivated by the need to improve their socio-economic situation and gain access to decent employment opportunities.

For Western media and decision-makers emphasizing the political demand for democracy and human rights almost exclusively permitted escaping the discussion of the negative socio-economic effects of implementing neo-liberal economic prescriptions and recipes that Arab countries have been following over the last decades under the powerful influence of the International Monetary Fund (IMF), The World Bank and the European Union. IMF annual reports based on Article IV Consultation on Tunisia, Morocco, Egypt, Syria and other Arab countries have shown a significant degree of optimism and approval of progresses realized in these countries thanks to the drive for liberalization. These reports have emphasized a number of issues including: (1) the improvement in fundamental macro-economic variables (inflation, budget deficit, balance of payment deficit); (2) the positive developments of local capital markets; (3) institutional modernization in terms of market liberalization (free trade,

---

†This paper was originally given as a presentation at the *Conference of the Circulo de Economia de Barcelone*, 22 June 2011, Barcelona, Spain.

free flows of capital, central bank reform, privatization and the reduction of the size of the public sector); and (4) improvement in banking market performance.

Both IMF and World Bank reports on the Middle East and North Africa (MENA) region analysed the lack of productivity and economic diversification or the moderate gross domestic product (GDP) annual growth rates as being due exclusively to the need to deepen the neo-liberal reform drive. In their view, Arab states should increase labour 'flexibility' and should not adhere to overvalued currencies so that their exports might be more dynamic. Government-funded social protection networks should be rationalized to target exclusively the poorest strata of the population only and thereby reduce the burden of state subsidies and the percentage of budget deficit in relation to the GDP. The World Bank reports look favourably on encouraging more emigration as a way to reduce domestic unemployment. In general terms, the IMF, World Bank and European Union considered Arab governments on the whole to be successful reformers implementing their recommendations consistently if rather slowly. No one within the Western donor community would have anticipated that revolts would erupt in the Arab world due in large part to deteriorating socio-economic conditions, which were neither properly monitored nor addressed.

What was actually happening in terms of real economy in Egypt, Tunisia, Morocco, Syria, Yemen, Saudi Arabia, Bahrain and Oman was out of their respective fields of vision. In spite of many studies by Arab economists indicating the deteriorating living conditions in rural areas along with the development and proliferation of shanty towns in the outskirts and suburbs of Arab cities, and despite available data on the burgeoning unemployment crisis and brain drain detrimental to the productivity of the real economies, Western attention has remained focused exclusively on macroeconomic balances and liberalization drives according to neo-liberal ideology. In general, pan-Arab financial institutions such as the Arab Monetary Fund or the Arab Fund for Economic and Social Development were not party to a markedly different attitude, except for their focus on rural poverty and on the widening trade gap in food products.

In fact, the recent economic history of the Arab world is one of an increasingly negative model of 'bad growth' to which few have yet paid attention which largely explains the vital socio-economic dimension of the Arab revolts. It is under this bad growth model that corruption has flourished and that unhealthy multifaceted links were created between the business establishment and the political establishment. Complete silence prevailed with regard to this phenomenon in the media as well as in academic research communities along with the technical reports of the international financial institutions (IFI), the European Union or the Arab IFI.

This paper will examine successively in the next section the components of this bad growth model and the subsequent section the way to transform bad growth into good growth.

The main characteristics of the Arab bad growth model

When compared with successful emerging countries, Arab economic growth and social performance have been characterized by average low rates of GDP per capita growth (with the exception of the Arab oil-exporting countries with small populations) as well as by very high rates of increasing unemployment, in spite of good endowment in natural resources. Eight strong indicators of the underperformance of the Arab economies can be mentioned here.

The lowest rate of active population to total population

International Labour Organization (ILO) statistics show that, on average, the rate of the active population to the total population in the Arab countries, which is 45%, contrasts sharply the with average world rate of 61.2%; and where the average rate in the East Asia region is as high as 70%. In addition, labour statistics in Arab countries show a very low participation rate for women in the labour markets and a very high rate of informal employment yielding very low revenues. This rate accounts for 70% of total employment in Morocco and 48% in Egypt (ILO 2011).

The highest unemployment rate to active population

If the overall average unemployment rate in the Arab world does not appear very high at around 10%, it remains the highest in the world (with the exception of Spain and Central Europe). The unemployment rate among young people (15–35 year olds) is much higher, hovering around 25%, while in other parts of the developing world the corresponding rate ranges between 8.9% and 15.7%. Another characteristic of youth unemployment in Arab countries is the very high rate of unemployment affecting young graduates of higher or secondary education. Thus in Tunisia, for example, the unemployment rate among higher education graduates jumped from 3.8% 1994 to 17.5% in 2006, while the share of jobseekers with degrees of higher education in the total rose from 23% in 2001 to 55% in 2007; and the percentages of job offers for the category were far lower. In Egypt the proportion of unemployed workers with a secondary education is estimated at 80% of the total number of unemployed; in Morocco the figure is 29.6%, in Algeria 37.8% and in Tunisia 42.5%.[1]

Stagnation of real salaries and poverty indicators

Furthermore, according to the ILO, real salaries in the MENA region have increased only minimally, if at all. Additionally, the productivity of workers, which is the reference for real wages, increased less in the 1990s in the MENA region than anywhere else except in Central Europe and Central Asia, which undertook extensive economic restructuring. In a sample of four Arab countries (Algeria, Jordan, Morocco and Syria) and Turkey the official minimum salary is extremely low, ranging from a low of US$164 per month in Syria to a high of US$425 per month in Turkey, while in Morocco the minimum salary for non-agricultural work is US$235 per month and for agricultural work a mere US$152 per month.[2] Another statistical source estimates that the average yearly per capita income in rural areas in the Arab countries did not exceed US$320 in 2008, against an average annual GDP per capita of US$5858 for the same year (including the oil-exporting countries of the Arabian Peninsula).[3]

Moreover, available statistics on poverty in the MENA region confirm the fact that the percentage of people living in conditions of poverty is probably greatly underestimated as the share of the GDP corresponding to per capita consumption in terms of US$ per day shows the extent of poverty at the national level in several Arab countries. It ranges between a minimum of US$2.34 per day in Mauritania to a maximum of US $11.05 per day in Jordan, though daily per capita consumption in most cases hovers around US$5 (with the exception of Lebanon at US$22.63 attributable to the highest level of emigrant remittances to GDP in the region).

A recent report charting the progress of the Millennium Development Goals in Arab countries (Economic and Social Commission for Western Asia (ESCWA) 2010) stated that although only 5% of the population in the Arab world falls within the definition of extreme poverty, which is pegged to people with an available income of less than US $1.25 per day, the figure under an adjustment of this definition of poverty to subsume those earning less than US$2 per day would account for 21% of the population. Moreover, 22% of the population in the area has *no* access to basic healthcare, education or a decent standard of living. The same report points out that infant malnutrition and malnourishment is still high and that in this respect the Millennium Development Goals are far from being attained. Furthermore, although there has been substantial progress in the primary and secondary education of girls, women's empowerment still remains a distant objective. Additionally, while infant mortality has been greatly reduced, recent statistics show an alarming rate of maternal mortality and premature pregnancies.

These poverty levels are especially shocking because not only is the MENA region very rich in energy and phosphate resources, but also some of its countries possess extensive areas of fertile land as well as water resources (Algeria, Egypt, Lebanon, Morocco, Sudan, Syria and Tunisia).

High economic growth rate dependency on external variables

Arab economies have become highly dependent on external variables to sustain growth rates, that is: oil prices, rainfall, tourism revenues and migrant/expatriate remittances. This why GDP annual growth rates are highly volatile for both oil-exporting- and non-oil-exporting countries. In the last 50 years international oil price variations (and accessorily phosphate and chemicals prices) have become the main determinant of the overall rates of growth in the region. This is due to the fact that oil-exporting countries are now importing manpower from other Arab countries and the demand for immigrant manpower increases with higher oil prices, while it decreases with falls in prices. Boom conditions in Arab oil-exporting countries due to sudden rises in oil prices activate foreign direct investment (FDI) by rich Arab nationals from these countries. Thus, growth rates in non-oil-exporting Arab countries have become dependent on Arab FDI and Arab migrant/expatriate remittances that accrue also from Arab emigrants to Europe or the United States and Canada.

Over and above this, in countries with agricultural potential like Morocco, Syria and Tunisia (in addition to Egypt and the Sudan), lack of adequate hydraulic infrastructure and water management programmes has largely kept agricultural income dependent on the amount of annual rainfall.

Finally, mass tourism from both Europe and the rich Arab oil-exporting countries is also an important source of income that is highly dependent on domestic political stability and on the variation in GDP in the countries of origin of the tourists. In fact, the main engines of growth in the Arab countries are *not* locally based (such as in industrial innovation, economic diversification or high value-added services that can be exported). These remain dependent to a large extent on external variables unrelated to the local economic dynamic.

Emigration and brain drain as a major indicator of deficient growth

Emigration is a consequence of the high unemployment rate, but in case of some Arab countries the dependence developed on remittances from migrants/expatriates has become very high. According to an ILO study, the flood of migrants from the MENA regions, especially the countries of the southern Mediterranean basin, is a major symptom of bad growth and of the resulting distortions in the labour markets. Between them the five Arab countries of the Mediterranean mentioned above (Algeria, Egypt, Lebanon, Morocco and Tunisia) have an emigrant population of over 8.1 million. These emigrants are distributed as follows: 55.44% in Europe (mainly Belgium, France, Germany and Spain), 23.76% in oil-exporting Arab countries employing unskilled workers and middle-management executives (see below), and 7.33% in traditional destination countries of immigration (Australia, Canada, New Zealand and the United States), the rest having migrated to various other Sub-Saharan countries of Africa and Central or South America (ILO 2010a).

It is worth noting that between 1998 and 2007, the flow of migrants from the five aforementioned Arab countries more than *doubled* in volume, in spite of the restrictive measures adopted by many European governments. Their numbers rose from 90 800 immigrants in 1998 to 195 600 in 2007. All in all, there were 1.55 million new migrants to Europe between 1998 and 2007. Some of them were students travelling to study abroad (an estimated 100 000 a year from the five countries plus Iraq), a large proportion of whom (recently estimated to be 54%) would never return to settle in their home countries. In point of fact, the surge in migration is increasingly taking the form of a brain drain and an exodus of qualified manpower, and this has led to an even greater decline in productivity as well as its becoming one of the primary features of the bad growth with which we are concerned.[4]

Of course, the Arab countries are not the only ones facing a surge in migration. The same phenomenon exists in other countries, whether in Sub-Saharan Africa, Central and South America, or Asia. Many studies have actually vaunted the 'merits' of emigration and the value of migrants' remittances to their countries of origin as doing much to resolve the problems of poverty and unemployment back home. However, it is now obvious that it is not the countries themselves that encouraged or even organized the extensive migration of their citizens abroad in order to benefit from their remittances whose economies have grown fastest. Indeed, in eleven countries that are particularly concerned by such migration movements (Algeria, Bangladesh, Egypt, India, Lebanon, Morocco, Nigeria, Philippines, Sri Lanka, Sudan and Tunisia), overall remittances increased by 800% for a total of US$800 billion between 1990 and 2008, whereas the average per capita increase in GDP during the same period was just 170%; in seven of the countries cited it was still under US$2000 per year in 2008, and in five cases under US$1000 per year (World Bank n.d.). Such statistics clearly show the absence of any appreciably positive impact of migration on the countries of origin.

Over the same period the group of countries exporting human and natural resources received over US$190 billion in development aid. In other words, between 1990 and 2008 they benefited from around US$1 trillion in external resources without a single one of them entering into a virtuous cycle of development based on dynamic local policies to acquire technology, unlike the Asian countries which instead of encouraging emigration opted for a proactive human resources mobilization policy and thus benefited from the spread of globalization by developing their capacity to export goods and services and then to satisfy domestic demand.

The cases of Nigeria (with its per capita GDP of US$1370 in 2008) and Algeria (whose per capita GDP rose to US$4845 for the same year after stagnating at under US$2000 for ten years before finally taking off in response to the boom in oil prices) are particularly dramatic, as neither managed to raise their domestic standard of living to any substantial degree, despite the additional advantage of a major inflow of financial resources from the energy sector – unlike some other countries that had no such rent-based income.

Indonesia provides another case in point. Although a major exporter of petroleum and also of wood, and for all its abundant natural resources, the country's per capita income between 1990 and 2003 was between a lowly US$640 to US$1000. As in the case of Algeria, Indonesian per capita GDP did not move substantially upward until the spectacular boom in energy prices from 2005 onwards bringing the per capita income to the level of US$2246 in 2008. By way of comparison, in 2008 three economies that were devoid of any natural resources but which did not encourage the emigration of their human resources had an annual average per capita GDP that was far in excess of those just mentioned: the Republic of Korea with US$19 115, Singapore with US$37 597, and Taiwan with US$16 988.

In fact, between 1970 and 2009 the Arab countries to the south and east of the Mediterranean received US$396 billion. The inflow of annual remittances has been steadily increasing over the last ten years – growing from US$10 billion per year in 2000 to over US$27 billion by 2009. Remittances constituted an ever-increasing proportion of the GDP of the countries concerned, reaching a level of around 20% in Lebanon but also 6% in Egypt and 9% in Morocco, according to World Bank (n.d.) statistics. Moreover, available data on the use of migrants' remittances confirm that when they are not used to increase consumption, these savings go towards financing the acquisition or construction of housing or of commercial businesses, which further increases the concentration of local investment in the property market (real estate) and local trade sector (European Investment Bank 2005).

As far as the brain drain is concerned, it is mainly attributable to the phenomenon of students studying abroad but not returning to their countries of origin, in addition to a high number of professionals who are unemployed or dissatisfied with local working conditions (like doctors, engineers, biologists) and therefore opt to leave their countries. Recently, an employment agency specializing in qualified manpower and operating in the Gulf Cooperation Council (GCC) countries estimated that over 54% of the Arab students abroad did not return home and that 70 000 university graduates from the Arab world emigrated each year.[5] It is also significant that the estimated 120 602 Arab students registered in foreign universities in 1999 was higher than the number of Chinese (106 036) or Indian (52 932) students (United Nations Educational, Scientific and Cultural Organization (UNESCO) 2005). It is also estimated that 100 000 scientists, doctors and engineers leave the Arab world *each year* not to return to their home country, constituting a brain drain that costs their countries of origin over US$1 billion annually.[6] Another study notes that the exodus of 450 000 'brains' from the Arab world, which has cost the countries from which they migrated upwards of US$200 billion.[7]

The high concentration of investments in a few sectors hindering economic diversification

Although foreign investment grew considerably in the Arab region, it did not revitalize the region's economies. In fact it remained well below foreign investment in other emerging economies. Moreover, it encouraged the concentration of investment in a few sectors, some of them offering little value added and entailing little risk (oil, gas and petrochemical sectors; luxury housing and tourism; the banking and financial sector; large retail outlets). This is clearly apparent from available data on some of the MENA economies. A recent ESCWA report for 2008, for instance, notes that the sectors that attracted the most foreign investment were energy and allied industries, services (especially financial services) along with real estate (ESCWA 2009, also United Nations Conference on Trade and Development (UNCTAD) 2008, n.d.).

In Saudi Arabia for the same year, the energy and allied industries sector attracted 41.2% of total FDI, against 20.8% for real estate, 25.5% for services and 6.9% for other activities: other industries attracted only 5.6% of the total. In the United Arab Emirates the structure of FDI was even more concentrated in 2006, with over 60% going to just two sectors: construction (29%) and financial and insurance intermediation (34.4%). That year only 10% of total FDI went to the industrial sector. In Lebanon 50% of the total in 2007 went to the real estate sector, while tourism and financial services attracted 33%. In Egypt the petroleum sector drew 57% of FDI in 2008. The same year, Jordan's hotel sector attracted 36% and its industrial free zones 56%. In Morocco the sectors that drew the largest share of FDI in 2001 were post and telecommunications services with 81% (because of the sector's privatization and the launching of the country's mobile telephone system) and real estate with 31% in 2002. The same happened in Tunisia, where privatization of the telecommunications sector attracted 45.2% of the accumulated total of FDI between 2002 and 2006.

It is clear that much the same phenomenon occurred with FDI as with migrants' remittances financial flows. FDI was massively concentrated on rent-based sectors while migrants' remittances were concentrated on consumption. Though this *did* create employment opportunities, notably in the mobile phone and tourism sectors, the fact remains that the increase in FDI did *nothing* to resolve the underlying problems of the employment market.

The very low level of research and development (R&D) and the absence of systems to support national innovation

Most Arab countries suffer from both very low level of research and development (R&D) and from the fragmentation of systems for acquiring and disseminating science and technology (S&T) in their societies. Because of its bad growth, the MENA region has one of the lowest productivity rates in the world, as shown by many indicators. This is particularly true of the number of patents registered by companies or individuals in the region compared with other countries and regions of the world. Thus, the total number of patents registered between 1963 and 2009 in all the countries of the MENA region was only 568, while the Republic of Korea alone registered 66 729 patents and Taiwan registered 77 285. Considering that all these countries were at roughly the same stage of development a mere 50 years ago, the figures illustrates just how little innovation has come out of the MENA countries.

This innovation deficit is also reflected in the very low level of expenditure on R&D – under 0.5% of GDP in most countries of the region compared with a world average of 1.9%, and 2.5% in the more dynamic and innovative countries. It is visible, too, in the small number of scientific publications in the region. This state of affairs explains why the relative technology content of the region's exports is so low, ranging as it does from 0.3% to a maximum of 7% of the region's total exports. The very small share of high-technology exports is in sharp contrast, for example, with that of the Republic of Korea (32%), Malaysia (47.1%), Singapore (49.1%) or Thailand (26.2%).[8]

Another indicator of the extent of the region's shortcomings in innovation is that of the brain drain, as already described. This has been a source of concern for years, but the fact that emigration has been encouraged in recent years by public policies advocated as a means of combating unemployment among university graduates and by policies pursued by many Arab governments has contributed to minimizing or diverting attention from the problem. A recent analysis of the subject estimated that nations to the south and east of the Mediterranean, with the partial exception of Turkey, have no human capital mobilization strategy conducive to the development of certain technological fields, especially those that constitute the driving force behind economic globalization.

This shortfall in S&T is not due to lack of universities – the region has many such institutions, some of a very high standard. Rather, it is because there is no integration into a national system for innovation that enjoys the strong backing of the state, the educational system and the private sector. Many recent reports and studies on the scientific and industrial lag of the MENA countries provide ample evidence that the few R&D institutions that exist have little productive potential (United Nations Development Programme (UNDP) 2010, UNESCO 2005, International Finance Corporation and Islamic Development Bank 2011). They all tend to be isolated from one another instead of forming a fully developed network integrated in all parts of the economy to provide it with an innovation capacity. And because there are no specific national technological or scientific objectives and no public policies to further them anyway, the fragmentation of R&D institutions tends to be self-perpetuating. Their usefulness is therefore not immediately apparent and the budgets they attract are correspondingly low. In addition, there is little contact between teaching institutions, private sector business associations, professional associations and trade unions, just as there is no established mechanism for consultations between the state, business and professional associations, and workers' and agricultural trade unions. This can be attributed to the absence of a national goal for them to attain in terms of acquiring and disseminating industrial technology as well as to the lack of any comprehensive industrial strategy or R&D policy to achieve such goals.

By way of example, UNESCO's annual report on the state of science around the world for 2005 (UNESCO 2005) drew attention to the knowledge gap in the Arab world, as evidenced by the following indicators: the low level of translation and publication of scientific articles and books; the almost total absence of scientific articles from the Arab world *cited in other scientific publications*; the lack of technological innovation as reflected in the very small number of patents registered in the Arab world; the minimal expenditure on R&D, making the region the least concerned with R&D in the world, especially when compared with military expenditure; the small amount spent on information and communications technology (ICT) and on higher education, as illustrated by the lack of autonomy of the universities and the rigidity of teaching curricula that are ill-suited to a knowledge-based global economy; the fact that the various levels of education are not linked to professional experience and human resource development in the public and private sectors; the very high rate of illiteracy; the poor distribution of university-level students among the various branches of knowledge – especially those concerned with science and technology; and poor standards for teaching of foreign languages.

The UNESCO report for 2010 focused on a description of the shortcomings of S&T systems (UNESCO 2010). It revealed that although many Arab countries established S&T institutions as soon as they acquired independence, they still have no national policy or strategy in this area. Sectoral policies for agriculture, water and the environment do exist, but budget allocations for their adequate implementation are rarely sufficient. Moreover, according to the report, many Arab states have established industrial parks affording a good infrastructure for the creation of new enterprises, yet only seven countries have an academy of science. As the report notes, ‘the indifference shown by decision-makers to S&T is a major contributor to the current vegetative state of S&T’.

UNESCO’s 2010 report refers once again to the small number of patents awarded in the Arab region, the small number of published scientific works and articles, high rates of illiteracy, the very low level of exports with a high-technology content, and the fact that the development of the university-level systems of education is driven far more by supply than by demand. It analyses all the deficiencies of these systems and the contradictory objectives they are supposed to achieve. It concludes by recalling that although most Arab countries have had scattered and disparate elements of a science, technology and innovation system for at least four decades, ‘little has changed in terms of the impact of science and the scientific enterprise for achieving socioeconomic development, or generating new knowledge’. Also, the report recalls in its Conclusion that the huge effort that is needed to catch up with other countries in the S&T field has been successfully accomplished in other countries that were once at the same stage of development as the Arab states, including the cases of Brazil, China, India, Ireland, Mexico and the Republic of Korea. Regarding the private sector, however, it does point out that there is little concern for S&T and that the sector is more attracted by trade in goods and services than in genuinely productive activities.

Finally, as in its 2005 report UNESCO (2010) or the conclusions of Antoine Zahlan analysis, the 2010 report refers once again to the problem of the S&T system fragmentation in the Arab countries and to the fact that their potential is championed only by individuals rather than by institutions. It urges the reader to bear in mind that the rentier economy is a key factor in the region’s technological and scientific stagnation.

Reference should also be made to the recent publication of a periodical report on the state of knowledge in the Arab world, published jointly by the UNDP and the Mohammed bin Rashid Al Maktoum Foundation (2010). The first report, for 2009, conducted an exhaustive analysis of the principal political and institutional obstacles to knowledge build up in the Arab countries. It takes up the well-known themes and indicators concerning the region’s stagnation in S&T and proposes ways and means of making up the knowledge deficit in the Arab world so as to bring about a change in the alarming state of S&T in the region. The report also contains a well-documented statistical annex concerning the relevant indicators.

Finally, the International Finance Corporation recently published a joint report with the Islamic Development Bank on youth employment and the adaptation of teaching systems in the MENA region to the requirements of development (International Finance Corporation and Islamic Development Bank 2011). The report estimates that youth unemployment costs the region some US$50 billion per year.

Deficiencies of external trade: another major symptom of bad growth

An analysis of the foreign trade of the countries of the MENA region points to another serious consequence of the shortcomings of the growth model and of the bad development to which they give rise. This can be seen from the deficit of over US$67 billion in the 2009 trade balance of seven countries of the MENA region (Algeria, Egypt, Jordan, Lebanon, Morocco, Syria and Tunisia), despite petroleum and gas exports worth over

US$57 billion in the same year. In other words, if one discounts energy exports, the trade deficit of this group of countries amounts to US$127 billion, which in per capita terms is the equivalent of US$675 per person per annum.

A slightly closer analysis of this group's trade reveals that their industrial sector is totally dependent on other countries, since their deficit in industrial trade is over US$82 billion, with a rate of coverage of imports of no more than 35%. And the figure would be even lower if one were to exclude products deriving from natural resources and allied industries, such as inorganic chemical products and fertilizers valued at about US$5 billion in export earnings. Furthermore, a large share of these countries' exports of manufactured goods is attributable to industrial subcontracting activities (US$23.9 billion), mostly in apparel and accessories, footwear, textile yarn, and fabrics as well as electrical machinery, apparatuses and appliances. All these industrial and manufacturing activities are undertaken in free zones under contract to European or United States' companies and not integrated in the local economies.

The most serious dependency is on medical and pharmaceutical products where the coverage of imports is no more than 19.3%, machinery and transport equipment where it is around 17.8%, professional and scientific instruments at 18.6%, and photographic equipment, optical goods and watches at 13.1%. However, one can also point to a very strong dependency on plastics in primary form with a coverage of only 14.8%, not to mention the enormous relative dependency of the road vehicles sector (6.7% coverage), specialized machinery and appliances (5.4%), metalworking machines and appliances (3.4%), other industrial machinery and machine parts (6.5%), and power-generating machinery and equipment (10.4%).

The foreign trade deficits of the countries analysed are also very high in terms of food products (US$12.16 billion) and even animal and vegetable oils, fats and waxes (US$1.64 billion), despite the considerable agricultural resources of Morocco, Egypt and Tunisia.

Meanwhile, it is instructive to compare these negative performances with the performance of four South East Asian economies that pursued dynamic and innovative industrial policies, namely, the Republic of Korea, Malaysia, Singapore and Taiwan. These four economies, with their combined population of 104.8 million inhabitants – roughly the same as that of the countries of the Arab East or Mashriq (Egypt, Jordan, Lebanon and Syria) managed to generate a foreign trade surplus of US$127 billion, in which the trade surplus in industrial products accounted for US$257 billion against a deficit of US$80 billion for the seven countries of the MENA region, with machinery and transport goods accounting for a surplus of US$178 billion against a deficit of US$46 billion in the MENA countries. At the same time, the four Asian economies registered a deficit of US$99 billion in trade in fuels against a surplus of US$33 billion for the seven countries of the MENA region. The net result was, thus, a trade surplus of US$127 billion where the MENA countries suffered a deficit of US$67 billion, despite their fuel export surplus.

These indicators and comparisons drawn from foreign trade figures all go to show how little industrialization there is in the MENA countries. This being so, it is hardly surprising that trade between the countries of the region remains so low. The share of inter-Arab trade in all foreign trade of Arab countries is still miniscule, hovering between 8% and 9% for exports and between 10% and 13% for imports (including oil and gas). In some of the countries the share of exports is much larger: Lebanon (47% in 2008), Jordan (41.7%) and Syria (40.1%). Tunisia sells only 9.7% of its total exports to other Arab countries, while Algeria, Libya, Mauritania and Morocco export no more than 3.7%.[9]

As to the composition of inter-Arab trade, the share of trade in energy products is just under 60% of total exports against 13% for food products, 9–10% for chemical products, 12–13% for manufactured goods, and 4–5% for machinery and transport equipment.[10] The level of inter-Arab trade is especially disappointing because an Arab free-trade area (the idea of which was first broached in 1996) has been introduced in several countries in recent years. This demonstrates once again that the rigidity of the economic structures described above is a major obstacle to the growth and diversification of these countries' productivity.

Conclusion: rentier economies and democratic systems are antagonistic

This short diagnostic can be summarized by a predominant specificity of the Arab economies which is their large rent base that prevents dynamism, economic diversification, real industrialization and high value-added service activities. It is not easy task to break with the trappings of bad growth, which depends essentially on a number of sources of state and individual rent-based revenues mainly in commodities exports, mass tourism, real estate, and import and local trade activities; these have contributed to the ossification of a socioeconomic structure characterized by a lack of dynamism and diversification and by increasing income inequalities between different regions in each country. These income disparities are most visible in the increasing gap between the rural areas in which a large population continues to live in many countries and affluent families living in large urban centres.

As history has shown, rent-based economies have always produced authoritarian political regimes, wherein the ruling elite will consider natural and human resources to be of its patrimonial inheritance of which it can freely dispose. The rise of democracy in Europe has been a long road towards dismantling the patriarchal state and substituting its economic and political culture so as to lay the bases for individual freedoms and accountability of the ruling elite towards its citizens.

What has recently happened in the Arab world in terms of mass revolts cutting across all age groups and all social strata of the population is an important historical moment, opening up new avenues to shift away from bad growth to virtuous growth and from dictatorship to democratic systems. We will try now to see how to shift from one economic model to a new one based on dynamism, diversification and full mobilization of hitherto neglected human resources. The future of these Arab revolts in terms of successfully establishing democratic systems is dependent on the capacity to implement such a shift from a deficient rent-based growth model to a virtuous innovation-based, dynamic, fair and sustainable development model. As we will see, this is not an easy task.

Shifting from bad growth to virtuous growth

Before considering what changes are required in macro-economic policy and sectoral policies to escape the rent-based system, this section will review briefly the obstacles to be encountered.

Difficult international environment

Several negative factors could be identified here that might hinder the shift from one model to the other.

A continued reliance on the approach to economic reforms based on the neo-liberal creed as ingrained by the Washington consensus

In spite of the deep financial and economic crisis that have affected Western economies, decision-makers at the level of the G7 and to a large extend the G20 (including the new emerging countries), the main dogmas of neo-liberalism have not been shaken. The recent document produced at the G8 Deauville Summit in May 2011 to support the Arab Spring movement – namely the IMF Memorandum on which financial support is to be disbursed to the new regimes in Egypt and Tunis – does not deviate from the economic stereotypes that have dominated the views of the IFI (G20-G8 France, 2011). What is being advocated is further liberalization of markets, greater labour flexibility, more privatization, a reduction in state subsidies, etc., all of which have been standard themes.

Some of the Arab new elite acceding to power after the revolutions have their careers in the IFI and are convinced that the main problems in the Arab economies derive from an insufficient effort to create the conditions for a better business climate, fewer state and public sector activities and interventions in the economy, along with more FDI and private investments.

This very traditional approach totally disregards the lessons of economic history, and particularly those of 'late industrializers', be they Germany and Japan in the nineteenth century or those of the Republic of Korea, Taiwan, mainland China, Singapore, Brazil and others in the twentieth century, whereby well-focused state interventions have supported and oriented private entrepreneurs towards the mastery of technology and innovation, full mobilization of human resources, and adequate planning of social and economic change to adapt to ferocious trade competition between nations. None of these models has been followed in the Arab world (except for very short periods in Egypt under Muhammed Ali in the nineteenth century and under President Jamal Abdel Nasser in the twentieth century). Over the last decades, no Arab government has attempted to follow the example of one of the new emerging countries in South East Asia.

Increase in budget and current account deficits

Given the political turmoil that has been created by the revolutionary movements and the necessity to yield to some of the demand for greater social justice, governments could not avoid increasing subsidies on essential goods and in some cases also increasing salaries. This will undoubtedly precipitate an increase in budget deficits. In addition, the instability has caused a sharp drop off in tourist activities and consequently a decline in foreign exchange receipts. Exports may also have declined due to weak demand in European markets and declining production due to the many days when protest demonstrations paralysed economic life. FDI will necessarily decrease as foreign investors wait for the political situation to stabilize. The result will most probably be a deterioration in balance of payment flows. In turn, these short-term negative developments have affected local markets.

The speculative nature of markets and the behaviour of rating agencies and the IMF

Domestic stock exchange and foreign exchange markets are highly volatile and investors, as everywhere else, like to speculate on any bad news. The Arab revolts have tended to depress markets and wealthy people have been transferring money abroad through official or unofficial channels, which has contributed to the depletion of foreign exchange reserves. Rating agencies in such cases can be prompt to downgrade the credit worthiness of large companies or state bonds, which only accentuates 'market fear'. Any broad change in traditional macro-economic policies as recommended by the IMF, World Bank and European Union to try and innovate in terms of growth models might attract sharp criticism of the sort that will also adversely impact markets and 'investors' confidence'.

In general, market investors make their decisions based on short-term considerations; seldom do they have a long-term perspective based on positive economic changes that might occur in the wake of a restoration of the previous stability.

This why we now need to consider the long-term perspective and the conditions under which specific reforms could possibly liberate repressed productive capacities due to the rent-based economic system and the bad growth model that has been analysed.

Six policy measures to shift from a rent-based to a productive economy

Curbing corruption and promoting the accountability and social responsibility of the private sector

The Arab revolts have undoubtedly uncovered the amount of corruption linked to the nature of political regimes as a rent-distributing mechanism among a closed circle of elite and promoted businessmen. Corruption cannot be curbed by exclusively designating state officials as being responsible for the corruption. Transactions based on corruption always require at least two partners: a businessperson, on the one hand, and an official, on the other. This is why the time has come in the Arab world to focus attention on both sides of the equation and to introduce through local legislation effective procedures to detect and punish misconduct by some of the private sector businessmen close to government circles who are taking advantage of such links and enjoying special privileges or confidential, insider information. This is not only contrary to the principle of fair competition, but also it creates economic wastage and maintains low productivity.

The private sector should also be made to realize its economic and social responsibilities. Managing a business operation is not reducible only to owning and maximizing returns of a 'profit-making machine'. Private sector companies are also part of the society and owe it to work for its benefit, in terms of the quality of products and services delivered, as well as the training of human resources and the provision of decent job opportunities. They should not predate natural and human resources of the country by underpaying for such natural resources or degrading the environment; and they should offer decent work and salary conditions to their employees and workers. For its part the judicial system of Arab countries should be well attuned and trained to judge infringements to fair competition, the degradation of natural resources and environment, the misuse of influence through friendship with officials, and other pernicious practices.

Better and more ethical behaviour by the private sector along with its adherence to its social responsibilities could greatly improve the productivity of the economy and reduce corrupt practices considerably between high officials and rich businessmen.

The diversification of investments and the curbing of the brain drain

This another urgent issue to be tackled. The Arab world has witnessed a very high concentration of local and foreign investments in a few production and services sectors with high profits but low value-added or low employment potential (tourism, real estate, banks, local trade distribution, in addition to traditional energy and petrochemical sectors). Diversifying investments into many other productive activities will reduce unemployment and the migration of skills and those with high professional or scientific qualifications. There are many fields in which the private sector – eventually with the support of the state along the lines of the East Asian growth model – can engage in activities, and among these are:

- Producing alternative and renewable energy (solar, wind, water).
- Producing equipment for such alternative sources of energy (solar panels) or for waste treatment or water purification.
- Medical research and pharmaceutical production.
- In-sourcing R&D from other more technologically developed countries in ICT sectors.
- Developing rural areas and macrobiotic food produce.
- Developing mechanical and equipment industries to reduce the total dependence on foreign suppliers.
- Halting desertification through reforestation.

Integrating the informal sector into the modern sector

Another urgent need in the Arab economies is that of integrating the very small informal and family enterprises into the modern production sector through outsourcing and subcontracting to them small parts of the production process, as has been done successfully by many other countries. This requires that local modern firms determine what parts of their production could be outsourced to indigenous informal producers and what training and equipment material would necessarily have to be supplied to the small enterprises.

Given the size of the informal sector and the role it plays in employment, this is an urgent task. It requires a very active policy that should be designed by the main business associations (Association of Industrialists, Chamber of Commerce and Agriculture) as well as the professional orders such as the Order of Engineers.

Private–public partnership in defining national objectives in terms of mastering clusters of technologies

In the context of economic globalization, countries need to progress in mastering science and technologies in basic fields of modern industry and services so as to provide for economic diversification and the full employment of its qualified human resources. This requires that national objectives for S&T be identified by common consent between the state, the educational sector and the private sector. A national system of innovation should be set up with funding of both the private and the public sectors.

Given the lag in S&T that affects all Arab societies and the absence of links between education, technical skills and innovation or the fragmentation of innovation systems and R&D institutions, this a field that demands a great deal of attention and funding. If productivity of the economy and the increase in high value-added export of goods and services are to be realized, the Arab economies need to adopt such policies urgently.

Suppressing pockets of illiteracy and caring for the development of rural areas

It is a scandalous situation that the Arab world still suffers from very large pockets of illiteracy in some important countries like Egypt, Morocco, Yemen, Sudan and Mauritania. The concerned states should adopt a plan to suppress illiteracy in a few years. The implementation could be outsourced to independent non-governmental organizations (NGOs) dedicated to alleviating poverty.

It should also be noted that illiteracy is concentrated in rural areas, which is an additional reason for Arab states to become more aggressive in implementing active policies to increase investments and well-being in such areas. Rural populations in the Arab world have not seen their socio-economic situation improved during recent decades, and this fact has hindered overall growth dynamism in the Arab world.

Reviewing the tax system to equalize rates of profits between technology sectors to be developed and traditional high-profit sectors

Arab tax systems are entirely maladapted to the main characteristics of their rent-based economies. Tax burdens on financial or real estate capital gains are in most cases non-existent. Rent revenues from investing in shares or bonds are taxed at low rates. Under the cover of investment codes, many tax holidays and shelters are applied to types of business that do not entail any economic or technological risks. In the rich oil-exporting countries of the Gulf income tax is either non-existent or does not persist except as *zakat* (alms for the poor) as in the case of Saudi Arabia.

Nowhere in the Arab countries is there an income tax based on external indicators of wealth in terms of real estate properties, the number of cars or yachts or private jets, while there is an increasing number of millionaires and billionaires. This is why tax systems have to be totally revamped and overhauled so that foreign and the local private companies will be induced to invest in new high value-added activities and spending on R&D within the framework of national objectives and an integrated system of innovation designed and implemented within the framework of an association of the public and the private sectors.

Conclusion: the long road to be travelled to extricate Arab economies from the bad growth model and orient it towards a virtuous model

There is no doubt that the greatest challenge facing the revolutions of the Arab Spring is changing the Arab rentier economy bad growth model. It has been the root of generalized corruption, state patrimonialism, nepotism and favouritism, and authoritarian political regimes. This bad growth model has created and deeply ingrained a certain number of socio-economic behaviours antagonistic to productivity, fair competition, economic diversification, and entrepreneurship and innovation.

The predominance of neo-liberal economic thinking has, up to now, not only prevented any in-depth analysis of the rentier model, but also it can be said that the way the prescriptions of the Washington consensus have been implemented in most Arab economies through IMF/World Bank/European Union assistance programmes has probably been responsible – at least partially – for the increase in corruption, the social marginalization of large segments of the rural and urban populations, and the huge wastage of human and natural resources in Arab countries. This is why continuing to accept more of the same in terms of financial assistance conditioned by greater labour flexibility, deregulation and lack of protection of natural and human resources will continue to be a formula for additional hardship that may lead to a radicalization of marginalized segments of the population. In this respect the IMF document adopted at the Deauville G7 meeting in May 2011 (G20-G8 France, 2011) to serve as a guide to financial assistance conditioned by new reforms along the neo-liberal agenda should be cast aside.

New ways of thinking about economic reforms that would help a real transition to democracy and the state of law should be developed as an alternative to traditional rigid and abstract neo-liberal thinking that leads to more of the same. The analysis of bad growth conducted here as well as the proposals formulated for a genuine transition in the Arab growth model are intended as contributions to help Arab citizens access a better life where their talents, intellects and energies can be mobilized to achieve economic diversification out of rent sectors and to promote real creative and productive entrepreneurship within the scope of national goals for mastering technologies and creating the conditions for a better life for each citizen.

In the final analysis, there can be no real democratic life in countries in which the economic base is entirely dependent on rent inflows that are not properly distributed and invested in the economy to promote social equity and full employment based on economic productivity and diversification.

Notes

1. According to data from a table in World Bank (2008).
2. Data are drawn from ILO (2010b).
3. *Unified Arab Economic Report*, published by the pan-Arab financing institutions and the General Secretariat of the League of Arab States, Kuwait, September 2009.
4. For the brain drain and its cost to the economy of the migrants' country of origin, see Corm (2010).
5. See http://talentrepublic.net/NewsDetails.aspx?ID=2/.
6. See http://talentrepublic.net/NewsDetails.aspx?ID=2; reference is made to statistics of the Arab League, ILO and UNESCO.
7. See http://www.scidev.net/en/news/brain-drain-threatens-future-of-arab-science.html/.
8. Figures are drawn from World Bank (n.d.).
9. Statistics are drawn from General Secretariat of the League of Arab States (2009).
10. Statistics are drawn from General Secretariat of the League of Arab States (2009).

References

Corm, G., 2010. Faits et méfaits de l'émigration des competences. Paper presented at a seminar on *Highly Qualified Migration From, Towards and Through the Countries to the East and South of the Mediterranean and Sub-Saharan Africa*, 27–28 September 2010, University of Saint-Joseph, Beirut, Lebanon.

Economic and Social Commission for Western Asia (ESCWA), 2009. *Foreign direct investment report*. New York, NY: United Nations.

Economic and Social Commission for Western Asia (ESCWA), 2010. *Charting the progress of the Millennium Development Goals in the Arab region. A statistical portrait*. Beirut: ESCWA.

European Investment Bank, 2005. *Study on improving the efficiency of workers' remittances in Mediterranean countries*. FTF/REG/01/2005, Final Report. London: European Investment Bank.

General Secretariat of the League of Arab States, 2009. *Unified Arab economic report*. September. Kuwait: pan-Arab financing institutions and General Secretariat of the League of Arab States.

G20-G8 France, 2011. *Renewed commitment for freedom and democracy: final declaration of the G8 of Deauville*. Available from: http://www.g20-g8.com/g8-g20/g8/english/live/news/the-declarations-of-the-deauville-g8-summit.1341.html

International Finance Corporation and Islamic Development Bank, 2011. *Education for employment: realizing Arab youth potential*. Washington, DC: International Finance Corporation and Islamic Development Bank.

International Labour Organization (ILO), 2010a. Migration for decent work. Economic growth and development. Unpublished report. Geneva: ILO.

International Labour Organization (ILO), 2010b. *Politiques et institutions du marché du travail. Avec focus sur l'inclusion, l'égalité des chances et l'économie informelle*. February. Geneva: ILO.

International Labour Organization (ILO), 2011. *Global employment trends 2011*. Geneva: ILO.

United Nations Conference on Trade and Development (UNCTAD), 2008. *World investment directory*, Vol. X: *Africa*. Geneva: UNCTAD. Available from: http://www.unctad.org/.

United Nations Conference on Trade and Development (UNCTAD), n.d. *FDI in brief: Morocco*. Geneva: UNCTAD. Available from: www.unctad.org.

United Nations Development Programme (UNDP) and Mohammed bin Rashid Al Maktoum Foundation, 2010. *Arab knowledge report 2009. Towards productive intercommunication for knowledge*. Dubai: UNDP and Mohammed bin Rashid Al Maktoum Foundation.

United Nations Educational, Scientific and Cultural Organization (UNESCO), 2005. *UNESCO science report*. Paris: UNESCO.

United Nations Educational, Scientific and Cultural Organization (UNESCO), 2010. *UNESCO science report*. Paris: UNESCO.

World Bank, 2008. *MENA development report. The road not travelled: education reform in Middle East and North Africa*. Washington, DC: The World Bank.

World Bank, n.d. *World development indicators*. Online database. Available from: http://www.worldbank.org

The 'Arab Spring': breaking the chains of authoritarianism and postponed democracy

Mohammed Noureddine Affaya

Faculty of Literature, Mohammed V University, Rabat, Morocco

While the events of the so-called 'Arab Spring' constitute movements of vast social significance within the Arab world, they have at the same time raised as many questions as they have hopes and expectations. Among the most pressing causes for concern and further research are the roles that Arab audiovisual media and satellite broadcasting have played in not only covering events, but also in possibly even *fomenting* them through selectivity, timing, high-technology decoupage of images culled from the internet and new forms of social media, as well as the introduction of themes and slogans into various Arab public arenas even before the locals have taken such up themselves. The connection of Arab media to the political agendas of their sponsors as in the case of Aljazeera, for instance, has also been brought to the fore and writ large, leading to questions over whether or not media discourse is dialogic and genuinely responsive to multiple voices in the sense envisioned by Habermas or whether it is a Machiavellian enterprise directed towards very specific political ends. The political role of the media and individual newscasters has assumed new dimensions during the course of the upheavals of the 'Arab Spring' where it has been difficult if not impossible to characterize the media as strictly a passive observer of events and not also an active participant in initiatives for 'democratic transition' and other. Finally, while previous incarnations of state control and censorship of Arab media have been diminished or shed outright in a number of Arab countries – including Egypt and Tunisia – there are questions about what sort of conditionalities new corporate sponsorship may evolve. This article examines the philosophical and sociological dimensions of the Arab media of the 'Arab Spring', which like the events that it has covered have taken the Arab world into uncertain and uncharted territory.

Preface

In a dialogical work that Michel Foucault published under the title of *Iran, the Revolution in the Name of God* (Brière *et al.* 1979) is a collection of essays and eyewitness accounts of the French philosopher who lived in Tehran during 1977 and 1978, and then again in 1979 during the tumult of the Iranian Revolution, when he was amazed by the explosion of religious 'passion' and the sweeping mass support for the overthrow of the regime of the Shah. In the Preface Foucault quotes a line from Karl Marx that 'Religion is the spirit of a world without a spirit.' He observes that many among the Marxists as well as their opponents have tended always to emphasize

Marx's famous maxim: 'Religion is the opiate of the masses', forgetting or ignoring that the term 'opium' had a particular connotation in the nineteenth century when it was not always used in the sense of drugs (and their abuse), but also as a means to which doctors in hospitals would resort to lessen the pains of the sick and to tranquilize them in their sufferings. Moreover in the view of Foucault, Marx in his youth was still under the influence of Ludwig Feuerbach, and especially the effect of the latter's (1841) book, *The Essence of Christianity*, when he expressed a heightened sense of awareness of religion and its utility in society across history to the extent that even if he took a critical view of it, he dealt with it on the consideration that it was an existential and symbolic matter of the greatest seriousness and importance.

Foucault's concern was to witness an historical moment – a major event transpiring in the name of religion. Even though this philosopher was among the greatest of those who confronted contemporary myths through analysis, exposure and deconstruction – and among these the mechanisms and myths of authority – he was not motivated by major expectations with regard to the course and results of the 'Islamic Revolution in Iran' because he was convinced that the mixing of religion and politics precipitated forms of deprivation, subjugation, tyranny and death.

Perhaps the uprisings and demonstrations that the Arab world is witnessing today constitute a historical event according to all criteria. This is true if what is occurring represents an expression – in diverse languages, styles and interventions – of a new pattern or mode of manifestations of the Arab political imagination. It is an imagination that is not entirely removed from its authoritative points of reference or its 'religious' symbolic order – in the general cultural sense and not its particular 'creedal' or 'ritual' connotation. This is to affirm that the spark of the *intifada* that moved from Tunisia to Egypt and then subsequently to other Arab arenas represented a call to liberate politics from its impenetrable moulds – ones that Arab political authorities were vigilant about fortifying and protecting with an unsurpassed Machiavellian proficiency. The events that are occurring and the transformations in actions, movements and discourses are indicative of a way of dealing with politics that is 'semi-absolute'. That is, *politics* – across all the public squares and venues of protest – is the one subject that is the passion of all, object of all animosities and daily manoeuvrings that has become the subject of utmost importance and seriousness which cannot be displaced by any other sphere – with the exception of religious changes – as its actors or those who speak in its name, and they are many and various, intend a redistribution of values on the basis that whatever is not political and whatever does not enter into its locus or serve its ends whether in terms of art or love or any sort of celebrations must be subjugated to it in one way or another![1]

The political imagination has emerged to impose its language on the spaces of discussion and action and in situations of tension and cooperation; religious expressions have come into prominence in politics along with the imitation of the call for building modern politics and whims in spheres that allegedly purport to respect rationalism. The matter pertains to a major event – or events – that audiovisual means and the internet have lent the appearance of a 'big show' or rather a 'spectacle' – even in its tragic moments – and have factored in all ways to create every sort of obfuscation and ambiguity where accuracy is lost in the transmission of information, as is clarity in analysis and commentary and the mobilization of all factors of impulsive reaction that produce observations and abbreviated judgments, which have no relation to life and sociocultural complexities in this domain or that.

We can observe this collusion of factors in some of the manifestations of this confusion of this obfuscation and ambiguity in the prevailing discourses today about democracy and the emergence from tyranny to pluralism/multiplicity, the resolution of controversies, and the roles of communication media in the process of transition.

Anxiety over understanding

In light of what is transpiring in the Arab world – *intifadas* and transitions, confrontations of various forms, including armed ones – any discussion of democracy and democratic values imposes upon us a need for caution and circumspection. It is a problematic discourse, not innocent, and has generated different states of bewilderment and anxiety. To confront the various forms of uncertainty and complexity precipitated by the ongoing movement in the world at large demands a very singular and penetrating vigilance over and above tackling the major ambiguities that attend emergence from Arab authoritarianism and different incarnations of autocracy together with the degradation of the individual. Likewise, the challenge hurls us into states of fear and embroils us in the difficulties that divide politicians and elites at all levels when they attempt to anticipate or imagine the future.

The human being is haunted most of the time by feelings of determinism or fatalism that are difficult to explain, as whenever he refers to what he assumed to be ancient givens and preconceptions, he finds himself confronted with doubt and apprehension. It is not always the case that such states are invariably non-productive in awakening the reason and spurring thinking and communication. However, what is tantalizing about approaching the question of democracy and (related) values is the attendant sense of grief or mourning over the passing of some of the principles or even some of the convictions that used to prevail. Yet, the pace of transformation – in economics, the broadcast media, internet communication as well as new forms of violence – all impel the human being either to transform doubt into an system and a choice, or fall in to the trap of dogmatism.

It is worth recollecting here that the lengthy quest of the individual for liberation – as proclaimed by modernity – is extremely costly. This is apparently not well understood or given much attention in many analyses and commentaries on the Arab *intifadas*, that do not take into account the (role of) historical or political conditions – and especially not the cultural ones. Abdelilah Belkeziz noted this hugely important aspect a number of years ago when he recognized that the state as well as society in the Arab countries is predicated on a 'grave deficiency', represented in essence in:

> the difficult birth of modernism in Arab political and civil societies; this structural difficulty is epitomized in the crisis of legitimacy in regard to the state and the weakness of the psychology of acceptance (i.e., the acceptance of modernism) within Arab society.
>
> (Belkeziz 2001, p. 39)

Every individual or every society pays the price according to the nature of the forces and actors in it. Although we could to an extent calculate the cost that must be paid for the sake of freedom, this does not prohibit acknowledging the paradoxical dimension as being a burden and responsibility – far from easy – to the extent that it might turn into exploitation of a new sort. The individual, when he is in the process of liberating himself from the dominance of the group, is at the same time placing himself in situations of weakness, loneliness and vulnerability. Many Western writers and Arab intellectuals residing in the West who have written about what is transpiring within some of the Arab *intifada*s see this movement as a licence for the Arab individual to come into prominence in the political sphere. Such writings appear to me to be very hasty and to exhibit poor assessment of the profound givens of these societies engaged in uprisings. Such can be seen in the case of what led Gilles Lipovetsky to assert that the collapse of traditional forms of framing and formation is not an indication of the creation of a *tabula rasa* or reaching a degree of 'zero' on the scale of values. Rather this collapse requires the individual to break free from the 'tried and true' guardianship (of the state) that suppressed the obligation to set out upon a path of ethics of responsibility (Lipovetsky 1996, p. 26).

The human being today in many of the countries of the West or those that have been exposed to the influence of the West – such as our countries – finds himself confronting two types of behaviour. The first is characterized by a 'boyish' or 'childish' avoidance of the responsible exercise of an individual's freedom which a person treats as though it is an amusement or passing fancy, The second is behaviour characterized by an individual who views himself as 'victim' exposed to an original or historic injustice and who views *himself* on the consideration that he *is* such, regardless of what this may incur of harm or what it may achieve of gains.

How, then, is it possible to live in a world without a compass? There are those who see, like Andre Comte-Sponville, that living in this wayward world, exploited by every form of tyranny and consumption, and immersed in the 'culture of perception' (as identified by ʿAbd al–Jābrī 1999, p. 191) is possible. However, this is so not through the imagining of new values, but rather by innovating a new mode of loyalty to that which human history has bequeathed to us or that which the particular history of each society has produced. This approach takes into account the realities of disputatiousness and hegemony, alienation and anxiety. And what are these values? They are those that maintain the integrity of the root principles or the four principles of ethics that are oriented towards life; toward society and its welfare; towards the mind or what is universal in it; and lastly that pertain to love and compassion. Vital interaction between these four orientations is what establishes loyalty on the consideration that life stops at the limits of the needs of society, which stop in turn at the limits of reason, in turn defined and perfected by love and compassion. Thus, the transition which we are experiencing today in the sphere of politics and values is not a step from one rung of the ladder of values to the ladder of principles and other values, but rather is a transition from extreme conviction or faith to loyalty to noble values on the basis that loyalty is what gives faith its permanence at a time when we reckon we have lost it (Comte-Sponville 1996, p. 138).

Among the terms of expression for this new loyalty is the question of the relation between theory and history and between reason and communication/interaction. This new loyalty is built on the basis of discussion between cultures and individuals on the frontier of reconstructing a new meaning for group action. This is not a call for discourse immersed in ethics and driven by romantic inclinations, which is absolutely impossible. The intersection between politics, philosophy and ethics is an axiomatic matter whenever the matter pertains to a historical turning point or a movement aimed at transcendence or beginning a process of transition. How could we contextualize a collective act to establish a 'democratic state' that liberates the Arab individual from the state of 'humiliation' and the 'psychology of subjugation' to the promulgation of a new social and political contract? And to what extent can we anticipate the reconstruction of a 'democratic' political sphere on the basis of forces that are still internally beholden to a 'Bedouin culture in rebellion against the urban/civil mode' of living (Belkeziz 2001, p. 45)? And does what we are witnessing of *intifadas* and protests really portend the existence of a collective consciousness that possesses what is necessary in terms of qualifications to administer and manage multiplicity/pluralism and differences?

On the consciousness of multiplicity/pluralism

Multiplicity/pluralism represents the basis of the democratic system where the styles and modes of administering it reveal the degree of conceptual, political, and institutional awareness of the intellectual and political elites responsible for facilitating public affairs or who aspire to bear the burden of their facilitation. However, what is occurring in the Arab countries undergoing revolutions, *intifadas*, armed confrontations and struggles that vary depending on the different chemistries within each country would suggest that there is a major ambiguity between democracy and political liberalism. If the latter is an expression of a political system that depends upon an agreed constitution and includes the undertaking of 'free and fair' elections, and which supposes a state based on truth, within which is a separation of powers and the protection of political freedoms, then all of these conditions refer to 'constitutional liberalism'. This *might* or might *not* be expressive of democratic choice which demands deference to rights that encompass and extend to economic, social and cultural dimensions. The slogans of 'freedom', 'justice' and 'dignity' that have been raised or are still being touted in the face of authoritarian regimes do not appear to transcend the threshold of demands possessed of a liberal frame of reference.

This is what the observer of the political movement notices – whether in the first country in which the spark of what came to be termed the 'Arab Spring' was ignited – Tunisia – or in what the various Syrian political forces are demanding in the way of a transition to a civilian political system that would admit and contain all the forces, currents and sensitivities.

Vis-à-vis tyranny and authoritarianism, it appears that there is semi-agreement over 'democratic choice', even from the perspectives of parties that have not ceased to criticize its cultural background and negative aspects. This is because it still represents the best possible way to administer public affairs. And whether this accord was initiated by tactical considerations, of this current or that, or clear intellectual or political convictions, all of the political and intellectual parties that emerge are presented as being representative of democracy or endeavouring to represent it. These include instigators of protests and opposition, or sides which are still clinging to power, or groups that have lost their protectors – as in the case of Tunisia and Egypt – but did not possess the requisite means and power to evade the process of transition to a different political sphere. Thus, democracy has not only become a system of rule or civilizational choice on account of its being a process for resolving differences and attracting more than one side to what it produces as gains for individuals and groups, but also it promises alternative ways to transcend systems of subjugation and tyranny. In fact, however, we find political parties and groups, particularly those affiliated to political Islam, have begun to present more than one justification for appearing in 'democratic' guise, even if that exposes them at a certain stage to distortion, and divests them from all their significations, especially given that most of its constituents 'want restricted democracy that does not contradict Islamic *sharīʿah*', and put preconditions on the principle of freedom demanded by the youth as well as other sensitive issues. These currents possess definite social bases and the ability to polarize and mobilize, given the nature of their discourse, and their organizational history, and they appear more and more every day to be elements entering into the scope of what we term as being 'impediments to democracy' (Namer 2003, p. 49).

What is the degree of influence of *thought* in presenting a concept conforming to what is happening in the Arab countries given the difference of their stressors, the degrees of their tensions and the diversity of forces active in the struggle? We pose this question because Arab thought has provided critically important enquiries, over the past three decades, on state, democracy and civil society, and has produced substantial conceptual inroads into these, since the writing of *Al-Īdiyūlūjīyā al-ʿArabīyah al-Muʿāṣirah* [*Contemporary Arab ideology*] (1970) and the *Mafhūm al-Dawlah* [*Concept of state*] (1981) of Abdallah Laroui, to the writings of Burhān Ghalyūn from *Bayān min ajl al-Dimūqrāṭīyah* [*Exposé for democracy*] (1978) to *Al-Miḥnah al-ʿArabīyah* [*The Arab inquisition*] (1993) and Aziz al-'Azmah, Ghassan Salame and Abdelilah Belkeziz. Also worthy of mention are the valuable intellectual works of various sources and the sensitivities that Dr. ʿAlī Khalīfah al-Kuwārī endeavoured to produce and publish in the framework of the initiative of *Al-Kutlah al-Tārīkhīyah ʿalā Qāʿidah al-Dimūqrāṭīyah* [*The historic bloc for the principle of democracy*] (2010). These works without exaggeration constitute an authoritative political reference rather than a 'school' in the context of inculcating democratic thought in Arab political culture. In the exploration of work ethics, discussion and commitment in the framework of what al-Kuwari, and those active with him in the initiative, termed the 'historical bloc on the foundation of democracy', these thinkers scrutinize in detail the prerequisites and the missions that must be undertaken in order to accomplish the transition to democracy.

Among the components required are:

> the emergence of a democratic leadership fit and qualified for responsibility, imbued with the value of collective endeavor, partnership with others and communication with them, as well as being free of the mentality of exclusion, egoism and pretensions of possessing 'absolute truth'. Also necessary is the practice of politics in a professional fashion along with what this dictates of professional politicians – pragmatism, planning, patience over the long haul, self-criticism, and circumspection, reliance on rationalism rather than emotionalism in propounding work agendas and meeting challenges, in addition to learning from past mistakes and the experiences of others. Meeting these requirements entails having faith in the existence of universal norms shared in common across different civilizations and regions around the world, as well as respect for the principle of the division of labor and consultation with experts and specialists/
>
> (Al–Kuwārī and Māḍī 2010, pp. 132–133; see also Al–Kuwārī and Māḍī 2009)

Some of the writings of these thinkers are a valuable aid to understanding and keeping abreast of many of the political trends and views being voiced in Arab societies, including those which anticipate what Laouri termed 'the future of the past'. Vis-à-vis what has occurred of transformations and what has accumulated of conceptual and intellectual analyses and open-minded enquiries, countering the high-handed and hegemonic onslaught of audiovisual media and its efforts either to mobilize or to justify developments, a question must be posed. Is there a way to create the necessary distance to understand the significance of what these transformations portend and arrive at a set of indicators suitable for application to the slogans and maxims being put forward for the aim of rebuilding the political sphere on the basis of contemporary democratic thought? We raise this question in this context, with a modicum of doubt because if democracy is considered a political choice, this relies on certain bases, the most important of which are the following: the promulgation of a constitution over which there is consensus; recognition of actual, effective political pluralism and not only multiplicity in the quantitative sense; establishing representative institutions resulting from fair elections; and the provision of conditions for the peaceful rotation of political authority/power. Then, in addition to the above, democracy is a translation of a mode of thinking, an order of values and an etiquette of discussion, competition and debate. Democracy is not – and never has been – a given that is conferred based on individual choices, the primary purpose of which is to evade demands, as much as it is a product of collective efforts beginning with family upbringing, education, plus the media, as well as the means for managing differences and disputes in the public sphere. This is with the knowledge that there are various sources of democratic culture and memories of pluralism in light of which it is not possible to impose a ready-made model for administering principles of the social contract or control of political struggles. What is important here is that all these movements do not produce regimes that will turn into a front for the protection of capital, or for the justification of thinly veiled autocracy, or to provide cover for blindly imitative choices that bring about autocracy according to a new paradigm.

Many people defend, from a philosophical or political standpoint, the principle of pluralism on account of its being a founding condition of democracy. However, is it sufficient to defend this principle in the absolute? That is, given that there are a number of problems that confront the institutional, political and cultural application of this principle, does the matter necessitate an 'acknowledgment of the multiplicity' of group identities? Alternatively, does it serve to negate or marginalize them as being incompatible with the components of the political system in the framework of the foundations and constraints of the state or *ummah* (the nation) that – in the first instance – has been predicated on a religious or cultural legitimacy or that of a historical legacy? How can we judge between the individual independence of the citizen and the independence of a particular group and the considerations and calculations of the state? Or, more frankly, how can we construct a group identity or a *collective* 'we'?

This is not the place to go into these questions in detail. What is important is that each discussion of pluralism calls for attention to the decisive importance of the principle of equality and renewable capacities that need to be created in order to construct a 'public culture' resting on shared values. A public sphere capable of enriching and protecting these values through group discussions – taking every word into account and meeting every argument with another – is the objective here. Since 2001, Fahmī Jadʿān has mentioned the complexity of the democratic question in Arab society and has confirmed the following:

> Our story with respect to democracy is now taking a new direction that demands examination of a set of essential issues:
>
> First, we must reexamine the concept in an enlightened fashion or critically – whether negative, positive or both – because we must not unreservedly concede to any given of which we are not absolutely certain.
>
> Second, we must confront the heap of discussions of democracies currently in circulation – especially those affiliated to liberal orientations – in conjunction with the general and regional conditions of the Arab world to arrive, if circumstances permit, at this or that appropriate model or mode of democracy.
>
> Third, we must answer the following question: should we begin only using the 'Western given' as a point of departure or must we necessarily summon up or retrieve historical or ancient precedents in this regard, if there are any which merit such a retrieval?
>
> Lastly, where does democracy fall – or in what sense – in the scheme of 'political pressure' that ought to be exercised on the Arab scene and in its [public] spaces?
>
> (Jadʿān 2001, p. 158)

He then adds that open democracy suffers from 'in many circumstances, a lack of maturity and political consciousness among the "popular masses"', and this means that:

> the majority lack the maturity and political consciousness to rule and promulgate laws regulating the matters of society and state, and that the 'minority' that possesses the requisite experience and consciousness will be barred from this … and thus it would be extremely easy to 'exploit' these masses and manipulate them though the use of the power of money that knows no limits and excessive and falsifying media orientations.
>
> (p. 158)

Yet, are there conditions conducive to engendering a political sphere responsive to these dictates? This question arises against the backdrop of what we have witnessed in the period of authoritarianism – which is still fighting to maintain the sources of its continuity – and what occurred in Egypt and Tunisia, along with what is happening in Yemen, Bahrain and Syria, where we have seen the transformation of the nature of the struggle from the natural general grievances – which should be accommodated into the proliferation of disputes, not subject to the norms of logical understanding, or amenable to control and framing or susceptible to being managed or resolved. Democracy is a long-term process not subject to the timetable of the dissolution of autocratic regimes. It is insufficient in this regard to trot out the 'bogeyman' of multiplicity, as witnessed today, nor is it sufficient to agree on 'constitutional' principles (such as having a constitution, elections and perhaps even rotation of power), 'but rather democracy requires a clear, collective political consciousness that differentiates between the period of protest and the period of construction, which is based on economic-, moral-, social-, political- and conceptual choices' (Ghalyūn 2001, p. 440).

This is why Ghalyūn considers that the provision of suitable conditions conducive to achieving democratic transformation requires accomplishment of the following five tasks. First:

> developing a new democratic culture … where here 'consciousness' does not imply merely belief in democracy or in it as a slogan or just knowing its simple connotation and content, but rather entails possession of a particular theory of it that is specific to the conditions of Arab societies in general, and to each society and its specific circumstances in particular.

This distinction is to be understood in light of the 'present weakness of democratic consciousness or its dispersion and lack of coherence due to the generalized poverty of the political culture in our societies' (Ghalyūn 2001, p. 440). The second task revolves around 'guaranteeing material and moral resources, without which no political movement can persist' (p. 440). As for the third task, it is represented in:

> the building of an active, democratic and pluralistic centre [literally *quṭb* – 'pole'] as well as avoiding a one-sided view of reality as well as learning how to absorb intellectual and organizational multiplicity … and this is the one way in our societies to transform democracy into a social choice, that is, into a common denominator and point of intersection among various social classes and groups and political forces.
>
> (p. 440)

The fourth task necessitates:

> changing the structures and reforming official and social institutions. There is no hope to advance along the road of democracy, and not only that but on the road of genuinely

> sound political governance – in contrast to the savage rule prevailing on control by force and the imposition of submission and deference – without working to uphold legal institutions of the state and to liberate them from the imperialism of political-, tribal-, clientalist- or family partisanship ... and the battle to change and reform the institutions ought not be delayed until after the triumph of the democratic movement. However, there must be work at the level of these institutions and departments in order to realize this reform, which itself constitutes an important instrument of leverage in democratic work.
> (p. 442)

This is at a time when the fifth task is embodied in 'constructing a unifying collective political credo or national consensus' (p. 443).

The question of the interstice in contemporary culture and the enigma of the incapacity to attain to democracy in emerging societies brings up another issue. It pertains to the capacity of the actors in the public squares of liberation and change to ameliorate and alleviate controversies and resolve disputes.

The battle over and within democracy

It is obvious to say that contention or struggle – in the broad sense of these terms – does not represent a confluence of interests, sentiments, choices and conflicting goals only, but rather it is a component of human and social interaction and a catalyst of politics. Likewise, recognition of contention or struggle as being a natural reality of democracy and in political competition is not a result of a particular interpretation – of this side or that or this group or the other – of the nature and degree of contention in the midst of transition.

Arab autocracy has produced societies that penetrate to the very heart of the meaning of humiliation and degradation and the acceptance of the loss of dignity, for people accustomed to suppression and deprivation. With the sparks of the *intifadas*, what was being held pent up inside has exploded forth and the barrier of silence has been broken. Tongues and pens have been unleashed to aspire to the heights of social eloquence. As much as there was a determination to bring down the regimes – even if only *some* of their symbols have gone in Tunisia and Egypt, for example – on the basis of such being an agreed-upon slogan, deep differences have erupted over the nature and components of the alternative or hoped-for political system – either openly or behind the scenes – between factions, parties and groups driving the *intifadas*.

How can we deal with these differences when they are natural, given that, in principle, all have the right to participate in the public sphere? Does this emerging political society possess the necessary means to resolve conflicts and effect the crystallization of a new social contract, establishing a democracy responsive – during this transitional period – to the minimal components of social liberalism?

Posing the question in this context necessitates confronting two problems at least: the first pertains to the nature of the conflicts that have erupted and which require resolution; the second pertains to the method or technique adopted to resolve them. Doubtless, every Arab society has traditional means for arbitration to resolve conflicts, some of which persist in resisting the onslaught of new forms of organization and in some cases authoritarianism has worked to crush and eliminate. Violence was and is a means of practising politics in Arab countries to a degree noted by Abdelilah Belkeziz:

> We have not known a stable political life free of violence except only very rarely! Those who have arrived in power since the end of the 'Liberal Age' got there through violence

> (military coups). And those who maintain power do so by violence. As for their enemies and opponents who are looking to remove them, they too unsheathe thoughts of violence and occasionally resort to its instruments.
>
> (Belkeziz 2008, p. 131)[2]

Apparently the tribal, clan, sectarian and factional grounding within the fabric of Arab societies has begun to reveal many of its symbols in a number of the *intifadas* indicating the tremendous possibilities for this tribal, clan, sectarian and factional rootedness to renew its components and replicate its expressions, according to the contexts and typologies of the struggles. There are a number of indicators that suggest that the Machiavellian style of expressing and resolving these conflicts is currently reigning supreme in managing these differences and disputes. Niccolò Machiavelli, as is well known, identified 'struggle' (*La Lutte*) as the preferred means of conflict resolution, or rather, it is the only possible way. This is unless – God forbid – domination over an opposing group or competing parties occurs by means of obfuscation/subterfuge, deception or lying. Conflict, according to him, is a confrontation between forces contending to remain in power or to acquire it. Resolving conflict, or neutralizing the opposition and creating the conditions for peace, cannot occur except as a result of fierce confrontation between these forces; that is, through the use of violence to seize power. So long as violence remains the essential means for resolving conflict, then the 'art of battle' becomes for Machiavelli the supreme art, the indispensible technique of political authority and power. To affirm this principle does not connote strictly physical violence alone as he advocates other techniques of a more 'enlightened' nature, such as the manipulation and utilization of people or various ruses – all of which are techniques tied to rhetorical discourse, movements and modes of communication (Lefort 1986, p. 71).[3]

Among that of which the *intifadas* have precipitated in relations of appeasement or conflicts with the prevailing political authority or in what is transpiring between driving forces in these *intifadas* are modes of exchange and interaction that most often betray carefully weighed tactical calculations and the adoption of Machiavellian styles more than any other option. In contradistinction to the Machiavellian approach we find contrasting exercises in *ijtihad* (independent reasoning) that view the subject of conflicts precipitated in the political arena as issues that may be resolved within the 'framework of dialogue' and thereby avoid all forms of violence – physical or ideological. Democracy, in the various modes in which it is practised and its institutional values, adopts a theory of the dialogic (*Dialogique*). Yet, how often is 'dialogue' and the Arab rhetoric deriving from and revolving around it employed in order to impose the will of one side on other sides? Dialogue, however, in its intellectual, political and contemporary connotation – especially according to Jürgen Habermas – is directed towards understanding and comprehension and presupposes a consideration of 'the other' as being *an end in itself* as opposed to a means to an end. Thus, it represents the only way for non-violent resolution of conflicts.

The goal of understanding or 'comprehending' the 'other' is predicated on a will to interact and cooperate with him as a person possessed of dignity. Whatever applies to him applies to all. This cannot possibly be realized unless we consider ourselves as ends rather than as a means to serve the ends of others. Acknowledgement of the dignity of 'the other' has great semantic and social weight; and in any contention the precondition of acknowledgement and respect is necessary in the view of Habermas. The question this raises, however, in many instances is reducible to one of means and the tangible forms for such that an actor innovates in order to convey respect in the context of dialogue. It might be said that this occurs by according priority to listening and respecting answers, in the first instance, in what Habermas (1992, p. 67) terms 'the will to search cooperatively for the truth' (also Habermas 1987a, pp. 416–417, Habermas 1987b, II, pp. 114–115, Affaya 1998).

Listening cannot possibly be circumscribed here as only the *intention* to listen – even if intention to do so is presumably integral – because if one side desires that listening should occur and be realized effectively, it must make allowance for the other side to enjoy freedom of speech and expression. The situation is that freedom pertains more to social, political or objective situations more than it does to personal circumstances of the self. It is incumbent upon 'the other' to bear responsibility for freedom of expression and what is said – that is, to express his choices, intone or make known his particular goals and to accept the premise that the other has the right to express a position or a legitimate and rightful demand too.

Habermas sees that it is within the capacity of dialogue or discussion to bridge the chasm between politics in all its incarnations – among which is the authority of the state – and the order of truth. It can also create conditions for reconciliation between the practical dictates of political authority and expectations of rights, in the interests of arriving at oversight of the state instead of the perpetuation of the 'state of surveillance'. This is achieved through depending upon plausible communicative mechanisms for cultivating or rooting – depending on the circumstances – the prerequisites of rights and freedoms. In mechanisms of communication, skills and acumen in negotiation, consultation and dialogue intervene to produce an entente between participants in the process and thence avoid betting on force, and accord primacy to establishing a consensus based on fairness and vigilance over interests and expectations of all actors. Moreover, in any situation where consensus is impracticable, it is possible to solve any conflict or difference through a temporary compromise to constrain any danger posed by one or other side looking for a way out from the principles of discussion. Where conditions for a genuine dialogue are provided, the best and most convincing argument is that which prevails on the basis of logic and persuasiveness, where other expressions might be added in the interests of national welfare, without resorting to violence, deception or manipulation.

It is certain that inculcation of the principle of dialogue in democracy is an essential and foundational task – not because it supports the construction of a peaceful approach to resolving conflicts, but because the mode of dialogue presupposes preparation and education. Likewise, proceeding according to dialogue and judicious use of its principles represents an opportunity to become conscious and aware of the differences that divide the different sides participating. To a certain extent, it also may also mitigate the reasons for struggle and potentially arrive at a peaceful solution by working to find compromise conditions instead of relying on a 'consensus' for which the necessary prerequisites might not be forthcoming at a particular stage. In any case, flexibility and the mutual ability to back down with the conviction that this will lead to understanding is what represents the goal of dialogue.

If the approach of Habermas pinpoints the cause of injustice in a lack of respect for the formal preconditions of public discussion, then there are other interpretations which hold that the experience of injustice expresses itself clearly when there are social, political and ethical motives underlying the contentions. Here, thought must be given to a type of 'ethical codes of conflicts' in the event it is not possible to prevent a clash or conflict of interests in social and political struggles only, given that a sense of belittlement is to be expected when hegemony is imposed. Thus it is necessary to analyse givens and circumstances in all their various formulations and active components, as well as the intents which drive them, in order to distinguish between types of conflicts and thence find a suitable means for resolving them. There is a need for a mode of arbitration between interests and aspirations, some of which dictate relying upon diverse means to determine and delimit primary and genuine interests or the social or ethical claims of contenders. The normative expectations referred to by individuals who are suffering from injustice and belittlement mandate interpretation because they are expectations directed towards a type of mutual recognition through which is produced a kind of positive relation with the self. However, this condition is not entirely sufficient as it is not possible to construct a theory of social justice where such a theory is absent from the catalysts of protests, *intifadas* and revolution – in the context of a society that guarantees all its individuals the possibility of developing a productive relation with the self.

John Rawls is not mistaken when he introduces the concept of 'the social bases for respecting the self' (Rawls 1987, p. 76) among the enumeration of primary social values, the guarantee of which is mandated equally for all citizens. At the same time, it would be an injustice to pay heed only reductively to this dimension given that 'a normative theory of democracy' works to posit a just working answer for treating social conflicts wherein at least three considerations must be introduced. It is not possible to conceive of a social or political controversy simply because there is a social protest on the part of one group (or more) occupying a place within the social structure. Here, it appears that the social and economic mechanisms have greater importance in this situation. Secondly, there occurs a social controversy every time the members of a group perceive a type of injustice as catalysing the protest. Thirdly, it is not possible to consider this protest acceptable except in the case that those carrying it out are expressing a situation of group dissatisfaction over lack of consideration for their political, social and even cultural expectations.

Conflict resolution necessitates – in all instances – a genuine and appropriate understanding of its causes, types and means of expression. This understanding rests on a communicative and groundbreaking pedagogy accompanying the manifestations of contention over and above their derivation from the principles of truth, equality and noble sentiments of equanimity. Here, controversies and conflicts demand intermediaries who possess sufficient cognizance and capabilities for understanding as well as sound management skills to arrive at just solutions.

On the basis of what has been presented it should be apparent that these normative stipulations are applicable to societies firmly rooted in democracy that refer conflict resolution to particular arbitration procedures resting on an axiomatic culture or ethics of discussion in political and social exchange. However, this also does not preclude affirmation that the various *intifadas*, arising over humiliating situations across the entire geographic expanse of the Arab world, are in dire need of principles and mechanisms of 'dialogue' in order to manage and mitigate the differences produced by the shake ups to which Arab authoritarianism has been exposed and to which it is still being exposed. There can be no escape from democracy carving out ways and means to deal with struggles and controversies. It is a forward progress that demands maturity, pedagogy and extreme patience. This is because democracy is a price that must be paid. There is no third option: either proceed through consensual efforts to construct a contemporary political sphere or deceive this major movement and depart from its goals by focusing on new modalities of autocracy – either veiled or open. Recourse to these alternatives rests on a social and political ground still congested and overcrowded, as Belkeziz (2001) has remarked:

> in traditional and inherited manifestations of a tribal, clan, factional or sectarian sort where these have not ceased to be renewed or to reproduce themselves (or to be reproduced) on account of their being a 'natural' part of the present scene and which haven't ceased to present themselves – in what is actually worse and more reprehensible – as political dynamics and structures capable of engineering numerous instances of political conjunction and its realities in our current age.
>
> (p. 443)

Have the upheavals underway in the Arab countries really shaken up these traditional phenomena rooted in the popular subconscious and the structures present upon which to affirm their pillars of support and reproduce the mechanisms of their continuity? Is the propagation of these 'revolutionary' protests truly impelled by and embracing a new and truly 'revolutionary' thought, holding out an alternative to what prevails in economics, politics and culture? Or, is the matter no longer one of an outburst of rage over humiliation, tyranny and corruption without political horizons or in particular a near-total absence of any shared conceptual or cultural referent, other than those alleged or raised by groups of political Islam or some youth groups which have liberal inclinations that profess secularism, in addition to very small nationalist, popular and socialist currents?

It would appear that thought is bewildered in the face of the vast scale of the eruptions and the types of umbrella groups precipitated by the movements in various Arab countries. What is occurring in this country or that precludes all stereotypical inclinations or predispositions as well as any all-encompassing assessment that purports to supply the requisite and applicable means for understanding all the *intifadas*. Likewise the unprecedented, excessive high-handedness of the audiovisual channels in their professionally dubious dealing and interaction with the images of the internet precipitate a genuine jolt to and distortion in thinking and the desire to understand. Aljazeera is not alone in infringing upon the principles of the accepted standards of audiovisual media, nor is it alone in presenting itself as representative of the voice of the 'revolutionaries' while at the same time giving special consideration – as per the different Arab arenas and the transformations of the chemistry of struggle – to the censure of some expression of pluralism. What is happening at the level of Arab satellite channels is startling where such channels are translating – as mediators or intermediaries – expressions of an Arab regional 'civil war' in a way that demands their accountability and requires enquiry and evaluation.

Undoubtedly the Arab world is witnessing a historic moment par excellence. Arab societies that had been ruled through complete subjugation and submission have risen. People have been liberated from fear and the youth have been the vanguard of the movements, utilizing all possible means – including the digital – and social, political and religious currents have ridden this wave to affirm their presence. Europe and America have mobilized every means and pushed every pen to decree that the youth of the 'Arab Spring' resemble 'us' as they are translating the principles of enlightenment into their public squares. 'Aren't freedom, equality and justice "our" principles?' they ask. Thus, overnight, the Western mode of perceiving the Arab has changed and the oft-repeated clichés embedded in the minds and imaginations with vigilant determination have been shaken. From societies stereotyped as producing violence, terrorism, emigration, drugs and images of veiled women come societies capable of raising contemporary slogans and thirsting for freedom and democracy; and Europeans have expressed, in an unprecedented fashion, intentions to help these countries – especially Tunisia and Egypt – politically, materially and militarily while at the same time they are intent on keeping out some thousands of Tunisian youth who are attempting to escape unemployment. This is even to the extent that France has demanded a review of the system of 'Schengen' visas and a return to the monitoring of borders between European countries as a result of what it has termed a 'flood' of young émigrés.

The media and the cost of transitioning to democracy

It is well known that institutions and research directives work, to the full extent of their capabilities, to study and follow the indicators and significances of these *intifadas* and through various means – in everything from descriptive to the reported – seek to observe the course of each particular Arab experience – even if much of what is published on the basis of these methodological *claims* does not measure up to the requisite standards – from texts, articles and writings characterized primarily by haste, entrenched positions and overgeneralizations. This is what causes the forfeiture of its intellectual merit and worthiness as well as the soundness of its deductions and inferences. Special editions of magazines are prepared and edited around these events, and research centres have sponsored meetings in order to comprehend what is going on and to predict what is expected to happen. However, all indicators suggest that television has played, and continues to play, a decisive role in presenting the events and airing deductions and commentaries on these. There are even channels that have entirely altered the structure of their programming so as to devote airtime exclusively to developments of affairs in some of the Arab arenas. Some have transformed into a factor/actor to motivate, provoke and goad the creation of an 'organized' web of reporters, commentators, 'eye witnesses', 'strategy experts' and specialists on revolutions. Rather, we have seen and heard channels raise the slogan of 'down with the regime' (*isqāṭ al–niẓām*) before demonstrators have raised this slogan themselves (and chief among these are the Qatari station Aljazeera and the Iranian al–ʿĀlam, by way of example, where there is more than sufficient material for researchers to uncover the political and ideological affiliation of the channels and the aims that are driven by the politics of the two states that fund them). We have also witnessed how the media has slipped into broadcasting a curious conceptual and political mixing between regime, state, political authority, the military and government, on the one hand, and reform, revolution, local divisions and democracy, on the other. Some of the channels adopted something of a policy of *confusion* from which they actually suffered in covering the events of Tunisia and Egyptian especially. They have also not ceased to follow particular – if nebulous – lines in their covering of the Yemeni schisms, the Bahraini movement, the armed fighting in Libya, and the savagery with which the Syrian regime has confronted demonstrations in its cities and villages. These news channels have followed a clearly war-like policy and style in language, editing, commentary and the compilation of images in addition to the ways in which they show them repeatedly; and this is what justifies the assertion that the audiovisual treatment of the *intifadas* in the Arab world, with rare exceptions, has fallen into consecrating and broadcasting states of impassioned emotionalism and participated in firmly rooting what Mohammed Abed al-Jabri referred to as the 'culture of perception' (*thiqāfah al–idrāk*) (ʿAbd al–Jābrī 1999, p. 191; also al–Ghadhāmī 2004, pp. 207–208) at the expense of news, edification and consciousness raising or respecting the freedom of viewers and militated against their right to choose the view they find most suitable.

How is it, then, that audiovisual media production can claim to cover *intifadas* over humiliation and belittlement and to anticipate the establishment and recognition of a contemporary democracy when it marshals all that it possesses editorially to 'advertise' and avoid all serious pluralism and multiplicity (of views). And it on the consideration that such propagandizing is the basis of the media that participates in reform and firmly anchoring the prerequisites of democratic choice?

It is obvious that there is no such thing as media or communications, or audiovisual broadcasting – Arab or other – that is motivated by 'angelic' intentions. This is because the audiovisual components, whatever their nature, and their technical and human elements as well as their editorial choices as well as their short- and long-range goals, are connected to a cultural model and political agenda. Thus, broadcast operations are not merely ones of transmitting and reporting because they are expressive of a desire *to produce an effect*, and occasionally *a reaction*. Likewise, most often they emphasize narratives of a culture or a society itself instead of the participation of audiovisual communication in expressing the details of group identity or the transformations that are occurring to the structures of mindsets, behaviours, political positions, and aesthetic sensitivities and sensibilities.

There is no argument that audiovisual communication operates in complex conditions in general as it is, in its essence, multidimensional and of manifold intent. It presents as if capable of anything and everything, and in a way that is sometimes excessive as in the matter of the Don Quixotesque style of some of Arab news satellite channels. Actual authority and power is represented in the relation of the media to various political and economic authorities and powers. Despite that to a certain degree the media avails itself of some of these possibilities, it suffers at the same time from a fragility the nature of which is constantly changing due to technological changes and changing calculations and political balances as well as the quality and value of human resources.

Television has an amazing influence, and it is not possible to consider new digital means of communication as constituting a challenge or detracting from the magnitude of this influence. We may observe the opposite in the complementary nature of the roles of television and these other digital media. Television broadcasts images and video recordings taken from the internet, which in turn embeds thousands of images and television programmes in its electronic websites and sites of social communication. Thus, television grants itself permission in everything. It makes public and reveals what it wants. It correlates and synchronizes the bit of information and the event that it has decided to present in a way and according to a timetable of its choosing. Similarly, it holds back occurrences and information and conceals them; and moreover, it is able instead to create distortion. It is a multifunctional tool possessed of multiple facets, influences and effects as well as a medium of 'strategic' importance in orienting policies and channelling expectations, needs, forms of deprivation, and even dreams and whims of a wide strata among the people.[4]

The Arab world has actually witnessed a carnival of satellite news, specialized and public/general channels in what exceeds more than 700 channels shown daily to Arab viewers. Approximately 20% of these are religious channels devoted to preaching and proselytizing and mobilizing. A massive group has invested and has vested interests in this sector, and states have come down with all their financial and political weight in a war by the various stations to influence people. These range from Aljazeera with which the state of Qatar does not hide its regional and political connection and agenda to al–ʿArabīyah, beholden to the major orientations of Saudi Arabia, to al–ʿĀlam which transmits the politics and positions of Iran vis-à-vis Arab issues, to BBC Arabic and France 24.

Those who follow the treatment of the Arab *intifadas* by these stations witness vast differences in approach, exposure and commentary. Some of these channels commit genuine 'violations' of news and plurality of opinion as well as infringements of practical media ethics even if they raise the banner of 'One Opinion and Another Opinion' ('*al–Raʾyu wa al–Raʾyu al–Ākhir*') as in the title of an Aljazeera programme, where this translates both editorially and practically into 'Opinion … the Final Opinion' ('*al–Raʾyu wa al–Raʾyu al–Akhīr*'). If these stations express the policies, interests and positions of those who fund them and if their satellite broadcast and viewability through the internet permits them to penetrate many boundaries and limits and bypass traditional modes of censorship, then their broadcasts raise serious and real questions about the role of the media in observing and monitoring the reality of the Arab movement in its various forms and expressions, and its participation in efforts of 'democratic transition' and the distortion of this in one or another Arab country.

What is the role of the media and journalism in democratic transition? If the newscaster has a role in democracy, is it incumbent on him to recommend or be a spokesperson speaking in the name of a socio-political project? Or should that role go back to the political actors? What are the limits and points of intersection between news, opinion and liability?

Heated discussion has erupted between newscasters and journalists in Tunisia, for example, over the means of administering this transitional phase that is witnessing major difficulties represented in an unprecedented recession in tourism, the effects of which have negatively impacted social groups that derive their living from it, who number in the millions. Such is also the case with the departure of a number of corporations and the closure of others in a trend that has exacerbated unemployment and the return of tens of thousands of Tunisians who were working in Libya and have fled the ongoing war there. Accompanying this has been a rise in the prices of basic living staples over and above the lack of security in some outlying districts far from the urban centres.

Newscasters and journalists went from being defenders of the previous regime, cooperating with it, seeking to appease it or being suppressed by it – where silence or fear was the guiding principle, with few exceptions – to a number of them expressing with incisive frankness a loss of identity that reflects an existential crises over their practise of the profession of journalism in a society that has just recently emerged with great difficulty from authoritarianism. Likewise, some others have proved hesitant to be forthcoming in a situation in which they are torn between a temporary government suffering from a deficiency in legitimacy and the expectations of broad groups among the people who have begun to demand rights and are occupying some positions in the public sphere in an unprecedented fashion. Along with this, followers of events may notice that newscasters in Tunisia have been liberated from many professional, psychological and political obstacles from which they suffered during the phases of autocracy that distinguished the rule of al-Habib Bourguiba and, in particular, that of Zein al-Abidin Ben Ali. Tongues and pens have been freed from their restraints and the Tunisian press has come to deal with all subjects without trepidation or fear of prohibition, censorship or penalties. Tyranny had produced atrocities that Tunisians are sometimes unable to describe because they were so horrific. All the sources of information were controlled. No news was leaked except that which the political authority decided to present to readers, listeners and viewers in ways, language and according to timetables that it chose. It exercised an extreme protectionism over the minds of Tunisians, which is what led a large number of people to abandon these means of media, or rather to 'despise and deride' them. If there was a group, aside from the police apparatus, that was exposed to scorn and ridicule – according to some – it was the group of newscasters to such a degree that they not only suffered from a lack of trust in them, but also some were harassed and even assaulted occasionally due to their positions or roles in justifying the tyranny of the previous era.

Doubtless, newspapers and journalists have maintained a minimum level of trust and believability and know-how to 'manoeuvre' around and 'negotiate' the previous era. Similarly, the internet exploded the calculations of the regime and a sizable number of newscasters set up sites expressive of the defiant desire of Tunisians for freedom, despite the fact that this transitional period in speech and expression has witnessed glaring slippages in professionalism. Thus, nothing is yet fully fledged and the maturation process requires time and accumulation in order to establish institutional bases – material and professionally – dedicated to creating a media that abides by a greater degree of fairness and objectivity in news and edification.

If previously the political authority publicly followed a strategy of containment with regard to 'independent' media initiatives, then a new amalgam has begun to appear by changing the logic of political pressure and following other methods of pressure exerted through and by those who possess the means of funding and the owners of capital. This is what will create new and pending obligations and conditionalities for the press, despite the palpable climate of freedom in the Tunisian media; and it is also that which will pose serious questions about the 'independence' of journalism, and the limits of criticism and accountability of various authorities.

It appears that the transitional period being experienced by Tunisia raises serious causes for concern in the statements of actors in national bodies (whether these be the 'Supreme Body for the Achievement of the Goals of the Revolution, Political Reform and Democratic Transition' or the independent body that oversees elections or the body that will prepare the guiding principles for regulating written and audiovisual media).[5] The major challenges confronted by the various planners in this new stage has produced a mature awareness of the difficulties involved and the complexities of transition as well as the preconditions for its success and the preparedness to bear the costs of this upheaval in Tunisian political society. At the same time an ethic of discussion and listening has begun to crystallize, piquing attention or even arousing wonder and occasionally bewilderment. There are wounds created by the *ancien* regime among workers in the same field. The newscaster today finds himself divided between the desire to be rid of his status as an employee subject to directives and instructions and his being someone demanding to be an actor in the transition, to practise his profession normally – respecting multiplicity/diversity and observing professional conduct. The situation is that the newscaster, according to those actually working in the field, enjoys freedom today but is bereft of the tools and editorial preparedness, where a large number of them suffer from a deficiency in training as to how to exercise freedom. This is what necessitates a rehabilitation and reformation in order to be able to cope with the pervasive factors of sweeping changes and to translate them into journalistic forms and treatments in the media that will factor genuinely in bringing about the transition. However, the crucial question remaining in this context, in my view, pertains to whether it is possible to conceive a course whereby the means of written, electronic and audiovisual communication will lead to the successful transition in disseminating the culture of citizenship and encouraging people to participate in making political and social decisions.

It might appear as though this question has something of a utopian nature, given that most of the means of communication are preoccupied with priorities other than those which might possibly be subsumed in efforts to deepen critical perception or encourage action and participation in public democratic discussion. Likewise, the websites and electronic journals have conditions more favourable to liberation from political bargaining and the constraints of money to which the written and audiovisual media subject them. However, how can it be expected that shackles might be shed and the heavy burden of advertising obviated along with the habituation of mindsets and imaginations and the instilling of habits of delegating trust and submissiveness in order to transition to an initiative of providing the requisite conditions for producing and distributing media qualified to assume roles of raising consciousness and deepening the culture of citizenship and participation?

Tunisia has come to know a raging activism, and it has problems beyond counting. Forward-looking expectations, intentions, and political and media projects make this country – which sparked the *intifadas* against Arab political autocracy – a genuine test bed for the promulgation of contemporary democratic principles, which many of those concerned predict will produce impacts and repercussions throughout the region. Doubtless, the ousting of the regime of Ben Ali created a huge vacuum in leadership, particularly in the political and media spheres, just as it appears that the country will pay a heavy price for transitioning to democracy. However, a modernizing elite coexisting alongside Islamists has led to calls for the emulation of the Turkish experiment in Tunisia (and it is a relation not incidental to the particular history of Tunisia with Turkey in any case, even if many Tunisian political bodies doubt the extent of commitment of the Arab renaissance movement to the intellectual orientations and politics of the Turkish Justice and Development Party).[6] This development is taking place in a civil society that has begun to organize itself on the consideration of it being a counter-authority and internationally supported even if it has not ceased to be a theoretical proposition that has not yet been practically translated into reality. All these factors taken in aggregate put Tunisians at a historic crossroads where there is no room for failure.

Of necessity, the course of transition imposes – in its obstacles and difficulties and the forms of interstices in the struggles for democracy – the necessity of liberating the media, and especially the audiovisual media. It also necessitates proffering new conditions for the presentation of a 'national' product capable of catalysing reconciliation with the expectations of the viewer instead of leaving him to Arab and 'Islamic' channels motivated by agendas that do not serve – and for which the passage of days *will* confirm that they do not serve – democratic construction. They are motivated instead by other intentions, among which is reverting Arab countries to something which predated the state and encouraging all the '*salafist*' trends who cast democracy in the framework of unbelief (*takfir*) to agitate for the Islamization of societies.

There is no argument that the 'arenas of struggle' are ablaze and in the process of transition, especially in the context of liberation from the chains of autocracy and compliant submission. Every society contains within it these arenas replete with questions and issues pertaining to the reading of history, the place of religion, the importance of language and status of women, etc. The media, in particular the public audiovisual forms, plays decisive roles in dealing with these arenas of struggle and presenting them in the service of promoting local peace and critical national integration in order to evade all the pitfalls that might dissipate or exhaust the efforts for democratic transformation, especially in a cultural context that has not ceased to produce obstacles to 'modernization' and which suffers from huge deficiencies in contemporary democratic culture.

Notes

1. The importance of the religious unconscious emerges here. It is necessary to re-differentiate between religion, as a sacred referential authority, and its practical, creedal translations, and also between various manifestations of religiosity that modern society produces. A number of sociologists and anthropologists have worked since the 1970s to study group-collective situations or occasions that produce manifestations of religiosity, especially during football (soccer) games and huge concerts. Among these researches are the works of Michel Maffesoli (Maffesoli 1993, 2000, 2007) and others. See also the works of Régis Debray, who is considered to be one of the Marxists who noted the importance of religion in politics and modern life (while he was still in prison) in the late 1960s when he published his referential book entitled *Critique de la Raison Politique ou l'Inconscient Religieux* (1981). The data of the technological world and the expressions of the religious imagination, both the violent as well as the pacifist, confirmed to him the deep influence of religion in politics and society (Debray 2000, 2001). It has been noticed that Arab uprisings have created their own spheres of demonstration and meeting points, such as Taḥrīr/Taghyīr Square, in which numerous slogans and placards of graffiti were held aloft dedicated to numerous themes such as the 'Friday of Rage', the 'Friday of the Masses', the 'Friday of Steadfastness', the 'Friday of the March', the 'Friday of Freedom', etc. Gatherings in these public venues acquired significant symbolic importance among demonstrators because they became occasions in which bonds, ties, connections, communications, discussions, and negotiations were made and created in what promoted forms of heartfelt, impassioned spiritual camaraderie, despite differences and contradictions that persisted among participants party to this public ritual.
2. Also since 1997 Muḥammad Jābir al-Anṣārī has observed Arab–Islamic experiments – from the Lebanese experience to the Somali one to the Afghani experiment – admitting the probability of other wider experiments in the Arab world that are equally dangerous in terms of schisms and insecurity. He has noticed that these pluralities and attendant groups are capable of 'revealing' their true 'naked' essence and transformation into what is genuine civil strife in nature in the framework of our socio-political reality, whatever we may raise of banners or slogans of nationalism and religion and however careful we may be in raising such or discussing them, or however we may confront the struggle with nationalist, regional or Islamic polemics (al-Anṣārī *et al.* 1977, p. 27).
3. It may be worth mentioning that the term 'Machiavellian' not only refers to the author of *The Prince* alone, but also is an indication of a collective representation attached to modern politics. It is, on the one hand, a term for politics attached to groups engaging in corrupt and deceptive behavioural conduct, while, on the other hand, it is indicative of the games played by the government/ruling authority which through various techniques ensures its tight grip and control of the people as being 'subjects'. Such ways include deception, lies, fraud and trickery, meaning the 'utilitarian and applied' aspect of politics (also d'Allonnes 1999, p. 222).
4. The broadcasting of the hearings of the trial of Hosni Mubarak, his sons and others accused beginning on 3 August 2011 was, incontestably, a political moment with historic significance heralding a massive political sea change, and indicative of the precursors of Egypt entering a new era of human rights, and that it was undergoing a qualitative change in audiovisual coverage and treatment of events. At the very least it is indicative of the opening of new innovative horizons for the professionalism and competence of Egyptian media.
5. Numerous analysts began to examine the reasons and repercussions of this anxiety, about which Waḥīd ʿAbd al-Majīd has written: 'the question being raised today is not about the time frame needed for the triumph of revolutions that seem to emanate from the desires of the majority of people, but rather pertains to whether or not they have actually succeeded in effecting change.' He adds that 'the scene in both countries [meaning Tunisia and Egypt]

is no longer indicative of the optimism which prevailed initially after the toppling of the regime, which perhaps dissipated a few weeks afterwards. The forward course is facing difficulties, and the transitional period is ridden with anxiety. Those who are leading it have committed and are accused, at most of conspiracy and at least of stalling and procrastination. Also the forces of the revolution and those who advocated it are divided and are unable to reach a consensus over the new regime' (Waḥīd ʿAbd al-Majīd 2011).

6. Rāshid al-Ghanūshī argues that 'the state in Islam is a *civil* state, and those who are responsible for it are always subject to criticism, and lack any sacred attributes … we oppose the notion that the state interferes in the creedal doctrines of people: in what they eat, drink or wear as such is the [private] affairs of the human being. And, if you wish consider this to be a form of laïcisme/secularism, then so be it' (al-Ghanūshī 2011).

References

ʿAbd al–Jābrī, M., 1999. *Al–Masʾalah al–Thaqāfīyah fī al–Waṭan al–ʿArabī*. National Culture Series No. 25. Issues in Arab Thought No. 1, Vol. 2. Beirut: Centre for Arab Unity Studies.

ʿAbd al-Majīd, Waḥīd, 2011. al–Taʾathur fī Tūnis wa Miṣr … wa Maṣīr al–Rabīʿ al–ʿArabī. *al–Ḥayāt*, 31 July. Available from: http://menber-11.info/pdf/show.php?id=9090 [Accessed 4 October 2011].

Affaya, M.N., 1998. *Al–Ḥadāthah wal–Tawāṣul fī al–Falsafah al–Naqdīyah al–Muʿāṣirah: Namūdhaj Habermas*. Casablanca: Dār Afrīqiyā al–Sharq.

al–Anṣārī, M.J., *et al.*, 1977. *al–Nizāʿāt al–Ahlīyah al–ʿArabīyah: al–ʿAwāmil al–Dākhilīyah wal–Khārijīyah*, Ed. ʿAdnān al–Sayyid Ḥussayn. Beirut: Centre for Arab Unity Studies.

Belkeziz, A., 2001. *Fi al–Dīuqrāṭīyah wal–Mujtamaʿ al–Madanī: Marāthī al–Wāqiʿ, Madāʾiḥ al–Usṭūrah*. Casablanca: Dār Afrīqiyā al–Sharq.

Belkeziz, A., 2008. *al–Dawlah wal–Mujtamaʿ: Jadalīyāt al–Tawḥīd wal–Inqisām fī al–Ijtimāʿ al–ʿArabī al–Muʿāṣir, Madāʾiḥ al–Usṭūrah*. Beirut: al–Shabakah al–ʿArabīyah lil Abḥāth wal–Nashr.

Brière, C., Blanchet, P. and Foucault, M., 1979. *Iran: La révolution au nom de dieu: suivi d'un entretien avec Michel Foucault*. Editions du Seuil.

Comte-Sponville, A., 1996. Une morale sans fondement. *In*: J.M. Besnier, D. Bourg and P. Bruckner, eds. *La Société en quête de valeurs: Pour sortir de l'alternative entre scepticisme et dogmatisme*. Collection Institut du Management. Paris: Maxima L. du Mesnil, 119–126.

d'Allonnes, M.R., 1999. *Le Dépérissement de la politique: Généalogie d'un lieu commun*. Paris: Flammarion.

Debray, R., 1981. *Critique de la Raison Politique ou l'Inconscient Religieux*. Bibliothèque des Idées. Paris: Gallimard.

Debray, R., 2000. *L'Emprise, Le Débat*. Paris: Gallimard.

Debray, R., 2001. *Dieu, un itinéraire: Matériaux pour l'histoire de l'Éternel en Occident*. Le champ médiologique. Paris: O. Jacob.

Feuerbach, L., 1841. *Das Wesen des Christenthums* [*The essence of Chritianity*]. Leipzig: Otto Wigand.

al–Ghadhāmī, A.A., 2004. *al–Thaqāfah al–Tilfizyūnīyah: Suqūt al–Nukhbah wa Burūz al–Shaʿbī*. Casablanca: al–Markaz al–Thaqāfī al–ʿArabī.

Ghalyūn, B., 2001. al–Dīmuqrāṭīyah min Manẓūr al–Mashrūʿ al–Ḥaḍārī. Paper presented at Naḥw Mashrūʿ Ḥaḍārī Nahḍawī ʿArabī, studies and discussions of a seminar held at the Centre for Arab Unity Studies, Beirut, 2001.

Al–Ghanūshī, R., 2011. Interview with Rāshid al–Ghanūshī by the Moroccan journal *Akhbār al-Yawm*, 23–24, July. Available from: http://www.maghress.com/almassae/137647 [Accessed 4 October 2011].

Habermas, J., 1987a. Logique des sciences sociales et autres essais. In: *Philosophie d'Aujourd'hui*. Paris: Presses universitaires de France, 121.

Habermas, J., 1987b. Théorie de l'Agir communicationnel. *In: L'Espace du Politique,* 2 vols. Paris: Fayard.

Habermas, J., 1992. *De l'éthique de la discussion*. Paris: Flammarion.

Jadʿān, F., 2001. Naḥn wal–Dīmuqrāṭīyah: Manẓūr Tanwīrī. *ʿĀlam al–Fikr*, 29 (3), 158.

Al–Kuwārī, ʿA.K., 2010. *Naḥw Kutlah Tārīkhīyah Dīmuqrāṭīyah fī al-Buldān al ʿArabīyah* [*The initiative of studies on democracy in the Arab world*]. Beirut: Centre for Arab Unity Studies.

Al–Kuwārī, ʿA.K. and Māḍī, ʿA.F., coords/eds, 2009. Limādhā Intaqal al–Ākharūn ilā al–Dīmuqrāṭīyah wa Taʾakhar al–ʿArab? Dirāsat Muqāranah li–Duwal ʿArabīyah maʿ Duwal Ukhrā. *In*: *Project on democratic studies in the Arab world*. Beirut: Centre for Arab Unity Studies.

Al–Kuwārī, ʿA.K. and Māḍī, ʿA.F., 2010. Mafhūm al–Kutlah al–Tārīkhīyah ʿalā Qāʿidat al–Dīmuqrāṭīyah. *al–Mustaqbal al–ʿArabī*, 32 (373), 132–133.

Laroui, A., 1970. *Al-Īdiyūlūjīyā al-ʿArabīyah al-Muʿāṣirah* (1970) [*Contemporary Arab ideology*]. Paris: F. Maspero.

Laroui, A., 2002. *Mafhūm al-Dawlah* [*Concept of state*], 7th edn. Casablanca-Beirut: al-Markaz al-Thaqāfī al-ʿArabī

Lefort, C., 1986. *Le Travail de l'œuvre Machiavel*, collection Tel, 2ème partie. Paris: Gallimard.

Lipovetsky, G., 1996. L'Ere de l'après devoir. *In*: J.M. Besnier, D. Bourg and P. Bruckner, eds. *La Société en quête de valeurs: Pour sortir de l'alternative entre scepticisme et dogmatisme*. Collection Institut du Management. Paris: Maxima L. du Mesnil, 23–30.

Maffesoli, M., 1993. *La Contemplation du monde: Figures du style communautaire*. Paris: B. Grassat.

Maffesoli, M., 2000. *Le Temps des tribus: Le Déclin de l'individualisme dans les sociétés de masse*. Paris: La Table Ronde.

Maffesoli, M., 2007. *La Connaissance ordinaire: Précis de sociologie compréhensive*, meridiens klincksieck. Paris: Klincksieck.

Namer, G., 2003. *Le Contretemps démocratique: Révolte morale et rationalité de la loi*. Paris: L'Harmattan.

Rawls, J., 1987. *Théorie de la justice*. Trans. from the English by C. Audard. Paris: Seuil.

War of Creative Destruction: the central tendency in the globalized Arab revolutions (a study in the formation of the future)

Fatḥī al-ʿAfīfī

Zagazig University, Zagazig, Egypt

The Arab world in the 2010–2011 period was subject to a massive and unprecedented process of 'creative destruction'. Despite its highly pernicious effects at numerous levels, including the distortion of political life and the stark polarization and increasing disparities between rich and poor, creative destruction is the instrument of choice in the process of globalization run by the major powers, and functions in place of more costly direct military interventions but can be used to serve similar ends. Major western powers engage in trafficking in protection, and American policies impose international axes conflicting by design for the purposes of managing their concerns whether such be through playing off political rivals against one another or running low-intensity wars that serve vested interests or grander imperial designs. Savage capitalism is an overt instrument and consequence of authoritarianism and corruption that justifies chaos, which also, in the context of globalization, gives just cause for revolution when it affirms social–Darwinian concepts that suggest 'victims deserve their fate' and 'whoever can save himself does'. The Neo-liberalism derivative of Adam Smith that is at the core of globalization and its logic vigorously promotes individualism at the expense of collectivism and group interests and encourages individual initiatives—all of which led to the major global financial collapse of September 2008, and it is this same logic that underpins the strategy of creative destruction. This article provides a theoretical framework as well as specific means for analyzing the process of creative destruction specifically in the Arab world during the period of the so-called 'Arab Spring' and deals with the various social matrices and movements along with the role of Arab satellite media, electronic chaos and cyber-mobilization. Additionally projects, justifications for, and hierarchies of creative destruction are detailed across various axes and different modalities including the American mode, the Arab authoritarian state mode and the popular mode. The force of creative destruction in the Middle East, in the final analysis, is more than a US scheme for dismantling the old Arab order; the Arab revolts constitute the catalyst and central tendency towards taking responsibility—as a concept and plan for the unleashing of the tremendous power and mobilization that are permitting Arab peoples to do more than react, but to have their say in history.

Introduction

Recently, the Arab region has been swept by an unprecedented wave of chaos, penetrating all aspects of the old and overturning decades-old convictions, in which concepts and practices have intermixed to spawn activism and debate over what is destructive and what is constructive. This has happened in a way that has catapulted all factions into the fray in hopes of prevailing, driven by the desire to exploit this historic opportunity, which might never recur – at least not in the foreseeable future. Hence, what is occurring is a type of multidimensional collapse and failure of all the policies – stemming from customs or laws – that had governed the region for more than 50 years. The earth has been split asunder by the emergence of a new seedling, still barely formed, fraught with danger and fear, yet which marks an historic turning point of reconciliation between the private and the global. For the first time, the Arabs have taken the initiative to act on the global stage, with repercussions for all humanity, manifesting their refusal to remain on the receiving end and merely respond to stressors coming from all sides and directions. The current globalized movement and its concomitant campaigns for liberty, democracy and the overthrow of autocratic, corrupt and dictatorial regimes is merely one facet of globalization, in which events appear to be possessed of a central tendency – the hidden and manifest aspects of which appear in attempts to channel its dynamics across different levels, in the violent birth of an Arab revolutionary movement.

This force of creative destruction in the Middle East is more comprehensive than a simple US scheme for the systematic dismantling of what was. The Arab revolts constitute the catalyst and central tendency towards taking responsibility, as a concept and as a plan, for the unleashing of the tremendous power and mobilization that are leading the Arab peoples to have their say in history. All the separate revolutions spell a single revolution across different regions. Perhaps, this time, the people have succeeded, where all previous attempts at unifying the Arab nation on elite or authoritarian bases have failed, and to affirm that this region constitutes a single organic entity, in which, if one 'limb' is subject to harm, all others rally to it in care and protection. The central tendency is manifest in the collective consciousness that was moved to revolt against injustice, oppression and blind might; and this historic development, despite its wide scope and variable effectiveness, is reducible to a 'central tendency towards creative destruction'.

What is surprising in this study is that creative destruction has evolved with the development of the methodology of analysis itself. When the American central tendency provided 'the essence, the concept, the plans and the initiatives', the ruling authorities could justify the chaos they had engineered, but which in turn stirred the embers and then caused the eruption of a counter-hierarchy. Subsequently, the people took control in the form of an electronic popular mobilization, and they went to the streets *en masse*, in a defiant image of chaos spreading across the Arab world, with an unprecedented determination to create a better reality by rediscovering life, and building a meaningful world according to new givens.

First: the central tendency of American creative destruction

Over the last decade, following the attacks of 11 September 2001, the United States has engaged in aggression against the Arab–Islamic world in a series of wars of revenge beginning in Afghanistan and then continuing with Iraq. Israel launched hostilities against south Lebanon in 2006 under the 'moral cover' of a 'War on Terror' and against the 'Axis of Evil', along with the dissemination of democracy and the overthrow of religious and political dictatorships in the region. Subsequently a new approach was adopted, oriented towards improving the image of the United States and transitioning it from an imperialist state into one that fosters dialogue between different groups. This transition was undertaken not for the sake of bringing these groups into agreement, but rather with the intention of directing and controlling them and directing the struggle according to new mechanisms of remote deconstruction.[1] These events were akin to a rude and violent awakening for autocratic regimes, and the people had no option but to enter into the fray. The plight of former Iraqi President Saddam Hussein, fleeing from one place to another, followed by his execution, rendered the toppling of draconian and excessive rulers possible, and the Arab nation dared to contemplate the nature of the coming change. They debated: would change be from within or without? The people of the region witnessed with their own eyes the precedents of Iraq and Afghanistan and what these have entailed in terms of interminable destruction and sectarian warfare. Thanks to the development of globalized social media, and after protracted and exhaustive negotiations and dialogue over the preferability of either of the two choices, the Arab peoples elected to act.

The term ‘creative destruction’ should not be repulsive or rejected on intellectual grounds, simply because it is of Western origin and reflective of detested and hostile American policies. Many are the things that belong to their culture, but despite this we use them and work without being beset by any sort of psychological complex or excessive sensitivity. Revolution is, itself, an operative practice of creative destruction; and it is the necessary and inevitable escape from the clutches of tradition and stability in a state of humiliation. When the masses revolted with such unprecedented anger against tyranny and, on this path, adopted the goal of bringing down everything that had a connection to tyranny, dictatorship and social injustice, this was an act of chaos – or creative destruction – in the interests of creating more just, free and democratic systems. Revolution, in any case, is the ultimate *intifada*; that emanates from chaos. The central tendency of American creative destruction proceeds along two orientations.

The essence of the central tendency towards chaos

In an attempt to maintain control, while initiating the twin political and structural changes intended to bring about the Americanization of the world, any regional structure deemed unsuitable for accomplishing the desired goal in American terms is targeted for destruction and its component capacities unleashed in processes of open-ended bloodletting and the dissemination of ‘chaos’. These are the alternatives confronting any scheme for stability that does not conform to the plans of global geo-politics (Kier and Krebs 2010, pp. 17–18).[2]

US intelligence played a major role in destroying the former Soviet Union, and engendering a state of chaos and the break up its institutional elements and satellite statelets. It built on the rubble of this a unipolar ‘New World Order’ (1991–1994); and as a result the term ‘globalization’ came into common parlance as both a concept and a practice (Neo-liberalism; free trade/liberalization of the market; and facilitation of the free movement of capital, i.e. the removal of barriers), while by force of arms and occupation new military bases were set up across the world. This strategy persisted throughout the tenure of President Bill Clinton (1993–2001).[3] When George W. Bush came to power the United States expanded the use of theories of creative destruction, at the behest and instigation of companies such as Halliburton and the Pentagon (the military–industrial complex), through the ‘War on Terror’ and ‘pre-emptive wars’ and reactivation of the ‘domino theory’ that signalled the gradual collapse of autocratic regimes, after Bush announced that ‘stability no longer served American interests’. Subsequently, the theory of ‘creative destruction’ (or ‘constructive *chaos*’) emerged as a grand plan for dealing with this region, involving:

> the breaking up of the Arab regional order through forging axes with America or against it, putting the order into a state of perpetual worry and threatening it with change; recasting the order where America will play the role of fomenting destruction (chaos) and leaving the region to its internal struggles so as to become in need of American intervention to impose order.[4]

What ensures the support for and perpetuation of imperialism, to a large degree, in all this regional revolutionary activity is the cunningly woven complex web that emerges from the interplay of the following stages or factors:

- The failure of the mechanism of direct military intervention along the lines witnessed in Afghanistan and Iraq, because: (1) direct military intervention has huge costs that are disproportionate to the benefits and outcomes, in addition to it being long-term; (2) it does not have the desired effect after the collapse of the regime, in the absence of a strategy for reconstruction after the collapse; and (3) it negatively impacts the image of the United States, when it is transformed into a 'policeman' for the world that does not hesitate to kill and destroy to arrive at its (illegitimate) ends.
- The existence of lobbies for globalization that have an interest in bringing about crises in weak regions of the world and are composed of the following three sectors: (1) weapons manufacturers that participate effectively in American presidential and congressional campaigns and that do not intend to find themselves out of work; (2) pharmaceutical companies, the mechanisms of which operate at full capacity during situations of wars spread around the world; and (3) media and print corporations that operate as a huge propaganda machine that remains in the background of events.
- In accordance with the above, the co-optation of the Arab revolutions in order to achieve: (1) the reproduction of hegemony through new means of globalization that are amenable to remote control and attempt to bring the region into greater geo-political proximity with the plan for the 'New Greater Middle East' (as introduced at the G8 Summit in 2004); (2) the organized theft of oil, where the absence of institutions paves the way for interim regimes to accept necessary concessions in order to secure their retention of power; and (3) firmly ensconce the regional position of Israel and limit the cost of the conflict when confronting Arab regimes experiencing a state of chaos. The final outcome is the attempt to punish in exemplary fashion and contain this region that from whence came those with the audacity to undertake a raid in the heart of America against its vital points and symbols of military and economic power (the twin towers of the World Trade Center and the Pentagon) so as to serve as a lesson to anyone and everyone who might entertain the idea of resisting American hegemony.

In this way, chaos, in the American approach, is nothing but a political injunction for an open massacre; a concept drawn from the physics of critical mass, where the greater the mass and the closer to the explosion, the greater are the reactions. It is a destructive orientation, as confirmed by Michael Ledeen,[5] one of the leading spokespersons of Neo-conservatism who asserted: 'Creative destruction is our middle name. We do it automatically … it is time once again to export the democratic revolution' (al-Ḥāj Ṣāliḥ 2005, p. 77).

American creative destruction focuses on what is termed the 'revolution of democracies', highlighting the themes of basic rights, freedom, justice, equality and the right to determine one's destiny, as global human values not restricted to any single nation and featuring the political theories espoused by the American ruling elite, which have an influential role in bringing about radical changes in stable states and ones where security is tightly controlled. Among the concepts espoused was that of 'constructive chaos', promoted by Madeline Albright, US Secretary of State at the beginning of the third millennium, which connoted at that time, creating a state of systematic chaos in order to shatter and bring down old prevailing patterns, where subsequently all the people will proceed to ballot boxes to come to know the real balance of forces, so as to adopt future strategies on the basis of these new givens (Zenko 2010, pp. 235–238).[6]

The polarization projects of creative destruction

The unleashing of chaos necessitates a series of polarization initiatives, that are like connecting neurons that feed its credo and which are generated in the name of globalization and absolute freedom of information, wealth, ideas and merchandise, necessitating a network of international services essential to the upkeep of the process. These demand a pattern of international relations that might not necessarily lead to stability and world peace, but which might lead in many areas to the instigation of revolutions and reactions. Whenever tyrannical autocratic regimes believe that external support connotes a guarantee of their continuity, in fact such becomes a *casus belli* for their overthrow, where logistical services are distributed across the following:

- Joint investments: this refers to the process of integrating local companies into global corporations, where the parent company appropriates the ideas and policies and implementation; and where, subsequently, absolute economic sovereignty comes under the domination of the market mechanism and the centralization of the global economy (Saʿīd 1986, p. 219; also ʿAbd al-Rāziq 2004, p. 66).
- Trafficking in protection: the security and protection provided by the major powers (the United States, Britain and France) to autocratic regimes in the Arab region demands perseverance in purchasing arms and military equipment from these countries under the pressure of the lobbies of the major weapons manufacturers. This is exemplified in Egypt, where economic assistance was earmarked in a particular fashion and went almost entirely towards supporting defence and thence the complete subjugation of the region to foreign colonial administration, over and above the scattered settlements of occupation and military bases, and the presence of foreign experts and technicians and vital apparatuses, to return Arabs to a state of colonization. In all cases the expropriation of sovereign decision-making of these countries is a result of the regional crises (Cordesman 1993, pp. 16–18).
- Conflicting axes: American policies impose a new pattern of international alliances, some of which are sectarian, such as the 'Shi'ite axis', the 'Sunni axis', as well as the other imperial ones such as 'moderate states' and 'extremist states', where this is tantamount to undeclared conflict in the way such axes feed and perpetuate tensions, such as those in Egyptian–Qatari relations. These conflicting axes collide and are either causes for low-intensity or partial wars or logistical manifestations of these and regional intifadas, in the service of the central agenda and point of reference.[7] Thus one finds that Iran behaves however it wills in Shi'ite regions, and practices systematic destruction, yet

when the countries of the Gulf defend their interests, pre-empting danger, Tehran threatens vociferously and does not hesitate to intimate war in defence of its ideological creed.

- The Gulf Marshall Plan: the United States resents any orientations or movements that are outside its scope and the designs it has for the region. From this standpoint the countries of the Arab Gulf have resorted to implementing a 'Marshall Plan' for the Gulf – to support Bahrain and Oman, such that the Kuwaiti Council of Ministers approved a grant to Bahrain in a number of instalments, the first of which was 40 billion Bahraini dinars, similar to the initiatives taken by Saudi Arabia and the United Arab Emirates (UAE). To this end, the Emir of Kuwait succeeded in repairing the cleavage in Emirati and Omani relations that had witnessed grievous tension in the wake of accusations by Muscat that Abu Dhabi was behind destructive activities there (Anon. 2011a). When the policy of the 'carrot' proved unsuccessful, the Gulf countries resorted to the 'stick' and sent the Peninsula Shield Force into Bahrain which took part in breaking up by force the demonstrations at Pearl Roundabout. This instance confirms that the Gulf Cooperation Council (GCC) is an autocratic association designed primarily to protect the regimes from being overthrown. All of this stirred up American resentment; and US Secretary of State Hilary Clinton announced that the Saudi intervention in Bahrain was a mistake and liable to instigate regional chaos (Anon. 2011b).

Second: creative destruction in the autocratic approach

Ruling regimes resort to bypassing and trampling on constitutions, doing away with law, and violating people's basic rights – and they become proficient in forms of discrimination, corruption, favouritism and usurping public monies, while inciting riots and fomenting chaos in parliamentary elections, in addition to taking advantage of all national resources and capabilities (oil, gas, land and weapons) as though they are in a state of ongoing and systematic war against their people. This is how these regimes use creative destruction to ensure their interests in monopolizing accumulated power and wealth, qualitatively and quantitatively, in ways that prolong autocracy and reproduce it in an endless dialectic of integration and fragmentation that does not end, except by revolution against it (Bajoria and Jerome 2011).[8]

Authoritarian justifications for creative destruction

The Arab countries differ from the standpoint of their staying power and the extent to which they respond to revolution and styles of resisting authority, in accordance with the nature of their demography and the political environment that nurtures their regimes. Thus what is correct in Egypt is not necessarily correct for another country. In Libya the situation necessitated entering into bloody battles and massacres of Libyans, given the 'tribal nature and geographic separation' that characterized the society (as well as the absence of a regime or system susceptible to overthrow in the first place). This nebulous and intricate tribal order interwoven with militias viewed the system as the state; where if the capital did not fall, then the authority could never be brought down. In Bahrain, sectarianism is one of the causes of weakness and power at the same time, where revolting against the ruler or supporting him reverts back to factionalism. Yemen, likewise, might witness civil wars and secessionist movements; and even when the revolution erupted in the name of bringing down the regime of Ali Abdullah Saleh, it was said that this was nothing more than riots and acts of rebellion (ʿAlam al-Dīn 2011, p. 1).

The one constant that constitutes a confirmed central tendency as a primary motivator for all these Arab revolutions is inherent in the notion of the 'inheritance' of political rule embodied in a voracious state that has possessed Arab rulers and their entourages. The philosophy of political inheritance is based on treating the people, or subjects, as though they are personal property, wherein the citizen is an employee of the ruler and his heir apparent, to be taken as though he/she were a sort booty in a system where the people do not choose their ruler or even criticize him and cannot undertake to replace him. And because this practice of inheritance of rule has become legitimized, societies have stopped developing and institutional structures have been rendered dysfunctional and ineffective. Additionally, both the concepts of power and state were abolished, along with all political methodologies and theories, and what they entail in terms of crippling and expunging enlightened elites, substituting in their place obscure elites predicated on allegiance and subordination, ignorance and oppression – rewarding the compliant and obedient with membership in representative or parliamentary councils of the government (Khalīl 2011, p. 17). Moreover, institutions pertinent to the relation between people and the state become family-run establishments, whence the old Arab ruler, having acquired the taste and appetite for power and its pleasures, endeavours to clone himself, and attempts to cover his flaws and escape being held accountable for what he did to his country, his people and their future, espousing misleading slogans about stability and continuity of the national course.[9]

The outcome of all this is an autocratic environment that justifies the rebellion of the people and their involvement in the process of 'creative destruction', and which may be defined as follows:

- The absence of proper constitutional arrangements. Constitutions should be contractual and not granted (i.e. be top-down or by royal decree), so that they establish the legitimacy of governance; shut the doors to civil strife; distribute powers and balance between them; and allow for the enactment of laws that specify and guarantee freedoms, rights and duties.
- The infiltration and manoeuvring of the ruling regime (family or party run) in all the apparatuses of the state, and their grip over sovereign offices that gives people a sense of injustice because they are not fairly represented in government or official bureaucracy.
- The systematic distortion of political life and the absence of genuine paths towards democracy so long as the process of forming political parties remains suppressed and rejected by authorities.
- Disparities in peoples' incomes that widen with the phenomenon of the polarization between the rich and poor in the era of globalization. It is necessary to search for means and ways to dismantle social and economic authoritarianism at the same time as adopting the path to political democracy.
- The absence of oversight and accountability standards and regulations in preference for normative justifications of the status quo renders these countries unresponsive to accountability and transparency, either internally or externally. Moreover, there is no alternative to oversight apparatuses and an independent judiciary as prerequisites for a true civil society.
- The malleability of authorities to the exigencies of Western strategies to dismantle regimes and societies in order to reformulate them in conformity with the

> West's new geo-political visions. This is in addition to the resort to oppression as the only mechanism of understanding between regimes and their peoples and the enactment of 'states of emergency' that permit the use of brute force by police and security apparatuses that eventually foments mobilization and justifies violent revolutionary reactions.[10]

Savage capitalism is an overt instrument and consequence of authoritarianism and corruption that justifies chaos, which, in the context of globalization, raises a quintessential banner for revolution when it affirms social–Darwinian concepts that suggest 'victims deserve their fate' and 'whoever can save himself does'. It is as though the Arab peoples were the like of a huge elephant trapped in the narrow tunnel of the state, or where the ship of state which they are aboard is about to sink; and that clear and present danger offers no other way out but for each group to save itself alone, according to the logic that 'might makes right'. Furthermore, the Neo-liberalism that is at the very core of globalization and its logic vigorously promotes individualism at the expense of collectivism and group interests and encourages individual initiatives, according to the exhortations of Adam Smith: 'let them act' or 'let them get on with it' (where *laissez-faire* literally connotes 'leaving one to do' or 'allowing one to act').[11] The concepts of non-interference of governments in the economy and restriction of the role of the state merely to protecting the interests of elite minorities – even though these are only frameworks and theories – led to the major global financial collapse of September 2008 (ʿAbd al-Safīʿ 2008, p. 38), immediately following on the bankruptcy of Lehman Brothers, which represented the first domino in a long chain of economic collapses around the world. However, despite this, capitalists did not reconsider their policies, but rather undertook measures to adapt and restructure the economic institutions in their countries, as advocated by The World Bank, the International Monetary Fund (IMF) and the World Trade Organization (WTO). These adaptive and compensatory measures did not aim to rectify the situation or quell the economic revolution aroused against greed and savage capitalisms, but rather to reproduce that very same corruption. Moreover, monopolization of wealth accumulation by other means, in accordance with mechanisms of globalization, requires a world where the public sector is ever more supplanted by the ever-more-powerful transnational corporations of the 'private sector'. As John Kenneth Galbraith has noted, this entails media advertising, in its various forms, which endeavours to promote a certain kind of merchandise and to whitewash reputations; security, which provides information (i.e. intelligence agencies); the necessary power to quash opposition; and research into public attitudes and how to control and guide public awareness (Karam 2005). These phenomena appeared in Egypt and the Arab world in general over a decade in which a group of businessmen prevailed by way of excesses, stealing and embezzling the countries' resources through the promulgation of laws, and official decrees, while monopolizing vital industries in the largest of fraudulent operations, that appeared – on the surface – to be innocent. All of this occurred within earshot and plain view of the people, a fact which mobilized the masses and galvanized their hatred and outrage towards the corrupt men and associates of the *ancient* regime, until on 25 January 2011 the whole society revolted against the savage capitalism that seemed to know no limits or end.

The hierarchy of the chaos and revolutionary nature of the outburst

To take the example of Egypt, the period of revolutionary gestation that represents the genuine historic roots of the revolutionary outburst of 25 January 2011 extends back an entire decade before this date when Egyptians were persuaded that the rule of President Hosni Mubarak had gone on for too long. This was because the regime seemed on the verge of adopting a dynastic approach, in the grooming of the President's son Gamal to inherit rule over the largest Arab 'feudal' state and all that this entailed in terms of sabre rattling among the elite, who were prepared to utilize excessive force, if necessary, to carry out such a scenario for the succession. None of this prevented people from descending onto the streets and formulating an alternative that would wash away the stagnant and filthy waters (Hafez 2011, p. 68). During this period Egyptian protests came in waves of increasing magnitude along the following three political, social and electronic axes:

- Political demonstrations: the banner of liberalism was carried by a number of actors and liberal parties. Notable among these were: the Kifayah (Enough) movement; the newspaper *al-Badīl* (*The Alternative*) of thinker Muḥammad al-Sayyid Saʿīd; the newspaper *al-Masry al-Youm* (*The Egyptian Today*); the perseverance of ʿAbd al-Ḥalīm Qandīl, Chief Editor of *al-ʿArabī*, who unleashed sharp words against the regime on numerous occasions in writings like dirges for the dead or the moribund, and who was therefore kidnapped, beaten and left naked by the side of the Suez Desert road one night in a despicable and reckless act by the regime that stirred the compassion of Egyptians and their ire over official brutality; and the newspaper *al-Dustūr* (*The Constitution*) which served as the platform for the provocations of journalist Ibrahim ʿĪsa who was audacious enough to take on the office of the presidency in his famous article 'Al-Ālihāt Lā Tamraḍ' ('The Gods don't get sick'), mocking the official protest of the state and its objection to his questioning the health of Mubarak.[12] The climax of the political conflict came when Muhammad al-Bareidi, former President of the International Atomic Energy Agency (IAEA), returned to Egypt and joined the National Association for Change. This marked the first time that a figure of this stature came out against the regime, and his demands for immediate change threatened its will to survive, given that al-Bareidi's insistence propelled the Egyptian case onto the international scene. The entire world was waiting and watching to see what he would do and what he was thinking, where some considered him to be a political inspiration for the revolution in addition to other human rights activities. This was over and above the strident efforts of the Muslim Brotherhood, who are tantamount to political masochists by demeanour – vacillating between conciliation, egoism and arrogance, and who, having feared that the regime would destroy them, set up their tents in Tahrir Square and embraced the wave of change (Caldwell 2011, Ḥasan 2011).
- Social protests. Mobilization of the hitherto unchanging and stagnant Egyptian milieu encouraged factions and groups to express their concerns over the process of privatization (the academic term for 'corruption') and the selling off of the public sector that brought about the layoff and unemployment of thousands of workers. The state seemed powerless and incapable when popular anger at this reckless and arbitrary injustice, which afflicted wide sectors of society, led protests to escalate from strikes and sit-ins to demonstrations, and then subsequently to mass mobilizations and nationwide strikes that spread from textile and cloth factories in the city of Mahallah to include all manner of employees, technicians, university professors and judges. This later phase was met with security measures that aggravated the unrest and galvanized the determination of protestors and the opposition, especially when police went after members of the judiciary and threatened them with verbal abuse and physical violence.

- Electronic contestation. Globalization has introduced a particular mode and culture of social communication and interaction, epitomized in such phenomena as the Internet, Facebook and Twitter and the pivotal role these have played in the mobilization, organization and formulation of the revolutionary discourse about the causes, justifications, methods and goals to be disseminated. Given that clientalism plays an essential role in the science of politics, it was natural for youth groups, given their familiarity and facility with the relevant technology, to constitute the most sizeable element participating in the processes of electronic contention and resistance through the Kullunā Khālid Saʿīd (We Are All Khaled Said) group, the Ḥarakah Shabāb 6 Abrīl (April 6 Youth Movement); the Shabāb Ḥizb al-Jabhah al-Dīmuqrāṭīyah (Youth Democratic Front Party); and the Shabāb al-Waṭanīyah li-l-Taghyīr (National Youth for Change), joined by other political groups or 'the revolution's newcomers' from various classes and factions. Thus, there is no doubt about the massive and deep impact of the forceful Egyptian revolutionary influence in fomenting chaos in the political arena of the Arab region. This has become evident at two broad levels:
- At the official level of the ruling authorities and its bureaucratic apparatus differences are most prominent and fierce between three camps. The first adopts immediate, decisive structural change with the aim of avoiding risks and preempting a popular outburst. The second supports measures constrained to mere formal reforms, along with some grants and concessions. The third trend is represented by those still living in the past, who hold the view that because there are differences in particularities from one Arab country to another, what is occurring in Egypt cannot be generalized or extended to other regions, and thus that there is no need in the first instance to change anything.
- At the popular level there has been a gravitation towards three distinct currents of chaos. The first pertains to some of the elites who obtained material and moral benefits under the aegis of despotism, who do not perceive the necessity for change that threatens the stability of the status quo, and who vigorously defend the continuation of autocracy. The second is a parallel current represented by the middle classes, who defend the legitimacy of their demands for freedom, justice and human rights as well as the inevitability of changing the essence of the regimes and their various systems in an era wherein the masses are protesting for their dignity. The third trend is at the base of the socio-economic pyramid, constituting the largest strata of society, which represents people who were systematically impoverished. They see corruption as a sort of primordial beast that consumes everything in its path and knows no limits. They are in fact the cannon fodder in the battle and the raw fuel of the revolution – they surge forward unprotected in defence of their right to live. Thus, it may be said unreservedly that this is an act of creative destruction.

Third: the communication revolution and the chaos of creative destruction

Herein lies the vice of a revolution that is unconcerned with construction and portends what is termed 'the revolution of increasing expectations' or 'political opportunism' – when separate interest groups take to the street, in the form of protests and strikes, for the purpose of achieving social and group demands. They consider that their creative destruction is justified by their desires to enhance their particular circumstances. They do not merely demand material goods, but demand the amendment of laws, administrative restructuring and the exile of corrupt figures. Electronic control and management was highly influential and present *en force* in directing and "riding herd" over the social mobilization process in order to marshal forces, unify ranks and efforts, and define the goals. The stage of mobilization in the period of revolutionary gestation was about arranging the cumulative development – the more the authorities resorted to draconian measures, the more the catalysts and causal factors for the outbreak of the revolution accumulated, along the following lines:

- Electronic chaos and cyber-mobilization. The period of revolutionary gestation was in fact tantamount to a gradual build up towards a declaration of war against the particular form of chaos and meddling imposed by the forces of tyranny within. This poses an essential question: how is it possible to create a revolution in a society that is knuckled under by despotism and strict security surveillance? Offering an answer to this question demands knowledge of the dynamics of revolution from the standpoint of very precise electronic technical capabilities.[13] Facebook, as is well known, served to bring about the horizontal networking of millions of people. Likewise, it was within the capability of any individual to set up a webpage and personal profile and then select others to join as 'friends' whereupon messages and information can be exchanged by 'posting' statements, announcements and details of events on the so-called 'wall' or 'message board' on the webpage. All these steps have their functions that range from mobilization, through 'joining' and participation, to organization and the marshalling of logistical support, directing field operatives and, finally, making decisions and determining orientations and plans. In other words, all these factor on a scale of responsiveness to challenges and threats, and all these operate in accordance with the complex electronic order in which the hallmarks of the revolutionary act are defined according to stages that can be understood to correspond to parts of a body where the initial phases are the most intense and in closest proximity to the 'heart' and subsequent phases are nearer the 'extremities':
- The 'beating heart of the revolution' is responsible for the vast majority of operations directed towards generating participation in the phase of electronic invitations to protests and demonstrations, then mobilization and subsequent commitments. Here two primary groups come into prominence: the group We Are All Khaled Said with a social communication rate of participation of 7.6% and with a comment rate of 79.4%; and the April 6 Youth Movement with a participation rate of 10.6% and a comment rate of 5.8%.
- The 'body' of the revolution comprises all the political, social and demographic groups that shouldered other burdens when the revolution began to intensify, when the 'heart' of the revolution became embroiled in managing the skirmishes and battles in the field, far removed from network communications.
- The 'extremities' of the body of the revolution comprise technical, professional and technology groups that constituted the outer periphery of the sphere of action of the revolutionaries and which absorbed pressures on the 'heart' of the revolution and frustrated the efforts of counter-forces allied to the government. The youth were the 'heart' of the revolution and society at large constituted the body.

Tracing the trajectory and dynamics of the revolution, it becomes possible to track how the handling of information proceeded across successive waves and stages along the following lines (Table 1):

Table 1. Dynamic waves of the revolution (25 January–25 April 2011)

The Revolution	The first wave	The second wave	The third wave
The body	Non-violent outrage confronts police brutality (25–28 January)	Documentation and reminiscence (i.e., collective memory) confronts the brutality of the ruling party (28 January–3 February)	The counter-revolution sparks a wave of purges (25 February–7 April)
The beating heart	Planning to counter ridicule (10–25 January)	Focusing on the goal, fighting the brutality of negotiation (28 January–4 February)	Making a complete break with the deposed regime (10–25 February)
The extremities	The justice of the cause confronts the tyranny of government-run media (21 January–3 February)	Defiance paves the way for the fall of Mubarak (4–10 February)	The trial: the army against the imprisoned president (25 April)

- Planning to counter ridicule. This phase extended from 10 to 25 January 2011, when Facebook performed the seminal role of inculcating the concept of revolution, positing its slogans and the approaches to execute it and preparing to unleash the revolutionary fervour – that was constrained at this stage to peaceful demonstrations and protests, as well as the synchronization and facilitation of these.
- Developing non-violent outrage. The phase devoted to generating non-violent outrage in the face of the brutality of the security services extended from 25 to 28 January, during which time violent intervention by the police galvanized the determination of protestors to maintain their position. A spirit of courage and sacrifice was imparted under the slogan coined by the youth: 'Jumʿat al-Ghaḍab' (The Friday of Rage) and Tahrir Square was specified as the rallying point. Protestors faced off against the corrupt and brutal state, which had bared its teeth and roared through a tactic of 'non-violent outrage'.
- Focusing on the goal and combating the brutality of negotiations. From the evening of Friday, 28 January onwards, the moribund regime introduced into the field a new counter-revolutionary tactic, which could be termed the stratagem of 'brutality through political negotiation'. It tasked the newly appointed Vice President Omar Sulayman and acting Prime Minister Ahmad Shafiq with circumlocution and stalling until 9 February. Their strategy constituted a cause for the obstinacy of the masses and the social revolutionary energies were refocused on the goal to plan what was subsequently called 'Jumʿat al-Raḥīl' (The Friday of Departure) that was actually carried out on 4 February.[14]
- Defiance paved the way to the overthrow of the regime. A mood of despair was only partly dissipated by a shift within some of the elites that had been sitting on the fence, siding neither with the protestors nor with the regime, but then came the tidal wave that confounded all expectations. This was the campaign to herald victory and push forward, and the idea of the 'Jumʿat al-Taḥaddī' (Friday of Defiance) and 'Al-Zaḥf ʿalā al-Qaṣr' (Marching on the Palace),

specifically on 10–11 February, was the *coup de grace* for the collapsing, moribund regime, which fell at that moment.

- Making a complete break with the deposed regime. Acting Prime Minister Ahmad Shafiq sought to stall and buy time in order to reduce the severity of the impact of the fall of Mubarak. Shafiq was confronted by two ethical imperatives: (1) he was obligated to stand by the former president, to protect him, and safeguard him and members of his family from humiliation; and (2) his desire to affirm that he was not a part of the regime, but that he wanted to rebuild with genuine integrity and patriotism. His dilemma failed to head off demands for his departure until he stepped down; and with this Egypt affirmed the complete break of the revolution with the *ancient* regime.
- Counter-revolution intensifies the wave of purges. In the lull in the fighting that followed Mubarak's fall, the remnants of the deposed regime gathered together to mount a counter-revolution to pre-empt their being taken to account. As they set about systematic destruction of the new social project, the masses returned to Tahrir Square on 'Jumʿat al-Ṭaṭhīr' (Friday of Purification), 7 April 2011. As a result, the former symbols of the *ancient* regime, one after the other, were sent to prison without any resistance worthy of mention. They lost all their outward aspects of pride and arrogance so that people began to ask in amazement: 'How was it that these people ruled us in all this humiliation for thirty years?' (Howeidy 2011, p. 16).
- 'The Trials' or the military versus the president. The deposed Egyptian president failed to learn his lesson even as he witnessed members of his entourage going to prison in shackles, and he insisted on condemning himself right up to the very end with his disgraceful last-minute address in which he alleged that neither did he or his sons have any monies outside the country nor that he had profited from his office. This was a manifest affront to the army, which wondered how a person under investigation could so grossly transgress all legal norms, over and above the shock to the masses, who saw that his rule for more than one-quarter of a century was predicated on lies and distortions. Thus, Mubarak lost his moral and official status, and his image was completely ruined for all Egyptians. It was a bitter end for him, his sons and the dramatic saga of a man who proved proficient only in the art of drowning.

Scenes of chaos and scenarios of construction

In the aftermath of the authentic revolution, the real impact began to be felt where it is difficult to distinguish between Cain and Abel, due to the advent of a flood of freedoms after years of coercion and suppression. In this tumultuous atmosphere it is possible to identify a number of approaches that may be something akin to feedback on the future and which may be summarized as follows:

- The impact of the image. The Egyptian revolution of 25 January was a revolution of the globalization of information *par excellence*, and it is a modern phenomenon that belongs to the 'virtual' world. This is not only because of the dawning of the electronic era, but also because of the ability of ordinary people to benefit from what they learned thanks to real-time broadcasting, as they did from the coverage of the US invasion of Iraq in 2003 and the descent of that country into a vortex of endless violence and counter-violence.[15] What happened in Iraq impressed upon the minds of Arabs that change instigated and supported from without might not at all be in their interests, and moreover such might carry huge costs. It imparted the idea that free peoples should not wait for a repeat of the Iraqi model, which over and above being a humiliation reverted the country back to the age of abominable colonial occupation. People, it could readily be inferred, should depend upon themselves if they desire genuine changes, as demonstrated by the Tunisian uprising that compelled the corrupt president to flee. This was what inspired Egyptians to enquire among themselves why they did not do the same? The Egyptians, along with the rest of the Arab world, were getting live broadcasts and glad tidings of the ouster of former President Zein al-'Abidin bin 'Ali through various electronic and satellite media and ultimately Facebook. Then when the spark of revolution was finally ignited the Qatari satellite television station Al-Jazeera stood firmly in the way of all attempts by the official Egyptian media to propagate an inaccurate picture of the number of demonstrators and their composition. The official Egyptian media and press misrepresented the revolution as though it were the product of external machinations, alternately accusing Iran, Hamas, Lebanon's Hizb Allah, and the United States and Israel of involvement, despite all the manifest conflicts of interest between these groups. Al-Jazeera alone, with the exception of a few privately run newspapers such as the Egyptian *al-Shuruq* and the London-based *al-Hayat*, took the side of the revolutionaries, and the Egyptian masses took to saying: 'Had it not been for the cameras of Al-Jazeera, Tahrir Square would have been obliterated along with everyone in it.' The Egyptian revolution is globalized in aspect and import, as all of Egypt was placed under the microscope at the international level wherefore it was problematic for the despotic clique to escape this time. The revolution similarly benefited in two key respects from the globalization of the image and the events at the scene. First, the brutal practices of the security forces and the sight of martyrs falling one after the other attracted a huge number of new recruits to the revolution, so that the demonstrations spread to different regions of Egypt. Secondly, the formation of international public opinion served to generate positive pressure, through supportive stances from people outside the country, backing and encouraging the revolutionaries within to finish what they had begun. This was over and above American and European government pressure that was initially remote and indirect, before coming to bear decisively in the final stages, and serving to compel the Egyptian president to relinquish power. Additionally, the shift in the US stance derived from a desire to avoid appearing to oppose the liberation, democratization and human rights movements or to give the impression that it supported dictatorships right up to the end – although the peoples of the region had long since noticed this tendency and had encountered it more than once along the road.[16]

- The counter-revolution. The phase of the revolution that brought down the regime had hardly subsided when a new storm termed the 'counter-revolution' suddenly blew in. It was comprised of an 'alliance of the vanquished'; and all of them had been influential forces under the old regime. They were termed the 'satanic triangle', which was made up of three types of forces:
  - The forces of hard power: these are comprised of the remnants of the detested and draconian security apparatus who were accustomed to using brutality and prospering through illegal means. They are unable to adapt to or coexist with

the new conditions. These forces act according to what they understand they can execute with extreme professionalism, being run by the 'state security' apparatus. They are not beyond drawing up political assassination lists targeting members of various religious sects in order to spread civil strife and chaos and thence undermine and derail the original revolution.

- Material forces: these constitute a group of businessmen charged with corruption in the wake of Mubarak's fall, who are ready to make exhaustive efforts to preserve their financial empires. They are engaged in funding all operations of brutality and systematic destruction as well as keeping the mother revolution from spreading to the infrastructure.
- The forces of soft power: these are the politicians and thinkers of the deposed government and its elite who are intent upon aborting the revolution, after fatiguing and incapacitating it by way of striking against the active bloc, also composed of politicians and thinkers, within the mother revolution. They cast doubt on the trustworthiness of their opponents through ridicule, scorn and satire, as well as engaging in 'character assassinations' by means of libellous and underhanded distortions, so as to debase their standing in the minds of the passive bloc among the masses of the people and supporters of the revolution, and get them in the end to abandon the prominent proponents of the revolution. These are among the most chaotic and cataclysmic forms of creative destruction, yet even so the core and vital bloc of the mother revolution stood firm against these threats, which proved unable to deter it from its goals (Salmān 2011a, p. 10).

Fourth: globalization and future repercussions on the geopolitical landscape

The analysis of scenarios for the future of the Arab world must necessarily take into account globalization and its repercussions on the geo-strategic landscape, before reaching an assessment of the potential for success or failure of the creative destruction that has swept the Middle East like a tsunami. This is not to mention what politics, i.e. the making of human beings, can precipitate in the way of calamities. For example, one may consider the sight of the Peninsula Shield Force moving from Saudi Arabia into Bahrain, and the passage through the Suez Canal of two Iranian ships headed towards Syria – something that has not happened in 30 years. Similarly, there is the return of Allied forces to the countries of the Middle East to impose no-fly zones, as in Operation Odyssey Dawn over Libya, along with Turkey rushing to fill the regional vacuum resulting from the absence of forces able to operate effectively in the field – due to their turning inwards and absorption in internal reconstruction and building. The official Arab order has been brought down under the violent blows of the Arab peoples and the collapse of the Middle East according to the traditional decades-old 'American' formula. All this has brought into being a new 'hybridized' Middle East that combines the sediments and accumulations of the past with the hopes and aspirations of the future. It is difficult to probe the contours of this new entity, one which has yet actually to be fully born. How this globalized scene and how politics are seen and heard for the first time live on air, in conjunction with the ambiguities of the present geo-strategic changes, can only be surmised. And two intertwined and nebulous vignettes will serve: first, the complexities of the situation in the Arab Gulf region; and second, the 'tyrannical despotism that attracts invaders' and leads them to undertake their doings in the Arab region in general.

- The Saudi–Iranian strategic skirmishing in Bahrain give rise to some potential scenarios along the lines of the following. The political upheavals that have beset Arabs from the Atlantic to the Gulf and surrounded Saudi Arabia in particular have affected the balance of forces and the geo-political map of the Middle East in a major way. The changes have created opportunities for Iran, of which it is attempting to take advantage, in order to increase its influence in the Gulf and in the Levant in particular. The strategic balance in the Gulf was historically predicated on a tripartite regional order of three powers: Saudi Arabia, Iraq and Iran (al-ʿAfīfī 2004, p. 66). This had persisted ever since the British withdrawal at the beginning of the 1970s, and even proved durable during the Iran–Iraq War (1980–1988), where neither protagonist was able to overcome the other. The dynamic changed, however, with the fall of the Ba'athist state in 2003, which transformed the Gulf power structure into a bipolar world between Iran and Saudi Arabia, where the latter was obliged to bear increased strategic burdens because of the fall of Iraq. At the same time, Iran oriented by stages to extend its influence to Iraq, Syria and Lebanon, using sectarian tensions and Shi'ite groups to exploit adverse circumstances and using American influence as a pretext in both Iraq and Lebanon (al-ʿAmrī 2011, p. 11). The only fact that can be confirmed as a result of this analysis is that the chaos of creative destruction leads to more creative destruction so that the manoeuvring and game-playing can continue along with the march of history.
- Tyrannical despotism attracts invaders. The problem now is no longer restricted to internal regional skirmishing, but also encompasses the counter-revolution of American making. From the Iraq of Saddam Hussein to the Libya of Mu'ammar al-Qadhafi, to the Yemen of 'Ali 'Abdullah Saleh to the Bahrain of the Al Khalifah family, the same catastrophes are being repeated. The local despots have prompted the call for American and foreign intervention, including Israeli, thereby turning their countries, formerly ruled by oppression, over to the foreigners. The people are losing their nations before their very eyes, the state is collapsing and the regional state system is reverting to what it was at its inception, where there is a scramble for power and resources among tribes, clans, factions, sects and fighting elements under the protection of colonialism that has regained its 'prestige' and returned in this particular moment as 'saviour' and 'protector'. Some of the Arab scruples and reservations that rejected intervention in Iraq in 2003 no longer existed in the case of Libya in 2011. NATO aircraft and the offshore fleet destroyed Libyan air and military bases with impunity, pummelling Libyan positions and armour with rockets and withering force; and the Western powers undertook this as though it were a matter of little concern, having convinced themselves that all of it was simply an operation to discipline a dictator who had mocked them repeatedly and degraded their achievements, and who had conspired against some of them – including kings and heads of state. This is not to mention the participation by the armed forces of the UAE and Qatar – with considerable Saudi moral support – in the rabid attack under the spurious presumption that they were helping the Libyan people in their moment of despair to build a democracy of the hollow and gilded sort they extol in their emirates (Salmān 2011b, p. 10)!

Before the Criminal Court in Cairo on 6 March 2011, the prosecution was represented by Muhammad al-Najjar, Deputy Head of Public Finance, who was unsurpassed in his quips that went straight to the heart of Egyptians and spoke to their conscience. Al-Najjar proved adept at getting to the essence of matters in the trial of the century, which gave a new name to corruption, saying:

> Egypt has been ruled by a group of kings, satans, traitors of the age and thieves as though history is repeating itself. This era produced the like of the 'drummer – *al-ṭabbāl*' of the Egyptian political order (Aḥmad 'Izz); and the Minister of Manpower and Migration ('Ā'isha 'Abd al-Hādī), and the unqualified Minister of Transportation (Muḥammad Ibrāhim Manṣūr) with a diploma in embroidery and the uneducated Housing Minister (Aḥmad Maghrabī); and O Egypt! Allah is the only one who can help you; 'Unto Allah belongs the past and the future' (Q 30:4).[17]

Conclusion

The violent political action that struck with force at the substructure of authoritarian power in the Arab world cannot be attributed to any single factor or constrained to just one political group to the exclusion of others. Neither can it be correlated to an exceptional period of history. Rather, it is the product of numerous factors, groups and developments, and in particular multiple foreign pressures that can be summarized as the strategy of creative destruction that contributed decisively to the destruction of the outer shell and pulled back the curtain on Arab autocratic regimes, so that the peoples might behold the inner sanctums of authoritarianism. The matter demanded penetration from every direction and the combination of all currents over a relatively protracted period of time, all of which was accompanied by an array of vital and necessary logistical support services, without which the resistance and revolutionary forces would never have been able to coordinate effectively over the various stages. This transpired at the same time that external and internal action fell under the rubric of globalization and its concomitant generative agency in transitioning peoples from a state of inaction to one of dynamic and effective action. The conclusions of this article can be summarized as follows (see also Table 2):

- The Arab peoples elected to depend on the mechanism of change from within after witnessing the huge costs of foreign intervention (as in Iraq) that relied on destruction of the moral, religious and nationalist values; the expropriation of vital resources; and exerting influence over these exposed and exploited countries under the pretext of bringing change.
- Responding to the forces of creative destruction does not mean subscribing to a conspiracy theory, as much as it is a reproduction of it, for the sake of doing away with external threats, even as it has served to turn the attentions of people to the internal chaos that regimes engineered in the name of the myth of stability.
- Electronic warfare and resistance, as well as mobilization through the Internet, were among the most significant gains of the people from globalization as nationwide groups came to know how it was possible to join the age, partake of its givens and interact with its new technologies, positively and effectively, after years of having utilized technologies only for the purpose of computer/video games, amusement and entertainment.
- Planning is a vital and essential component for the success of all movements of liberation, on the condition that it appropriates cumulative development, since change is a complicated and composite process that demands exhaustive efforts.
- The image as transmitted across the web or through televisions factors extremely effectively in engendering a rationale and cognisance for change as well as guiding,

Table 2. Combined dynamic model of the work mechanisms of creative destruction

Creative destruction	The American mode (2003–2011)	The authoritarian mode (2003–2011)	The popular mode (2005–2011)
Essence of creative destruction	Destruction of state infrastructure; access points for intervention in regional wars; altering geo-political topographies	Absolute power, absolute corruption; accumulated provocation of the revolution; abject disregard for constitutions and the law	Legitimate destruction by the right and construction by the right; political and factional opportunism; exhausting the mother revolution and causing its failure
Projects of creative destruction	Occupation, dismantling and division of Iraq in 2003; economic annexation of Iraq via privatization; axes of autocratic regimes	Falsification of the election processes and results; oppressive security control; distortion of political life	Resisting the tyranny of despots and invaders; ending the oppression and subjugation of society; state mobilizing the public to revolt
Justifications for creative destruction	Reproducing hegemony; systematic theft of oil; guaranteeing the security and stability of Israel	Myth of growth and stability; protecting national security; combating 'terrorism' and extremism	Bringing down the dictatorial state; transition to a free democracy; shaping the future
Hierarchy of creative destruction	Surveillance of public liberties and minorities; democratic shake downs; violent polarization initiatives	Expedient oppressive power; eliminating political parties; ascendency of programmes to effect dynastic succession or inheritance of rule	Organic intellectual elites; neo-liberal youth vanguard; various sectors of the people
Electronic cyber-creative destruction	Exporting electronic chaos; Freedom House website; motives for electronic communication and social networking	Electronic assassination of sites; electronic predation of the revolution and its sites; broadcasting and disseminating counter disinformation	Electronic resistance sites; mobilization through networks; combating electronic counter measures
Manifestations of creative destruction	Occupation of Manhattan (Wall Street) 2011; joining the Arab revolutions; geo-strategic skirmish	Symbols of the period of revolutionary gestation; despotism attracts invaders; desertion of the police and the opening of prisons	Centricity of mass gatherings in the field; thugs on camels and horses; aftermath of the fall of tyranny (the trials)

orienting and encouraging it. Those individuals, groups and nations who entered into the revolution after the initial phase were influenced by the scenes they witnessed transmitted from one place to another, which spread like wildfire and co-opted the global conscience in support of those hastening towards liberation.

Notes

1. The strategic application of Josef Schumpeter's concept of 'creative destruction', attributed to former Secretary of State Condoleezza Rice since 2005, is but another encounter with other provocative terminology of human history such as 'the cycle of civilization' originally attributed to Ibn Khaldun and subsequently to Georg W. F. Hegel, or the 'new world on the ruins of the old' as according to Friedrich Nietzsche or in the words of the Arab poet Muẓaffar al-Nawāb: 'Oh God, begin the destruction now, for destruction by right ... is construction by right.' It also pertains to the British colonial dogma of 'divide and conquer', where 'divide' implies 'chaos' and 'conquer' implies colonial construction. However, America undertook to divest these slogans of their content and to repack them with political plans and policies, just as 'creative chaos' is the logical extension of the concept of the 'sick man [of Europe]' applied to the waning Ottoman state to suggest its disintegration. In this context, the Soviet Jew who immigrated to Israel and worked in the United States government, adopted in his book *The case for democracy: the power of freedom to overcome tyranny and terror* (Sharansky 2004) the principle of destroying the Arab nation – a concept that only a religious and racial minority would adopt. Former President George W. Bush adopted this book as the essence of American Middle East policy (Rafīq 2008, p. 74).
2. The American war did not result in any sort of democracy. On the contrary, it hampered civil liberties and inflicted a state of futile and catastrophic chaos.
3. On the role of Israel in the 'creative destruction' strategy, see Fleshler (2009), pp. 162–164.
4. On the change in the strategy of 'creative destruction' after the failure of the Iraqi model, see Pollack *et al.* (2011), pp. 17–21.
5. Ledeen is a prominent and outspoken Neo-conservative advisor to former President George W. Bush and Vice President Dick Cheney affiliated to the American Enterprise Institute (AEI) and the Project for a New American Century (PNAC).
6. This political theory applies in the frame of the limited US military alternatives of crises administration.
7. On the subject of retaliation and vengeance in international relations there are rules, regulations and many narrations (to be told). For more details on this subject, see Sami/al-Biḥīrī (2011).
8. Many specialists relate between the fall of the regime of Mubarak in Egypt and the end of the US era in the Middle East.
9. The Egyptian Fact-Finding Commission published its final report on 'The 25 January Revolution' and its ambiguities, which asserted the Egyptian people had, in all their various strata and factions, revolted against tyranny and political corruption and in protest over the absence of social justice and repression of freedoms, the wide spread of graft and favouritism and the control of money over governance as well as the disinformation of the media. For more details, see Anon. (2011c).
10. The problem of alliances and authoritarianism with the West, and the United States in particular, has evinced widespread debate and elicited palpable contradictions. The United States conferred upon itself the right to intervene in Libya at the head of NATO forces, following on from United Nations Security Council Resolution 1973 (issued on 18 March 2011), while at the same time the United States criticized the deployment of the Peninsula Shield Force in Bahrain. Yet, the forces deployed in Bahrain at the behest of Saudi Arabia and the UAE were the same as those that participated in the 'international alliance' of forces on the side of the Libyan opposition in order to bring down the regime of the Jamahiriya. The chain of repeated mistakes has put the interests of the United States in the Arab region on the edge of a volcano. For more on this, see Freeman (2010) and Pollack *et al.* (2011).
11. Editors' note: For more on this, see http://dictionary.reference.com/browse/laissez+faire [Accessed 17 February 2012].
12. For works and literatures on non-violent resistance, see Sharp (1973/1984–2005).
13. The electronification of chaos is 'chaordic chaos'; 'chaordic organization' was coined by Dee Hock, founder and former CEO Emeritus of VISA USA and VISA International. It most often refers to the order that integrates between chaos and the system on the basis of coexistence, as a harmonized coexistence, which sees the manifestation of both without the hegemony of either one over the order. For more on this, see Zahlan (2011).

14. For more on this important informational analysis, see Ghīṭās and al-Ghamrī (2011).
15. On the bitter Iraqi experience, see al-ʿAfīfī (2005; also Cordesman and Mausner 2007).
16. On the abandonment by the US administration of support for Arab democracies, and recourse to the support of allied and 'moderate' countries before the revolution in the case of Egypt, see Ottaway *et al.* (2008), pp. 16–23.
17. 'The drummer' (*al-ṭabbāl*) is Aḥmad ʿIzz, the dismissed Organizational Affairs Secretary in the National Democratic Party (NDP); ʿĀ'isha ʿAbd al-Hādī is Minister of Manpower and Migration, who only holds a primary school certificate; Minister of Transportation is Muḥammad Ibrāhim Manṣūr; and (former) Housing Minister is Aḥmad Maghrabī, in addition to Anas al-Faqīh, former Information Minister of Media, who had worked when younger as a dancer in a band called 'Riḍā' (Satisfaction) (Abū Shanab 2007, p. 5)

References

ʿAbd al-Rāziq, Fāris al-Fāris, 2004. al-ʿAwlamah wa Dawlah al-Riʿāyah fī Aqṭār Majlis al-Taʿāwun. *Al-Mustaqbal al-ʿArabī*, year 26 (no. 302, April).

ʿAbd al-Safīʿ, ʿIsā, 2008. Al-Khalīj wa al-Iqtiṣād al-Siyāsī li-l-Istithmār al-Ajnabī. *Al-Siyāsah al-Dawlīyah*, year 44 (no. 171, January).

Abū Shanab, Fāṭimah, 2007. ʿAhd al-Mamālīk wa al-Shayāṭīn, al-Muḥākamah. *Al-Masry al-Yawm*, 7 March. Available from: http://www.almasryalyoum.com/node/389630 [Accessed 15 February 2012].

al-ʿAfīfī, Fatḥī, 2004. *Al-Tawāzun al-Istrātījī fī al-Khalīj al-ʿArabī Khilāl ʿAqd al-Tisʿīnīyāt.* Emirati Lectures Series. Abu Dhabi: Emirates Center for Strategic Studies and Research (ECSSR).

al-ʿAfīfī, Fatḥī, 2005. *Amrīkā fī al-Khalīj: Suqūṭ al-Iqlīmīyah wa al-Mustaqbalāt al-Baldīlah.* Cairo: Markaz al-Ahrām li-l-Tarjamah wa al-Nashr.

ʿAlam al-Dīn, Bāriʿah, 2011. al-Baḥrain wa al-Ḥiwār: al-Yaman wa Lībyā wa Irān ʿalā Khaṭ al-Infijār. *al-Ḥayāt newspaper*, 22 February.

al-ʿAmrī, Ṭrād bin Saʿīd, 2011. Al-Baḥrain ʿUqdah al-Khalīj al-ʿArabī. *al-Ḥayāt newspaper*, 19 March.

ʿAlī Ḥasan, ʿAmmār, 2011. al-Ikhwān al-Muslimūn wa Ghazwah ʾUḥud. *Al-Masry al-Yawm*, 5 April, 17. Available from: http://www.almasryalyoum.com/node/405447 [Accessed 15 February 2012].

Anon, 2011a. Mashrūʿ Marishāl al-Khalīīj li-Daʿm al-Baḥrain wa ʿUmān. *Al-Masry al-Youm*, 4 March, 6. Available from: http://www.almasryalyoum.com/node/338337 [Accessed 15 February 2012].

Anon, 2011b. al-Waḍʿ al-Kārithī fī al-Baḥrain, Ikhlāʾ Dawwār al-Luʾluʾah bi-l-Quwwah. *Al-Shurūq newspaper*, 17 March, 9.

Anon, 2011c. al-Taqrīr al-Nihāʾī li-Lajnat Taqaṣṣī al-Ḥaqāʾiq bi-Shaʾn Aḥdāth Thawrah 25 Yanāyir 2011. *Al-Ahrām newspaper*, 20 April, 4. Available from: http://www.ahram.org.eg/Al%20Mashhad%20Al%20Syiassy/News/73695.aspx [Accessed 15 February 2012].

Bajoria, J. and Jerome, D., 2011. *Egypt's post-Mubarak path.* Washington, DC: Council on Foreign Relations, 11 February. Available from: http://www.cfr.org/egypt/egypts-post-mubarak-path/p24085 [Accessed 15 February 2012].

Caldwell, C., 2011. Egypt shakes a distant dictator from his dream. *Financial Times*, 11 February. Available from: http://www.ft.com/intl/cms/s/0/31aa808c-361d-11e0-9b3b-00144feabdc0.html [Accessed 15 February 2012].

Cordesman, A.H., 1993. *Trends in the military balance and arms sales in the Southern Gulf States after the Gulf War, 1990–1993.* Washington, DC: Center for Strategic and International Studies (CSIS).

Cordesman, A. and Mausner, A., 2007. *Iraqi force development: conditions for success, consequences of failure.* Washington, DC: CSIS Press. Available from: http://csis.org/files/media/csis/pubs/070910_cordesmanexsum.pdf [Accessed 16 February 2012].

Fleshler, D., 2009. *Transforming America's Israel lobby: the limits of its power and the potential for change.* Washington, DC: Potomac.

Freeman, Jr, C.W., 2010. *America's misadventures in the Middle East.* Foreword by W.B. Quandt. Charlottesville, VA: Just World.

Ghīṭās, Jamāl Muḥammad and al-Ghamrī, Khālid, 2011. Al-Facebook Qalb al-Thawrah al-Nābiḍ: Suqūṭ Dawlat al-Balṭajah wa al-Marāḥil Mukhtalifah li-l-Thawrah. *Majallah Lughah al-ʿAṣr*, March.

Hafez, Ziad, 2011. Thawrah Yanāyir fī Miṣr: al-Ḥāḍir wa al-Mustaqbal. *Al-Mustaqbal al-ʿArabī*, year 33 (no. 385, March), 68.

al-Ḥāj Ṣāliḥ, Yāsīn, 2005. al-Siyāsah al-Amrīkīyah fī al-Sharq al-ʾAwsaṭ min al-Istiqrār ilā al-Fawḍā al-Khallāqah. *Ḥiwār al-ʿArab,* year 1 (no. 12). Beirut: Arab Thought Foundation.

Howeidy, Fahmy, 2011. Muwāṭinūn ʿĀdīyūn Jiddan. *Shorouk News*, 4 April, 16. Available from: http://www.shorouknews.com/columns/view.aspx?cdate=20042011&id=380296d2-e4c2-40d3-9ad9-07b6c38a70c4 [Accessed 16 February 2012].

Karam, Samir, 2005. Book Review: 'The Economics of Innocent Fraud: Truth for our Time', by John Kenneth Galbraith. *Al-Mustaqbal al-ʿArabī*, year 27 (no. 314, April), 169.

Khalīl, Aḥmad Khalīl, 2011. *Tawrīth al-Siyāsī fi al-Anẓimah al-Jumhūrīyah al-ʿArabīyah al-Muʿāṣirah*. Beirut: Arab Institute for Research and Publishing (AIRP).

Kier, E. and Krebs, R.R., eds., 2010. *In war's wake: international conflict and the fate of liberal democracy*. New York, NY: Cambridge University Press.

Ottaway, M., Melhem, H., and Diehl, J., 2008. *Democracy promotion in the Middle East: restoring credibility*. Policy Brief No. 60, 12 June. Washington, DC: Carnegie Endowment for International Peace. Available from: http://carnegieendowment.org/files/0612_transcript_restoringcredibility2.pdf [Accessed 16 February 2012].

Pollack, K.M., *et al.*, 2011. *Unfinished business: an American strategy for Iraq moving forward,* with contributions from J. Hiltermann. Washington, DC: Brooking Institution Press. Available from: http://www.brookings.edu/~/media/Files/rc/papers/2010/12_iraq_strategy_pollack/12_iraq_strategy_pollack.pdf [Accessed 21 March 2012].

Rafīq, Abd al-Salām, 2008. Al-Wilayāt al-Muttaḥidah al-Amrīkīyah bayn al-Quwwah al-Ṣalbah wa al-Quwwah al-Nāʿimah. *Awrāq al-Jazīrah*, 6 (Doha, Markaz al-Jazīrah li-l-Dirasāt).

Rivil, Sami, 2011. *Qatar et Israël, dossier des relations secrètes;* trans. into Arabic by Muḥammad al-Biḥīrī. Cairo: Maktabah Jazīrah al-Ward.

Saʿīd, Muḥammadal-Sayīd, 1986. al-Sharikāt ʿĀbirah al-Qawmīyah wa Mustaqbal al-Ẓāhirah al-Qawmīyah. *ʿĀlam al-Maʿārif,* no. 107. Kuwait: National Council for Culture, Arts & Letters (NCCAL).

Salmān, Ṭalāl, 2011a. al-Shuʿūb Taktub Tārīkhuhā ʿan (al-Mīdān) wa al-Thawrah al-Muḍādah. *Shorouk News*, 23 March. Available from: http://shorouknews.com/columns/view.aspx?cdate=23032011&id=fa06783d-b06f-4140-9f13-56cec1f872e8 [Accessed 16 February 2012].

Salmān, Ṭalāl, 2011b. al-Hujūm al-Muḍād ʿalā al-Mīdān: al-Ṭughyān Yantahī Ḥalīfan li-l-Haymanah al-Ajnabīyah. *Shorouk News*, March 30. Available from: http://shorouknews.com/columns/view.aspx?cdate=30032011&id=98a175d8-6785-4996-9961-ff82f13d2c68 [Accessed 16 February 2012].

Sharansky, N. and Dermer, R., 2004. *The case for democracy: the power of freedom to overcome tyranny and terror.* New York: Public Affairs.

Sharp, G., 1973/1984–2005. *The politics of nonviolent action,* with M. Finkelstein, 3 vols. Boston, MA: Extending Horizons Books; repr. Boston, MA: Porter Sergeant.

Zahlan, A., 2011. Al-ʿIlm wa al-Siyādah: al-Āfāq wa al-Tawaqquʿāt fī al-Buldān al-ʿArabīyah: al-ʿIlm wa al-Jāmiʿāt wa Muʾassasāt al-Aʿmāl. *Al-Mustaqbal al-ʿArabī*, year 33 (no. 386, April), 29.

Zenko, M., 2010. *Between threats and war: U.S. discrete military operations in the post-world.* Stanford, CA: Stanford Security Series.

The revolutions of the Arab Spring: are democracy, development and modernity at the gates?

Michael Sakbani

The Herbert Walker School of Business, Webster University, Geneva, Switzerland

The paper places in historical perspective the current Arab uprisings. It argues that the reasons behind them lie in the comprehensive political, social, economic and educational failures of the Arab regimes. It documents these failures statistically and analytically. It goes on to provide analysis of the current developments in Egypt, Tunisia, Libya, Syria, Yemen and the rest of the affected states. It concludes by drawing up the implications on the Arab future of these uprisings.

The current revolutions of the Arab World are, according to many observers, the most important and exciting events the world has seen since the collapse of Communism in 1989. By their sheer scale and potential, they are truly seminal events. If successful, they promise a radical change in the conditions of 340 million people and a transformation in one of the most significant areas of the world. For the Arab people, they might signal rejoining history.

Placing the current Arab revolutions in a historical perspective

The Tunisian and Egyptian revolutions and the revolution-in-making now in Libya, Yemen and perhaps elsewhere, are to be seen as the fourth phase of the historical evolution of the Arab World in modern times. The first phase started with the Great War of 1914–18 which broke up the Ottoman Empire. Instead of realizing the promised and cherished goal of establishing an Arab state in Greater Syria and Iraq, the Sykes-Picot Pact divided the Arab countries of the Middle East into five statelets. The years between the end of the Great War and that of the Second World War were times of struggles for national independence in Egypt and these statelets.

The priority attached to national liberation in countries suffering from underdevelopment due to over 700 years of multifaceted stagnation did not allow time for maturing an experienced leadership. In the event, a modest class of political leadership with limited horizons was in place. The nationalist leaders of the struggle for independence were rather sincere traditionalists who had little know-how and practically no living experience in how to build and run a modern state.

Emerging from the Second World War, the creation of Israel in 1947 and the war with the Zionists the year after diverted the Arab World from following a development and modernization path into one of facing a national calamity. The establishment of

Israel in 1948 and the war that followed it was a cruel test for the leaders of the newly independent states. It exposed their lack of seriousness and the deficiencies of their states and societies. In a short time thereafter, a series of coups-d'états started in Syria in 1949 and was followed by Egypt in 1952, Iraq in 1958 and Yemen in 1963. These brought forth a new nationalist leadership with instincts for reform. The new leaders however, were militarists with more political nationalists' zeal than know-how about state building and society transformation. Although Egypt had the luck of still having the state built by Mohamed Ali, the other Arab countries had to start from scratch. Nonetheless, the military coup in Egypt brought forth the charismatic leadership of Jamal Abdul Nasser, who was able to evolve his coup into a revolution and set in motion several important reforms in Egypt. Nasser espoused effectively a Pan-Arab cause with a Pan-Arab unification program, and mobilized all the Arabs behind his leadership. However, the Pan-Arab Program was not developed on the social, economic and political fronts. Whether it was the Baath or the Nasser variety, it lacked an effective development model and copied the socialist economic model without having the necessary preparations for growth led by a public sector. It also applied the model of a one-party state dependent on the security apparatus and based on the absence of freedom. In the social arena, the new regimes held a truce with the traditions of society without offering any critical examination thereto. This second phase continued till 1970.[1] The 1967 war tolled the defeat of this system militarily, but perhaps more importantly, sounded the failure of its programs. There was significant rethinking of the model after 1967 but the division of views between advocates of opening up and those of more affirmation of the socialist state model did not allow the swift corrections necessary – so the exigencies of the war of attrition dominated everything.[2]

The unexpected demise of Nasser in 1970 allowed the emergence of a new leadership with regional rather than national perspective, and an enhanced sense of political domination and security preoccupation. Thus, the Arab World entered into the third phase of its modern development. The new leadership had only one program: to abandon the previous policies in all the domains: foreign and domestic, social or economic. In Egypt, the traditional Arab leader, Sadat, marked the end of the Nasser era. He played upon the contradictions of the society rather than dealing with them, and abandoned the Arab leadership role of Egypt.

In Syria and Iraq, the divided Baath regimes slumbered into more dictatorship, more control and more economic restrictions. The dominant public sector allowed no room for a market-based mixed system, and in itself, produced little economic development. Parallel developments took place in Arab North Africa and in Yemen. In the traditional monarchies and principalities of the Gulf, the rent-based oil economies postponed any serious social and political transformation.

Over almost three decades these systems became frozen in time. Their lack of legitimacy and popular accountability bred in them a sense of ownership of the state and its resources. In some countries, the president had a budget independent of the general budget and classified as a state secret. A beneficiary class developed around the regimes which operated a Wild West type of capitalism with no regulations or effective market checks. This new class used its proximity to the regime and connections to its dominant public sectors to enrich itself and wallow in pervasive corruption.

A disturbing development was the abandonment of the concept of the modern citizen state and the descent into a pre-modern norm of state based on family, region, tribe, sect or party. We saw that in Syria, Iraq, Libya, Yemen, Egypt and Algeria. One result was the disregard of public opinion and the total absence of the will of the populace in the regimes' choices and political calculations. As a matter of fact, support of foreign powers came to substitute for popular legitimacy; Mr Mubarak spent his last two years lobbying for US support for his succession by his son! The other states close to the US believed that the US holds all the cards and all the power in the region, and thus followed what it asked them.

The Arab regimes started after 1970 to cohabit with a dormant, but always present, current of political Islamists. This current started a societal movement towards authenticity based on referring backwards to traditions, upholding the old historical example as a political program. It bolstered its legitimacy with clear reference to the failure of the prevailing autocratic regimes.[3]

With the advent of the twenty-first century and its revolution in communications, social networking and information, the regimes lost their monopoly on information. The Arab societies started to realize that their governments have not only denied them political participation and control over their lives, but have produced nothing in the social, economic and educational domains. The old references to nationalism, Palestine, the struggle for patriotic sovereignty and social redistribution of wealth became empty and obviously self-serving slogans. Instead, the new generation, aware of the world and other societies, and capable of expressing itself through the new media, and even the old generation with their disappointments and stoic sufferings, started to long for freedom, for liberal democracy, for reforms of everything around them. It was no longer ideology that they sought but dignity and respect of the individual. This is how we enter, with these revolutions, the fourth phase of modern Arab development.

The current Arab revolutions, more than anything in recent memory, might reveal the irrelevance of much of the received political wisdom about the readiness of Arab society for democracy. Often one has wondered why the Arabs, people of great wealth, talent and major civilization, have been so far behind others in the march to freedom, political liberalism and democracy. There was no dearth of facile explanations, ranging from the tired clichés about Islam, to the imperialist anthropology of condescendence espoused by the Orientalists, to the fundamentalists' rejection of democracy. The successful but unfinished Tunisian and Egyptian revolutions together with what is now unfolding in Libya and Yemen and elsewhere, simply discredit much of all that. The youths of these countries showed that the oppressive autocratic Arab regimes and their security apparatuses are not to be feared; they can be challenged and even thrown out. The psychological barrier of fear was thus broken. Henceforth, the tyrants who have been in power for a generation and plan to have hereditary republics could no longer sustain the status quo. While the ultimate outcomes of these popular revolts are yet unknown, the future will not include despots with a one-party system, militarists with the power of the gun, and even hereditary autocrats with wealth and tribal alliances. The Arab street is discovering its power to say: enough, no more.

Why have the despots collapsed so quickly?

Some observers have expressed their astonishment that such long-repressive regimes could collapse as quickly as if they were made of cardboard. The observation is rather too simplified, for most of them have indeed stood for a very long time. When their end came, one could see that their accumulated failures and inability to change made the end inevitable. The failure was multifaceted enough that it left their citizens incapable of answering for themselves the purpose of having such governments. The irrelevance of government to the average citizen led to a stoic resignation enforced by fear and hopelessness. But living is all about hope; and this is especially so among the young. The young who could not emigrate were caught in the syndrome of despair of Mohammad Bouazizi, the fruit vendor arrested by the police: immolate yourself or rise against those who deny you a decent existence; the cost of the choice being the same, fear should no longer be there. This is what ignited the revolution of the despairing youth, the youth that has been outside the compass of the regimes and what is left of the feeble opposition.

A catalogue of failures

The political system

In the catalogue of failures, the political one is obvious to all; in the Arab World politics ceased to exist. The one-party state anchored on the security apparatus and possibly the army, which has been the norm in the Arab republics, has bulldozed the political and civil scenes and left no civil institutions. The old political parties were banned and, in time, disappeared. The permitted opposition parties live by the grace of the regime and in obedience to it and generally lack popular bases. Civil-society institutions like trade unions, professional associations and advocacy institutions are under the control of the regime. Without freedoms of expression, of assembly and of association, society has no opinions, no views and above all no public debate. In short order, the insular leaders trusting only their cliques and beneficiaries and having no independent expertise in the public function, trapped themselves in a bubble. Their disconnection from their people was semi-complete, and their dispossessed citizens came to feel the alienation of outsiders. In this world of a dysfunctional state living in an eternal status quo, the decision-making circles are the protectors and beneficiaries of the regime; they function in perfect insularity and often lack expertise and empirical knowledge. We now know the delusional hubris under which Saddam Husain, Bin Ali, Hosni Mubarak and Mouammar Gaddafi labored.

To a larger extent than the rest of the Arab World, Gaddafi dismembered the Libyan state institutions in addition to the institutions of civil society. He replaced these institutions with popular committees, which are sort of his security militias. One of the main victims is the Libyan Army, which has been kept weak and small. Mr Gaddafi, who holds no institutional position, is, however, in full and single control of the country. In this system without institutions, Gaddafi and his son, who also claims no positions, appeared on Libyan public TV to threaten the revolutionaries and promise a fight to the finish. We are thus in the realm of a family state.

The Arab leaders did not come to power by popular choice; they came by military coups, party takeovers or hereditary means. On the whole, they seem to have had no vision or intellectual capital. Perhaps some, like Nasser, had an instinct for reform. In his book on his years in the White House, Henry Kissinger remarked that one enters government service with a certain amount of intellectual capital and vision. After four to five years, according to Kissinger, one has to come out for renewal of one's exhausted capital. In the Arab countries, the leaders did not have this problem; they entered to govern, and to govern they stayed until the onslaught of political Alzheimers. The people they saw and consulted were like themselves: exhausted old hands. Some ministers and councilors were in the same place for two decades; the Prime

Minister of Bahrain has been in office for 42 years. The insularity of the regime led to thinking that after the Pharaoh leader is no more, the best replacement is his son.

Political failure also includes the absence of freedoms. Limitations on freedom in politics, civil society and the economy together with state domination over citizens, lock up the capacity of society for self-help and deprive the country of its elites. Time and again, the lack of freedoms along with the dearth of economic opportunities, have been the driving forces of brain drain in the Arab World.

Failure of economic and social developments

A second class of failures is in economic and social developments. In the early 1950s, many Arab countries, like Syria, Lebanon and Iraq were as well off as South Korea, Malaysia and several Latin American countries. In some indices – literacy and gross domestic product (GDP) per capita – Syria and Lebanon were favorably compared to Turkey. Five decades on, they remain underdeveloped while the comparers have become dynamic developed countries. The failure here is undoubtedly due to the wrong policies, the wrong choices of economic systems, the enchainment of society and the inability to review and reappraise these choices. A closed system neither knows what is happening around it nor what is happening to it.

In Tunisia, Libya and Egypt, where half of the population is below 30, the respective economies proved incapable of offering jobs, basic necessities and hope for a better future. The rate of unemployment among the youth in Tunisia, according to statistics from the International Labor Organization (ILO), has been 31%, and 44% among some university graduates. In Egypt, youth unemployment is estimated at 21%, almost double the general unemployment rates (Haq *et al.* 2011, pp. 2–4). In Egypt, the economy creates 65% of the jobs needed to accommodate the new entrants into the labor force, while in Tunisia it creates 75%. In Libya, the unemployment rates were 40% for the youth and 30% for the general population (ILO 2011a). These dismal statistics are in the same league as the rest of the Arab region. In comparison to other developing regions, the Arab region has 10.5% of its population unemployed – 10.5% in the Middle East and 10.2% in Arab North Africa – whereas East Asia has 4.1% and South Asia 4.3% (Haq *et al.* 2011, p. 3).

Interestingly, neither Egypt, nor Tunisia nor Libya has been doing badly with regard to their per capita incomes and their rates of growth. The rate of GDP growth in Tunisia has ranged from 3% to 4.7% in the last three years (AMF nd, World Bank 2010a). In Egypt, the GDP growth rate over the last five years ranged from 4.5% to 7%; it has averaged 6% over the last decade (World Bank 2010d). In Libya, the GDP rate of growth has run between 3.7% in 2006 and 9% in 2007, but an odd 2.1% in 2009. The GDP per capita is a high $12,020 (World Bank 2010b). These rates are higher than most European and developing countries. Yet, the growth of the economy has not generated enough jobs. This is due to the significant increases in trend productivity relative to labor inputs growth. In contrast, the Libyan economy generated a lot of jobs for trained and skilled workers, but those were filled by foreigners. According to the Central Intelligence Agency (CIA), 30% of the Libyan endogenous labor force is unemployed.

Perhaps, the spotty increase in income, by virtue of its skewed distribution, brought about rising expectations. In any event, the oligarchic nature of the ruling regimes seems to have skewed the distribution of income and wealth: thirty percent of income growth in Egypt accrues to the top ten percentiles of the population and 3.7% to the lowest ten percentiles. In Tunisia, the respective figures are 33% and 2.3%.[4] We know from comparative economic statistics that the distribution of wealth is usually considerably more skewed than income distribution. Mr Bin Ali's family, friends and other beneficiaries certainly became very wealthy, as did the Mubaraks and their business clique. The Press reported, without documentation, billions of dollars stowed away in various places. According to the *Guardian*, the Mubarak family has amassed a fortune of US$30 billion, whereas the CIA places it at a modest US$4 billion!! In the event, the skewed distribution of wealth and income created impoverished masses with disappointed expectations and withered away the middle class. Forty percent of the Egyptian population lives below the poverty line, on less than two US dollars a day. Tunisia is better off, but not in relation to its per capita income, which is 3.7 times higher than Egypt's. This descent into misery has taken place in full view of the social media, with the TV screens displaying daily the comings and goings of the lifestyle of the rich and the corrupt.

Another aspect of the economic failure has been the emphasis on imported consumer goods in the context of the total liberalization of trade. In 2010, Egypt ran a trade deficit of US$22 billion and its current account was US$5 billion in the red. Egypt's foreign debt now exceeds 75% of GDP (Central Bank of Egypt 2009). Tunisia's deficit was US$4 billion in 2010 (Banque Central de la Tunisie 2009). Both countries were severely hit in 2010 by the increase in international commodity prices, in particular food prices. In 2010, the overall rate of inflation was 13% in Egypt and 14% in Tunisia (CIA 2010). In both countries however, given their dependence on food imports, the rise in international food prices, which has exceeded 25% in some basic staples, hit the budgets of the poor consumers with full force. Had the two countries been to some extent self-sufficient in food and basic goods, the impact would have been significantly attenuated. In the event, the poor came to be squeezed mercilessly where their demand is perfectly inelastic. Economists and market analysts are unanimous that food prices will follow a rising trend in the foreseeable future. Thus, the Arab countries would be better served to work at substituting food imports through local or regional food production schemes.

The industrialization of the Egyptian economy and the technological development of its agriculture and infrastructure started in the late 1950s under Nasser. It was led and dominated by an unprepared public sector. However, this process was effectively aborted in the 1967 war and its aftermath. At any rate, the public sector-led growth had only limited success. Thus, it was effectively abandoned under Sadat and rejected under Mubarak in favor of the private sector. The experience of Egypt over the last twenty years shows that the private sector has proved, on the whole, disinterested in agriculture or industry, except in light of two to three-digit type transformations. The bulk of investments have been in commercial activities and tourism. In Egypt, the value added of industry to GDP ranged between 28% and 30%, whereas services ranged in the last five years from 66% to 70% of GDP, and agriculture, only 4% to 5% (World Bank 2009). Given the limitations on arable land in Egypt and the size of its population, neglect of industry and technology-based products is rather the wrong choice. In Tunisia, the pattern of growth emphasized the service sector, in particular, tourism in addition to light transformative industries. Services accounted for 59% to 62% percent of Tunisian GDP in recent years (World Bank 2009). Tunisia also developed pockets of its infrastructure here and there, especially in human resources. To be sure, it is perfectly acceptable for an economy to develop its service and commercial sectors. However, if economic dependence on foreign imports is to be at acceptable levels, it is imperative to couple that with productive real sectors capable of producing jobs and essential real goods in a sustained fashion. Libya's pattern emphasized its oil and oil-derivatives industries. Lately, foreign direct investments have begun developing some service and transformative industries. It is telling to note that almost all the autocracies have palliatives like food and fuel subsidies to defray the burden of the populace instead of developing their productive capacities. This composite failure was on display in the recent revolts, as we saw on TV screens in Cairo and Tunis the coming together of the poor, the unemployed youth and the withered and diminished middle class.

Education, knowledge and research and development (R&D)

In the non-oil economies, the above failures are associated with the deterioration of the quality of education and learning. Given the dearth of resources, pressure on the education system due to the double coups of more egalitarian educational opportunities and galloping population growth, has resulted in the deterioration of quality and the neglect of specialized technical learning. According to United Nations (UN) reports, only two Arab countries, Libya and Bahrain, can provide all their youth with the opportunity to acquire appropriate education at high levels (UNDP 2010). The UN Report on Arab Education documents (in Table 3.3) the inferior results of the test scores of degree holders; only 12% scored good results (UNDP 2010). In higher education, there is not a single Arab university among the top 400 universities in the world (WCU nd). The picture is more somber if the oil-exporting countries are excluded, as they have spent significantly on education in recent years.

Of particular alarm is the widespread illiteracy of Arab women. The Human Development Report estimated that in 2005, 60% of females were illiterate (UNICEF nd). Despite the increased enrollment of women in all levels of schooling, especially at university level, their stock is still limited. The energy-exporting Arab countries, plus Jordan and Tunisia, have boosted the number of women in tertiary education significantly, but the problem is that higher education in the Arab countries remains separate from employment needs, and in the case of women, not fully deployed. It should be recalled that many of the manifestations of social development are associated with the spread of literacy and availability of jobs for females. Outside the agricultural rural sector, female labor-participation rates are less than a fourth of the males' rates. The received traditions of Arab societies are not helpful in this regard; women's labor-participation rates in the Arab countries are much below those of other developing countries, and ironically, Tunisia has one of the best. No society can become modern and fully productive if women are relegated to home and household work. On the basis of a capital output ratio of three to one, and using Ockun's Law, it can be shown that raising the participation rate of women to 40% of the national labor force would add 1.2% to the trend of GDP growth. The revolutionary republics proved to be just as backward in their orientations as the traditionalist kingdoms and principalities. Finally, the refuge over the past three decades into authentic traditions, known as the 'Islamic Awakening', has reinforced the referring back to ancestral traditions in Arab societies, thereby increasing their disconnection from contemporary modernity. This adds to the failure of modernization and feeds into social obsolescence.

The total expenditure on research and development in the Arab World does not exceed 1% of the GDP in the highest-ranking country, Tunisia. The United Nations Economic, Social and Cultural Organization's (UNESCO) Science Report of 2010 estimates R&D expenditure in Egypt at 0.23 of 1% of GDP and in Libya at 1.2% (UNESCO 2010). This compares with an average of 2.2% in the Organisation for Economic Co-operation and Development (OECD) countries and higher than that in the US, Japan, Israel, Malaysia, China and South Korea. Qatar has set an ambitious 2.8% to be reached in five years. Saudi Arabia and Libya also have ambitious plans. But the rest of the Arab countries rank among the lowest in the world in spending on R&D. Without governments' commitment to R&D, the private-sector expenditure operates in a vacuum. Development of knowledge and knowledge applications are the bedrock of advance and the source of the growth of productivity which has historically accounted for two thirds of GDP growth in almost every country. After the passing of the fossil-energy era, the Arab countries' future problems will be in water resources, in desertification, in food production and in coping with climate change, all of which needs knowledge and research.

The failure of educational transformation condemns social and economic transformation. In the global economy, only the educated and well trained will have a chance, and only economies with a capacity to export and trade have been successful. Egypt, Libya and Tunisia, like all other Arab countries, are insignificant participants in world exports outside the oil sector.

Egypt and the Arab vacuum

Rounding up this catalogue of failures is the feeling of most Egyptians, and other Arabs, that the absence of Egypt under Mubarak from playing an Arab role has created a regional vacuum. Mubarak egged on the US in invading Iraq. The Wikileaks papers reveal his contribution to the false intelligence about Iraq's claimed weapons of mass destruction.[5] He kept silent during Israel's attack on Lebanon. His Foreign Minister and the Egyptian-controlled media blamed the Lebanese resistance for provoking Israel's attack on Lebanon. When Israel attacked and savaged Ghazza, Mubarak stood silent and continued his blockade of the tiny sector, thus effectively becoming an objective ally of Israel. During the last five years leading to the division of Sudan, which is the strategic depth of Egypt, Mubarak was a passive observer toeing the US line. The same can be said regarding both Egypt's role in Somalia and after the invasion of Iraq. The shrinkage of Egypt's role in the region created a vacuum filled by the new non-Arab players, Turkey and Iran, who have their own agendas. Egypt also abandoned its old role on the world scene under Mubarak. All of that rendered Egypt a third-rate state.

Social media and communication technology

The widespread use of the new communication technology and its associated social media among the young turned out to be decisive in these youth revolutions. A quarter of the population in Tunisia has computers and there are an estimated 10 million users in Egypt. In addition, there has been an enormous spread of satellite TV outside government control (around 100 such channels), some of which, like Al Jazeera, are among the most effective in the world. Given the very high ownership of portable devices, the media brought the world to Arab citizens. It informed their vision of it and opened their eyes about their marginality in their own countries. In addition, they were able to circumvent the restrictions of martial law on assembly and association, and to open a digital space of communication. Years of advocacy on satellite channels of human rights, of lamenting the absence of representativeness of Arab governments and the lack of freedoms, entered the cultural consciousness of the youth. For this youth, rising expectations juxtaposed themselves against their reality of economic misery and, in the process, created the combustible material from which the sudden revolutions ignited. On the TV channels and on their smartphones, they saw the events in Tunisia. Their phones and computers also enabled them to communicate and spread the facts without censure or 'retouching'. On the occasion of the death under torture of blogger Khaled Said, they called on 25 January 2011 (the day of the police) for a day of rage. The youth went to Tahrir Square in their thousands and held there bravely for two days. The authorities' response was violent repression. This violence solicited a popular response. Soon, they were joined by others and thus the seminal events of the last weeks were set in motion. When the regimes faced large masses of the population, the army was neither able nor willing to protect them, nor were the security forces capable of killing enough people to maintain their masters. In the end, the people proved to be the only force that determines who governs.

Contagion and prospects

The various Arab countries still under authoritarian autocracy have different conditions and dissimilar backgrounds. But they share the failures expounded above. They also share, to varying degrees, the pervasiveness of corruption. This is both a source of susceptibility for contagion and a caution about possible failure. On objective grounds, contagion is likely in Yemen, Sudan, Jordan and the Palestinian territories.

Candidates for the first wave

In Yemen, President Ali Abdullah Saleh has been in power for 32 years, and despite his consummate skill in manipulating the various opposing groups and his gift for political theatre, he has achieved very little outside securing Yemen's unity and building a unified Yemeni state. Large chunks of the country are excluded from executive power and the North and South are in quasi-open rebellion against him in the center. He has run a family and tribal-based regime. Yemen is among the least-developed countries in the world. It boasts 40% unemployment. Ninety percent of its exports are accounted for by the little oil it has, and 75% of its government revenues come from this single source. Of the arable land, 35% is used for cultivating the hallucinogenic kat. Its tribal society has built-in fissures. Interestingly however, during the recent demonstrations, Yemen's national unity was not in question. President Saleh's problem now is that he promised much in the past but delivered little.

The political opposition, the 'Joint Rally', has used the freedom margins allowed by the regime to demonstrate and ask for political reforms. This was soon joined by the youth from Sana'a university. In a few days, various personalities and various other groups joined the demonstrations. By the third week of March, the protest movement has gathered momentum, become continuous and countrywide. On 10 March, President Saleh offered to change the constitution and turn the system into a parliamentary democracy at the end of 2011. He also invited the opposition to join a national unity government. Finally, he proposed full decentralization of the administration into three regions. Had such a package been offered two months before, Yemen would have probably kept quiet. This is again too little too late.

The momentum of the drive for regime change has led the protestors to promptly refuse the offer and to insist on the President's immediate departure. As the protest became overwhelming, President Saleh's regime, in obvious panic, struck with force against the demonstrators. Fifty-two people were killed, and hundreds injured on

18 March. In the wake of that, several ministers and ruling party officials, plus army generals and ambassadors, resigned in protest and joined the demonstrators. In the throes of the 'finale', President Saleh offered to resign in 2011 after organizing elections. But again, there were no takers. As the demostrations continued unabated, the security forces once more struck in Taaz and Hudayda, killing some 30 people and injuring hundreds.

The armed tribal composition of Yemen does not permit complete triumph of either party. Thus, a compromise must be found for an exit for Mr Saleh that preserves Yemen's unity and paves the way towards a federated sharing of power among its three regions. Indeed, the states of the GCC offered on 11 April to mediate and invited all concerned to a meeting in Riad to work out a compromise.

In Sudan, President Omar al Basheer came to power with the Islamists in 1991. In a few years, he kicked out his original partners and clamped military control over the political life of Sudan. Over the past five years, he has managed to lose South Sudan by making all kinds of wrong decisions. He has devastated Darfur and brought upon himself an indictment for crimes against humanity. Two months ago, he got himself re-elected unopposed for another term. And after the dismemberment of his country, he refuses even to change his cabinet.

The Palestinian Authority on the West Bank and Hamas in Ghazza have both become illegitimate as their terms expired more than a year ago. The Palestinian Authority has been negotiating with Israel for nineteen years without results. As the Wikileaks papers show, its policy seems to consist of offering Israel one concession after the other without a quid pro quo. Its lack of strategy and accomplishment is only matched by Hamas whose avowed resistance is negligible and its strategy leads nowhere. Meanwhile, the Palestinians' suffering continues under occupation and, given the split of the Palestinian leadership and the aggressive colonization policies of Israel, their cause has never faced bleaker prospects. In full frustration, hundreds of thousands started demonstrations in Ghazza and the West Bank on 14 March to force reunification and new elections for Parliament and the Executive.

King Abdullah II of Jordan, who came to the throne on a promise of openness and reform, has achieved very little on this score. He is far from a constitutional monarch, and acts more like a dictator. To his rather modest economic record, he has added a deepening division between Palestinians and Jordanians among his citizens and tolerated rampant corruption by, inter alia, using many of the old hands and scions of the same families used by his father. While Jordan has done well in education and public health and allowed a measure of freedoms, its social development has been rather modest. Right on the heels of Tunisia and Egypt, Jordanians of all ages started popular demonstrations asking for reforms and changes. The King twice changed his cabinet and formed a Commission for Dialogue, which met on 19 March to discuss comprehensive reforms. The Commission has prepared laws for elections and political associations and some guidelines for constitutional reforms.

Candidates for the second wave

If the rulers of Syria, Algeria and Iraq do not heed the urgency of reforms, they might also be facing popular revolts. It will be more difficult and more bloody in these cases, but still inevitable.

Algeria, with its bloody experience of Islamist revolt, has a measure of freedoms, but its political system has been dominated by the same ruling party and the military oligarchy behind it for two decades. The country has a massive unemployment problem, especially among the youth, but holds US$80 billion in Central Bank reserves!! President Boutaflika is facing riots and repeated protests. He has to start overdue political and economic changes. He abolished the emergency laws in effect for nineteen years, distributed social state aid and promised more reforms.

Syria, long isolated and ruled for 41 years by the Asad family, has not been doing well economically since the mid 1990s. After an explosive growth of 360% in the 60s and 70s, GDP went down 33% in the 1980s. In the 1990s, average GDP growth was only 1.1% per annum (Wikipedia 2011). In the years since 2001, GDP annual growth has averaged about 3.0%, while population growth has run at 2.7%. From 2008 to 2010, GDP grew by 4.3%, 5.0% and 4.0% respectively (ILO 2011b, Economy Watch nd). These are modest and unstable figures in comparison to well-performing developing countries (World Bank 2010c, ILO 2011b). There is rapid population growth and consequent high unemployment at 20% (ILO 2011b). Adding to these problems is the secular decline in oil revenues and the failure of agricultural crops in the last four years. As a result, the Syrian per capita income has fluctuated at staggering amplitude over the years. Over 2008–10, the per capita income (on a purchasing power parity [PPP] basis) ranged from US$4600 to $4800 (ILO 2011b).

The Syrian economy remains state-dominated and inefficient (54 of 93 state enterprises were in the red in 2010), and suffers from low investment rates. Part of the explanation is the decline in public sector investment in recent years and the modesty of private sector investment. Despite laws and measures to encourage foreign investment, Syria's share of all types of such flows is modest. The lagging investment was not helped by the private sector's seeming practice of exploiting its connections to the decision makers to invest where quick monopoly profits can be gained rather than adding them to the productive capacity of the economy. In general, there is an aura of mistrust and apprehension about the public sector in evidence. The Syrian middle class is reputed for its entrepreneurial spirit. Yet, the policy makers are advancing hesitantly towards liberalizing and opening up the economy.[6] The liberalization efforts of the last four years still fall short of what is needed and the government still lacks economic credibility.

The Syrian political system is frozen into a one-party system with nominal, essentially approved, opposition. Despite Syria's clever foreign policy and honorable stands on various Arab issues, its population needs besides that to see improvements in living conditions. Official statistics put 12% of the population below the UN poverty line.[7] This is a counterintuitive underestimation given the population growth and the distribution and level of income. After 48 years of rule by martial law, Syria needs liberalization in the economy and in the laws and practices covering expression, association and assembly. There is also an urgent need for improving Syria's record on human rights and the protection of individual dignity, as well as curbing corruption. Against this background, demonstrations erupted in Syria over the past ten days. The government first dismissed the demonstrators as bands of terrorists and hired agents, and reacted with a security reflex, killing several people. In the city of Daraa, security forces fired on the public funerals that ensued. Five days later, the security forces killed 21 people and injured more than a hundred in a crackdown on demonstrators barricaded inside the Omariah Mosque in Daraa. On Thursday, 24 March, Ms. B. Shaaban, a senior aide to President Asad, announced in a press conference several decisions of the Regional Command of the Baath Party. The most important were to appoint a committee to study lifting the 48-year-old martial law, another concerned with forming political parties, and a third for the freedom of the press. She also promised laws and government action for fighting corruption. These are positive steps, but they are promises from authorities that have been notoriously slow in everything. Part of what has to be reformed in Syria is the one-party system, and yet the reform seems to be under the auspices of the Baath Party. The power structure in Syria, namely the state security, family and other beneficiaries and the party, surely have a vested interest in the status quo, and they may very well obstruct reforms.

Due to the absence of transparency in decision making in Syria, we do not know who in the regime is for or against reform. The day after Ms Shaaban expressed the sorrow of President Asad for what had happened, the security forces opened fire on demonstrators in several Syrian cities, killing and injuring dozens of people. So, is this double talk or are the security forces really in charge?

President Asad inherited a heavy history with a power set-up afraid of change and averse to openness. He must face this reality assured in the observation that he has popular backing for overdue change. He faces now the choice of his life: will he announce to his public a clean break with the past, or will he make another set of promises to patch up the system, which like their antecedents will continue to be unfulfilled?

The Syrian regime faces unavoidable issues in the need for immediate decisions, even though some, such as economic issues, will take time to bear results. Nevertheless, the survival of the regime depends on its alacrity and decisive sense of reality.

The first issue is the abandonment of the special status of the Baath Party enshrined in article 8 of the Constitution; there is no such thing in the world today as one party that is the leader and sole representative of society. Opening up the political system to electoral competition is not only imperative; it is the guarantee of continuity for the party. The second is freeing the system from undue clan sectarian specificity. This has been started by the President and it needs continuity and further demonstration. There are those who want to transform the political issues of Syria into sectarian ones. Iraq furnishes a lesson regarding the dangers of such a deviant slope. The Latakia riots on 26 March, in which 12 were killed, are a warning that Syrian sectarian pluralism can be exploited by the forces of religious intolerance and those who do not wish Syria and the nationalist causes it supports well. The third is to convince all power centers of the regime that popular legitimacy under liberal democratic freedoms offers the best protection for them and for all citizens. It is also the only guarantee for the safety and stability of Syria. Fourth, the President has to embark on fundamental economic reforms, which include revamping the role of the public sector in a market economy along the lines of the successful models of Turkey, Malaysia, Brazil, Chile, Taiwan and South Korea and not on the empirically unfounded claim of specificity of Syria. The economy needs to be further opened up and the state should do all it can to promote small- and medium-size enterprises, which worldwide generate the most employment. Syria also needs to develop its export capacities, in particular technology-based products. The lagging investment can be helped by liberalizing, under wise regulations and enforced competition laws, access for both foreign and domestic investors. Syria should take advantage of Arab foreign direct investment as well as FDI from technologically advanced sources and encourage, through industrial policies, any investment of strategic economic potential. The President has to face up to the dissolution of the government security apparatus and the termination of its practices outside the law; a state that sees danger in its people is a failed state. Egypt has recently offered a good example of security reorganization. Finally, the regime must chart out a road map for democratic conversion, which includes new laws for parties and civil society bodies, new laws of press and public assembly, juridical control of elections, new election laws which open up the electoral process to all, and transformation of the parliament to a fully elected and representative body.

President Asad, a modern man attuned to his times, enjoys a favorable public image and wide popular sympathy. The demonstrations seen on 29 March attest to that. This should embolden him and the Party to move swiftly on reforms and attain due popular legitimacy.

On 30 March, the President gave a long awaited speech about the Arab events and Syria's reforms. The speech basically endorsed the need for reforms and explained that external circumstances had changed priorities and caused delaying reforms. It portrayed the pro-democracy events in Syria as part of a conspiracy to seed sedition and division under the guise of demanding reforms. The speech announced nothing concrete. With more than 200 dead reported by Human Rights Watch and large scale arrests, the real stance of the system is in question. With all the mixed signals, one cannot at this point predict the future course of reforms in Syria.

Iraq presents a special case. The invasion of Iraq broke up the institutions of the Iraqi state, ignited ugly sectarian divisions and brought Iranian influence into Iraq. It has also devastated the Iraqi economy and annihilated public services (Sakbani 2010). One result of the US occupation was to put in place an imperfect political process. This process is exclusionist and plagued with corruption and political shenanigans. After a record eight months of no government, the irremovable sitting Prime Minister, Mr Nouri al Maliki, with help from Iran and the acquiescence of the US, succeeded in forming a coalition with promises and political deals. As has become his style, Maliki reneged on some of the deals he cut, and several key ministries remain in his own hands.

In February, demonstrations took place all over Iraq protesting corruption, lack of public services and political abuse. In March, the demonstration spread to the Kurdish area as well. In their wake, Maliki promised one month ago that he will solve all the public service problems in 100 days – something he had not been able to do for five years. This is indeed a bold theatrical gesture. It would be in character that he will use this probation period to fire the ministers he does not like at its end.

Maliki's twists, turns, dealings and broken promises are typical of the culture of the sectarian political class of occupied Iraq. These politicians have proven themselves incapable of building a state, of serving the public or running a clean government. Iraq's future will only be clear after the US withdraws all its troops at end of 2011. Iraq, rich with natural and human resources, is for the time being, the throbbing Arab tragedy.

Before 17 February, nobody would have picked Libya as the site of the next eruption. But 42 years of Colonel Gaddafi's dictatorship and rule without institutions or civilized norms have been enough to mobilize another youth-led revolt. In Libya, it is not primarily economic misery that is the motive, although Libyans are neither prosperous nor fully employed. The real problem is the dysfunctional non-system in control. Having squandered resources on adventures and misdeeds and corrupt use of public finances with no accountability of any kind, Gaddafi has ran a type of feudal lordship in which he decides what to do with the public purse. Lonely in his bubble, he appeared one week after the revolution unaware of what was happening. He dismissed the revolution as riots of drugged youth and a conspiracy hatched by the US, Israel and al Qaeda – an imaginative combination indeed. With megalomania galore and psychopathic determination to defend his power even by bombing his people, he pledged to fight until the last person and the last house. The Libyan revolution, peaceful and unarmed, was forced by Gaddafi to defend itself against his all-out attacks. Although Libya is a tribal society that owes its present unity to Gaddafi and the Sanousi King before him, the revolution is supported by all segments of Libyan society and all its regions.

At the beginning of March, the revolution formed an Interim Libyan National Council (INLC) to focalize its leadership. The composition of the ILNC is not clearly known, and the young occupy only two seats out of 31. The ILNC is led by the former Minister of Justice and has in majority respectable, albeit traditionalist, figures. It is still somewhat unclear what type of alternative to Gaddafi it might provide. The ILNC made some strides in the second week of March in securing international recognition, notably from France and the European Parliament, and its envoys were received by countries including the US. But it has a nasty war to fight with inferior weaponry and untrained volunteers. In his latest past-midnight TV appearances, Gaddafi warned Europe about al Qaeda in Libya, illegal immigration swamping European shores and even discomfort for Israel if he goes. It seems that there is nothing the revolutionary colonel would not do or offer to stay in power.

From where we are now, it looks that Gaddafi's time is up and he most likely will soon join the circle of despots in exile. However, in the recent fighting, Gaddafi was gradually getting the upper hand. The fighting has become bloody, costly and devastating to Libya's future. The military difficulty of both the regime and the revolution is the vastness of the terrain. Occupying land is not as important as having an assured control of the four oil pipelines and the refineries in al Zawya, Ras lanof, Brega and Tubrok, which quickly fell into the hands of the revolution. Aware of that, Gaddafi launched a counter-offensive to gain back these objectives.

The ILNC as well as the Arab League endorsed on 12 March the idea of requesting that the UN Security Council impose a no-fly zone over Libya to stop Gaddafi from using aerial bombardment, especially of civilians. On 17 March the Security Council passed with a majority of ten to zero (five abstentions) a strong resolution not only to impose the no-fly zone but also to empower members 'to protect the civilian population by any necessary means'. Gaddafi, who appeared on TV the day before threatening vengeance and destruction, and promising to wipe out the revolution in 48 hours, immediately declared a ceasefire; his calculations shifted when he was no longer facing unarmed people. Naturally, the ceasefire was a cloak under which he continued his assaults. In the event, the international community started military action on Saturday 19 March to enforce the Security Council resolution.

The international intervention in Libya raises several issues. The first is the demonstrated failure of the Arab states to take up the task of protecting Libyans. The Arab League once again showed itself as an umbrella of the Arab regimes. The second issue is that this will be a precedent for the UN Security Council to intervene to protect a population from the actions of their governments: '*le droit d'ingérance*'. This is a welcome evolution which might serve as warning to abusive governments, like the Arab dictatorships, that crimes against their peoples will be punished. However, since military action is difficult to control and wind up, it is a dangerous precedent as far as weak countries are concerned. Finally, the Arab consciousness is seared by the catastrophic consequences of the Iraq intervention. Even though this one involves no land troops, it will bring destruction upon Libya and its population. Like Saddam before him, Gaddafi has brought this upon himself and his people. The international action will eliminate Gaddafi's offensive power, but will not be sufficient to remove him. If the purpose, as President Obama said, is to remove Gaddafi, then the no-fly zone will not be sufficient and there has to be a land force to take him out. A prolonged struggle would be tragic. The revolution must prepare itself to take Gaddafi out by force with Arab or international help. It is incomprehensible how Gaddafi can conceive of returning to power after all he has done. But at every turn, he has proved determined and psychologically prepared to inflict on Libyans any price for his survival in power.

The monarchies

The monarchies: Saudi Arabia, Bahrain, Oman, Qatar, United Arab Emirates, Kuwait and Morocco face the problem of lack of popular participation and basically, royal-family monopoly of power. The struggle of the people there is about establishing constitutional monarchies rather than removing the kings. With the exception of Morocco, the economic conditions in these countries are quite good and the motivating force is political.

Bahrain was the first to erupt. The central question is about freedom, political participation of all citizens and social modernization. Bahrain's problem is compounded by its vertical sectarian divisions and the growing influence and mischief of Iran in the Gulf. Yet, if the King were to open up the political system and allow full equality and opportunity to all citizens regardless of sect, the country would perhaps not have experienced the current political protests. In response to the demonstrations and after initial repression, the government formed a Commission of Dialogue under the Crown Prince to find a compromise.

The Commission came to a deadlock as the opposition raised the ceiling of its demands and the government drew red lines around certain issues. Behind the back of the Commission and perhaps the Crown Prince, the Prime Minister took advantage of scattered acts of violence by a part of the opposition demanding the establishment of an Islamic Republic to repress the demonstrators. In addition, his government invited Gulf Council intervention. On 14 March, Saudi Arabia sent 1,000 soldiers to bolster Bahraini authorities. There is no doubt that if more soldiers are needed, more will be sent. With the arrival of these troops, the Interior Ministry dispersed by force the demonstrators and inflicted significant casualties. The next day, it arrested several of the opposition leaders. The GCC intervention might have unwittingly transformed the Bahrain problem into a sectarian conflict and furnished extra reasons for Iranian meddling and mischief. The challenge now is to find a compromise forged by moderates from the opposition and the royal family. This must succeed, for Bahrain will not at any cost be allowed by Saudi Arabia to become an Iranian-influenced state. Bahrain's stability requires broad equal political participation of all its citizens.

Demonstrations also took place in Oman. The Omani Sultan promptly replaced twelve members of his cabinet and promised political reforms. He also announced the formation of a Commission to look into modifying the constitution, including his own authorities, and to set provisions for establishing a Parliament with unrestricted authority. Again, it is the representation of the people in the political decision that is demanded rather than changing the regime.

The biggest, richest and by far the most influential monarchy in the Gulf, Saudi Arabia, will not be immune to the current wave for long. King Abdullah, a respected moderate Arab Nationalist and a potential reformer, is hampered from taking the necessary bold and far-reaching political and social reforms required by the times by his age (87) and succession, by some members of his family and by the religious establishment. Despite questions about the type of education instructed, the kingdom has generously spent on education and has produced an able and modern cadre. It has also built considerable economic and human infrastructures. However, it has remained tradition-bound and obsolete in many respects. The political system is based on the royal family and allows only a non-binding consultative role for others. Popular political participation and accountability are absent and the expression of opposing views, public assembly and political parties are not allowed. The Saudi economy is in need of structural reforms and considerable reorientation for meeting the post-energy era. Buying people's acquiescence by $30.5 billion of social expenditures, as done recently, is no substitute for deep reforms. Saudi Arabia's increasingly educated population cannot be kept at bay forever.

In Morocco, King Muhammad VI has introduced many political reforms and has opened the records of the previous tyranny for national reconciliation. The Moroccan economy has been growing at a moderate pace. But the regime is far from being a constitutional monarchy. To his credit, the King declared on 8 March that he is going to constitute a commission to modify the constitution to turn Morocco into a constitutional monarchy. He also said that he will have the government look into some pressing economic problems.

Failure in Egypt, Libya and Tunisia is still possible. The leaderless popular revolutions in Egypt and Tunisia have no pre-thought-out programs, no charismatic leaders and, for the time being, no agreed tactical plans. Their visions of freedom, democracy and social justice are long-term strategies without operational signposts. In effect, these three popular revolts do not obey the norms of revolution models. Revolutions require programs, leadership and popular insertion. These are partially absent in the event. Thus, they need in the transition common agreement and joint tactical aims among all the political participants. They need the emergence of political leaderships and the mobilization of expertise, which has been long-absent from the public function. Unlike Iraq, they should attract and accept the participation of the uncompromised and able elements of the old regimes. Their aim must not be revenge and the settling of accounts, but turning a new page. But in all of that, they should take the time necessary to prepare for the organized participation of all parties in future elections without exclusion. Without adequate preparations, the revolutions risk being hijacked by the better-organized groups, (for instance, the Muslim Brothers), even if the latter play by the rules and have bumbled throughout the early phase of the Egyptian and Tunisian uprisings.

Democracy is an institutional envelope which requires many building blocks: an independent judiciary, the rule of law, the existence of civil and political institutions, the freedoms of expression, assembly and association, free and universal elections and the vigil of a liberal society. The culture of Arab society has not always evolved along a liberal and multi-vision path. Its tendency to accord acceptance to traditions without critical examination is not conducive to the acceptance of differences in thinking and in values. This has also been reinforced by the failure of the nationalist secular regimes and the closed horizons of their dictatorial orders. There should be full awareness of these self-limiting factors in perceiving the future. However, these shortcomings should not stop the march towards democracy. Some commentators, including the Arab regimes, have made the false and historically invalid argument that democracy needs special preparations; yet all peoples started from a zero point and learned by doing as they went along. India, for example, should still be non-democratic according to this assertion.

The challenges of the transition

The responses of the authoritarian regimes in all the Arab countries were similar: they accused the demonstrators of following a foreign agenda or being at the service of subversive parties or as Gaddafi did, being drugged children and nobodies. Another common refrain was to accuse the Media, in particular al Jazeera, of fomenting the troubles. They all claimed specificity and differences from other Arab countries. In Tunisia, Egypt and even Syria and Yemen, the regimes acknowledged the shortcomings and the grievances and endorsed in principle democratic reforms. However, in all cases the regime tried to play musical chairs by firing their cabinets and installing other old hands in power and promising future reforms. This was obviously an attempt to get around the revolutions and contain their impacts. The first reflex of all the governments was the security one; the police and state security charged the demonstrators, opening fire and killing many of them. This was then followed by arresting many activists in an attempt at quelling what they thought were passing disturbances. By the time they understood these popular uprisings for what they are, they came up with unacceptable promises, and it was the case of too little too late. On 11 February Mubarak finally gave in and resigned, handing over his authority to the Supreme Military Council (SMC). Ben Ali ran out after four weeks.

The SMC had an auspicious start by dismissing the two houses of Parliament and forming a commission to look into the constitution. It also declared its aim of handing authority to elected representatives in six months if possible. Two weeks later it dismissed Mubarak's last cabinet and appointed a respectable Prime Minister, Dr Isam Sharaf, nominated by the revolutionaries. The new cabinet replaced the contested ex-Ministers of Foreign Affairs, the Interior and Justice. The new Prime Minister started by dismissing the old State Security Service, which has focused on surveying its citizens rather than anything else. A new national service will replace it with the explicit mission of state external security.

On Saturday 19 March, the proposed amendments of the Commission were put to popular vote. There were eight articles in play and a ninth which, if accepted, would provide for a change of the whole constitution after the upcoming elections. The referendum was hurried and its scope severely limited. The Constitution in effect endows the President with enormous powers. It has many provisions that are questionable. Changing it in good time would have been a better choice. The period up to the elections provided in the amendments is too short to allow enough preparation for new political groups. The organized groups, viz, the Muslim Brothers and the National Party, would certainly be at an advantage. The referendum took place in order and peace under full judicial supervision; by a 77% majority the 'yes' side had it. It was overwhelming evidence of the populace's embrace of democracy and the feeling of empowerment. Instead of the miserable 15% participation of the last Mubarak elections, preliminary reports claim more than a 41% turnout and thousands were not able to vote due to limited polling time.

Subsequently, the SMC put into effect a constitutional package of 62 articles including the nine passed in the referendum. The package spells out the transition authority of the SMC, the rules for future elections and for political organization.

Consequently, the date of the legislative elections was set for September 2011, followed by presidential elections and then drafting a new Constitution.

The old regime's set-up, laws and faces are still much in evidence and in administrative charge. To be sure, it takes time to clean up the state. But cleaning up the state, revising the biased laws in effect and preparing politically to fight the elections are the future challenges.

The road for creating viable democratic institutions and practices will be long and difficult. Nobody should underestimate the difficulties attendant upon creating viable democratic institutions and practices or the length of the road ahead. We know that the old dictatorships have fallen but we do not know yet whether their replacements will be another set of dictators in military or religious garbs. Nonetheless, the collapse of fear and public passivity will allow no renewal of authoritarian autocracy. If the Armies want to help their peoples, they should become the protectors of democracy and constitutional legitimacy.

Egypt and all the Arab countries need fresh faces capable of leadership, possessing vision, exposed to the outside world and conversant with it. Many of the names of presumptive candidates in Egypt are unfortunately not of this type. The exception, Dr. al Baradie, would make an excellent candidate, but he lacks a popular support base and party organization. Egypt is rich in human resources. Let us hope it comes up with an excellent pick.

The Egyptian Army has behaved admirably during the revolution. However, it has been the power behind the regime for 59 years. During this time, it has acquired privileges and vested economic interests. Will it allow the changes that people want and the liberal democracy needs? That is the question. The Egyptian revolution has succeeded but it remains incomplete; it has changed the government but not yet built a state, and its ultimate results are still unknown.

Implications for the Arab future

The revolts of Egypt and Tunisia and the ones following them in Libya, Bahrain and Yemen will have significant historical implications. It took the French Revolution 26 years to settle, the Bolshevik revolution twelve years to steady itself. The Arab masses, led by their youth, seem to have triumphed and ushered the beginning of liberal democracy in a few weeks. When the fresh new wind will have swept the others, it is likely that the Arab revolutions will be the briefest in history. Unlike military coups, party revolts or de-colonialization movements, the Arab street moved into a new path with minimal bloodshed and no national fragmentation. The revolutionaries were peaceful, civilized and non-ideological. They aim to free man and better his conditions rather than to transform societies and their governance into a new ideological state of being. These have been revolutions of modernization using the technologies of their age. They also constitute a new model for the genre: no leader, no ideological program and no organized popular bases, rather, an accumulated popular demand for change.

After the 1967 war and the demonstrated failure of Arab Nationalist regimes and their programs, Arab Nationalist consciousness appeared to many as a hollow sentimentality devoid of tenability on the ground. The revolutions have startlingly showed that Arabs feel their tragedies and their triumphs in common and experience some kind of joint destiny. The revolutions cascaded from each other bringing the same slogans and sounding the same cry for salvation. Thus, we are witnessing the emergence of a new Arab dawn. It is one of many commonalities, but of differences as well. It evokes an interdependent destiny in a decentralized future Commonwealth of co-operation. The political systems of this new dawn, as one gleans from the revolutionaries, stand on respect for the citizen, on his right to choose his governors and to call them into account. The revolutions are instructing their citizens that their social contract is based on citizen-sovereignty and not on state subjugation, and that open and liberal democracy is what gives expression to that. The way the various strata of society came together means that all freedoms must be rooted in tolerating differences in ideas, values and traditions. Hopefully, the Arabs will have no governments above the people and in disregard of public opinion; nor will they have governments tolerant of privileges and corruption.

The street revolutions proved that successful economic and social performance is what determines the legitimacy and continuity of any government in the long run. Governments are there to serve their people and improve their economic wellbeing. The ushering in of democracy in the Arab World with all types of freedoms will inevitably improve economic performance. Modern history shows that failure does not last long in democracies.

Given the labor and capital resources of the Arab World, there is no reason that real GDP growth should not be three to four percentage points above the growth of population. We are therefore talking about a 6% to 8% growth per annum in real terms. To achieve this range of growth, which many other developing countries have done, women must join the labor force. As we argued above, such participation can add 1.2% to the secular growth of GDP and can also diminish population growth as demonstrated in all comparative demographic data. According to statistical evidence on growth and unemployment, Okun's Law, the Arab countries need some 3% to 4% growth in per capita income to tackle their unemployment problem. In the long run, the Arab World is called upon to invest heavily in education, knowledge and public health. This has been the secret of the success of the emerging economies like China, India, Malaysia, Brazil, South Korea and Turkey, and before that the US and Europe. Education has quantitative and qualitative dimensions. The quality side has been missing in Arab education as shown above. The decision to shift resources from armaments, privileged patronage and budget subsidies to health and education implies a shift of some 8% to 10% of GDP into such expenditures. This will only be possible under democratic authority.

The revolutions, if successful, will change the role of Arabs in the contemporary world. Democracy will give expression to the will of the Arab masses and bring forth the independent foreign policies of the Arab states. For the first time in three generations, the Arabs will determine what happens in their region. The Palestinian problem will have a new lease on life. The new Arab state system will result in revising the institutions of Arab co-operation, the Arab League, and will express the communality of the Arab people in some form of meaningful regional Commonwealth of co-operation. The spread of democracy will bring Egypt back to its leading role. With that, both Iran and Turkey will have a smaller role than at present.

Fears are expressed in the West that the Islamists will take advantage of democracy or hijack the Arab revolutions. These are rather understandable but unjustified fears. The Islamists will be present in the future political scene; they are a part of the people. But they will be forced, by their minority status, to play by the democratic rules. Islamists prosper when they are an oppressed opposition. If they are allowed to compete, their deficiencies will become apparent: they have no specified program, they have no particular expertise, their record where they gained power is hardly impressive and their attachment to the past will always render them out of touch; it is not enough to be a good Muslim to run well a government. Among the young crowds in Tahrir Square, the Islamists were followers and not leaders, and their appeal among the educated young was limited. It would seem that robust liberal democracy is the best protection against such fears.

The self-image of the average Arab has been long warped by frustration and a deep sense of failure resulting in low self-esteem. There were Arabs and outsiders who wrote books psychoanalyzing the Arabs and the Arab mind-set. For the entire modern era, the West, in particular its self-satisfied elites, have considered the Arab uncivilized, prone to emotionalism and irrationality and incapable of good governance. In the last two decades, Islamists succeeded in adding another slur: that Muslims are violent, intolerant and a good many of them, terrorists. These revolutions will transform these caricatures and discourage stereotyping. Their results will in time remove failure from being a fixture in the contemporary Arab condition and psyche.

When achievement and success become apparent, the spirit and the face of the Arab World will shift. A period of failed Nationalist militarist and dictatorial governments over the past 60 years will have come to end. This part of the world will no longer be associated with wealthy petrol Sheikhs riding in dark limousines and holding absolute power, or megalomaniac psychopaths like Gaddafi and Saddam, who bombard their own people, or incoherent half-educated leaders incapable of sustaining serious thinking. The Arabs will be ruled and represented by their betters and not by the adventurists of fortune and beneficiaries of accidents of history. Their elites will undoubtedly participate in the public function. The youth of the revolutions were the first installment of such a change; and what a difference in spirit, enthusiasm and hope that will make.

Geneva, 14 April 2011

Notes

1. See for an extended discussion, see Sakbani (2007).
2. Mohammad Hasanain Haykal, the well-known Egyptian collaborator, journalist and adviser of President Nasser, reported on these differences in his Al Jazeera program, 'With Haykal', in 2010 (Haykal 2010).
3. For a detailed discussion of this cohabitation, see Sakbani (2007, pp. 8–14).
4. World Bank, *World development report*, various issues, especially 2008 and 2009.
5. Wikileaks, second set of papers.
6. Syria forwarded its candidacy for joining the World Trade Organization (WTO) some time ago. The WTO decided in 2010 to take up the matter. It will be imperative to liberalize the economy and decrease state-sector domination if this candidacy is to go anywhere.
7. The author believes this to be an underestimation in view of the unemployment and income distribution figures as well as the demographic growth.

References

Arab Monetary Fund (AMF), n.d. *Unified Arab economic report.* League of Arab States, Arab Monetary Fund, Arab Fund for Economic and Social Development and AOPEC.

Banque Central de la Tunisie (BCT), 2009. *Rapport annuel* [Annual Report]. Available from: http://www.bct.gov.tn/bct/siteprod/francais/publications/rapport.jsp [Accessed 22 March 2011]

Central Bank of Egypt, 2009. *Balance of payments.* Available from: www.cbe.org.eg/public/Annual_2008-2009.pdf [Accessed 12 March 2011]

CIA, 2010. *World fact book.* Central Intelligence Agency. Available from: https://www.cia.gov/library/publications/the-world-factbook.

Economy Watch, n.d. *Syrian economy.* Available from: http://www.economywatch.com/world_economy/syria/ [Accessed 23 March 2011].

Haq, T., Schmidt, D., and Tzannatos, Z., 2011. The labour market after the crisis in the Arab States. Paper presented at: Research conference on key lessons from the crisis and way forward, International Labor Organization, 16 February, Geneva. Available from: http://www.ilo.org/public/english/bureau/inst/download/rc_confdownload/tariq.pdf [Accessed 22 March 2011].

Haykal, Mohammad Hasanain, 2010. 'With Haykial', Al Jazeera TV.

ILO, 2011a. Libya: international employment statistics. *CIA World Factbook.* Washington: Central Intelligence Agency. Available from: https://www.cia.gov/library/publications/the-world-factbook/geos/ly.html [Accessed 23 March 2011].

ILO, 2011b. Syria: international employment statistics. *CIA World Factbook.* Washington: Central Intelligence Agency. Available from: https://www.cia.gov/library/publications/the-world-factbook/geos/sy.html [Accessed 23 March 2011].

Sakbani, M., 2007. *Islamic militancy and the failure of economic and social development in the Arab World.* Available from: www.michaelsakbani.blogspot.com [Accessed 23 March 2011].

Sakbani, M., 2010. *Iraq: the epilogue of a tragic decision.* Available from: www.michaelsakbani.blogspot.com [Accessed 23 March 2011].

UNESCO, 2010. *Science report.* Available from: http://www.unesco.org/new/en/natural-sciences/science-technology/prospective-studies/unesco-science-report/unesco-science-report-2010/download-report/ [Accessed 22 March 2011].

United Nations Childrens' Fund (UNICEF), n.d. *Human development report.* Available from: http://hdr.undp.org/en/countries/ [Accessed 22 March 2011].

United Nations Development Program (UNDP), 2010. *Arab human development report: Arab education,* chapter 3.

Wikipedia, 2011. *Economy of Syria.* Available from: http://en.wikipedia.org/wiki/Economy_of_Syria [Accessed 23 March 2011].

World Bank, 2009. *Egypt: development indicators database.* Available from: http://data.worldbank.org/country/egypt-arab-republic [Accessed 22 March 2011].

World Bank, 2010a. *Egypt: data & statistics.* Available from: http://data.worldbank.org/country/egypt-arab-republic [Accessed 22 March 2011].

World Bank, 2010b. Libya: development indicators database. Available from: www. World-bank.org/country/Libya [Accessed 12 March 2011].

World Bank, 2010c. *Syria: economic development indicators.* Available from: http://data.worldbank.org/country/syrian-arab-republic [Accessed 22 March 2011].

World Bank, 2010d. *Tunisia: development indicators database.* Available from: http://data.worldbank.org/country/tunisia [Accessed 22 March 2011].

World-Class Universities (WCU), n.d. *Academic ranking of world universities* (ARWU). Available from: http://www.arwu.org/ [Accessed 22 March 2011].

On the Arab 'Democratic Spring': lessons derived

Khair El-Din Haseeb

Over the last three months a wave of revolutions, uprisings and strikes – aiming to realize democracy according to its primary concepts – and which began with a peaceful, non-violent revolution in Tunisia that then spread to Egypt, has occurred in a number of Arab countries.[1] As a result, regimes in both countries were brought down, and both countries are taking important steps in order to consolidate the primary elements of the revolution and establish a new system in each, despite some fears which have not ceased but which are diminishing. Subsequently, these peaceful uprisings spread to Yemen where they began with demands to undertake radical reforms which did not preclude 'negotiations' with the regime as a means to achieve this aim. After the authorities used violence in confronting demonstrators, demands shifted to the overthrow of the regime of President 'Ali 'Abdullah Saleh; subsequently, the government on 23 March – and after it was too late – offered to submit to terms previously proposed which it had initially refused. Simultaneously, it declared a state of emergency, and the situation appears to be on the brink of a revolution. 'Demonstrations' occurred in Oman; however, up to the present, the regime has wisely managed to contain them and to respond to and constrain principle demands.

Similarly, a peaceful 'uprising' occurred in Bahrain, undertaken primarily by groups deprived of their rights – representative of the majority of the Bahraini people – most of whom had reached a consensus to demand radical modifications to the system and transformation to a constitutional monarchy. These were confronted by an offer from the regime for dialogue along with stern repressive measures that pushed other factions to join the opposition under the banner of bringing down the regime. Subsequently, events developed until they reached the point where the Bahraini government sought and received military support from Saudi Arabia and the United Arab Emirates (UAE), when it declared a state of emergency and martial law. The Bahraini regime deployed the mostly hybrid army and used excessive violence with the unquestioning support of the Gulf Co-operation Council (GCC) regimes. There were signs of demonstrations and limited protests in Saudi Arabia and Kuwait; however these have, until now, been contained through the undertaking of a number of measures of a material nature, which involved too much money but little freedom. Yet this is a wound which has been bound only temporarily.

This phenomenon has transitioned to Jordan but yet remains limited. Demands have vacillated between 'constitutional monarchy' and 'overthrow of the regime'. The Jordanian government is attempting to contain and placate elements seeking changes and has formed a dialogue committee to deal with the draft demands. Similarly, Syria is witnessing demonstrations in various cities, most of which are fielding demands for democracy, with a few local social and economic concerns, with some casualties in Dar'a and Latakia. The Syrian authorities promised to meet some of the demands of the demonstrators shortly, and seem to have contained the demonstrators for the time being. Demonstrations have spread to most population sectors in Iraq where most demands have revolved around public services with some others being political in nature; these have pervaded both Arab and Kurdish regions.

In the countries of the Arab Maghreb and Morocco, in particular, King Muhammad VI anticipated demonstrations by forming a constitutional review committee to increase the powers of the Prime Minister and the Council of Ministers in addition to other matters for the purpose of diminishing the present nature of the 'absolute monarchy' and moving it towards a 'constitutional monarchy'. Despite this, demonstrations were sparked on 21 March in more than 60 Moroccan cities, calling for political, constitutional and economic reforms. Tens of thousands participated in the demonstrations that took different forms of expression aiming towards realizing a 'constitutional monarchy'. In Algeria, some demonstrations which were put down with force occurred; however, the situation differs dramatically from that in other previously mentioned Arab countries to the effect that it is often said: 'If every state has an army, the Algerian army has a state.' The upshot of this is that the Algerian Army represents the liberation army that brought Algeria to liberation and independence, since which time it has exercised power sometimes directly, especially after Boumeddien, and at other times indirectly and clandestinely. The Algerian leadership is currently attempting to pre-empt events, being facilitated in this through its significant fiscal capabilities deriving from oil and gas revenues. It is attempting this by taking political and economic measures to contain probable demands by nullifying the state of emergency and undertaking other social and economic action.

As for Mauritania, the 'tsunami' has yet to reach its shores in a significant fashion, whereas Lebanon is a different case: there are impracticalities to undertaking popular action that transcend sectarian and confessional lines as well as the material interests of some of the ruling class. Lebanon is currently witnessing initial and limited, but diffuse, attempts, where there are weekly youth demonstrations on Sundays (this being the official day off in Lebanon) calling for: abolition of confessionalism and sectarianism; promulgation of a democratic elections law; and a unified civil-status law. These demonstrations have been increasing in number, but their future impact will depend to a large degree upon their ability to persevere. However, it is not anticipated that the tumultuous Arab democratic tidal wave will reach Lebanon due to the complicated nature of its political and social structure.

In terms of lessons which may be drawn, it is possible to note the following:

(1) There is an erroneous overgeneralization in the use of the term 'revolution' with regard to all of the aforementioned events. The term 'revolution' is seldom employed without confirmation of the proper significations of this expression when it is most typically employed to describe a military *coup*, an uprising or a temporary mass insurrection that leads to some sort of cosmetic change restricted to the existing ruling regime. Whereas, the precise definition of 'revolution' connotes 'all actions and events that lead to radical changes in the political, social and economic reality of a given people or group in a comprehensive and persuasive way over an extended period of time and from which results a modification to the structure of social thought among the revolting people as well as the re-distribution of resources and political powers'. Many social scientists insist on defining 'revolution' as connoting a 'comprehensive fundamental change in the distribution of the sources of wealth and the production processes in society'.[2] While this definition is

applicable to a great extent to the revolutions of Egypt and Tunisia, it might also be applicable to the uprising in Yemen, provided that President 'Ali 'Abdullah Saleh's regime is toppled, which is quite likely. As for Libya, the term may be appropriate if the opposition there is able to extirpate what still remains of al-Qadhafi's regime, a mission that might take relatively longer to accomplish in comparison to the timeframes of Egypt and Tunisia.

Until such occurs it is problematic to term what is currently transpiring in Yemen and Libya as 'revolutions', as until now they are more apt to be termed 'uprisings', which might later be considered revolutions if the regimes are deposed and the outcomes are radical changes in the nature of both systems. As for events taking place in other Arab states, these are not showing signs of being more than limited uprisings: expanding horizontally without discounting the possibility that they may transform into far-flung and total rebellions, and possibly into genuine revolutions.

It is important to emphasize the peaceful and non-violent nature of these revolts and uprisings, even in cases of self-defense, with the exception of the Libyan opposition forces that were compelled to resort to violence in order to defend themselves. This represents a substantial and qualitative development in the means to which the Arab opposition movements can resort, which would never have achieved what they have today had they resorted to violence or had they been drawn into using it in their bid to achieve their demands.[3]

(2) Practical experience in Tunisia and Egypt, and contrary to the preconceptions of many, has shown that radical change from within is viable without resort to outside intervention, as in the case, for instance, where some have attempted to justify seeking foreign intervention for precipitating change in Iraq.

(3) It is also evident that it is relatively simpler to topple a regime than to construct a new one, as is suggested by the experiences of Egypt and Tunisia. For the purpose of reaching a consensus among opposition forces – whether they be individuals or groups – agreement on overthrowing an autocratic regime is much easier than reaching agreement on the nature of the new system and the means to achieve it. Moreover, establishing the foundations of a new system is considerably more exposed to risks and threats of conflict between the revolutionary parties, which gives an opportunity to counter-revolutionary forcers to maneuver and sabotage the establishment of an alternative system. Until now, Egypt and Tunisia have been able to overcome some of these obstacles and succeed in imposing a timetable for undertaking parliamentary and presidential elections as well as drafting a new constitution. There are still, however, obstacles and challenges lying ahead of these two countries which they will need to surmount.

(4) In an attempt to clarify and pursue the point raised above, it is necessary to stress that in order to attain social justice and real development that deals with the issue of unemployment, establishing a democratic regime alone is not sufficient to achieve the social and economic goals of the revolutions completed thus far and the ones expected in Yemen and Libya. Since democracy is an 'obligatory and requisite condition and not a sufficient one' it is therefore necessary to accomplish the economic and social aims of every revolution, but democracy alone is not sufficient. These objectives of the

revolution cannot be attained without sustainable economic and social development in tandem with social justice. Social justice means the 'increase of production and a fair distribution', which is a more complicated and problematic matter than bringing down a despotic and corrupt regime. Furthermore, the revolution in both Egypt and Tunisia has temporarily eliminated country revenues from tourism, reduced production and services in some sectors as well as precipitated some capital flight from the country among other negative results, and this is among that which necessitates making people aware that they should not harbor excessively high economic and social expectations so as to prevent falling into major disappointment.

(5) Tunisia ought to be granted a patent in pioneering the revolutionary movements as the Tunisians were the first to break the barrier of fear, which constituted the major obstacle in the face of unleashing popular fury and resentment over deteriorating economic, social and political conditions which needed only a spark to explode forth. The Tunisian revolution was the catalyst that instigated the Egyptian revolt and uprisings in other countries. Despite the limited significance of Tunisia in the regional Arab system, its role in breaking the barrier of fear was of paramount importance, which should not be underestimated, and which exceeded Tunisia's traditional role in the regional scheme.

(6) The most important event that has occurred in the Arab World until now is the revolution in Egypt – due to its weight in the Arab regional system and which has long been absent – and the absence of which constitutes one of the factors in the collapse of this system. It is temporarily both understandable and acceptable that the revolution in Egypt has yet to exhibit its Arab dimension so as not to incite opposition because, for the time being, Egypt is passing through a critical period that entails a grave need to mitigate and immobilize opponents. Therefore, we see no serious Arab criticism leveled at the absence of an Arab dimension to the revolution, and we see the announcement of its intention to abide by international agreements (which include the Camp David accords). Nevertheless, Egypt needs to send messages of reassurance to Arabs concerning its Arab viewpoint while at the same time avoiding new problems at the international level. Among these long-awaited messages and actions is the opening of the Rafah border crossing between Egypt and Gaza, and not on a temporary basis restricted only to individuals, as has been the case until now, but rather on a permanent footing for both people and goods alike. The second required message and action is to stop pumping gas from Egypt to Israel, regardless of whatever pretext might be offered for such, where some conflicting reports have been issued on this subject, and while realizing that the agreement between Egypt and the Israeli corporation involved does not fall under the rubric of international accords. Also among required measures is cessation of the joint Israeli–Egyptian industrial production initiative – the Joint Qualifying Industrial Zones Agreement in Egyptian territory known as 'QIZ' – for the reason that it represents a form of normalization which is not binding on Egypt as per the Camp David accords.

(7) What is currently transpiring of revolutions, uprisings and their symbolic implications suggests a total Arab awakening to unity and massive interaction in the Arab consciousness. If it is not the case, then why is it that these Arab events did not diffuse to some of the sub-Saharan African countries, some of

which suffer from the likes of the despotism, poverty and corruption experienced in the Arab countries?

(8) It is arbitrary to term the revolutions of Egypt and Tunisia and all the revolts and uprisings currently being witnessed as 'youth revolutions'. For while it is the youth who instigated these events, all or most classes of society who suffered the injustices of these regimes in Egypt, Tunisia and Yemen have participated and played a significant role in these revolts and uprisings. Thus, objectively, it is appropriate to term the revolts in Egypt and Tunisia as 'popular revolutions' and those in Yemen and Libya as 'popular uprisings'.

(9) Experience of what has transpired up to now confirms that the uprisings, which have succeeded and transformed into realized revolutions, are those which have been able to secure the neutrality of the army and preclude it from opposing or quashing them after the inability of other security apparatuses to do so. The Tunisian revolution succeeded because the Tunisian Army is small in size, poorly armed and not politicized. Similarly, the revolution in Egypt succeeded because it was able to secure the neutrality of the army initially to prevent an attempt to quash the uprising and subsequently to oblige it to accede to its goals once the revolution expanded and increased in scope and the dimensions of its success had become clear. The situation was different in Yemen and Bahrain where it appeared initially that the respective armies had stood by the regimes, but where subsequently – in recent days in Yemen – segments have broken away and a majority has sided in support of the uprisings, with the exception of the Republican Guards and the Supreme Command that has not ceased to support the Yemeni President. Likewise, the Bahraini Army, which is composed by a majority of non-Bahrainis, has backed the regime and acted to suppress the uprisings.

(10) Events have clarified the error of adopting slogans identical to those of the Tunisian and Egyptian revolutions – in regard to regime overthrow – in all cases of change. Where there were monarchial/royalist regimes (or what resembled such), the slogan of overthrowing the regime connotes overthrow of the King or the monarchy, which has impelled these monarchs to rely on every internal and external means, including foreign military bases, in order to quell these uprisings.[4] What is more correct – both theoretically and practically – is the demand for 'constitutional monarchy', which bears the possibility of favorable reception among Arab peoples as well as foreign; and moreover, its implementation is considerably less complicated than other options.

(11) It can be inferred, with a measure of confidence, that that the role of Islamic fronts and currents – with the exception of Bahrain – has not been primary, without discounting their participation wherever they were found.[5] Thus it is no longer possible for these regimes or the international forces which back them to operate on the pretext or maintain the claim of fear that Islamists will take control over these regimes. These recent events have also shown that the role of 'social communication' means, such as Facebook and others, is surpassing that of the 'mosque' in mobilizing people in uprisings. Similarly these revolutions, uprisings and have weakened 'al-Qāʿidah'.[6]

(12) There is an overemphasis on the role of social means of communication (Facebook, Twitter and others) in effecting these revolutions and uprisings. It is true that such means facilitated initiating and igniting these events;

however, these uprisings and revolutions could not have marshaled all these various social factions if there had not been a sufficient accumulation of consciousness for the requisite radical reforms in which different political and conceptual orientations have factored over the past 40 years. This is in addition to the fact that that revolutions have occurred in contemporary history in Iran and Indonesia without the availability of these and similar means of social communication.

(13) The position of Arab media vis-à-vis these revolutions, uprisings and their effects and implications has been varied, and especially that of satellite channels. At a time when the Al Jazeera satellite channel played an important role in the Tunisian and Egyptian revolutions and the opposition uprisings in Libya and Yemen, it has exercised considerable restraint in regard to what has occurred and is transpiring in the countries of the Gulf Cooperation Council – especially in regard to Oman, Bahrain and Saudi Arabia – and this has had an impact on its credibility among both Arab and foreign audiences. This applies to Arab satellite channels and media, in general, and in particular to Gulf news services as well as Moroccan and Algerian media where silence or partisanship and bias was overt, which – regrettably – led Arab viewers and readers to rely on satellite broadcasts of the Arabic-language BBC as being relatively more objective in the comprehensiveness of its coverage than Arab news media in general.

(14) There is a fear that consensus will not be reached among the various social and political forces that participated in bringing down the regimes in Tunisia and Egypt. That is, they do not agree on the characteristics of the new regime which they are attempting to establish and which might pave the way for a counter-revolution to exploit these differences and factions as well as derail the process of realizing the general goals of the revolution in the new system. This demands the establishment of a 'historical bloc' or 'front' or 'coalition' through which agreement may be reached for an interim transitional program for a period of two to three years, to comply with this and enter into elections for parliaments, the promulgation of new constitutions as well as establishing a new system on this basis in general. In addition to the danger of leaving the way open for counter-revolutionary activity if this is not achieved, there is also the danger that there will be difficulty in holding new parliamentary elections due to the inability to achieve a concordant majority agreeing on a transitional program. Also, there is a risk that these elections may precipitate the formation of small parliamentary blocs that will stand in the way of the elected parliaments and keep them from adopting what is expected of them in terms of radical modifications; moreover, this is one of the possible and sometimes probable negative potentialities in democratic parliamentary elections.

(15) The positions of regional Arab regimes towards these revolutions, uprisings and their implications is divergent and sometimes contradictory – in accordance with the nature of their political structures and their interests – and constitutes an expression of dichotomous dual standards, worthy of concern. At a time when Arab Gulf regimes kept silent about what occurred in Tunisia, Egypt, Yemen, Jordan and Syria, they enthusiastically supported the Libyan uprisings, while simultaneously standing by the current regimes in Oman and Bahrain. In particular, they supported the Bahraini regime and Saudi and UAE military intervention against a large segment of the Bahraini population. Likewise, with

the exception of Qatar, they took a negative stance towards the uprisings in Yemen and are vigilant about the continuity of the current regime. Iranian and Turkish positions towards events in the Arab World have diverged, with Iran supporting all that has transpired with a failed attempt to cast it in terms of a 'Middle East Islamic revolution' and with Turkey remaining hesitant and neutral given the clear impact on its economic interests in the region.

(16) As for Israel, it was panic-stricken over changes occurring in Egypt and Tunisia, and it took a negative position towards these incidents. As for the international positions, especially those of the United States, the European Union (EU), Russia and China, we must dispel illusions about the reality of the US position in particular, and that of the EU to a certain extent, towards Arab regimes and their willingness for these to transform them into democratic ones. Despite some of the slogans that they iterate at times, the essence of their genuine position is to preserve corrupt Arab autocratic and undemocratic regimes, as these realize their interests which conflict with those of the peoples of Arab countries. Transformation of these regimes into democratic ones which incorporate the participation of their peoples in primary decision-making processes will preclude their national security from remaining at the mercy of the United States and its allies as well as what is connected to this of imposed billion-dollar arms sales without defining the real enemy. Similarly, such a transition would adversely impact US military air- and naval bases which it maintains currently, the cost of which is paid by some Arab Gulf regimes. Likewise, these peoples will not permit the continued pilfering of oil and gas revenues by their rulers, with the exception of Kuwait, and to earmark and apportion whatever they will for the national budget of their populations. Additionally, investments will not remain with their public and private dividends what they are, without consideration of genuine interests. The people of these countries will not tolerate Westernization and distortion of their Arab identity through the imposition of English-language educational curricula at all levels as a first language, in addition to the role of non-Arab expatriate workers in misrepresenting and maligning this identity. The Arab peoples will demand 'just' prices for their vital oil and gas resources, commensurate with the price increases of various goods in the West. They will not permit their regimes to continue to sell oil at current prices, which despite recent increases is still almost equivalent to 1970s real prices, after taking into account the inflation which has occurred during the intervening period.

As for Russia and China, they will proceed essentially according to their economic interests in the Arab World, with concomitant consideration of their obligations to the United States and Europe and their interests which lie therein.

(17) In general, the double standards of the US and the European Union have become clear vis-à-vis current democratic changes transpiring and those which might occur in other Arab countries. The US and EU remained silent then neutral until the fall of the regimes in Egypt and Tunisia became evident to them. Gradually, a change was precipitated in their position towards lukewarm support for the revolutions in both countries. They tentatively supported the Libyan uprising then adopted – under the rubric of humanitarian objectives

and under the cover of the Arab League and a Gulf initiation – the imposition of a no-fly zone over Libya to prevent al-Qadhafi's air forces from attacking civilians. Yet it has maintained silence over the hostilities of the Yemeni regime against demonstrators and many casualties and, similarly, has backed regimes in Oman, Bahrain[7] and Saudi Arabia in their positions towards the uprisings in them, with modest reservations over the use of violence against demonstrators. N.D. Kristof says: 'Today the United States is in a vise – caught between our allies and our values. And the problem with our pal Bahrain is not just that it is shooting protesters but also that it is something like an apartheid state. Sunni Muslims rule the country, and now they are systematically trying to crush an overwhelmingly Shiite protest movement.'[8]

(18) As for Russia and China, they both avoided taking clear positions due to their desires to abide by economic interests. Furthermore, during the United Nations Security Council meeting they abstained from voting on the Libyan no-fly zone draft resolution, where if they had utilized their veto powers, the resolution would not have passed.

As for the future and the possible development of these events in the relevant Arab countries and their related needs, the following may be reasonably asserted:

(1) The success of the democratic revolution in Egypt and Tunisia and later in Yemen requires economic and fiscal support in order to realize its purpose and social and economic promises to the respective peoples, for the reason that their internal revenues do not enable them to achieve the necessary growth with the requisite speed which is in order. In order not to leave them at the mercy of the conditions of American and European aid and assistance which may or may not come – with all the associated political and economic pressures which can be expected to accompany such – there is certainly urgent and pressing need for the establishment of an Arab financial support fund that should be created swiftly through an Arab Economic Summit, in which Arab oil producing countries with financial surplus, such as Saudi Arabia, Kuwait, Qatar, the United Arab Emirates and Algeria, would create a fund as a reflection of their good intentions and in expiation and atonement for the negative positions of the majority of them towards the revolutions.

(2) It is expected that the 'democratic spring' will complete its course successfully and that the uprisings in Yemen will culminate in a revolution that will bring down the regime of 'Ali 'Abdullah Saleh in the near future.

(3) As for Libya, it is predicted, unfortunately, that the current bloodbath will continue for some time and that Colonel Qadhafi will persist in destroying hearth and home. However, the regime will fall and come to an end after a high price in human lives and material is paid. It is incumbent upon the opposition, despite its understandable circumstances and its being compelled to resort to outside support to impose a no-fly zone against al-Qadhafi's regime, to distance itself from seeking support of the West on the ground in the completion of its revolution. This must be the case no matter what it entails of extended time and greater sacrifices and casualties, as to seek the aid of the West on the ground would be 'the kiss of death' for it.

(4) In the case of Bahrain, wisdom may yet prevail, and the regime may transition to dialogue with the opposition in its entirety to realize essential graduated and

continuous constitutional reforms which will lead eventually to 'constitutional monarchy'.

(5) In Morocco, it is anticipated that the perspicacity of the King and what he will undertake of immanent rapid changes towards constitutional monarchy will obviate the need of the Moroccan people to resort to revolution.

(6) As for Algeria, the lifting of the state of emergency indicates the awareness of the regime of the danger of situation; however, much depends on the extent of the limited scope of the capacity of the President to pre-empt matters and to achieve the minimum in terms of steps towards establishing genuine democracy in the country.

(7) In Jordan, it is hoped that the regime will act rationally in facilitating what will realize genuine reforms on the path towards constitutional monarchy. Perhaps establishing a committee of national leaders in Jordan to propose these amendments would constitute a step in this direction.

(8) In Syria, where the situation differs to a large degree from that of other Arab regimes due to the American stance towards it and its policies towards Palestine, it is compelled to introduce serious political and economic reforms and fight corruption within. It is hoped that it will comprehend the lesson from current events before it is too late.

(9) In the case of Saudi Arabia, it is doubtful that the nature of its regime and the mindset of its rulers will permit the realization of a sufficient measure of reforms that might be able to shield it from the winds of change in the Arab World.

Conclusion

In conclusion, it might be said that whatever the extent of difficulties and hardships in consolidating the successes that have been achieved up to now, what has happened is significant and there is no going back. The new Arab renaissance is knocking on the door of all Arab regimes where the choice is between that of the regimes submitting themselves to gradual peaceful and orderly transition towards democracy or a revolutionary change. It is our hope that this will be without violence and imposed from within by the peoples who are still under the yoke of tyranny. Thus, some of the corrupt and autocratic Arab regimes have met their fate, and there are those that are still awaiting it. And as it is said in the holy Qur'an: 'And We did not wrong them, but they wronged themselves.'[9] The revolutions of Tunisia and Egypt have shown us that 'the nights are yet pregnant with all manner of wonders'.

Notes

1. I completed writing this editorial on 24 March 2011. Therefore I could not attend to the development of events after this date and before the publication of this issue of *Contemporary Arab Affairs*.
2. 'Arʿūrī, Nassīr (2011).
3. It is not obvious from the interviews that I conducted recently in Egypt that the youths of the revolution in Tunisia and Egypt were aware of Gene Sharp's literature on the subject of 'non-violent revolutions'. However, an article by Ruaridh Arrow (2011) indicated that

when he visited the liberation square in Cairo on 2 March 2011, he found that some of those who were trained in Gene's work were either under arrest or under surveillance. Also see Sharp (1984–2005).

4. In his article 'Is Arab spring over for youth?', Michael Slackman (2011) says that 'the Arab Spring is not necessarily over, but it has run up against dictators willing to use force to preserve their power'.
5. Slackman (2011) adds, 'what surprised many was the absence of religious discourse and the embrace of pluralism'.
6. See Scott (2011).
7. It is worth noting that 'it's almost impossible for Shiites to be hired by the army or police' (Kristof 2011, p. 7); he adds: 'The Arab democracy Spring that began with such exhilaration in Tunisia and Egypt is now enduring a brutal winter in Libya, Bahrain, Saudi Arabia and Yemen.'
8. Kristof (2011).
9. Reference is made to qur'ānic verse 101 of *sūrat hūd* (Q 11:101).

Bibliography

'Ar'ūrī, Nassīr, 2011. Istishrāf lima'ālāt al-Thawrāt al-'Arabīyah. Available from: http://www.aljazeera.net/NR/exeres/61D2E551-B85B-470B-BB9F-C0F22648B8BB.htm [Accessed 30 March 2011].

Arrow, R, 2011. Gene Sharp: author of the nonviolent revolution rulebook. Available from: http://www.bbc.co.uk/news/world-middle-east-12522848 and in Arabic in *Al-Quds Al-Arabi*, 7 March 2011, p. 10 [Accessed 30 March 2011].

Kristof, N.D., 2011. Bahrain pulls a Qaddafi. *International Herald Tribune,* 18 March. Available from: http://www.post-gazette.com/pg/11077/1132725-109.stm [Accessed 30 March 2011].

Shane, S., 2011. As regimes fall in Arab World, Al Qaeda sees history fly by. *New York Times,* 27 February. Available from: http://www.nytimes.com/2011/02/28/world/middleeast/28qaeda.html?_r=1 [Accessed 30 March 2011].

Sharp, G., 1982–2005. *The politics of nonviolent action.* 3 vols. Boston, MA: Porter Sargent Publishers.

Slackman, M., 2011. Is Arab Spring over for youth? *International Herald Tribune,* 18 March. Available from: http://www.pressdisplay.com/pressdisplay/viewer.aspx [Accessed 30 March 2011].

Post-Gaddafi Libya: Interactive Dynamics and the Political Future*

Youssef M. Sawani

Acting Director General, Center for Arab Unity Studies, Beirut, Lebanon and Professor of Political Science, University of Tripoli, Libya

Libya's contemporary history has been dominated by the interplay of the perpetual dynamics of religion, tribalism, oil and ideology. After 42 years in power Gaddafi was killed at the hands of revolutionaries and the final chapter of his dictatorial reign was terminated. With direct and powerful support from the North Atlantic Treaty Organization (NATO) and some Arab governments the revolution was another reflection of the supremacy of the perpetual dynamics. The purpose of this chapter is to examine the interaction of these dynamics and how they are echoed in post-Gaddafi Libya. An assessment is made of the manifestations related to these dynamics by providing a sketch of existing social and political features. This will help determine the fundamentals that shape the foreseeable future of the country and predict the role of the various political forces interacting in the field. The role of foreign powers in the downfall of the Gaddafi regime is also analyzed and developments related to it are reflected upon in an attempt to evaluate their impact on Libya's present and future. The chapter is a product of direct research, analysis, eye-witness accounts and discussions in Libya with important personages and representatives of powerful currents now currently competing on the scene and vying for influence in the determination of the future of the country after Gaddafi.

Foreword

An assessment of the future of post-Gaddafi Libya must address questions and challenges related to the war that led to Mu'ammar Gaddafi's fall, in which forces of various orientations were involved and in which foreign forces played a highly influential and decisive role. Of equal concern is the fact that Libya today lacks an effective political authority, just as it lacks an accumulated political experience of the sort that might be of assistance in contemplating the future of the country, even if one can discern something about the future by examining the orientations of the major forces prevailing in the field and their political and social topography. The course of events that have unfolded in Libya since 17 February 2011 was unexpected. Military operations ended on 20 August 2011 and the National Transitional Council (NTC) became the formal authority of a Libya free of Gaddafi. However, the situation on the ground is far from one of peace, law and order since armed clashes are a daily norm while the edifices of state or an effective government are missing, at least in the civil sense.

Libya has witnessed a massive influx, if not to say a *scramble*, by various international powers, keen from the inception of the revolt in February 2011 to play a role in

* This is an updated version of 'Post-Gaddafi Libya: Interactive Dynamics and the Political Future', *Contemporary Arab Affairs*, Vol. 5, No. 1, January-March 2012.

shaping the outcome of the fighting and controlling the dynamics of the combatants as well as limiting and defining the form of political society or the future state in Libya. There had been no common cause that brought together the Libyan political or armed forces except the goal of completely overthrowing Gaddafi's regime. The strength of this unifying factor appears to have waned after the killing of Gaddafi and with the cessation of military actions. The ensuing situation will open up new and potentially unlimited frontiers of possibility for the future of Libya at the levels of identity, national integration, democratic transformation and determinants of the whole new political order.

An attempt will be made here to sketch the features of society and politics in Libya from political, economic and social perspectives. The aim is to bring into focus the dynamics that constitute the fundamentals shaping the foreseeable future of the country. After this, the analysis will proceed to present a map of the various political forces and currents now interacting in the field. This will serve, to the degree that such is possible, to predict their future trajectories, on the basis of the elements and referents from which they have emerged. Lastly, analysis of the transitional phase and its various components appears necessary in order to formulate and hazard a preliminary response – by no means conclusive – to the question of where Libya is headed. However, this subject will be delayed until the end of the discussion. This study derives, in the main, from observation of the developments ongoing since the spark of revolution was ignited, as well as what has been written about these. It also takes into account first-hand information about the activities of the various political forces, in addition to discussions and personal meetings with their representatives, and discussions the author undertook with persons of numerous orientations and views.

Libya and the political–economic dynamics of society: the constraints of the future

The relation between society and state in Libya has remained subject to constraints to do with ideology, tribalism and oil. These were the primary factors that defined the relations of the structure of political authority with the social structure over the past four decades. It is highly probable that these dynamics will play a similar role in the future of the country after the fall of Gaddafi (Mislmāni 1999, pp. 66–75).

In order to grasp these dynamics, it is necessary to deal with the matter in some detail so as to sketch a panoramic view of contemporary Libya. This should be helpful in anticipating the foreseeable future in terms of the influence of these dynamics. The chapter will begin with the factor of religion that has a clear and fundamental relevance in Libya's history and culture. Religion also has a palpable influence given its association to the expressions that have become abundantly familiar in all the news about the revolution of the Libyan people and the ensuing debate and political contest that have characterized post-Gaddafi Libya.

Religion and politics

Libya has been a Muslim community ever since the advent of Islam in North Africa, and Islam became the religion of all its inhabitants. The vast majority of Libyans are Sunnis who adhere to the Maliki madhab (school of fiqh). Attempts at spreading Shiʿism during the period of the Fāṭimids failed completely, as did attempts to spread other *madhabs* aimed at changing this predominant orientation. The only exception is the existence of a small percentage of Libyans (the Amazigh) who follow the Ibāḍi madhab, which has remained restricted to the region of the Western Mountain. Almost all authorities that ruled Libya including the Ottomans attempted to employ Islam and display that they had credentials attesting to their adherence, care and respect for the people's religion.

Just as Idris and the Sanusi Order proved incapable of bending Libyan Muslims to suit particular ends, failure also proved to be the fate of attempts by Gaddafi's regime to reformulate the Islam of Libya in accordance with its political or religious theses, especially those pertaining to the *sunnah* (i.e. the normative practice of the Prophet Muhammad as reported in the hadith literature) and its status with regard to law and legislation. Despite Gaddafi's suppression of Islamist orientations and the injustice of his regime, fundamentalists (uṣūliyin) and *jihadists* have appeared, especially in the region of the Green Mountain, but their open appearance on the scene has not obscured the tolerant and moderate nature of Libyan Islam.

Undoubtedly, religion has remained a central component of the cultural composition and the definition of Libyan identity. Despite the attempt of Gaddafi to substitute the ideology of the *Green Book* in its place, Islam remained basic and essential to the value structure of Libyan society and the primary formative element of the social system itself. This matter has had special significance after the fall of Gaddafi's regime that unleashed ideological currents deriving from particular and contrasting views of Islam, life and politics. Thus, the ability of Libyans to hold on to their moderate Islam will be subject to a serious test as they contemplate the positions they ought to take towards extremist trends. The debates that have characterized post-Gaddafi Libya attest to the waning of whatever influence his ideas on religion may have acquired. Though echoes of his stance against the Muslim Brotherhood can be traced in the discourse against them, Libyans seem well determined to distance themselves from any politicized views that depart from their moderate Islam. Libya's first democratic elections held in July affirmed a tendency against extremism. The results showed that moderate liberals and nationalists made gains at the expense of Islamists.

Tribalism and political authority

Libya is home to a rich tapestry of tribes scattered across the country with numerous small tribal enclaves. This proliferation of tribes leads to complexities that render differentiation between them anything but simple. Both the regimes of King Idriss and Gaddafi relied on tribal alliances in the administration of power and recourse to such always had a role in stirring up tribal and regional sensitivities.

It is important to note the amorphous nature and fluidity of tribal alliances in Libya along with the pronounced desires of many tribes to ally themselves with the political authority. This tendency helped Gaddafi to implement a strategy that inflicted severe damage on the tribes and destroyed their power structures, such that they ceased to be an effective force in the political and economic sphere. Gaddafi's regime, its various policies and the repeated abolition and undermining of the various administrative institutions, bodies and formations deepened the crisis of state and, in many instances, paved the way for regime domination of tribal alliances, thereby exacerbating factionalism. This raises questions pertaining to the state and its very existence. It also highlights the possibility of reverting to a federal system in Libya, such as existed before 1963 (Mislmāni 1999, pp. 72–82).

As an indigenous socio-political structure, the tribe did not transform into an institution that works in parallel with modern institutions of state and its central bureaucracy. Researchers suggest that this failure has contributed to diminishing the chances of building a strong civil society. However, it can probably safely be inferred that tribalism in culture and the tribe as an institution will continue to exert influence on socio-political interactions and on individual and group identities in Libyan society. This will be the case so long as Libyans do not perceive the existence of alternative institutions and civil society organizations. It goes without saying that the existence of a civil society that enjoys independence and effectiveness relies on the existence of civic culture and citizenship, wherein individuals discover modern expressions and forms for their orientations and demands (Obeidi 2008, p. 16).

The regime, with the desire to avoid being left without the strong support Warfellah had afforded it, created the People's Social Leadership (PSL) in 1993 to fill the void and institutionalize the security role of all tribes in protecting the regime. Though this institution and its branches were intended to represent tribes and their leaders, it was designed and run for the purpose of maintaining strict control. Most members were Gaddafi loyalists, comrades, revolutionary elements and security and army generals with close personal connections to Gaddafi who entrusted them with the institution. As the PSL was very closely connected to him its longest serving heads were from his own tribe.

In terms of its function in reality, however, the Social Leadership was a parallel institution and used to counter any other manifestations of social entities or structures that proved difficult to control. Since these leaderships were *artificial* creations of Gaddafi, they proved unable to resist pressure or sustain their role in supporting the regime during the uprisings. Notwithstanding that some social leaders were active in rallying the support of their tribes for Gaddafi through propaganda-like tribal conferences, even if the majority of Social Leaders faded away out of the picture or sided with their tribes in revolt.

This phenomenon may be explained by the deep roots tribalism has maintained and its influence on Libyans. Although 80% of the inhabitants of Libya 'live in urban areas', as Libyan sociologist Mustafā al-Tir asserts, 'the vast majority of Libyans still speak of tribal belonging'. Al-Tir (2011) attributes these orientations and self-described affiliations to what he has termed the 'ruralization' of cities where:

> The major urban areas developed as a result of emigration from the countryside and not as a result of natural increase [in population] ... thus, the tribe is still present today in the memory of a large number of urban dwellers. This is especially true since instead of those coming from the countryside integrating into the life of the city and adopting the ways and modes of urban life, they entered the cities, over the last forty years, as though they were conquerors and they imposed on the city and its inhabitants various particulars of rural life.

This persistence of tribal loyalty impinged on the entire process of modernization, and the power of tribal loyalty factored 'in obstructing the transition of society to the stage of modernity'. Though al-Tir considers modernity a precondition for political modernization, he quips that 'when loyalty encroaches upon necessary qualifications, then discussing modern institutions becomes meaningless!' (Al-Tir 2011).

It should be indicated that the revolt against Gaddafi's regime was not based on tribalism and did not witness tribal battles in any readily perceptible or significant sense.

However, the war against Gaddafi was undertaken via means that *did* employ tribalism. It was utilized by both the Gaddafi regime and the NTC. Gaddafi did everything possible to portray the uprisings and their leaderships as driven by tribal interests and separatist orientations. For its part, the NTC was very active in consolidating its legitimacy through tribal declarations of allegiances and thereby discrediting Gaddafi's tactics and claims. The NTC could at least claim that people were brought in to attend the Tripoli tribal gathering, organized and staged by the regime out of fear of reprisals by Gaddafi if they had acted otherwise (Leitsinger 2011).

Gaddafi endeavoured to represent the revolution as though it was limited to particular regions or tribes in an attempt to foment schism, contention and gain control. It is noteworthy that the NTC, which led the revolt, also utilized tribes in order to win advocates – as vividly demonstrated in the Council's co-option of members of Gaddafi's tribe itself in order to undermine his efforts and deprive him of tribal legitimacy at any level. Such tactics serve as a reminder of the role tribalism played during the Italian occupation of Libya when the war of resistance was waged with tribes as its focus. Tribal loyalty or identity, therefore, has proven a suitable instrument to generate tribal consensus for the purpose of affirming the legitimacy to rule the country; and there is no doubt that it will retain weighty influence in the future (Chersstich 2011).

Though foreign intervention inspired various regions and tribes reluctant or hesitant to join the revolution – thereby prolonging the struggle and increasing the numbers of its victims, Gaddafi's regime failed in rallying more lasting support or playing neighbouring tribes off against each other even in places where civilian casualties as a result of NATO operations were experienced directly. Tribalism was not reflected in the uprisings in any manner that suggested lack of national sentiments or unity. As for the public squares of protests in Benghazi, Misurata, Zintan and other towns, the surge of national patriotic sentiment and the insistence on national unity (unity of people and territorial integrity) were among that to which rebels were most devoted and which they stressed and displayed in many ways. Banners and placards were put up and held aloft in squares decreeing that 'Tripoli is the eternal capital of Libya', 'Neither Eastern nor Western; ours is a national revolution', 'Libya is immune to partition' and 'O Gaddafi – death, death; Libyans are brothers' (Anonymous, 2011a).

Oil and the challenges of modernization

Oil was and will remain an essential factor in the process of political, economic and social transformation in Libya. Al-Tir has noticed, with a degree of anxiety, that the approach of modernization did not establish itself completely in the case of Libya when the oil boom failed to generate a change in economic-, social- and political structures. Gaddafi's regime attempted to restrict oil-related transformations and contain their impact. The regime was keen on combating forces of political, social and economic modernization. The outcome of this was effectively to place obstacles in the path of the modernization of Libyan society and state (Al-Tir 2011).

Oil raises challenges for the future of Libya other than those connected to modernization.

It was the primary driving force that fuelled Gaddafi's internal and external adventures. Yet, the most dangerous repercussion of oil wealth was that it accorded the regime the material power necessary to achieve two ends simultaneously. The first pertained to providing the state with favourable conditions to penetrate society and create a system of local compradors. The abundance of petro-dollars enabled the state to practice subjugation in all its forms without the need to impose taxes. Secondly, oil wealth liberated the government from any need to conciliate the people politically or to accommodate democratically their demands. Huge oil revenues were behind the conviction of the political authority that excluded any social contract. Since the government had all the means it needed derived from this resource at its disposal, any notion of democratic credentials was not deemed necessary, so long as it had the backing of an oil rentier economy to impose its control (Sawani 2006, pp. 23–38; al-ʿAwkali 2007, p. 95).

Oil has maintained its hold on Libyan politics and foreign relations. Long before the land was declared Gaddafi-free, reports emerged that oil and gas deals were being struck between the NTC and western governments and their transnational oil companies. Though the NTC denied such deals and in a counter-move announced that all deals during Gaddafi's rule will be subject to review, many observers consider this to be a deceptive smoke screen, sceptically referring to the irony that while all other sectors including security are either nonexistent or dysfunctional, the oil and gas sector has almost fully resumed its pre-February 2011 production and export levels.[1]

The interaction of perpetual dynamics and their political manifestations

On the basis of the foregoing presentation and analysis it appears clear that pre-existing dynamics have figured prominently both politically and socially since the onset of the revolt against Gaddafi. By utilizing such information as is available, in conjunction with direct observation and experience, it is possible to delineate and analyze the manifestations of these dynamics.

The most prominent manifestations are those associated with religion and its anticipated political role in the new, post-Gaddafi Libya. Domestic Islamist movements today share a commitment to an Islamist project and the goal of realizing an Islamic state. None of the political trends that have come into prominence have rejected democracy, although the *salafist* current underlines the contradiction between democracy and the historical precedent course of the 'pious ancestors' (*al-salaf al-s ā li h in*). Salafists stress the historical precedents of *shūrā* (consultation) and the role of the *ahl al-ḥall wa al-ʿaqd* (those charged with the authority to conclude and dissolve agreements).

Overall, the present Libyan scene reflects the fact that the Islamist forces are the best organized of the various forces and currents in the field. They proclaim their adherence to the Islamic religion and its value system, and politically they exploit the hold Islam has on the minds of people. Islamists are eager to multiply the force of their political presence and reinforce a desire to replace the *ancien régime* that they criticize in every way possible as a source for augmenting their popular support (al-Dāli 2011, pp. 6–7).

As for liberal, nationalist and leftist currents – despite the existence of those speaking in their names – they do not constitute a clearly organized entity. Their representatives advocate a civil state and warn that the danger to democracy lies not only in its being divested of any social or economic content, but also in its potential to be hijacked under an Islamic rubric. They criticize the use of religion to control the public and accuse Islamists of camouflaging their real intentions by employing democratic facades, where the appearance of democracy is maintained only until their arrival in power, at which time the democratic system will be overturned completely. These currents suffer from lack of organization and, in particular, at the grassroots level. Their leaderships have not yet paid sufficient attention to conceptual and organizational questions and seem content to wager on the traditional moderation of Libyans.

However, these assertions may not be relied upon to quell the Islamists. This is particularly the case given the readiness for adventure among some quarters known for extremism. The heated debates that went on over the last several months elucidated the sharpness of the differences between liberal and Islamist currents. This was abundantly evident in reported incidents of political assaults on the leadership of other currents on various grounds, and related statements, including personal defamation and assorted accusations. This level of disagreement appears most clearly in the case of Islamist forces, at the forefront of which is the Islamic Movement for Change (IMC, i.e. al-Ḥarakah al-Islāmiyah li-l-Taghyir) led by ℵAbd al-Ḥ akim Bilḥāj, one of the leaders of the Libyan Islamic Fighting Group (LIFG, i.e. al-Jamāʿah al-Libiyah al-Islāmiyah al-Muqātilah). Bilḥāj resigned his post as the chairman of Tripoli's Military Council and publicly affirmed his belief in democracy and a civil state. He formed a political party (*Al Watan, the homeland*) and ran for elections achieving very moderate gains. However, many still question his real intentions and close links to Qatar, seeing him as intent on plunging into the fray of the political battle, as well as being prepared to resort to violence and force.

What also commands attention is the emergence of particular factional orientations or narrow regionalism. This includes advocacy for the establishment of a federal system in Libya. In eastern Libya, where tribalism plays a conspicuous and influential role, the call for federalism or a particular position for Benghazi does not necessarily coincide with the interests of the Islamist trend. In fact, the tribal factor has more at stake here in many ways. This emerged clearly in the numerous tribal gatherings that have been convened, the last of which was called 'The National Gathering for the Inhabitants (of Barqah/Cyrenaica), or the Eastern Province' that was held in the city of al-Bayḏāʾ at the beginning of October 2011. The communiqué of the Conference affirmed support for national conciliation and the national bond. However, the fact that a delegation from the Conference visited Qatar, where it consulted and discussed Libyan issues with the Qatari government, lends support to the view that regionalist sentiment predominates here. Moreover, the Conference called for Libya to be administered regionally and rejected any centralism. This led observers to perceive a strong indication of the predominance of a spirit of regionalism and the ascendancy of tribalism. Many commentators consider that what was going on behind the scenes at the gathering was in marked contrast to what was announced publicly. There was – in other words – an effort to endorse federalism and, thereby, threaten the unity of the country (Libya al-Youm Journal 2011b; Al-Mahir 2011).

The situation differs in the region of Miṣrātah where there appears to be a connection between the Islamist current and local sentiments. This was clear when calls came from both for the censure of some leading figures of the progressive and liberal current in the interim government and the NTC and to bar them from the political arena. Along with this development the local orientation appears to be very pronounced and strong so as to suggest that Miṣrātah currently is almost independent in its administration, decisions and external relations.[2] Similarly, the position expressed by the leaders of Miṣrātah towards dark-complexioned inhabitants of the town of Tawergah went so far as to reject their continued co-existence in the border area contiguous with Miṣrātah and called for their displacement. Naturally if practised, this will set a very risky and problematic precedent.

The repercussions as well as the potential for a similar position and stance to be imitated in other regions are greater than any have anticipated. Even though there is a near national consensus over what many Tawergahans have done to Miṣrātans, which ranges from killings, rape of women, assault and destruction to acts of theft and robbery, the call to displace them exceeded all expectations and preconceptions. This issue clashes with the concept of Libyan citizenship and imposes numerous questions about the future.

As for the Western Mountain region, the situation seems to be one of a polarization in an Arab–Amazigh dichotomy. The early phases of the revolution saw increasing manifestations of this schism. Attempts at repairing the rupture succeeded in quashing any confrontations, particularly after Gaddafi's attempts to play on the issue in order to abort the revolt against him. However, the fact that the Arab tribes of al-Zintān have acquired a huge cache of all types of weapons has led other Amazigh tribes to follow suit. This renders the situation subject to change. It is also connected to what may be characterized as the existence of sensitivities between some tribes in the Western coastal region and along the border with Tunisia. Some of these sensitivities fall along tribal lines, while others have a connection to the Arab–Amazigh dichotomy. Information points to al-Zintān engagement in alliance-building in an attempt to offset the ethnic dichotomy.

It is important, however, to appreciate the fate confronted by the Mashāshah and other tribes in the Western Mountain area for reasons similar to the case of the Tawergah. In a visit to the area during the third week of October 2011, the author identified four towns and villages that were completely deserted. All inhabitants of these are now displaced and cannot go back to their homes for fear of persecution. They are labelled as Gaddafi loyalists and accused of supporting his killing machine during the revolt. The author's discussions with leaders from the local council of al-Zintān reveal that the return of thousands of displaced people to their homes remains very problematic. This clearly indicates the negative dimensions of the issue that has become a problem in itself (Affāya 2011, p. 21).

In connection with this it is possible to categorize the Amazigh current that held a general conference in Tripoli on 26 September 2011 – in a move unprecedented in the history of contemporary Libya. The Conference was the platform for advocating and securing the rights of the Amazigh, the constitutionality of their language and its written script known as Tifināgh. Even though the general orientation does not betoken anything that threatens national unity, some of the leading figures of the Amazigh movement in Libya have gone further than this. They have voiced a desire for a type of independence for or affiliation to the Amazigh of North Africa. A prominent leader expressed hostility towards Arabism and proclaimed a readiness to cooperate with Israel, while considering the Palestinian issue a concern of the Palestinians alone (General Administration of Al-Shouraffa on-line 2011a).

On the centrality of the transitional phase: defining rules of the game

The NTC that convened its initial meeting in Benghazi on 27 February and was officially established on 5 March 2011 assigned to itself the task of leadership during the entire transitional phase.[3] It obtained international support and the recognition of various Libyan cities sufficient to enable it to impose its control and authority. It set out to carry its self-defined mandate until after the realization of liberation in order to supervise election of the founding assembly that will draft a constitution for popular referendum and form a transitional government to initiate free elections. Despite all this, the Council did not have any authority backed by force other than moral or ethical authority.

It proved difficult for the NTC to put in place the transitional programme and implement it on the ground. Though the Council had established a number of institutions, these were unable to implement policies or programmes except when agreements were possible to reach. Most institutions, including those related to defence and security were virtually dysfunctional. Bold action by the NTC was lacking and even in instances when it was attacked itself by armed militias or when armed confrontations and clashes broke out between some areas, the NTC's actions were subject to negotiations involving political or tribal elements. In the early phase of its authority the NTC could have taken bold actions as people were more inclined to listen and be responsive to it. However, once liberation was achieved and the NTC showed hesitation and in many instances *inaction*, it almost lost the popular leverage it had initially. This had the effect of putting the Islamists and militia leaders in a stronger position with regard to refusing to acquiesce to these steps unless they got what they had wanted. Thus, the NTC lacked what would have enabled it to impose its political will on the ground. It had been exposed to criticism and rejection as well as calls for its dissolution and the setting up of an alternative elected body, which would have led to the protraction of the transitional phase.

The NTC, in affirmation of its determination to fulfil its perceived obligations, issued a Constitutional Proclamation on 3 August 2011 that defined the signposts towards establishing the new political system. The temporary Constitutional Proclamation contains 37 articles distributed across five sections dealing with defining the state and the values upon which it rests, just as it delimits the general principles of the political process. The second section is dedicated to rights and public liberties; whereas the third deals with the system of governance through the interim phase; and the fourth clarifies judicial/legal guarantees. The fifth section contains transitional regulations. It is a salient point that the Council relies on the legitimacy it derives from the revolution. It also considers its undertakings to originate from its responsiveness to the desires of the Libyan people and their aspiration (Al-Majlis al-Watani al- Intiqāli 2011, pp. 2–3).

This Constitution endeavoured to address the hopes of the people and their aspirations by clarifying its orientation towards 'a society of citizenship, justice, equality, renaissance, progress and comfort in which injustice, autocracy, tyrannical excess, exploitation and rule by a single individual are impossible' (Al-Majlis al-Waṭa ni al-IntiqāII 2011, pp. 2–3). The Constitution which sets out a road map for the transition to a permanent democratic government reflects and echoes the interaction of the numerous and diverse political and armed elements that made up the NTC itself. In this document it is obvious that the emphasis was placed on generalities and commonalities that brought these elements together. However, it reflects ideals and aspirations that were agreed upon during the struggle against Gaddafi. The fact that the desire to oust Gaddafi was the common denominator and unifying objective meant that the Constitution was reflective of the situation and meant to serve the purpose of consolidating the uprising by catering to all factions in a generalized way. Once the common goal was reached, problems came swiftly to the forefront and led to strong disagreements.

Early on, it was evident that Islamists took a hostile position towards the temporary Constitutional Proclamation and this reflected dissatisfaction with the NTC itself. In this context ʿAli Ṣalābi, Sālim al-Shaykhi and Ismāʿil al-Quraytli – all of whom are presumed to be affiliated to the Muslim Brotherhood – published on the Islamic website al-Manārah what they termed the 'Draft Interim National Pact'. This initiative specified that:

> The Transitional National Council shall be responsible for the administration of the affairs of the country until elections for the National General Conference have been completed. The temporary National Transitional Council is obliged to call, within seven days of the announcement of liberation, for the convening of the General National Conference comprised of all the representatives of the local councils of the cities. Failure to establish it during the aforementioned timeframe, tasks local city councils with convening their gathering as a General National Conference in Tripoli no later than a week from the date of notice. With the convocation of the first session of the General National Conference the trusteeship of the temporary National Transitional Council will come to an end and all of its powers and areas of jurisdiction will be transferred to the General National Conference (al-Ṣalābi *et al.* 2011).

Representatives of civil society considered such proposals that contradicted those issued by the NTC to be attempts to impose the will of a particular political faction upon the consensus of the rest. Such amounted to acting against the will of the people who are abiding by the continuity of the NTC, until such time as authority is turned over to a government duly elected on the basis of a permanent constitution.[4] To opponents of the Islamist current undertaking elections during the interim phase, before the permanent constitution is ratified, is tantamount to embarking on a dangerous adventure that puts national security and citizenship in jeopardy. They viewed this as extremely dangerous since the overthrow of the NTC would inflict considerable damage on the fragile stability that characterizes the transitional phase (al-Mismāri 2011, p. 12).

In the end, however, the most vociferous reservations vis-à-vis the temporary Constitutional Proclamation were those voiced by the Group of the ʿUlamāʾ (scholars) of Libya (hayʾat ʿulamāʾ libyā). This body was initially formed by a number of Islamists amongst those connected to the Muslim Brotherhood in Benghazi several months before the liberation of Tripoli. It is doubtful, given the circumstances that it resulted as a result of any widespread consultation or consensus, any government decision or the endorsement of the ʿulamāʾ of the country. It may also be noticed that this group was late in commenting on the Constitutional Proclamation. Its communiqué was not issued until 10 October 2011; and it is possible to explain their delay in responding in a number of ways. Regardless, it certainly is interesting to know the conditions that the self-appointed members of this group specified for the Constitution and imposed upon the Interim Council.

The Group has defined its position with regard to the provisions pertaining to public freedoms, demanding definition of the freedom of women, the freedom of opinion and expression, the freedom to form political parties and associations, and other human rights including the freedom to practice religion. Accordingly, these freedoms must be restricted so as to remain in conformity with and not in opposition to 'Islamic shariʿah'.

The most dangerous item in the communiqué was an objection with regard to women. The Group objected to 'equality between those two of different creation and nature and capability because this nullifies the justice that Allah the Most High has commanded'. Likewise, it objected to the quota specified by the Council for 'inappropriately' represented groups, such as women, by saying:

> To alter the will of the people by conferring on those whom they did not choose from within their strata or groups the task of representing them in the Council of Representatives (Majlis al-Nuwwāb) in a special quota destroys democracy and smashes its structures. (The Board of Trustees of the Council of Ulema (Hay'at al-ʿUlamā'), 2011)

Lastly, the Group wants to restrict the legislative jurisdiction of the future *majlis* or parliament by formal textual specification of the prerequisite condition that there is no contradiction of shariʿah. It vehemently demands a requirement to solicit the position of the ʿulamā' (scholars) of the shariʿah with regard to any initiative. Following the same logic the Group wants its inclusion and agreement in any work which the founding body (for drafting the Constitution) undertakes, by specifying that:

> The ʿulamā' of the sḥariʿah will have an influential representation in formulating the Constitution in order to avoid what occurred with the temporary Constitutional Proclamation and to insure that there is no possibility of its contravening the shariʿah. (The Board of Trustees of the Council of Ulema (Hay'at al-ʿUlamā'), 2011)

On the face of it, it would appear that this position confronts and rejects the principle of democracy and stridently refuses any viewpoint, legislation or legislative institution that does not enjoy the sanction of the 'ʿulamā' of the shariʿah' who alone have the authority to decree what is in conformity with it. Soon after the declaration of liberation disagreements became even bolder and more explicit on the Constitution as well as the role and future of the NTC itself. Disagreement was largely centred on the role of the NTC in the transitional period that was the subject of article 30 of the Constitution that stipulates a road map for the transition. The NTC had adopted an election law, set up an electoral commission, passed a law of political parties, amended the transitional constitution and organized Libya's first post-Gaddafi elections with remarkable popular participation of well over 60%.

The NTC, just few days before the elections, amended Article 30 of the Constitution thereby redefining the scope and nature of the National Council (NC) that will replace the NTC. As originally drafted, this article stipulated that the NC would assume the role of a national parliament with profound powers that include the most vital task of appointing the 60-member Founding Body for the Drafting of the Constitution, appointing a new government and organizing national elections within the framework of the road map outlined in the Constitutional Proclamation. Article 30 was amended to the effect that the elected national conference should choose, excluding its own members, a constituent body of 60 members to draft a constitution for the country. Its membership now equally represents east, south and west Libya with 20 members for each region along the lines of the 60-member body that had been formed to prepare a constitution for the occasion of Libya's independence in 1951 (Anonymous 2012).

If Libya moves in the direction the road map determined 'the draft constitution will be approved by the General National Conference which will recommend submitting it to referendum with a "yes" or "no" vote within thirty days from the date of its approval by the Conference. If the Libyan people approve the Constitution by a two-thirds majority of voters, the Founding Body will ratify it as the Constitution of the country, and the General National Conference will adopt it.' "If the Libyan people do not approve the Constitution, the Founding Body will be charged with re-drafting it and resubmitting it again for referendum in a period not to exceed thirty days. The General National Conference adopts the General Elections Law within thirty days. General elections will be organized within 180 days after the adoption of laws regulating them. The General National Conference and the Interim Government will attend to all requirements for a democratic and transparent election process. The Supreme Elections Commission (that will be formed by the General National Conference) will initiate general elections under the supervision of the national judiciary, the monitoring of the United Nations and international- and regional organizations. The General National Conference will ratify and announce the results of the elections and call the Legislative Authority to convene in a period not to exceed thirty days.

The latest amendment of Article 30 stripped the NC of its role of appointing the Founding Body that, accordingly, will be directly elected by popular vote. A debate ensued and many commentators were very critical of the amendment and considered the NTC's act as that of an attempt to derail the democratic process. The critics also highlighted the NTC's statement recommending that Islamic shariʿah be the fundamental source for legislation. Critics were dismayed by the suggestion that such an issue should not be subject to any sort of democratic popular referendum (Maghour 2012). It remains to be seen if the elected NC will honour such a view but Libya will have to go through another election to select the 60-member committee responsible for drafting the permanent constitution. The fact that this committee will have a direct popular mandate may very well prove problematic and raise issues with the NC which may also choose to nullify the NTC's amendments. In the case of such events, the transitional period is bound to become further protracted with achieving the desired outcomes more difficult without the need to resort to consensus-building measures that have thus far proved cumbersome to put into motion and effect.

Upon the convening of its first session, the General National Conference will be dissolved and the Legislative Authority will assume its tasks. Also the convocation of the first session of the Legislative Authority, the Interim Government will be considered a care-taker government until such time as the Permanent Government is convened in accordance with the Constitution.' (Al-Majlis al-Waṭa ni al-Intiqāl 2011, pp. 2–3).

The topography of the institutionalized forces

The National Transitional Council (NTC)

The violence and killings that took place at the hands of the Gaddafi Brigades had a decisive impact on many officials and moved them to defect from his regime. The course of severe repression and killing on which Gaddafi embarked impelled them to adopt stances in line with the dictates of conscience and patriotism. This translated into a number of resignations and scores of dissidents joining the ranks of the uprising. As a result, the uprising came to benefit from the services of many experts qualified to deal with the crisis who understood the ways and means for obtaining global support while addressing the challenges associated with the *intifada* and ensuring the protection of the people in the entire country (Anonymous 2011b). This was one of the elements of political power made available to the uprising that led to thinking about the creation of institutions to represent the rebels and the people who otherwise had no viable means to express their opinion. Mahmoud Jibril, the first chairman of the NTC's executive arm explained the origins of the NTC, and confirms that the idea of setting up the NTC was his brainchild. He had thought about the need for such a mechanism to represent the people and solicit international support and proposed it to 'Ali 'Isawi, Libya's ambassador to India. The two decided to pass on the concept to Mustafa Abd al-Jaleel in Baida through 'Isawi's brother living in Benghazi who received a document outlining the proposal by fax and drove to Baida to deliver it (Jibril 2012, p. 103).

During the uprising the NTC spoke on behalf of the rebels and played the role of the political leadership of Libyans who had joined the revolt. Once liberation was accomplished this body assumed the highest formal authority recognized internationally and possibly nationally as well. It announced its abidance by a commitment to democracy, the rule of law and constitutional legitimacy. Given Jibril's account, the Council was not formed by design but by the incidental reaction to the situation and gathering of personalities from various regions. Some members are independent while others belong to multiple political trends. The nature of the composition of the leadership of the uprising who comprised the NTC goes some way to explaining the fact that Libyans' revolt against Gaddafi's regime reflected the fragmentation and dispersal that have long characterized opposition.

The NTC was a mix of former opponents who lived outside Libya as well as intellectuals and academics, journalists, lawyers and human rights activists along with defectors from Gaddafi's regime and many others who had spent years in the dark in Gaddafi's prisons (Achcar 2011a, 2011b). It also included representatives of regions and tribes who reflected the diversity of Libya's tribal structure. Consensus around a unified position was indeed difficult to attain given this composition that also comprised pragmatists who were willing to negotiate with Gaddafi in order to avert further bloodshed (Pelham 2011). Only in later stages after the liberation of many regions did representatives of local or regional councils join the NTC but then only in a further reflection of the primacy of regional and tribal dynamics.

For these reasons, the NTC was from the outset a heterogeneous mixture by any standards, and there were no common denominators except for the will to stand up against Gaddafi. The NTC's success in gaining approval and recognition may be partially attributed to the failure of Gaddafi to depart from his views and perception of world politics. Gaddafi believed the West to always be hypocritical and driven only by its interests. He wagered that since he himself posed no threat this should serve his purposes in convincing the West that it was the *intifada* that actually constituted the threat to its interests instead, and not his regime. For this reason, Gaddafi, while failing to grasp that he had no real friends and that his policies were actually to the disdain of world leaders, committed the mistake of underestimating the hold public opinion has over democratic politics.

Subsequently these individuals opted to institutionalize their activities and the Council assumed the power of a parliament that also exercised some executive authority. NTC's scope of authority was widened, in theory, however, such expansion did not lead to a consolidation of power. This was a source for concern given the weakness of the leadership of the Council. It had been noted by numerous observers from the standpoint that members of the NTC were involved or complicit in contentious issues, thus exposing a weakness that cannot be ignored. Clearly, the Council had become the target of many criticisms. Calls were voiced for the need to expand its representative base so as to encompass all the regions as well as thinking about a source of legitimacy other than 'revolutionary legitimacy'. The NTC had displayed a willingness to heel to pressures to transform coming from regional, tribal and ideological quarters. The expressed desire was to accommodate and build consensus with the end result only being further fragmentation and the NTC's power and legitimacy suffering in the process. The attacks on the NTC and its leadership had come from all directions but the most obvious danger stemmed from the armed militias that have maintained an independence from the NTC and its policies. The Council was not able to embark on strengthening national institutions or to maintain law and order and its position suffered further. The most striking developments were all the more ironic since the membership of some NTC members was revoked by the very commission they had set up for – presumably – other purposes! The Transparency Commission decreed that some NTC members representing Tripoli, Sebha and Khomes were not fit to continue their duties as there was ample evidence to suggest that they ought to be disqualified and removed. As it was, further rifts within the NTC were avoided since the Commission's decisions were overturned by the courts.

The local councils

Local councils (majālis maḥaliyah) are entities that were mostly established through secret initiatives for the purpose of assuming the responsibility of administering cities and regions after their liberation from the control of the *ancien régime*. It is indeed ironic that the cynical reality of Libya under Gaddafi, that was typified by a contempt for institutions which he continuously sought to undermine or destroy and where he completely underestimated the importance of building a modern state, would go on to provide a model for a sophisticated and institutionally well-developed revolution. This was ironic especially since Gaddafi failed to establish an effective system of committees and congresses to perform local government duties because of his clinging to absolute power. The outbreak of fighting and armed clashes notwithstanding, once liberated from his control, Libyans were – given the circumstances – able to a remarkable degree to make a similar and analogous system operate efficiently as well as succeed in the setting up of effective local authorities throughout the entire country, perhaps taking advantage of their previous experience and expertise in the management of service organizations and government (Pelham 2011).

Local councils' elections were held in many areas including Zwārah, Misrātah and Benghazi where councils are presently entrusted with the role of local administration of the various government and service sectors. Some of these have military wings subject to their authority, formally at least. The majority of the military councils, especially in major cities like Tripoli are independent and make their will effective by employing force. Many councils are facing the problem of controlling armed formations while the legitimacy of these local councils, the capabilities of its members, their political orientation and their performance have come into question. There have been calls to dissolve the unelected councils and initiate elections to select new ones in a manner that reflects the struggle between political or ideological currents as well as factional/regional and tribal struggles.

The February 17th Coalitions

The February 17th Coalitions are associations comprising political and human rights activists who participated in the first wave of protests. It appears that city coalitions are closed organizations that do not allow outside membership. They draw their discourse and justification for their actions from 'revolutionary legitimacy' while exercising effective authority without recourse to any side. This has given rise to problems and contradictions that appeared early in Benghazi and subsequently spread to Tripoli where the Muslim Brotherhood controls the Coalition. The vast majority of the members of the Benghazi coalition have elected to dissolve it or to withdraw from it. They explained this by their desire to submit to a single legitimate authority which the NTC represented. Muhammad Zāhi al-Mughayrbi, one of its founders, explained, in a phone conversation with the author, that they took this decision so that the Coalition would not assume a position similar to that of a 'revolutionary command council' in reference to Gaddafi's RCC that had announced that it would hand power to the people only to consolidate one-man rule instead. This is a clear indication of fear on behalf of the Coalition over resort to 'revolutionary legitimacy', which threatens stability and democratic transformation. Recently, the Coalition in Benghazi transformed into a civil society organization.[5]

In Tripoli the Coalition has not yet ceased to engage in a wide range of activities under the cover of 'revolutionary legitimacy'. However, a number of its members with whom the author met expressed their anger and resentment over these practices that they attribute to the Muslim Brotherhood. This has led many Coalition members to desist from participating in its activities. One member characterized this sentiment in an article published recently. He expressed disdain for the Muslim Brotherhood because it had 'hijacked' this Coalition and taken control of its leadership. The Brotherhood is criticized for using the Coalition as an instrument to serve its political ends. They are also accused of using it as a means to extirpate and wage war on anyone who does not agree with them politically (Al-Mashirqi 2011, p. 2). Though the importance of coalitions seems to have waned at the regional level, many have been set up in ministries, government agencies and state-owned companies and corporations. These entities have been exercising influence in all matters that involve most issues within their respective organizations.

Islamist groups

Despite their small size in terms of membership the Islamists are highly organized groups whose members have excellent self-discipline and respect for their leaderships. The most prominent of these is the Muslim Brotherhood which has an organizational history in Libya dating back to the 1950s. The group experienced various vicissitudes until it was reorganized a few years ago following the period of détente (infitāḥ) that Libya witnessed. They engaged in a dialogue with Gaddafi's regime that resulted in the freeing many of their members from prison. The regime engaged all Islamists and particularly the Brotherhood whose members assumed official responsibilities. Many of their elements were involved with activities related to Saif Gaddafi's reform agenda. During the early days of the uprisings, the Islamists' position was impartial, reluctant or not supportive of the uprising. The Salafists were initially against the uprising and the Brotherhood asked its members to use their own discretion when choosing where they stood. As soon as Libyan regions were free of Gaddafi's control, the leadership emerged to occupy a prominent place, especially in the spheres of influential media such as Aljazeera satellite station, the internet and the pulpits of mosques for Friday prayers.

In March 2012 the Muslim Brotherhood formed their own political party, the 'Justice and Construction Party', and the group has been engaged in setting up new civil and religious organizations as well as infiltrating similar entities. It exerts great effort to affirm its media presence through new satellite channels, mosques, charitable foundations (awqāf), the issue of fatwās, committees of ʿulamāʾ, public lectures, etc. Nevertheless, they do not ignore the importance of a military wing of their own. Historically, the Libyan Muslim Brotherhood had an intellectual affinity and proximity with the Brotherhood in Egypt. There does not seem to be any considerable departure from this position. The Libyan Brotherhood has a manifest presence with members in all groups active in the revolution. They have professed their intention to abide by a civil state and democracy or a 'moderate' Islamic state; and the encouragement of civil society.

The gains they made in the first elections the country had in July indicated that the Libyan Brotherhood has popularity in some areas but almost no influence in most of Libya's regions and constituencies. Their share of the 80 seats devoted to political parties in the 200-seat National Conference was only 17 seats while their competitor, The Alliance of Nationalist Forces led by Mahmoud Jibril won 39 seats (Higher National Elections Commission 2012).

The NFSL which transformed in March 2012 into a political party 'The National Front' had historically been the largest of the Islamist movements and associations with an Islamists membership of multiple orientations. Its current leadership apparently has Sanusi, Sufi tendencies. This may be traced in that the political programme of the NFSL and the statements it issued, which express a clear attachment to the Constitution of the Sanusi monarchy and accord Idriss the role of a historical founder of Libya. In its life over the years the NFSL has been subjected to dispersion and the desertion of many from its ranks. This fragmentation was attributable to many reasons including differences that characterized the Libyan opposition outside the country since the failure of what was known as the National Conference of the Libya Opposition. This was set up to unify and coordinate the efforts of opposition forces opposed to Gaddafi. However, despite the shrinking of its ranks, the NFSL constituted a pre-eminent media and political presence throughout the revolution and before the liberation of Tripoli though with very few spokesmen. What is worthy of mention is that the Salvation Front might be alone in having put forward the most clearly defined political programme outlining the features of the new Libya and many of its constituents were appointed to senior government positions including Prime Minister Abdulrahman El Keeb. However, the results of July elections showed that NFSL lacked a real power base or wider popular support as they gained very few seats in July elections (Higher National Elections Commission 2012).

Coexisting in the field are other movements, the most important of which are those influenced by the Wahhabi sect and *salafists* affiliated to well-known *salafist* thought expressed in their vigilance in following those 'who have been delegated responsibility for affairs' (i.e. the so called *ūli al-amr* to use the Qur'anic term in the sense understood by *salafists*). Despite the ambiguous position of this current, many of its leaders took a position that might at least be described as negative towards the revolt against Gaddafi. Nevertheless, the trend has spread with rapidity among the ranks of the lesser-educated groups of the population and the youth. These are connected to the larger Arab *salafais* movement and especially with Saudi Arabia, which exploits the presence of Libyan youth during the *ḥajj* season or off-season pilgrimages to Mecca (*ʿumrah*) in order to disseminate its doctrine and call (*daʿwah*).

The *salafist* movement that has begun to make its presence felt publicly has organizations and branches in many cities. They have not as yet expressed a political position vis-à-vis the struggle of forces. They do, however, exploit the absence of a (governmental) authority in carving out what they desire of control over various spaces such as the mosques, or daʿwah efforts in the street. Some of its members are directly engaged in 'commanding what is right and forbidding what is unjust' (*al-amr bi-l-maʿrūf wa al-nahi ʿan al-munkar*) in some neighbourhoods of Tripoli. This includes, for example, informing ladies' hair stylists and beauty salons that they are no longer tolerated and will have to close their doors once and for all. They have also struck public opinion hard with their destruction of conspicuous funerary monuments with prominent tomb markers in marked contradistinction with other political currents and parties are preoccupied with serious matters of public policy and competing over everything. It might be more than a bit ironic to note that while Libyans have been embattled in many regions and taking casualties, the *salafist* movement has been concerned, in one of the most recent circulars that its members distributed in the streets, with warning and admonishing Libyans, all of whom are Muslims in a Muslim society, against *shirk* (idolatry).[6] The results of the elections confirmed their limited influence and popularity amongst the electorate.

Extremist Islamist orientations or *jihadists*, upon whom Gaddafi's regime had inflicted the greatest damage, have yet to announce themselves clearly or openly. Observers and analysts believe that these orientations are presently focusing on and preoccupied with acquiring weapons and financing. They are preparing for a decisive entrance onto the scene once the process of restoring stability and reconstruction has begun. Historically the Libyan Islamic Fighting Group was the most prominent among these. After suppression and executions of its rank and file by Gaddafi's regime, its imprisoned members entered into a dialogue with the authorities. This resulted in an avowal to undertake intellectual reviews, best known as 'renunciations' (*murājaʿāt*) through which they renounced violence and opted to undertake peaceful work (Bilḥāj *et al.* 2010, pp. 4–16).

The dialogue resulted in the release of members from Gaddafi's prisons in contingents, the last of which was set free only a few days before the 17 February revolt. These were vital fuel for the revolution. Tripoli had barely been wrested from Gaddafi's grip before one of its leaders, Bilḥāj, appeared as head of the Tripoli Military Council. It was not long before he began to play the role of the military governor of the city with thousands of armed supporters who have rallied to his banner.

Bilḥāj has stated on numerous political occasions and media appearances his commitment to the establishment of a democratic state. Despite his acceptance of democracy and a civil state in numerous interviews, the reality of Bilḥāj leading armed brigades that receive outside support is cause for resentment among others (Beaumont 2011). As soon as the electoral process was initiated with registering voters, Bilhaj gave up his official post as leader of Tripoli's Military Council and announced he was entering into civilian political life (Shuaib 2012).

Concern over the situation stems from the fact that the process of rehabilitating elements of the Fighting Group was not completed or entirely successful. Gaddafi's regime did not implement a comprehensive programme with enduring results. Therefore, the effectiveness of the 'renunciations' was potentially limited to the threshold of the prison doorstep. In addition, hundreds of prisoners who were not part of negotiations between the regime and the Islamists were released in the first days of the revolt in a desperate attempt by the regime to conciliate the street. Hundreds and perhaps even thousands more prisoners were released from prisons in Benghazi and subsequently in Tripoli after the liberation of the two cities.

Liberal, nationalist and secularist (i.e. non-Islamist) currents

Here there is an array of political factions of various dispensations. They are not Islamist and range from the leftist and the liberal to popular and Arab nationalist forces, etc. They express loyalty to liberal democracy. Some of the leaderships of these orientations belonged to old political parties or were intellectuals active politically and in the field of human rights during Gaddafi's reign. Others were members of the opposition in exile. They generally lack organization at the popular level and it appears that their leaders did not pay attention to this deficiency except recently when they witnessed the effectiveness of the activities of the Islamist trends.

Only lately have some of these elements begun to set up political parties or organizations of civil society that generally echo their views. However, these have yet to crystallize into any clear form with distinct features. This comes at a time when many of those involved find themselves drawn to political side-battles imposed upon them by the Islamists waged to dissipate their forces. It is difficult to produce a detailed outline of the political parties that have been publicly announced or that are undertaking preparations to emerge. Benghazi witnessed the birth of the first political parties just as Libyan opposition members formed a political association in a meeting in Tunis, while some individuals have been reticent to announce parties revolving around personalities. In addition to these may be added a sizeable number of small movements and organizations that comprise limited membership or which are controlled by families. These organizations emerged from the womb of opposition to Gaddafi abroad since the early 1980s but have managed to cling on to existence today.

Another organization that surfaced is the Libyan Democratic Gathering, which is a front association for activists, politicos and human rights activists comprising organizations of civil society with liberal and progressive tendencies. It issued a founding communiqué in Tripoli on 17 September 2011 and attacked the position of the Muslim Brotherhood and their stand vis-à-vis the NTC and the Executive Office. They considered such positions to be merely attempts to impose the will of the Brotherhood and dominate, while contending that there is no guardianship (*wiṣāyah*) for any party over the people (The Founding Committee of the Libyan Democratic Forum 2011).

Former Chairman of the NTC's Executive Council, Mahmoud Jibril, viewed as a prominent leader of the liberal trend, set up a political organization, the Alliance of National Forces, in February of 2012 and was officially elected as its head on 14 March. The Alliance is an umbrella organization comprising 44 political parties including the National Centrist Party that 'Ali Tarhouni, Minister of Finance in Jibril's government formed in February (Libya Herald 2012). The Alliance also has in its membership a whole host of organizations, 236 NGOs in addition to several hundreds of persons and regional leaders who share a liberal nationalist orientation. The Alliance has expressed its commitment to democracy and a moderate Islam and competed in the first elections in Libya. Jibril explained that his Alliance is guided by a commitment to preserving Libya's sovereignty, moderate Islam, national unity and territorial integrity in a unified state that while acknowledging the need for decentralization, sustainable regional development and local administration, has no room for federalism (Jibril, 2012, pp. 110–112). The Alliance made considerable gains and succeeded in getting 39 seats out of 80 seats devoted to political parties in the first elections. Such gains will position the Alliance as the leading political entity in today's Libya most likely to control the NC (Higher National Elections Commission 2012).

Since the liberation of the country from Gaddafi's regime political parties have mushroomed in all Libyan regions, cities and towns. Therefore, it is clear that long before the NTC adopted legislation governing political parties and entities in March of 2012, these mushroomed in almost all Libyan cities and regions with estimates exceeding several hundreds of parties, organizations, entities, and coalitions or alliances. One hallmark of these political movements is reflected in the similarities of their visions and goals as outlined in their political manifestos. They may well be classified into major trends: regional, ideological and personality-centred. Observers of activities connected to the founding of political parties can attest to the vagueness or lack of clarity in the many attempts and incapacity to formulate well-defined political programmes. They also lack clear-cut political identities and positions towards current issues. Though many lack a genuine popular base and an organizational coherence, approximately 100 parties competed in the country's first elections after Gaddafi. Many of these parties gained a limited number of seats or won none at all, but nevertheless indicated willingness of Libyans to participate in the new political process (Higher National Elections Commission 2012). However, the increase in the number of political parties was not matched by an ability of most of them to secure any sizeable number of seats in the July elections. Therefore, most of these parties will not be able to play any effective role in political life in the short-term at least.

Civil society

The process of incepting organizations of civil society bears fruit almost daily in all major cities in Libya. These organizations revolve around issues centred for the most part on human rights, women's rights or humanitarian issues. While it is apparent that there is an active presence of Islamist currents in a large number of these organizations, it is also clear that other trends find them to be a suitable forum for representation. The internet is brimming with Libyan websites and social networks that host growing numbers of web groups and communities. The fact that there is an absence of organization and effective political authority in the country renders this phenomenon more related to what is transpiring on the ground and less an expression of a phenomenon connected to a culture supportive of civil society.

Despite the announcement of the formation of a union of civil society organizations, it is dubious as to whether this genuinely reflects what the name implies. Given the small number of associations that constitute this union, it does not have a presence in all Libyan regions. This reflects a practice and mode of political control through the initiation of organizations, associations and unions. In fact most of these entities lack popular manifestations in all the reaches of the country. This also applies to unions and religious associations such as the Society or Union of Libyan ʿulamāʾ, the Student Union and others. There is a feeling that Islamist forces figure prominently in the inception of these organizations as a means for taking greater control of them. This has also become apparent in the leading role of Islamists in establishing charitable or humanitarian associations.

The danger of political currents and political parties exploiting the institutions of civil society to their own ends has come to the fore. As a result, these new and nascent institutions are cast into the unknown. Tribalism will likely predominate and serve as the axis for political work in which case factionalism/regionalism will dangerously impinge upon identity, integration, national unity and the democratic process.

The challenge before the Islamist currents lies in the extent of their ability to facilitate the process of democratic transition through their commitment to liberating the sentiments and attitudes of individuals from the dominance of the state. This, in turn, will lead to the creation of a wider sphere for democracy without hindering the realization of democracy itself (Obeidi 2008, p. 16).

The Amazigh: a cultural or ethnic challenge?[7]

Gaddafi's rule was characterized by a denial of Amazigh, particularly the Berber, rights to exercise their freedoms and rights associated with their unique cultural and linguistic identity. Gaddafi, for example, deprived the Amazigh from the right to give their children Amazigh names in a blatant denial of their cultural identity. He had always maintained that they were ancient Arab migrants from the Arabian Peninsula. As for other minorities, the revolution against Gaddafi was marked by the active participation of the Berber tribes in the Western Mountain while the Tabu remained reticent about joining the revolution. On the other hand, Tuareg fighters were an essential component in Gaddafi's forces in the face of the popular revolution, and as a result the Tuareg at large became the target of much of the violence and discrimination during the revolution and beyond.

Libya did not witness a struggle between the Berbers and their fellow Arab citizens except in the case of limited clashes between gunmen from the town of Zwārah and those from nearby Arab cities. In the event, these clashes were not primarily for reasons attributable to cultural or ethnic fault lines but as a consequence of the polarization wrought by the revolution between supporters and opponents of Gaddafi's regime. Some of the incidents were also related to conflicts of interests over smuggling goods, drugs, alcoholic beverages, arms and fuel cross the border with Tunisia. Once liberation of the country was announced Amazigh began expressing their demands and rights openly and peacefully through holding conferences, seminars and the media. Tripoli witnessed intensive Amazigh activities. The highlight of these was, perhaps, the convening of the 'National Congress of the Libyan Amazigh', which focused on the issue of enshrining the Amazigh language in the constitution. This was a reference to the desire for the adoption of the Amazigh language as a second official language of the country in the constitution (Anonymous 2012a).

After long decades of suppression by Gaddafi of the Berbers, the current state of political fluidity and the absence of any strong political authority have opened the doors to all forms of expression among the Amazigh of Libya and particularly the Berbers. The revolt against Gaddafi in the region of Jabal Nafūsah was characterized by clear expressions of its Berber Amazigh make up. Tripoli witnessed the convening of an Amazigh (basically Berber) conference (Libyan National Amazigh Conference on 26 October 2011, www.lnac.ly). This event was an indication of the commonalities of Berber demands with Amazigh of North Africa in general. Despite the fact it was the first such conference on Libyan soil, its organizers were keen on linking it to other non-Libyan Amazigh conferences; and this connection has been a cause for resentment among many non-Amazigh commentators. The Conference's main point of concern was expressed in its logo and slogan of 'constitutionalizing Tamazight … support for national unity' (Anonymous 2012a). The Conference decided a number of steps for the promotion of Amazigh demands. The 'organizers agreed to form committees representative of the various Berber towns and villages to follow up their demands and recommendations presented to the NTC regarding making the Berber language official in the constitution, and calling for Berber lawyers and law experts to assist in formulating provisions and legislations in a legal document which then can be presented to the interim Justice Minister for consideration as a set of temporary provisions until the full constitution is drafted' (Temehu 2011).

The demands expressed by Libya's Amazigh range from enforcing identity and culture to upgrading the Amazigh language to the status of an official or at least a national language. Though questions about the script for writing the Amazigh language (whether this should be Tifināgh, Arabic or European/Latin) remain unanswered. The fact that the Conference was connected to foreign conferences raises ambiguities. There may be questions as to the suitability of this with respect to the Tuareg and Tabu though a similar gathering (the Second Gathering of the Libyan National Amazigh Conference) connected to the Conference was held in Ubari in the southwest on 1 September 2011 with representatives from among Berbers and the Tuareg who called for similar demands.[8]

Amazigh activists called for Amazigh political rights and appropriate representation at all levels. They have been clear in their demands and in highlighting the need to involve them in determining national choices and according them representation in all political, legal and governmental organs. The Amazigh felt that the NTC ignored their demands and began to organize protests and sit-ins in Tripoli. The last three months of 2011 saw a number of such protests, the most notable of which was a large demonstration in Tripoli on 6 December 2011. They demanded respect for the Constitutional Declaration and the application of its provisions related to democratic government, freedoms, equal opportunities, equality and respect for cultural and linguistic diversity.[9]

The response of the NTC and the government to the demands of the Amazigh was lukewarm and tantamount only to lip service. The NTC and the interim government did not enter into a constructive dialogue aimed at integrating them in the political process. Leaders of political movements and parties also took positions similar to those of the NTC. Some Islamist leaders considered the demands of the Amazigh unacceptable and a danger to national unity, while asserting that Arabic is the language of the Qur'an, where Arabs and Berbers belong to an Arab-Islamic culture that does not discriminate between its various components and that an Islamic state accommodates and best serves the demands of the Amazigh.[10]

For some Amazigh activists it became obvious that their calls fell on deaf ears, and they inferred that they are bound to be excluded and neglected. Some Berber authors have suggested the government lack of attention to the needs of wounded and sick Amazigh rebels was nothing more than a reflection of policies of exclusion. The response of the NTC and government failed to go beyond the content of a speech that Mustafa 'Abd al-Jalil gave in the Berber town of Nalut on 6 December 2011 in which he only gave verbal assurances to the Berber that 'Tamazight culture and language are respected by all Libyans' while also explaining that the Berbers need to '*integrate*' into the Libyan society and avoid '*exclusion*' (Temehu 2011). Thereafter began another manifestation of protest expressing outrage. The most prominent expression of this discontent was what happened on 8 May 2012 when Western Mountain gunmen attacked the headquarters of the Prime Minister in Tripoli in an expression of the growing frustration and sense of marginalization amid demands for fair treatment.[11]

These expressions have best been portrayed in the writings of Amazigh activists – the most powerful and visible of such being expressed by Fathi Ben Khalifa, a Libyan national who is the President of the World Amazigh Congress. Ben Khalifa demanded that the NTC listen and act on the demands and rights of the Amazigh or they will have to boycott elections and will not accept their outcome. He also called on Amazighs to withdraw from the NTC and other state institutions. In what appeared to be the like of an ultimatum he indicated that given the failure of the NTC to engage and include the Amazigh their next step is to go directly and officially to the United Nations and international organizations and to call upon them to address the Amazigh cause (Ben Khalifa 2012).

The inability of the NTC to respond to demands of Amazigh has emboldened action on their behalf. If such issues remain unattended to and no clear-cut policy is adopted to cater to the express demands and aspirations of the Amazigh this may open up questions about ethnicity in the widest possible sense where the Amazigh may move towards demanding their own political entity, which would threaten the national unity of the country. This is particularly significant since that the Tuareg on the border with Mali have announced their 'Azwad Republic' – a Tuareg statelet, which enjoys indications of support from Libyan Amazigh and a statement of support from the World Congress of Amazigh.[12] This also has wider implications for the region extending from Egypt to Mauritania where the Amazigh have a presence. In the Libyan context many tribes such as the Qabaiel in Zawia, Hawrah in Elmaia and Janzour on the coast and Warfellah all have Amazigh origins and have been mentioned on many occasions by Amazigh activists, thus potentially widening the scope and receptivity of any Amazigh call for self-determination (Amareer 2010).

The new Libya: challenges and opportunities

Libya represents an exceptional case that involved the transformation of peaceful protests into a full-fledged violent popular revolt against the totalitarian dictatorship of Mu'ammar Gaddafi. Moreover, the uprising rapidly evolved into a sanguinary and protracted struggle as protesters and the regime alike resorted to arms. Calls for nationwide protests were launched via social media websites to commemorate the anniversary of 17 February 2006 when security forces opened fire and gunned down peaceful demonstrators in front of the Italian Consulate in Benghazi who were demonstrating against the disparaging caricatures of the Prophet Muhammad.

Peaceful protests were tolerated briefly before the regime resorted to its art of repression and violence. The spree of killing and extermination of which Gaddafi's regime availed itself and his call for the physical liquidation of protestors was something of a more diabolical revival of his old standing orders to the Revolutionary Committees in the late 1970s and early 1980s to carry out 'physical liquidations' but on a much vaster scale. The uprising summarizes the long history of Libyans' dismay with Gaddafi's regime at different levels including political, social, and economic that found appropriate expression in this movement. The protests began rapidly in the city of Benghazi but the violent confrontation by Gaddafi's forces and the shocking use of a killing machine directly against Libyans and from the first day of the demonstrations, resulted in a spill-over effect to other regions that also proved a force-multiplier.[13]

Therefore, limited protests transformed into a mass uprising that engulfed Benghazi and the surrounding areas before widening and spreading to towns and villages in the entire country. Only certain areas were not swept up in the momentum, for one reason or another, but not necessarily in a demonstration of any allegiance to the Gaddafi regime.

Some had reservations about engaging in collective action and directly expressing opposition to the regime. However, it should be noted that these islands, which abstained from active involvement up until the last days of the conflict and which could not join in the revolution had nevertheless suffered from the misdeeds of the regime, as had other regions. *All* regions of Libya exhibited something of a continuum of alternating opposition as well as support for Gaddafi. The city of Bani Walid inhabited by tribes of Warfellah, for example, which was the last city to be liberated before Gaddafi's killing and the liberation of Sirte had been a source of the opposition in the 1990s. A highly sophisticated coup attempt against Gaddafi in 1993 was primarily the work of Bani Walid natives. The Warfellah were penalized and other tribes stood by in silence over the imposition of sanctions on Warfellah tribes while its sons, both military and civilian alike, were brutally eliminated by the regime (Murphy 1993).

Thus, what may give the impression of a sudden and surprise surge of protests and uprisings reflects, in fact, a cumulative outpouring after four decades of Gaddafi's rule. The last decade in particular witnessed the further expansion of the chasm that separated society from state, ironically in a country where the ideology of the 'Brother Leader' espoused and advocated the merger and fusion of the two! In other words, Libya in recent years was living a glaring contradiction in the obvious divorce between Gaddafi's rhetoric and his actual practices.

Lastly, in this context, is appropriate to devote some attention to the role of Libya's women in the February revolution. Libyan women had recourse to and could benefit from the very effective and socially-binding respect traditionally bestowed upon them by society, and they utilized this to considerable effect in engendering greater popular agitation. Women took part in many protests and as soon as oppression and violence resulted in victims, they deliberately clashed with security elements, thereby provoking violent reactions and inviting even more protests (Tekbali 2011). Once an uprising began to take on form and gather momentum, women contributed through activities as diverse as the sewing of flags, making banners and billboards, and cooking meals as well as nursing. Women helped with communication, delivering light arms and ammunition and in some instances used them (Assed 2012).

Given the nature of the struggle and its consequences, Libyans are in need of a lengthy period in order to deal with the consequences of Gaddafi's rule and the negative impact of his policies. Gaddafi destroyed the concept of state and institutions and made war on society and its political and civil organizations. The worst of his deeds were not those connected to repression and killing or squandering the national resources in comparison with his role in shaking the value system of society and upsetting the components of its political culture. This places Libya before many challenges that demand patience and the marshalling of all energies to ensure the shortest possible interval of time necessary to embark confidently on a process of building.

The February Revolution in its initial stages had no leadership and was not expressive of any political or ideological orientations. This conferred on the revolution a capability to liberate itself from the impediments and sources of weakness associated with ideology and partisanship and the shackles they impose (Ulrichsen *et al.* 2011). The fact that after liberation ideological divisions ensued to become highly influential in determining the context and the transitional period is a reflection that these initial strengths have transformed into elements of weakness impeding the development of political organizations and an effective genuine civil society conducive to democratization. Only genuine civil society, responsible media and political parties based on programmes can militate against the potential danger of exploitation of the revolution and the blood of its martyrs for whatever political agendas. Similarly they may safeguard against forces desiring to preserve the status quo in order to exercise influence and any foreign desire to play a dishonest role by intervening in defining the form of the new Libyan political society.

The Libyan revolution was popular in origin and orientations. Libyans ventured into the midst of the revolution without any political experience or political culture or mass movements that would lend support to strengthen their ability always to maintain their revolution as they desired. Libyans were compelled to accept the intervention of NATO in face of the savagery of Gaddafi and his brigades. The moral and political instigation of the politicians and opposition figures and the highly influential role and media blitz of satellite channels, at the forefront of which was Qatar's Aljazeera, played a decisive role in charging their emotions. While Gaddafi's killing machine was committing barbaric acts, Libyans sensed that their country was susceptible to a war of extermination without mercy, and that there was no choice but to resort to world conscience and their revolution became immersed in the game of nations.

Doubtless, the world responded to various calls, and it cannot be denied that one of these was the plea for humanitarian intervention. The world was not prepared to repeat the tragedy of Rwanda in Libya or to see another Srebrenica in Benghazi. Libyans did not find any way out of the situation. The most the Arabs could do was to provide a measure of cover (necessary?) for the legitimacy of NATO operations. And while Libyans joined forces with the West, they did so with the determination that they would not accept the presence of foreign forces on their soil.

Nevertheless, the Libyan case within the Arab Spring raised and will undoubtedly raise many captivating, if problematic, questions concerning not only the ability of a local uprising to stand against a dictatorial regime and garner international support to achieve its goals, but also in regard to the legitimacy that an effort to topple a government of a sovereign state may accrue. This also introduces issues related to the extent to which the R2P principle may be expanded and how it may be interpreted (Etzioni 2011). It can also be argued that the Libyan case reveals new facets in the relationship between the Muslim and Arab world and the West. The fact that Gaddafi's regime was overthrown and Gaddafi himself was killed at the hands of rebels due to the unlimited support and direct intervention of Western powers touches upon the very salient issues that have long characterized this relationship and which are linked to Huntington's thesis of a 'clash of civilizations' and the broader Middle Eastern context. Moreover, the events that Libya witnessed and its results will potentially have far-reaching repercussions for the future of the country.

In the first few weeks after liberation the West and the United Nations advocated and marketed plans for the longer term and beyond the task of bringing down Gaddafi and protecting civilians. There were ideas and plans that had been laid down and prepared without revealing the extent of Libyan participation in their process. It was not clear the degree of the involvement of the leadership of the revolution either in preparing such plans or whether they had been consulted. Had these plans been implemented that would have transferred the task in Libya to the locus of building the state or the nation (*ummah*). These plans were not also divorced from the liberal peace project laid out according to the assumptions of the Washington Consensus and the principles of free market economy and neo-liberalism (Heleta 2011).

Most of these seem to have been abandoned though some of the components and policy recommendations they included are acutely needed in today's Libya. These refer to the plan proposed by British diplomat Ian Martin's UN special mission to Libya. Some of the declared objectives of the plan endeavour to guarantee a direct presence for civil groups of the United Nations on Libyan territory to assist the transformation. The initiative highlighted the need for the provisions of security, rule of law, political dialogue, reconciliation, transitional justice, human rights protection and expanding the powers of the state and the emerging institutions while restoring effective public services. Such interventions are indeed a prerequisite for any successful democratic transition and economic revitalization.[14]

Though these elements of the plan are desperately needed an obvious weakness hindering their implementation has been that they had transpired without a clear role for Libyans who have not had an opportunity or the time even to express their opinion in accordance with democratic mechanisms such as elections or referenda. Understanding Libyans' genuine anxiety that foreign intervention in Libya may lead the foreign interests moving to the fore at the expense of national needs and interests, the UN has modified the tasks entrusted to its mission to those of rendering to Libya what its infant authorities identify as areas of UN assistance and to embark on their implementation.

Libyan people do not easily rest content that their country should become merely a petrol station for Europe or that it should be run by Western embassies. Libyans who fought fascist Italy for decades put on record testaments to the heroics of an unarmed people who will not be deceived. The failure of Libya to achieve stability or transcend the negative impact of hasty arrangements for rehabilitation, reconstruction, democratization and liberalization of the economy may only multiply the dangers of schism and protract the period of instability. Similarly, if Islamists increase the use of techniques of elimination and exclusion or resort to liquidating opponents stigmatized as secularists or affiliated to Gaddafi's regime, this will open up the possibility of a war that will transcend politics. An even more horrifying prospect would be the possibility that large groups of individuals and specific regions or tribes might be banned from the right to participate on the pretext that they were Gaddafi supporters or on grounds that they took a position against the revolution or were not affiliated to it.

These possibilities are in play while principles of transitional justice have yet to be implemented. The legislation the NTC adopted imposing a ban on improperly or unclearly defined elements of Libyans associated with the old regime, has been considered flawed by many commentators and human rights organizations. Meanwhile, however, there is no agreement on the restrictions to be imposed on the practice of such elements of political activities prior to any relevant judicial process. In addition to the direct dangers related to these challenges, inaction opens up possibilities of resort to tribal, regional or factional protectionism and, hence, the potential corruption of the climate of political competition. The transitional phase will be decisive and the policies the NTC and its successor, the NC, adopts will define the form and rules of the game.

The guarantees of success rest on the transitional phase just as they rest on the extent of the ability of Libyans – and particularly the youth – to comprehend the prevailing contexts and to initiate action at all levels related to modern democratic society. In Libya, youth constitute the majority of the population and have been the human arms and ammunition of the revolution. They were frustrated by Saif Gaddafi's ill-conceived and apparently ill-fated reforms. Events in major cities after the liberation connoted the youth's disenchantment with both government and political movements. Such attitudes will not have any detrimental impact unless they show more resilience and determination in acquiring the political power that matches their place in society and the economy. Unless the youth are aware of the challenges the country is facing their potential contribution and energies will be appropriated by conflicting agendas (Sawani 2011).

A look ahead: concluding remarks

The crimes of Gaddafi exceeded those of material and human destruction and wastage and extended to the inflicting of serious harm on the foundations of the Libyan value system as well as disrupting the culture of political community and thereby undermining the potential for the growth of cultural components required for development. Furthermore, Gaddafi's foreign policy and misadventures greatly distorted Libyans' self-perception and that of the world beyond. Taken in aggregate, this bespeaks of enormous challenges that may hinder social conciliation, democratization, reconstruction and therefore lay obstacles before state building (UN General Secretary 2011). Arguing that the uprising was dominated by the periphery Jason Pack and Barak Barfi believe that '(Libya) is not prepared for the shocks that the periphery can deliver to the center', the fact that the country lacks civil society institutions and local governance implies the need for 'a paradigm shift (and) recogniz[ing] that connecting the periphery to the center has become the top priority' (Pack & Barfi 2011, p. 15, p. 40).

Present and future Libyan governments will have to face the enormous task of managing the high level of expectations that Libyans have while serving any interests that may have contributed to its composition. Striking the balance will prove cumbersome but the challenge remains that of acting in accordance with the ambiguous road map that the NTC adopted for the transitional period.[15] A rush to make hasty constitutional arrangements will only render the situation more fragile, and this was evident in recent calls for federalism, for example (Anonymous 2012c).

Despite the importance of balancing national expectations and taking into account foreign interests – particularly those of countries that supported the revolution – the real objective remains that of reinventing the Libyan polity that Gaddafi liquidated. This is also linked to the institutional and leadership weakness experienced by the country at various levels. There are visible negative effects of this vulnerability whereas conventional wisdom affirms that the most important components for successful transition and democracy building are those related to the availability of receptive leaders prepared to adopt democracy as a strategic choice and political commitment. The fact that Libya's present leaders are more concerned with partisan, regional and tribal politics suggests the greater need for consensus-building measures. Leaders confront serious challenges that are not divorced from their ability to provide elements for the success of the process to make democracy a reality along the lines of the pioneering founding fathers who drafted the Declaration of Independence and the Constitution in the United States of America.

Given the link developments in Libya have to the roles played by foreign powers, lack of strong leadership opens the door to yet more foreign influence. Analysts can only speculate as to the potential impact and manipulation exercised through tactics of playing Libyan factions against each other or – more evidently – through the support Islamists receive from abroad. Although all foreign powers publicly expressed respect for the will of the choice of Libyans and pledged support for the process of democracy building, questioning the actual and un-biased extent of support for democracy in Libya they tender remains undoubtedly a legitimate concern (Roberts 2012). More pressing questions arise, namely those relating to the formation of an alliance to intervene and 'assist' in building post-Gaddafi Libya (Anonymous 2012d). The real goals or intentions behind this alliance and its role and precisely how it functions on the ground have given rise to serious and heated debate in Libya. Many Libyan commentators, analysts, members of social networks, politicians and indeed people on the street have raised eyebrows as to the real aims behind such an alliance, headed as it is by Qatar (Hounshell 2011).

While Libyans expressed joy and excitement after the first post-Gaddafi democratic and successful elections, their failure to achieve democratic consensus will impede not only rehabilitation, reconstruction and the healing of society but will increase the risk of schisms and prolong the term of instability thus rendering the revolution absolute. Such would imply the opposite of the emphatic popular slogan: 'Blood of martyrs should not be shed in vain'.

Notes

1. Libya's Oil Production is above 1.5 mb/day, <http://www.febpress.ly/details.asp?id=20454&page=1>, viewed on 12/5/2012.
2. It is worth noting that the chairman of Barqah Council considered Misuratah independent of the NTC which, he claims, is turning a blind eye to this. Ahmad Z. Sanusi, Interview published in, <http://www.libyaalmostakbal.net/news/clicked/22573>, viewed on 15/5/2012.
3. NTC Website, <http://www.ntc.gov.ly/index.php?option=com_content&view=article&id=4&Itemid=2>, viewed 7/5/2012.
4. Statement of Civil Society Organizations on Libya's draft interim constitution, mentioned by A.S. al-Mismāri, 'Hal Nuldhagh Marratayn: Qirā'ah fi Bayān al-Tanẓimāt wal-Tajammuʿāt wa Munaẓẓamāt al-Mujtamaʿ al-Madani Ḥ awl al-Iʿlān al-Dustūri', *Ṣaḥifat Fibrayr*, 22 September 2011, p. 12.
5. Mohammad Zahi al-Mghayrbi, telephone conversation with the author, 13 October 2011.
6. Al-Ḥarakah al-Salafiyah [the Salafist Movement] 2011. 'Iḥtharū al-Shirk', document distributed by the movement in Tripoli on 2 October. Salafists, especially those influenced by Wahhābi thought, are extremely vigilant about anything that might give an appearance of idolatry – or shirk – taking partners in the worship of Allah. In particular, Wahhābis in Saudi Arabia undertook to demolish or otherwise completely level ancient tomb structures and markers (replacing them with simple stones) of even prominent Companions of the Prophet Muḥammad in the city of Medina. This was for the reason that they believed that tomb visitations – especially as in the cases of Shiʿite and Sufi praxis – had taken on particular dimensions of religious and spiritual significance, where people were making 'pilgrimages' to and seeking blessings at tombs of deceased 'saints' or prominent persons. According to narrow readings and interpretations in fiqh, such as those advanced by Ibn Taymiyah (d. 1328 CE) in this regard, such practices can be potentially construed to connote a kind of shirk. This severe approach towards graves and cenotaphs is generally uncommon in the Muslim world.
7. For two views on Libyan identity and nationalism see, Frank Ralph Golino, ' Patterns of Libyan National Identity', *The Middle East Journal*, Vol. 24,No. 3 (summer 1970), pp. 338–352, and Benjamin Rivlin, 'Unity and Nationalism in Libya', *The Middle East Journal,* Vol. 3, No. 1 (Jan. 1949), pp. 31–44.
8. See, http://ossanlibya.org/?p=22618>, viewed 11/5/2012.
9. See, http://www.bbc.co.uk/arabic/middleeast/2011/11/111127_lybia_demostration.shtml> viewed 3/5/2012 and for the statement issued see, < http://www.ahewar.org/news/s.news.asp?nid=745414>, viewed 3/5/2012.
10. See, http://libyafirst.blogspot.com/2012/04/blog-post_14.html>, viewed 12/5/2012.
11. See, http://ossanlibya.org/?p=26041#more-26041>, viewed 13/5/2012.
12. See, http://www.rif7.net/details-2251.html>, viewed 13/5/2012.

13. Timeline of the events is available in many sources, see, for example, Let us make it a day of rage http://fr-fr.facebook.com/17022011libya Accessed 17/2/2012.
14. For the Plan, see: <http://www.innercitypress.com/martin1unlibya1icp.pdf/.>
15.

References

Achcar, Gilbert, 'Libya: a legitimate and necessary debate from an anti imperialist perspective', <http://www.zcommunications.org/libya-a-legitimate-and-necessary-debate-from-an-anti-imperialist-perspective-by-gilbert-achcar>, viewed 27/2/2012, and Gilbert Achcar, 'A Revolution, with Qualifications', http://www.foreignpolicy.com/articles/2011/08/19/a_revolution_with_qualifications>, viewed 26/1/2012.

Anonymous, 2011a. http://libyanchants.blogspot.com/ viewed on 14/3/2012.

Anonymous, 2012. 'NTC adopts amendments', <http://www.thawralibya.net/index.php?option=com_content&view=article&id=4121:2012-03-14-02-30-32&catid=77:policy&Itemid=510>, viewed 2/5/2012.

Anonymous, 2011b. 'Timeline of Libyan Revolution', http://blogs.aljazeera.net/live/africa/libya-live-blog-march-23>, viewed 23/3/2012

Anonynmous, 2012a. http://chaabpress.com/news5214.html> , viewed 13/5/2012

Anonymous 2012c. 'Autonomy proposal triggers Libya clash', < http://www.upi.com/Top_News/World-News/2012/03/17/Autonomy-proposal-triggers-Libya-clash/UPI-75981332005384/ >, viewed 17/3/2012.

Anynonmous 2012d. Friends of Libya Alliance,< http://af.reuters.com/article/commoditiesNews/idAFL5E7LQ4V620111026 >, viewed 16/3/2012

Affāya, M.N., 2011. al-Taḥarrur min al-Sulṭa wiyah wal-Dimuqrāt ị yah al-Muʿallaqah. al-Mustaqbal al-ʿArabi, 391, 21.

Amareer, 'Is There Really an Arab Homeland?', http://www.libya-watanona.com/adab/amarir/am03047a.htm, viewed 12/5/2012.

Assed, Nafissa, 'Women's role in the Libyan uprising', http://www.libyaherald.com/opinion-womens-role-in-the-libyan-uprising/ Accessed on 10/3/2012.

Al-Tir, M.ʿU., 2011. Taḥaddiyāt al-Taḥawwul ilā al-Dimuqrāt ị yah fi Libyā. Ṣaḥifat al-Waṭa n al-Libiyā al-ʾIliktrūniyah [on-line]. 23 September. Available from: http://www.alwatan-libya.com/more.asp?ThisID=16855&ThisCat=22/ [Accessed 19 October 2011].

Beaumont, P., 2011. 'Qatar accused of interfering in Libyan affairs'. The Guardian, [on-line]. Available from: http://www.guardian.co.uk/world/2011/oct/04/qatar-interfering-libya/ [Accessed 19 October 2011].

Ben Khalifa, Fathi, 'Amazigh Libya ila ain wa ila matta', (Libya's Amazigh: where to and until when?', <http://ossanlibya.org/?p=25771>, viewed 12/5/2012.

Bin, ʿĪsā, F., 2011. Tahdidāt bil-Taṣfiyah al-Jasadiyah li-ʾIskātihā: ʿArūs al-Baḥr Tuḥammil al-Waṭa ni al-Masʾūliyah. Ṣaḥifat ʿArūs al-Baḥr, 6 (22), 3.

Bilḥāj, ʿA.Ḥ ., Dhawād ī, M., and al-Saʿdī, S.M., 2010. Murājaʿāt Tasḥ iḥiyah fi al-Jihād wa al-Ḥisbah wal Ḥukm ʿalā al-Nās. Cairo: Madboli.

Chersstich, I., 2011. 'Libya's revolution: tribe, nation, politics'. Open Democracy [on-line], 3 October. Available from: http://www.opendemocracy.net/igor-cherstich/libyas-revolution-tribe-nation-politics/ [Accessed 19 October 2011].

al-Dāli, F., 2011. Ḥ iwār maʿ al-Shaykh Sālim al-Shaykhi. Ṣaḥifat ʾĀfāq, 1 (1), 6–7.

Etzioni, Amitai, 'The Lessons of Libya', http://usacac.army.mil/CAC2/MilitaryReview/Archives/English/MilitaryReview_20120229_art011.pdf Accessed 29/2/2012.

General Administration of Al-Shouraffa on-line, 2011a. Amāzighiyi Libyā: Amāzigh Libyā LāYajidūn Ay Ḥ araj fi al-Taʿāmul maʿ Isrāʾil mn Ajl Maṣlaḥat al-Amāzigh fi al-ʿĀ lam [on-line]. Al-Shouraffa. Available from: http://www.al-shouraffa.com/?p=4030/ [Accessed 19 October 2011].

Heleta, S., 2011. 'Post Gaddafi Libya: a liberal peace project'. Transconflict, [on-line]. Available from: http://www.transconflict.com/2011/09/post-gaddafi-libya-a-liberal-peace-project-079/ [Accessed 19 October 2011].

Hounshell, Blake, 'Libyan diplomat unloads on Qatar', http://blog.foreignpolicy.com/posts/2011/11/04/libyan_diplomat_unloads_on_qatar>, viewed 4/3/2012.

Jibril, Mahmoud, 'Libya: where to?', Al- Mostaqbal Al-Arabi, No.399, May 2012.

Leitsinger, Miranda, 'Gadhafi, rebels vie for loyalty of Libyan tribes', http://www.msnbc.msn.com/id/43049164/ns/world_news-mideast_n_africa/t/gadhafi-rebels-vie-loyalty-libyan-tribes/#.T2M894FqO1s viewed on 4/3/2012.

Libya al-Youm Journal, 2011a. al-Ṣalābi wal Shaykhi wa 'Ākharūn Yuqaddimūn Mashrū' liMithāq Waṭa ni Intiqāli [on-line]. Libya al-Youm Journal, 28 March. Available from: http://www.libya-alyoum.com/news/index.php?id=21&textid=3654/ [Accessed 19 October 2011].

Libya al-Youm Journal, 2011b. Mu'tamar Sukkān al-Minṭa qah al-Sharqiyah wal-Khawf mn al-Fidrāliyah [on-line]. Libya al-Youm Journal, 2 October. Available from: http://www.libyaalyoum.com/news/index.php?id=21&textid=7965/ [Accessed 19 October 2011].

Libya Herald, <http://www.libyaherald.com/mahmoud-jibril-elected-head-of-alliance-of-national-forces/>, viewed 3/5/2012.

Maghour, Azza, iskaliaat al-jalsah al-oula lil mo'tamar al-watani al-a'am(al-tawaqu'aat wa al-moktarahaat, (on-line). Available from: http://www.libyaalmostakbal.net/news/clicked/24918 (Accessed 24 July 2012.

Al- Mofawadia Al- wataniah al- O'ulia lil intikhabaat, (Higher National Elections Commission),

Al-Mahir, I.K., 2011. Taḥarrukāt Qabaliyah Muqliqah Sharqi Libyā. al-Jazeera.net., [on-line]. Available from: http://www.aljazeera.net/NR/exeres/CAEEACC4-5691-4952-A6E8-F48F57D2349C.htm/ [Accessed 19 October 2011].

Al-Majlis al-Waṭa ni al-Intiqāl i, 2011. al-I'lān al-Dustūri al-Mu'aqqat. Ṣaḥifat Fibrāyr, 12 (September), 2–3.

Al-Mashriqi, A. H, 'Kawālis I'tilāf 17 Fibrāyir: Khada'ūnā fa Iltahamūnā wa Qālū I'tilāf', *Ṣaḥifat 'Arūs al-Baḥr*, 6 (22) 2011, p. 2.

Mislmāni, A., 1999. Ḥ uqūq al-Insān fi Libyā: Ḥ udūd al-Taghyir. Cairo: Markaz al-Qāhirah li-Ḥ uqūq al-Insān.al-Mismāri, 'A.S., 2011. Hal Nuldhagh Marratayn: Qirā'ah fi Bayān al-Tanẓimāt wal-Tajammu'āt wa Munaẓẓamāt al-Mujtama' al-Madani Ḥ awl al-I'lān al-Dustūri. ṢaḥifatFibrāyr, 11 (22 September), 12.

Murphy, Kim, 'Kadafi Quelled Libya Uprising, Sources Report, Warfillah', http://articles.latimes.com/1993-10-25/news/mn-49650_1_moammar-kadafi , Accessed 20/3/2012.

Obeidi, A.S., 2008. al-Thaqāfah al-Siyāsiyah fi Libyā [Political culture in Libya]. Trans. by M.Z. al-Mghayrbi. Benghazi: University of Garyounis.

Pack, Jason and Barak Barfi, 'In war's wake: the struggle for post-Qadhafi Libya', p. 15, p. 40, <http://www.washingtoninstitute.org/pubPDFs/PolicyFocus118.pdf>, viewed 22/3/2012.

Pelham, Nicolas, 'Libya, the Colonel's Yoke Lifted', <http://www.merip.org/mero/mero090711>, viewed 12/3/2012.

Roberts, David, 'Behind Qatar's Intervention in Libya: why was Doha such supporter of the rebels?', <http://www.foreignaffairs.com/articles/68302/david-roberts/behind-qatars-intervention-in-libya>, viewed 23/2/2012.

al-Ṣalābi, 'A.M., 2010. al-Shūrā. Beirut: Dār al-Ma'rifah.

al-Ṣalābi, 'A.M., Salem Shaykhi and Ismail al-Quratli, 2011. Mashrū' li-Mithāq Waṭa ni Intiqāl i.al-Manara media, [on-line]. Available from: http://almanaramedia.blogspot.com/2011/03/blog-post_3481.html/ and http://vb.7mry.com/t88212.html/ [Accessed 19 October 2011].

Sawani, Y., 2006. Libyā al-Mu'āṣirah: Qaḍāyā wa Taḥadiyāt. Tripoli: al-Markaz al-'Ā lami.

Sawani, Youssef, 'Challenges and Prospects in Post-Gaddafi Libya', Available from: http://www.iar-gwu.org/node/368?page=0,2 Accessed 16/3/2012.

Shuaib, Ali, 'Libyan Islamist quits militia to enter politics', <http://www.reuters.com/article/2012/05/14/us-libya-islamist-belhadj-idUSBRE84D1B120120514> viewed on 15/5/2012, http://www.temehu.com/imazighen/berberism.htm#libyanberbers, viewed 11/5/2012.

Tekbali, Yusra, 'Libyan Women Active Force In Revolution', http://www.huffingtonpost.com/yusra-tekbali/libyan-women-active-force_b_930995.html Accessed 26/2/2012.

The Board of Trustees of the Council of Ulema (Hay'at al-'Ulamā'), 2011. 'Bayān Ḥ awl al-I'lānal-Dustūri al-Mu'aqqat' [on-line]. al-Manara media, Available from: http://almanaramedia.blogspot.com/2011/10/blog-post_8451.html/ [Accessed 19 October 2011].

The Founding Committee of the Libyan Democratic Forum, 2011. Bayān al-Lajnah al-Ta'sisiyah lil Multaqā al-Libi al-Dimuqrāṭ i bisha'n al-Taṣr iḥāt al-Akhirah ḥawl Adā' al-Majlis al-Waṭa ni al-Intiqal̄ i wa Tashkil al-Ḥ ukūmah al-Mu'aqqatah. Al-Watan Libya, [online]. Available from: http://www.alwatan-libya.com/more.asp?ThisID=16807&ThisCat=40/ [Accessed 19 October 2011].

The National Front for the Salvation of Libya (NFSL), 2011. Ru'yah lil 'Amaliyah al-Siyāsiyah Khilāl al-Marḥalah al-Intiqāliyah. 27 June. Available from: http://libyanfsl.com/PDF/VISION1.PDF/ [Accessed 19 October 2011].

Ulrichsen, K.C., Held, D., and Brahimi, A., 2011. 'The Arab 1989 revisited'. Open Democracy [on-line]. Available from: http://www.opendemocracy.net/kristian-coates-ulrichsen-david-held-alia-brahimi/arab-1989/ [Accessed 19 October 2011].

UN General Secretary Report on UN Mission in Libya, 1.12.2011, <http://unsmil.unmissions.org/LinkClick.aspx?fileticket=v_-F2Xr3c9I%3d&tabid=3543&mid=6187&language=en-US >, viewed 17/3/2012.

Libya … hopes and fears

Khair El-Din Haseeb

Arab Thinker, Editor-in-Chief of Contemporary Arab Affairs, *and Chairman of the Executive Committee and Board of Trustees of the Centre for Arab Unity Studies*

September 1, 2011 would have marked the 42nd anniversary of the 'Libyan Revolution' of 1969 that the Arabs anticipated would support Egypt's Revolution of 23 July. However, as fate would have it, Gamal 'Abd al-Nasser would succumb to a heart attack on 28 September 1970, just one year after the start of what was then termed the 'Libyan revolution'. Nasser's untimely passing came at a moment when he was engrossed in a battle of attrition and preparing to regain the Sinai and other Arab lands occupied by Israel, and in the absence of the guiding light and of his idolized mentor, the young and impetuous Colonel Qadhafi, proved incapable and out of his depth. While he imagined that he might be able to fill something of the void left by the passing of Nasser in leading the Arab nation, such never materialized and Qadhafi would ultimately vacillate between 'Arab unity' and 'African unity' – not being qualified to assume a leading role for either and being unsuited for such on account of his upbringing, experience and acumen as well as due to the prevailing objective conditions of the country he ruled. After his failure in this endeavour, he took to distinguishing himself from other Arab rulers by arbitrarily adopting iconoclasm as a policy – to garner attention by 'going against the grain' (subverting the dominant paradigm), whether such was positive or negative, and where most often such was decidedly negative. Qadhafi undertook to change *names* including the well-known ancient names of the months (as well as altering the start of Muslim calendar so as to commence from the *death* of the Prophet Muhammad in 632 CE as opposed to his *hijrah*/emigration to Medina in 622 CE); the name of the country itself; and the names of ministries and embassies. This was accompanied by the publication of the *Green Book* and the setting up of 'Basic People's Committees' and 'People's Conferences' in his new system for which he coined a term and which he called the Jamāhīriyah (theoretically connoting 'rule by the masses') – in addition to dissemination of the 'Third Universal Theory' whereby he imagined and promoted himself as a 'king of kings' of Africa over and above his role as the de facto leader of Libya, despite his claims to the effect that he exercised no political authority. This is to say nothing of the Revolutionary Committees – which served as Qadhafi's 'extra-governmental' paramilitary apparatus to keep the People's Committees in line and handle 'physical liquidations' of opponents both inside and outside Libya – which were subsequently replaced by the 'Guards of the Revolution' and later augmented with 'Purification Committees' in 1996, followed by 'Volcano Committees'. Noteworthy also is the very sizeable share of the Libyan gross domestic product that he channelled into coups and to various groups (including the Palestine Liberation Organization (PLO), the Provisional Irish Republican Army (IRA),

Baader-Meinhof, among others) in addition to numerous foreign revolutions and intrigues both within the Arab World and without as well as connections to and/or support for a motley collection of African leaders of questionable stripe from Idi Amin to Jean-Bédel Bokassa and Charles Taylor. He also practised the ugliest forms of brutal oppression and injustice at home, where assassination of political opponents and the mutilation of their bodies – among the things in which he was proficient – could be subsumed under and pressed into the service of his policy of 'going against the grain' (subverting the dominant paradigm)!

Instead of transforming Libya with its huge oil revenues and limited population, through peaceful democratic rule, into a state that might serve as a shining model in the Arab World and elicit positively in the African sphere, the country became an object of scorn and ridicule representing one of the most viciously repressive Arab regimes and thereby distinguished as most deserving to be brought down. Such was the end of what was optimistically termed the 'Libyan revolution' at the outset, but which came to be the despotic regime of an individual and his family practising every shade of corrupt rule to the extent that its being brought down and its passing will not be regretted.

Theoretically, it might have been possible for the Libyan people to rise against Qadhafi's regime and bring it down along the lines of what the Arab peoples in Tunis and Egypt accomplished and what is attempted by people in other countries through peaceful, unarmed popular revolutions in which all strata of the populations participated – especially in major cities – and where the neutrality of the army was secured or it was brought over to the side of the people. However, not all of these conditions or factors were available to the Libyan people, where events compelled some to undertake an 'armed *intifada* (uprising)' where, whatever the justifications advanced for this, the conflict between the opposition and the heavily armed and well-trained forces loyal to Qadhafi – most of whom were led by his sons – was still a highly asymmetrical one. The 'National Transitional Council', created during the first days of the uprising, was composed of a mix of Libyan nationalist elements at the forefront of whom is Council President Muṣṭafā ʿAbd al–Jalīl, Chairman of the Executive Board of the council Maḥmūd Jibrīl, and official spokesperson for the council ʿAbd al–Ḥafīẓ ʿAbd al–Qādir Gogha and possibly other personages as yet unnamed for security reasons or among those inside or outside the country. When the Libyan people in the major cities, with the exception of Benghazi, did not take part in the uprising, the National Transitional Council incorporated a mix of Libyan elements rumoured to have foreign connections, which raise serious and dangerous questions about repercussions for the future of the 'Libyan intifada'. Subsequently, the leadership of this uprising engaged, with the encouragement of dubious parties both inside and outside Libya, in a suspicious move with the Gulf Cooperation Council (GCC) and then with the League of Arab States, which resulted in UN Security Council Resolution 1973 to protect Libyan civilians, which provided the justification and grounds for seeking the intervention of NATO air forces. This has caused a tumult and raised doubts and fears about the goals of NATO in backing this uprising and what will be its position and role in the new Libyan regime, a fact which mandates caution and close observation. Despite the existence of reassuring nationalist elements in the leadership of the revolution and which afford a measure of assurance, the West has proven to us that it is not some sort of 'charitable association' but rather it has rapacious vested interests that it seeks to advance in the background of any action or initiative it undertakes.[1]

The rejection in principle of foreign intervention that is fraught with the bitter precedents of experience stems from a stance of prudent caution over what might come to pass subsequently in Libya; especially if it is endeavouring to establish a mode of resistance to any future foreign intervention after the revolution has stabilized just as the Arab popular mobilizations have hastened in general to guard against a syndrome of dependency on foreign intervention.

What we have witnessed and what we see in Iraq after the occupation more than justifies these apprehensions, and commends raising of voices of caution and warning as both legitimate and prudent. Similarly, this reliance for assistance on the outside to bring down an oppressive Arab regime should not become a precedent to be emulated by other Arab oppositions. In addition, the eighth article of the Pact of the Arab League specifies that

> every state among the states party to the League shall respect the prevailing system of rule in the other states of the League and it is considered a right of these states to be respected; furthermore, each member state pledges not to engage in any act aimed at changing a regime in any one of them.

It is not permitted for the Gulf Cooperation Council (GCC) or the League of Arab States to intervene in order to change an Arab regime, however despicable it may be and regardless of whatever opinion of it we may hold.

***

Presently, Qadhafi's regime has breathed its last, and although his whereabouts remain unknown, it seems clear that he will either be killed, commit suicide, be arrested or obliged to flee into exile as members of his family have done in Algeria. Despite all the remarks I have made with regard to external foreign intervention in bringing down this regime, what is necessary is to focus on the future of Libya and to lay down decisive criteria for assessing the nationalism of the coming regime, which will be formed in the very near future, and the extent to which the incumbent Libyan national leadership will be able to alleviate fears and remove doubts about foreign intervention.

These criteria may be summarized as follows:

- Vigilance in establishing a democratic system that guarantees the provision of basic democratic rights for the Libyan people, first among which are liberties including: freedom of opinion and expression as well as freedom to publish and to assemble and organize, etc. That is, the sum total of liberties that renders individuals/citizens who exercise their right to citizenship without fetters on their freedoms other than what respect for the freedom of others dictates; without surveillance and censorship of their ideas, with the exception of what threatens the system of democratic freedoms or encourages civil–political violence; and without diminishing the right to organize and form political associations except those which persist on racial, factional, sectarian or tribal bases.
- Political pluralism and the right to participate, i.e. politics according to the dictates of public rights or the recognition that it is a public right of the various classes of society, its groups and elites, in what implies the prohibition of any form of monopoly of political representation by a single ruling party or a party heading a front of 'ruling' parties or any type of expropriation of political life or the bringing down the multi-party system – on the pretext that such tears

part the unity of the people! It is not sufficient merely to endorse political pluralism if all parties and organizations are not afforded the rights of political participation and legitimate competition over political representation and garnering public opinion through democratic means.

- A representative system (local and parliamentary) comprising legal and constitutional guarantees that ensure the following:
  - The freedom to vote for all citizens who have reached the requisite age and who are registered to vote in lists of voters where the electoral process is characterized in all aspects by transparency and impartiality as well as the prohibition of any form of expropriation of the will of the people or misrepresentation – either through illegal intervention in administering elections or counting ballots or by the usage of political monies to buy votes and allegiances – at the expense of conscience – or otherwise to control or impact the choice of voters.
  - The right to oversee and monitor political authority and its practices through the following various means of oversight: the deputy council's oversight of the executive authority; oversight of expenditure of public monies; and popular oversight of the administration of state authority. The representative system in modern democracies is the institutional form of expression of the principle of popular sovereignty or the principle which specifies 'the people are the source of authority', which they exercise through their freely elected representatives.

- The establishment of the political system on the basis of separation of powers (i.e. into executive, legislative and judicial branches), and respect – in particular – for the independence of the judiciary.
- Democratic rotation of power and endorsing the principle of the right of the political majority chosen through impartial elections in the formation of the executive authority and its administration, working according to the principle that exercising political authority is a public right of the people and the nation and not the special privilege of a political party, class, family or individual.
- That the aforementioned principles rest on a constitutional system that constitutes the essential order of the state that systemizes all its powers and relations between its various apparatuses in conjunction with the civil and political rights of its citizens. It is a system, the drafting of which should be entrusted to a duly elected founding commission, and the ratification of which should occur through a popular referendum.
- A just socio-economic system wherein citizens enjoy equal rights applied equally in such a way as to provide them with protection against infringement upon their political will, or their freedom to express their opinions or to choose whom they see fit to represent them.

A few further points should be noted with regard to these aforementioned principles:

- The application of one of these principles at the exclusion of another causes the system to forfeit its democratic identity as democracy is a comprehensive system all the tenets of which constitute an indivisible whole.
- That all Libyans should be granted the right to participate in this democratic system without any political isolation, political or social prejudice, and on a basis of complete rights for all Libyans.

- Avoidance of any polices of political retribution with resort to due process of law and fair trials for any previous violations or infringements (i.e. by members or supporters of the former regime).
- Fortunately for the Libyan *intifada*, Libya possesses superabundant funds estimated to be more than US$140 billion, whereby the new regime will be able to benefit considerably from these in rehabilitating the country as well as compensating those who were harmed during the uprising. It should also be able to provide health, educational and other services to Libyans rapidly and in a way palpable to citizens. Presently, arrangements are being made through the United Nations Security Council to lift the partial embargo of some frozen Libyan funds for this purpose; and this was something unavailable to the Tunisian and Egyptian revolutions, which might possibly constitute one of the sources of success for the nascent Libyan regime. Likewise, it should enable the new government from being subjected to a need to borrow from international organizations and the conditions to which they subject debtor nations. Tom Coghlan, in *The Australian* (2011), reported a source in the *London Times* to the effect that the preparation of a plan for the transitional phase after the fall of Qadhafi was completed by a group of experts of the temporary transitional council in Benghazi with Western assistance and consists of some 70 pages.
- Vigilance must be maintained against the intervention and interference of foreign forces, and Western ones in particular, in domestic and foreign policies of the new regime in Libya. This is what will partially unfold following on the results of the international meeting scheduled with regard to Libya for the beginning of September 2011 in Paris, where *only* projects to obtain Libyan oil and multiple bids to rebuild Libya – in an open and 'legitimate' competition – will be open to all external international parties, and wherein there will be no blackmailing of the new regime over what outside forces provided of material and air support for the uprising.
- A professional national Libyan army must be established swiftly, far removed from tribal or party influence, and political parties must be prevented from setting up bodies within the armed forces. The army must be armed and equipped only to the extent necessary to defend Libyan national security, with the proviso that the country may seek the assistance of other Arab armies during the transitional phase until such time as the training, equipping and formation of the national army is complete.
- The new Libya must rise to a positive role in the new Arab order, and particularly in the framework of reviving, developing and empowering the 'Union of the Arab Maghreb' for which Qadhafi's regime posed one of the factors of its stagnation. The future Libyan regime must also transcend sensitivities resulting from the stance of the Algerian regime in regard to the fall of Qadhafi.
- The Arab-Islamic identity of Libya must be persevered in all its component elements with reinforcement of its role in bearing responsibility for Arab-Islamic issues at the forefront of which is the struggle with the Zionist enemy.

The Libyan *intifada* is on the verge of a decisive point. Bringing down a dictatorial regime might, indeed, prove much easier than setting up a genuinely democratic system that will represent aspirations of the Libyan people. The success of Libyan national elements in transitioning Libya to the new system will be the true national criterion whereby to assess its nationalism, maturity and wisdom; and it is this alone that will serve as a response to all the doubts with which it has met through its work and cooperation with external forces. The entire Arab *ummah* is looking towards Libya with great hope to contribute new momentum to the Arab Spring.

Note

1. See: F. William Engdahl. "NATO's War on Libya is Directed against China: AFRICOM and the Threat to China's National Energy Security". Global Research, 25 September 2011. Available at: www.globalresearch.ca/index.php?context=va&aid=26763 (Accessed 10/10/2011). Also see: "Libya Invasion Planned by NATO Since 2007 with the Support of MI6; Mustafa Abdul-Jalil and Mahmoud Jibril have been paving the way for NATO's conquest since 2007" posted on rebelgriot.blogspot.com on 11/09/2011 and on Global Research 27/09/2011. Available at: www.globalresearch.ca/index.php?context=va&aid=26804.

Reference

Coghlan, T., 2011. Leaked plan of Western governments for 'post-Gaddafi Libya'. *The Australian*, 9 August.

Syria … the road to where?

Michel Kilo

Syrian thinker and writer

In this article, drawn from a presentation at a seminar held at the Centre for Arab Unity Studies on 9 September 2011 in Beirut, veteran Syrian writer and political thinker Michel Kilo analyzes the situation on the ground in Syria in the midst of the 'Arab Spring', unrest and violent clashes between the state and various forces. The reforms President Bashar al-Assad initially mentioned when he replaced his father in the summer of 2000 – when he endeavoured to open up the country to a degree – were accorded low priority until the events of 2011 obliged his government to readdress them. Kilo argues that the Ba'athist ideology has long since been obsolete and ill suited to present realities, that regime priorities have been misdirected and that while the entrenched security apparatus is still a force to be reckoned with, genuine reforms are inevitable if a major catastrophe is to be averted. Gross income disparities and inequalities such as those the author details, which are intrinsic to the system, must be rectified; and in what is most germane in the present context, the Syrian middle class can no longer be placated or controlled through the typical strategies that the regime has historically employed. Syria at large, and especially the youth, has come to experience the wider virtual public space afforded by the internet and its social media websites, and they are eager to transfer the freedoms of cyberspace to the real political sphere. Kilo also asserts that there is a grave danger of civil war in the event that Syrians and the regime prove unable or unwilling to sort out their issues, and the presence of armed Islamist groups at the local level is a genuine threat where such are capable of drawing elements of the general population closer and into the sphere of radical political Islam if the regime continues its draconian tactics and opts for a 'security solution'. Kilo argues that Syrians themselves must rectify the situation and that foreign intervention will only ultimately play into the hands of the regime or the Islamists or both, and that such would be highly detrimental to the project of democratic transition via apparatuses of civil society in which Syrian intellectuals and the middle class play a vital role. Syria is at a precipitous crossroads – a breaking point – and Kilo, as an insider long affiliated with the Syrian intellectual opposition, provides essential reading for comprehending the players and dynamics of the crisis – one which will have serious implications for Lebanon and the rest of the region.

Presently, Syria is passing through one of the most difficult and complicated moments in its modern history. Among the indications of this is the ongoing struggle in most of its cities and villages between official and semi-official military apparatuses, which are defending the current regime, and wide sectors of the population who want to change it or bring it down.

The social disobedience surprised many, and not only from the standpoint of its spread and its determination to achieve its goals, but also in what it revealed of the depth and pervasiveness of the general crisis – the political, economic, social and cultural/spiritual crisis precipitated by the single-party rule of the Ba'ath for almost half a century, throughout which Syria appeared to be distant and far removed from the intractable and stubborn crises persisting in the rest of the Arab countries. We ought not to forget the discussion in the Arab press after events in Tunisia and Egypt about the possibilities and probabilities with regard to the Syrian situation, when many asserted that Syria was insulated and removed from the sort of eruptions that had occurred in these two countries, at a time when some voices did acknowledge the existence of limited difficulties, which the regime ostensibly could eliminate with a degree of effort. We also should not forget President Bashar al-Assad's frank remarks to *The Wall Street Journal* (2011) to the effect that Syria is not Tunisia. This he attributed to two reasons: firstly, that Syria is an opposition and renegade state in which both official and popular views are in conformity within the framework of a general national consensus; and secondly, on the basis that Syria is a state that respects and shares in the beliefs of its people, where there is no dispute between the state and the people in these two important matters. Assad also asserted that the limited economic difficulties faced in Syria, that he acknowledged, were insufficient to instigate or serve as a *casus belli* for an insurrection of the sort that occurred (in Tunisia or Egypt), and according to him political reform is not a pressing issue, but one which can be delayed for a future generation.

***

The crisis of Syria appears manifestly in the political, social and national spheres.

In the political sphere

Syrian society has grown tremendously both quantitatively and qualitatively during the past half century and its structure has learned, advanced, become progressively more civilized and changed; whereas its political system has remained static and in its original state of inception for five decades. Moreover, changes in society have even exacerbated the regime's insularity and caused it to rely increasingly on its security apparatuses – as its means for controlling and containing modern social change. The structure of the political regime remains the one relied upon since 1970, that sees in the middle class the one potential political contender in an underdeveloped society, and, therefore, the one possible alternative and primary source of danger to it. Syria, in the belief of the political regime, is not a candidate for a bourgeois or socialist revolution, and therefore it considers the neutralizing of the middle class and the removal of it from politics to be a guarantee of the stability and sustainability of the regime. Thus, there is little doubt that it must focus its efforts on keeping the middle class in check within its political framework or by compensating this class economically and through granting it some authority (in positions within the state) in lieu of permitting it an independent political role. This is the view upon which the regime relies vis-à-vis hostile groups in general; where this view establishes a structure, the centre and axis of which is an authority that reproduces political reality and uses it as a point of departure and in keeping with its interests. Thus, the regime pacifies society under the aegis of a security apparatus that has permeated the political sphere or penetrated it *en force* and which behaves as though social development will remain static without political ramifications or repercussions, given that the regime will find a place in its ranks for anyone who rises to prominence or emerges in any sector among those of society, and will assimilate him into its structure.

This structure resembles an inverted cone or funnel, with its base in society – where it persists in drawing in whomever it needs or desires to neutralize and eliminate from its components and structures, by giving them a share of the booty or a position of power that will afford them the possibility of promotion, yet compelling them to cut off ties with the social milieu from which they came. In addition to this mechanism of assimilation and containment, the political party expressions either are integrated into the regime (the National Progressive Front), or are marginalized, pursued and semi-paralysed as an opposition. Given that civil society has yet to crystallize and local society is immersed in dealing with its own vital concerns, afraid of politics and distancing itself from the political sphere, or even that large segments of it have renounced the world altogether, we will realize that the regime's faith in its ability to contain social development within its own particular framework has not been entirely unfounded despite what this structure has precipitated in the way of problems and the turmoil it has caused, but which it has been able to control and suppress through security measures.

During the period following on the death of Hafez al-Assad, the regime changed its technique and attempted to keep the political sphere fixed: containing those problems that had become readily visible and fettering the movement of some of the intellectual forces that had begun to develop and become active outside its political equations, by using the economy as leverage and a means to expand its social base and thence to smash preliminary indications of a return of particular sectors of the middle class to the public arena. On the basis of this conception, there began a kind of intervention and expanded interaction between the ruling authority and the 'traditional Syrian bourgeoisie' as well as the nouveau riche – most of whom were drawn from the ranks of the government and who put their hands on national resources and increased their monopoly over them, to the extent that they considered such resources to be their private property, along with their fellows among the bourgeoisie.

This was the Syrian version of the Chinese experiment, modified and Syrianized, where China had contained stagnation of the political arena through mobilization of the economic sphere, and contained the political demands of society by providing them with consumer booty made possible through the prevailing political–economic alliance. This recourse meant the preservation of the system in its existing form and containment of social movement within its framework thus witnessing – after the suppression of an armed Islamist movement between 1978 and 1982 – a transformation that effected the handing over of the keys of authority to the security apparatus. This in turn had expanded and was transitioning into what resembled a society unto itself – penetrating all the political, social, cultural and economic components of Syria, taking hold of the helm – independent of Syrian society at large – steering its course and deciding its destiny without there being any serious influence on or repercussions for it. Under the shadow of this structure, which persisted in preventing the middle class from re-establishing itself as an independent political entity and arresting reforms – despite the general and persuasive need for such – tensions began to mount between a wide sector of groups belonging to this class and the political authority, which were dealt with through security measures.

However, this situation only further charged the atmosphere in the public sphere and precipitated phenomena unfamiliar to Syria in the form of continuous demands from different quarters for structural reform that would encompass the political authority and not stop at setting it in order at the administrative level or its external institutions (such as the government, the People's Assembly or local administrations, etc.). Those involved found unity and expression within the opposition forces for the first time since the Ba'ath Party arrived in power on 8 March 1963 and in the unmistakable escalations that would rock the regime, such as the defection of Deputy to the President of the Republic ʿAbd al–Ḥalīm Khaddām and the suicide of Minister of the Interior Ghāzī Kanʿān. After a conference convened by the Ba'ath Party in 2005, decisions for various reforms were taken, most of which were not implemented on the pretext of the American invasion and occupation of Iraq which gave the security question absolutely top priority. Reforms were inevitably delayed indefinitely, and – chief among them – political reform, that seemed imperative according to the consensus of most Syrians, and if not for this pressure then President Bashar would not have pledged to endorse such reform, as of July 2000, before delaying this indefinitely – due to its difficult nature – and delegating it to the coming generation, until just before the most recent popular explosion.

It should be acknowledged that the President had restricted some of the powers of the security apparatus, but then – given the priority of the security question – derailed the course of reforms, which broadened his influence. After a period this then began to shrink, amidst clear complaints from his leadership and apparatuses, so he seized the opportunity and tightened his grip on authority, so as to militate against restriction or nullification, and politically Syria went in the opposite direction to the one he had promised to follow. There began to appear a practical divide – much remarked upon – between the political authority of the presidency and that of the security regime. This divergence contributed to the proliferation of problems including one, pertaining to rule, which had not existed before and which aggravated tensions and took the country to the brink of the very 'surprise' that all were anticipating and warning of – and about which tens of articles were written and numerous lectures given – with regard to the increasing probability of its eruption. This was especially true, in the context of the information revolution outside and against the regime, after a new appetite for discussion, the exercise of freedom and access to open information developed across a wide spectrum of Syrian youth. Around 79% of the population were under the age of 34 (according to a study undertaken by an American corporation for the Syrian government, but never published), most of whom had obtained acceptable levels of education but found no opportunities for work or rights to exercise their freedom or to obtain information openly or engage in unrestricted communication with others due to their absence or being absented from public life.

Given the various experiences in other nations – both foreign and Arab – the most recent of which were Tunisia and Egypt, it was expected that the voice and demands of Syrian youth would be heard: group acquisition of freedom and the right to information, along with the actual extension of freedom into their society after they attained this individual freedom in the virtual society (of the internet). The political 'shirt' had been outgrown, putting pressure on forces most of whom had come into existence outside this 'straightjacket', who felt that they were suffocating in it and unable to find any understanding or response from a political authority that, for its part, clung stubbornly to its right to reproduce it. Thus, the political authorities still sought to regulate and control the political milieu within its own particular framework, which served its interests, even as it marginalized the youth and pushed them out of public life just as they were beginning to possess the keys to working within the framework of a public sphere they had rediscovered, following the failure of the translation of the prevailing pan-Arab socialist ideology into reality. That ideology demonstrated its failure when it became apparent that it did not possess the instruments or mechanisms requisite to reform the regime that had produced it or from which it had emerged. It became clear that the world of the political authority was a closed one and it was no longer able to block an alternative path, which is a process of completely re-establishing consciousness and reality outside its order. Therefore, a demand to reform the system from within is no longer being contemplated or put forward, but rather 'reform' has come to connote what crystallized increasingly as the 'substitution of a system based on freedom and citizenship and a civil state with a separation of powers, democracy, social justice and equality in place of the prevailing system', which lacks these characteristics altogether and is incompatible with them. Thus, a conceptual order came together and stabilized, expressive of the effectiveness of the cultural and political sphere interacting with social forces of the masses that the regime had removed deliberately from politics, yet these forces were to return in another way: through the rage that had accumulated over decades, which finally turned into open rebellion.

At the level of society

Social trends have been shaped by a combination of stagnation and political retrogression and a marked deterioration in the standards of living and life across a wide strata of civil society. This was apparent especially after the implementation of the 'liberal' policies intended to create the 'social market economy' that actually destroyed the sources of income of huge numbers of the rural population and urban dwellers of the small- to mid-size cities. Some persisted on the basis of the rural economy but from the bulk were compelled to leave their historical places of residence and their mode of living and customs were changed drastically. Given that the countryside is the repository of human resources on whom the regime relies and derives protection for the centralized, military security order, by introducing market reform the regime destroyed its relations with its primary human political base. That base was exposed to unbearable violations, including: the expropriation of its lands by processes of seizure said to be for public purposes and general welfare; impoverishment; and forced migration. People were uprooted from some their historical homelands: the Jazirah (the region said to be the breadbasket of Syria and a part of the Arab World), has seen more than 1.3 million citizens obliged to leave over the past six years (*Jarīdat al–Waṭan*, various issues between 2006 and 2010).

International organizations distributed nearly 23,000 food baskets daily to those affected, and refugees were drawn to tin-roofed shanty towns in the suburbs of the cities, surrounded by older shanty towns, deprived of most of the regulated public services and utilities. In point of fact, 42% of Syrians live in shanty-town regions, whereas the worldwide average is 8% ('Ali Dib 2011). The general purchasing power of people has dropped by approximately 28% over the past decade ('Ali Dib 2011), along with the transformation of the economy from a generally rentier–productive one to a luxury goods–consumer one with a glaring rentier character, shrinking the income share of the labour force of 16 million Syrians to only 24% of the national income, compared with 32% in India and between 60% and 70% in European countries (Nasr 2000). At the same time the quality of public services has declined, while their costs have increased, along with the corruption of the administrative apparatus that puts an ever-increasing price, without a ceiling, on any cooperation – however simple – with the political authority and its institutions.

An increasing number and diversity of people across society have experienced deprivation in both human terms and with regards to their access to information and, thence, freedom. The deterioration in living standards across a range of social and economic sectors, with people unable to maintain their right to work or a just share of income, has been coupled to the arrest of reforms and rampant corruption. Income disparities between the 'haves' and the 'have nots' and the astonishingly disproportionate concentration of resources in the hands of the few means they live in aristocratic opulence and indulgence (such that, for example, it is said that a wedding in the city of Ladhiqiyah cost approximately 100 million Syrian lira or the equivalent of almost US$2.02 million). This excess exists in conjunction with a rate of unemployment among the youth that has reached a staggering 70% of the total unemployed (Khaddūr 2010) – officially estimated to be at 7% and unofficially at 32% ('Ali Dib 2011). A concomitant exacerbation of the poverty rate has been observed. Though government numbers indicate a drop to 7%, an independent economics expert estimated the rate to be at 52%, when the threshold of poverty is pegged to an income of US$3 per day, and at a rate of 37% when calculations were made on the basis of a threshold of income at US$2 per day (Jamil 2010). Lastly, the tight grip of the security apparatus must be mentioned, given its role in maintaining the status quo and shutting all doors to any sort of reform. Combine all these factors and those who want a say and a role in public affairs joined with those who want their share of resources and income constitute the makings of an explosion simply waiting for an opportunity, or an accident waiting to happen.

At the national level

At the national level the position of the regime on the Israeli occupation correlates with a fundamental point of weakness for many Syrians, which is epitomized in the fact that the regime supported Hizb Allah in its liberation of south Lebanon, *en force*, while at the same time it abstained from using force to liberate the Golan Heights notwithstanding its incapacity to exert pressure – locally, nationally, regionally and internationally – to compel the Israeli enemy to withdraw peacefully from the Golan. Thus, it appears as though the national issue of the regime is extant in Lebanon, but it does not see the occupied Golan Heights as a national issue in light of which the reproduction of Syrian domestic and foreign policy is mandated. The regime does not even take this as a point of departure, with the mobilization of its symbolic connotations and national popular content in order to erase the negative perceptions that have accumulated in the group consciousness of Syrians in the course of the continued occupation of the Golan for more than four decades. During this time it has come to seem that this important part of the nation has been lost forever, without the political authority transforming it into a pivotal issue in its polices and relations towards the entire world as well as the Arabs and their peoples. What amplifies the danger of the matter is the incongruity of the foreign side of Syrian politics with the domestic one, where the former was predicated on defiance of what the latter could not bear or guarantee its success. In fact, an increasing number of Syrians have become convinced that the perpetuation of the domestic order is effected through the utilization of the foreign policy as an instrument – voiding it from its general national content, and linking it to the private aims of the regime, tied exclusively to the political authority remaining in power, which directs the complicated, intractable internal crises of Syria and essentially perpetuates them without a solution.

***

These three factors – political, social, national – merge and intersect in the consciousness of a new generation of the youth, mainly educated and unemployed, who constitute a wide sector of civil society, and who are looking to acquire that from which previous generations were deprived. They want a just share of freedom and resources at a time of deprivation, impoverishment and the shattering of local society as a result of the 'social market economy' policies adopted. By way of illustration, 12% of farmers in some regions of Syria abandoned their farms during the last few years as a result of the increase in the price of a litre of fuel oil from 7 to 25 Syrian lira and a rise in the price of 1 ton of manure from 12,000 to 48,000 lira. Syrian farmers transformed approximately 15% of their farmlands into feed for livestock after they found themselves confronting one of two choices: either crop failure or the loss of their livestock! (*Jarīdat al–Waṭan*, various issues in 2010). In the context of the political occlusion and economic standstill, it is no surprise that apparently contradictory developments coincided and conspired to precipitate a widespread social insurrection. It erupted after most citizens had spent several months sitting in front of their televisions witnessing and drawing lessons from the successful Tunisian and Egyptian insurrections. This experience led them to see with their own eyes how weak and unarmed people could defeat a security state armed to the hilt; and how effective and coercive their soft power could be when supported by legitimate rights and when a people determined to gain their rights combined with the persistence of those who no longer had before them any choice other than freedom and dignity or martyrdom. This transpired after half a century of enduring a regime that had nothing new to offer, even in the realm of promises; is unable to extricate itself or society from the depths to which it has sunk, and is unwilling or unqualified to achieve any one of the promises it had made and then abandoned.

Civil and local societies united and converged with the combined power of information seeking a role, labour in despair, unemployed elites, and a broad and deprived popular sector. The force of modernity united with the force of tradition, the power of thought waiting to be put into practice, and the power of local peoples seeking a practical escape – all these combined for the first time in contemporary Syrian history. When opportunity presented itself (in the arrest and torture of children in the city of Darʿa), the populace came out into the streets demanding what they lacked: freedom and social justice. Their consciousness had been raised about the significance of civil society movements after these had begun to form in 2000[1] and which imparted to them values that modern society had created: freedom, citizenship, human rights, a civil–democratic state, justice and equality, the rule of law, the separation of powers, the defining of the identity of the political sphere, the practices of the actors within it in accordance with the general popular will, etc. This focus caused the insurrection to occur as though it were taking place in a post-regime phase; that is, to overstep or sidestep the current political authority and its political world and to transcend these, as though the insurrection belonged to a future realm – and the people had begun to become free merely as a result of their demand for freedom. In fact the articulation of demands emerged over a brief period just before the uprisings through a confrontation with the closed official realm that belonged to the past and an ideology that had completely lost its practical utility and no longer had any function except to manage the suppression of society, the affairs of state and the corruption of both.

This regime, which claimed that it was in the vanguard working on the transition of society from a stagnant and underdevelopment state to a progressive and civilized one, was itself affirmed by the insurrection to be backward and stagnant when compared with society which itself had confirmed through peaceful means in the face of huge sacrifices that it in fact was progressive and civil. If not, it would not have demanded values that can only be restored through the formation of a state, society, political authority and sphere of public affairs with the goals of freedom, equality and justice in its very bones,. As it was, society compelled the regime to reveal its conservatism and reactionary nature and the point of collapse to which its utilitarian ideology had taken it when it refused to respond even to the demand for freedom, despite this having been one of its slogans and promises. The regime attempted to depict the insurrection (based on legitimate demands) as what they termed, some of the time, a foreign conspiracy of obscure and indistinct features and, at other times, a conspiracy by extremist Islamist forces. The identity of these forces could not be determined and as yet there has been no evidence offered to confirm their existence or activities notwithstanding the fact that the regime has arrested tens of thousands of Syrians and killed thousands of them. At the same time, the regime has refused to consider events as a social response to a historical crisis of multiple dimensions, which it is not only incapable of solving, but also for which – at one time or another over the last 30 years of its mismanagement – it has forced society to pay a heavy price. All this despite the crisis being of its own making and having become more complex and protracted in all spheres of existence of the people, state and political authority, to say nothing of individual life.

In the end, the regime dealt with the 'conspiracy' through violence that has begun to appear excessive and has escalated to modes and tactics of actual warfare to the extent that one might imagine that the army and security forces are fighting an external enemy that has occupied the country as opposed to dealing with the crisis through political means. There is no need to assert that repelling the conspiracy necessitates the preservation of the regime, when actually it calls for a change of regime and undertaking pervasive reforms appropriate to the depth and seriousness of the problem. In truth, the issue is one of escaping from reforms and change and a suppression aimed at not only the avoidance of making any serious change in the system, but also locking society in a hermetically sealed container in which it can compel it again to submit to a reality as close as possible to the status quo that prevailed before 17 March. That was when the social civil insurrection first broke out. Latterly, day after day, it is increasingly taking on the form of a full-blown rebellion.

***

The present Syrian crises bears characteristics that render it one of the most difficult compound crises that the country has faced during the course of its modern history. The way in which the regime has elected to deal with it has only increased its danger and has led to it losing its characteristic of being a general crisis with a political and social content connected to the life of the state and public society and their relations. The solution is not to be found in expanding the scope of violence as it is *not* a security crisis nor has it been of a violent nature. The regime does not believe in freedom even if it raises its banner, nor does it want democracy even if it makes pretensions of 'dusting its boots on its doorstep', and this on the pretext that democracy is sectarian and extremist, the activities of which threaten the unity of nation and people. Therefore, there is no benefit of a political solution or an option other than violence, and the government moved to suppress the uprising with the necessary severity as happens with the occurrence of any outbreak of domestic violent struggle in any place.

The regime called up and mobilized social and official forces as well as military and paramilitary ones and pressed them into battle to achieve two goals. First, the diversion of the popular action away from peaceful means in order to transform it to violence that would thence be easily overcome – given that the masses who are descending onto the streets now will not remain there if their struggle on the path to freedom and rights is transformed into armed action. Second, benefiting from points of structural weakness in Syrian society as well as various differences, may be exploited, whether these be class differences, regional, sectarian or ethnic ones, could effectively transform the struggle for legitimate rights into an internal conflict between contradictory and hostile social groups in what would also transform the political authority from a side in the conflict into that of a mediator or arbiter, and would lessen the pressure that the insurrection is exerting on it, thereby allowing the regime to play off one side against another. This is despite the fact that President Assad decreed in his first address to the People's Assembly (Majlis al-Sha'b) that there *were* just popular demands and that reform must be undertaken with regard to political authority, and he also acknowledged that there were sources of strife. However, in its actual dealings, the regime ignored demands for reform and focused on civil strife.

The assumption that strife was the goal of the popular movement was the motivation – even though this did not come from the people in the first instance but rather was instigated by the behaviour of security officers against children from Darʿa who were not more than 15 years of age and who were arrested and tortured with ferocity because they scrawled anti-regime slogans on the walls of their school. When the clan sheikhs and heads of families of Hawran demanded the release and parole of these minors and that they themselves be arrested and incarcerated in their stead, they were treated with harsh words and their women and daughters slandered obscenely, such that they exploded with rage and the situation blew up the following day. The security forces started things off by opening fire on the protestors and demonstrators on the first day, killing eight of them – some inside their own houses. The protests, which did not demand anything more than reform and freedom, widened from Darʿa to the other regions of Hawran, and from there to the rest of Syria.

In the beginning the demands were only for the cessation of hostilities against Darʿa and an end to its suppression. Vociferous demonstrators appeared everywhere – from Duma on the outskirts of Damascus to Ladhiqiyah on the Mediterranean coast to al-Qamishli and al-Bukamal in the furthest east and northeast areas of the country: 'In spirit and by blood we will ransom you O Darʿa.' They were met, in turn, with live fire, and demonstrators in Banyas, Homs, Dayr al-Zur, Idlab and Jisr al-Shaghur declared their willingness to sacrifice themselves to ransom the residents of the regions who were being suppressed. Their cries were the first clear expression of a genesis of nationalism possessed of a new content and taking a firm hold at the level of the popular social base which produced something new, something unimagined by even the most extreme critics of the regime. This was a social nationalism bearing the stamp of general popular consensus in confrontation with the nationalism of the political authority that appeared no longer able to generate any measure of voluntary consensus. Its nationalism was nothing but the nationalism of regulation, control, suppression and division.

What has increasingly become clear over the past six months in the period of the new relationship between the political authority and the people is the impossibility of building or reconstructing any new political initiative on the basis of what was, in a situation where the regime wants only the reform of its circumstances. In other words, it has become clear that the regime is no longer – in its present form – the referential authority for anyone, including its own leadership who reject any reform that would change it; even as they promise to undertake some reform in it. Moreover, there is no escape from it paying, in the upcoming period, the price of transformations that Syria desires and which have become inevitable. There is no doubt that if it truly desires a solution to the problems and crises that its polices have produced and for which it has waylaid solutions for over a quarter of a century, then the regime must take all of these reforms and transformations in a direction desired by the people – towards freedom, democracy, citizenship, pluralism and a civil state.

The regime chose the security solution for problems that *cannot* be solved through such means and it plunged the country internally into the unknown and opened the doors to a struggle susceptible to violence which might lead to civil war – expose it externally and put it in the path of a whirlwind of numerous interventions that can neither be stopped nor checked, thereby severely limiting its regional and national influence. Syrian society is confronted by two choices, without there being any third option. In the first instance, society could elect to be exposed to successive violent blows of ever-increasing intensity and harm with the hope that continuation and escalation will eventually force the opposition to respond in kind with violence of its own or to accept defeat and return to a state of compliant subservience that prevailed in the period before the insurrection. In the second instance, given that so much blood has already been spilled since the first days of the protests, whatever deal or settlement that the regime offers will not be accepted on the street. More likely, extremist parties to the situation – now playing a very limited role – will resort to moving the street towards violence, whereupon the official security forces are betting on the strengthening of these movements which will then allow them to kill a number of birds with one stone and to transform the struggle into a fight between the regime and armed extremist gangs, the existence of which will confirm the conspiracy theory that the regime has adopted. The regime is clinging to the security solution instead of opting for change and making the minorities increasingly disaffected with the majority. It is putting the country on the verge of sectarian infighting with which wide secular sectors of society are not willing to associate themselves and furthermore which they condemn and resist. Thus, a large peaceful popular sector has exited the street; and the inversion in the situation renders this, by rule of foregone conclusion, to the regime's benefit as the change in the structure of the insurrection will be a *fait accompli*. Those who are participating in the uprisings can be categorized as follows:

- A political party opposition with leftist, nationalist, and socialist roots and predilections, expressing itself in two blocs, which are: 'The National Democratic Assembly' and the 'Damascus Declaration', in addition to two Kurdish assemblies, which comprise more than 15 organizations.
- A very active and effective intellectual opposition, the most prominent expression of which is in the 'Committees for the Revitalization of Civil Society'.
- A youth opposition or what is termed 'the opposition of the Facebook youth', which is expanding and organizing itself to an ever-greater degree in what has come to be known as 'coordinating groups/coordinators (*tans īqāt*)'; that is, youth corps who manage the insurrection and drive it and who played a decisive

role in getting it started and who have also succeeded to this today in expanding the movement and controlling its actions.

- A local society opposition that contains the primary social base of the insurrection, which has been exposed to major structural changes over the last 20 years, some of the characteristics of which were mentioned above, and which has not ceased to make sacrifices daily of a sort hard to conceive of several months earlier. What has facilitated this is its solidarity as a traditional integrated society; its ethics as a Muslim society; and its peripherality to a regime focusing its efforts on controlling the cities – especially the major ones – as the well as the difficulty of penetrating local society and the relative ease of mobilizing it and the primacy of its group character and sentiment over the individualism of those belonging to it.
- A miscellaneous Islamist opposition, unknown and hidden for the most part, some of whom are *salafists* and others Wahhābis or affiliated with al–Qāʿidah.

In this reality, there is a latent danger lurking in the genesis of an armed reaction on the part of the Islamist opposition, which might be capable of winning over sizeable sectors of local society to its cause, who are not as yet inclined to political Islam, in the event of the security solution and official state violence coming to bear as well as the perpetuation of the situation of people in insurrection in an ever-tightening state of siege and daily killings where they have found themselves compelled to defend themselves. This situation, which, as mentioned, is one of the ones the regime is betting on – even though its *last* resort is to incite and exploit the internal divisions, especially ethnic ones – will put the leadership of the insurrection in the hands of extremist Islamist centres of power, whereupon and as a result of which two dangerous scenarios could ensue:

- Taking the leadership of the street out of the hands of those who can mainly be described as modernist and belonging to civil society, as well as circles within the regime itself who are inclined to reform, where already the relative weight of all of these is decreasing in the current movement and broad peaceful segments are withdrawing from the street. The danger is that the situation will be transformed from one of a struggle for freedom, justice and equality into another characterized by sectarian infighting, the extinguishing and termination of which will shatter society and destroy the state. In the event of such an occurrence, extremism will drive local society with all its various sizeable blocs; and the political, cultural and modernist youth opposition will increasingly lose its effectiveness as, given the nature of such a situation, it will not participate in such violence or support it.
- The second scenario sees the descent of Syria as a state and society into a destructive conflict in every sense of the word, pitting the political authority against traditional society, which has modernist demands, but which, in such an eventuality, will adopt sectarian/factional demands that are without doubt the necessary fuel for a civil war that will have an impact everybody. Syria, in the aftermath of such an eventuality, will not be what it was before, especially since expansion of the protests across the majority of the land and their spread to even the most remote rural areas, along with the joining of a huge swathe of humanity in the social movement, will bring death and destruction to every inch of the land that the army, the security forces and whoever supports them among paramilitary forces can reach. It should be known that the regime adopted from the first hours of the protests the security solution option in order to compel the other

> side to use violence and adopt violent factional or prejudicial positions. It did this despite the fact that this 'solution' opens the doors to foreign intervention and precludes the realization of the demands of protestors – demands which the political leadership has itself admitted to be rightful. It will prevent any reform of the regime before the end of the internal battle – so long as such demands are to the benefit of the regime, i.e. only partial and limited reforms that will preserve the regime's essence and only serve to improve its image. Moreover, such a strategy will also neutralize and effectively paralyse reformist forces both within the political authority and outside it and quash their role and the possibility of following it up, putting the country into a fatal 'zero-sum game' solution that can benefit no one and through which there cannot be a solution for any crisis. The proof lies in the recent issuing of laws on the press, political parties and elections: shoring up the stability of the political regime rather than taking it apart and confirming that the political authority is not paying heed to the demands of the people and is not serious about positive interaction or any 'give and take' with their legitimate demands.

In contrast to these two scenarios, reality also proffers two possible solutions. First, a new historical bloc combining the forces of reform in the political party and the political authority in the opposition with the intellectuals, youth and sectors of local society in order to isolate extremism and extremists and confine them to the sidelines of the conflict, stop the violence, and open the door to a general national dialogue about the issue that will pave the way for a historical settlement – one which will take the country to a transitional stage of a compromise/civil mode that will establish a democratic state where the bloc is adopted by the President and sustained by politics. Second, an alternative, historic bloc combining two oppositions – the political party and the intellectual opposition with the youth and local society ones – to resist simultaneously together peacefully, and in a popular fashion, both the regime of the security solution – which, in reality, suppresses the people and destroys both society and state – and the extremist forces operating within the societal base who, without doubt, must be isolated from local society. Such a new opposition bloc must take a firmly entrenched and frank stance in confrontation with them both.

Although neither of these two options is easy, and as it appears today – hypothetically dictated by the desire to win the battle for freedom – the exit of Syria from the current situation into an alternative one depends in truth on citizenship, the civil state, freedom, justice, equality and the rule of law central for its realization. However, if the second scenario should occur and the security solution can effect a quick victory of the sort that its proponents are counting on, and the regime elects to undertake superficial reforms to its external form and with regard to some of its practices, while maintaining its prevailing essence (and whereby it will be enabled to reproduce society and regulate it in accordance with what agrees with its nature as an authority representing a ruling minority fraction that possesses great assets), the crisis appears today as though there will be no improvement through the art of rule other than the use of weapons and the committing of fatal mistakes.

Where is Syria going? If the efforts of those whom I have termed 'a new historic bloc' do not coordinate and take shape in and outside the regime, or in the sphere of the opposition, the youth and local society as well as moderate Islamist currents, then things will swing back and forth to the point of rupture between a security solution from above and an opposing security solution from below, and overcoming the political regime will become an impossible dream!

What might be the national repercussions of this crisis that apparently will not be resolved in the near future – given the severity of its complexity and far-reaching implications and when it is entirely possible that it may take new and different forms that will persist for a long time? What will be the consequences in the event of the defeat of the popular insurrection or if the regime preserves its present structure, especially if the regimes in major Arab countries fall or if serious reform is undertaken in them so as to cow the Syrian regime into doing the same, or if there comes to power an Islamist or democratic current? What if – by and by – the regime comes to appear strange and alien in the context of an Arab World that differs from it and does not accept or is not able to co-exist with it? There is no final answer to these questions, even if what can be said at this point is that a regime that smashes its own people will invariably be reduced to rubble or nearly so in what is essentially a battle against itself, and it certainly forfeits any national or reluctant legitimacy, and finds itself confronting two sharp forms of isolation. It will face internal isolation from a people subjugated by brute force, where violence transforms its nation into the rubble of a nation; and an external isolation surrounding its symbols and institutions, with the awareness that either of these two types of isolation will have results and effects that will persist for a long time and make the victors wish they had been defeated!

Most recently, there have been indicators that point to the increasing danger of foreign military intervention in the debacle in Syria. There is action taking place along three axes:

- A hasty attempt to set up a Syrian national council of a Western orientation and identity from which will emerge a transitional national council composed of a limited number of persons who will be considered, as a number of various sources say, to be representing the Syrian people after the regime is considered to have lost its legitimacy and a demand for President Bashar Assad to step down has been signed.
- An attempt to get a decision issued for the protection of civilians that will give nations in the United Nations Security Council the right to humanitarian intervention against the Syrian government. There is an effort being made in the Arab arena to find an Arab position and Arab-backed settlement to be issued by the Arab League or a number of its members demanding a decision like this along the lines of what occurred with regard to Libya or with some modifications.
- Talk has begun to increase recently about the use of weapons to protect civilians on the inside, just as the remarks of some dissident officers have been published to the effect that they will protect the people with weapons.

These indicators imply, in the first instance, the marginalization of both the regime and the internal opposition at one and the same time; and secondly, the possession of the requisite legal corpus to cover any military intervention. French President Nicolas Sarkozy wants such an intervention to be made under the aegis and cover of the UN Security Council as he stated frankly in a remark during his meeting with French ambassadors in the Middle East on 31 August 2011. Resort to weapons means the marginalization of the popular movement, and the result is to put the destiny of Syria in foreign hands in a fashion that is fraught with danger and that will tie any internal solution to the desires and politics of the outside if the regime does not decide to desist in its internal military solution which opens the doors to all types of foreign intervention.

This, then, opens up real possibilities of direct foreign military intervention in the foreseeable future and that will head rapidly to a pre-emptive internal solution with strategic dimensions and import in which the opposition and the street are two partners and guarantors of its success, after it has become clear to them the American/Western solution will go against what they want for their nation and that such will also be at their expense in the event that the state is taken out.

Will the regime take the initiative, after the entire world has demanded – and among them its friends and allies in Tehran and Lebanon – for 'serious and pervasive' reforms and after Russia has delayed for a period of two weeks in order to find an acceptable solution, but which might be obliged to withdraw its support and compelled to side with a decision of the Security Council against Syria that will cover American/European intervention? This is the main question upon which all subsequent dangerous and risk-laden developments depend.

Note

1. Former Syrian President Hafez al-Assad died on 10 June 2000. Previous to that time, all but charitable non-governmental organizations (NGOs) had been effectively barred from entrance into or operation in Syria. The situation changed dramatically after his son's inaugural address which included themes of 'plurality' and the 'role of society', when incoming President Basahr briefly opened the doors to the influx of NGOs (Aoudate 2011, NGO Regulation Network 2011).

References

'Ali Dib, S., 2011. Social repercussions of economic policies. Paper presented at the University of Economics, Damascus, Syria, 10 May 2011.

Aoudate, H., 2011. *The harsh path of NGOs in Syria*. Available from: http://www.eurojar.org/en/euromed-articles/harsh-path-ngos-syria/1132/ [Accessed 23 September 2011].

Jamil, Q., 2010. Inflation in Syria. Paper presented at the Arab Cultural Center, as part of a seminar held by the Syrian Economic Socity, Damascus, Syria, 9 March.

Khaddūr, R., 2010. Regional developmental failures in Syria. Paper presented at the Arab Cultural Center, Damascus, Syria, 2 March 2010. Available from: http://www.iqtissadiya.com/print.asp?id=6110 [Accessed 18 October 2011].

Nasr, R., 2000. Poverty in Syria; alternative conceptions. Paper presented at the University of Economics, Damascus, Syria, 3 May 2011.

NGO Regulation Network, 2011. *Syria*. Available from: http://www.ngoregnet.org/country_information_by_region/Middle_East_and_North_Africa/Syria.asp [Accessed 23 September 2011].

Wall Street Journal, 2011. Interview with Syrian president Bashar al-Assad, 31 January. Available from: http://online.wsj.com/article/SB10001424052748703833204576114712441122894.html [Accessed 17 October 2011].

Morocco and democratic transition: a reading of the constitutional amendments – their context and results

Abdelilah Belkeziz

Hasan II University, Morocco

This article, originally delivered in the Fall of 2011 at a seminar held in Beirut at the Centre for Arab Unity Studies, examines the 2011 amendments to the Moroccan Constitution in light of the historical background. The tumultuous events of the so-called 'Arab Spring' brought new urgency to the issue of constitutional reforms that had been broached initially on the accession of Muhammad VI to the throne in 1999. Since independence, Moroccan political society has typically been vibrant, democratic and home to numerous political parties of various orientations and, since the 1970s, has witnessed calls by various sides for constitutional reforms as well as for the institution of a constitutional or parliamentary monarchy. On 9 March 2011 Muhammad VI gave a momentous address subjecting the issue of royal authority to public deliberations. This topic had previously ranked as one of the few unapproachable taboos of the political scene. A vital driving force in the process of constitutional reform has been the youthful February 20 Movement that was instrumental in the mobilization of millions of Moroccans and led to submitting the new draft Constitution to popular referendum and its ratification on 1 July 2011. Unlike other Arab countries, Morocco's functioning democracy, its well-established political parties and the fact that the issue of constitutional reforms had already been on the table meant that when Moroccans descended into the streets they had a set of clearly defined demands – demands that were also less drastic than those being made in other countries. Yet while Moroccan politics have been highly developed and articulate since the 1940s, the events of the Arab Spring provided the necessary shock and catalyst to transform relative complacency into action. The dense topography of mature political parties and organizations in Morocco factored in two ways: first, it permitted a stable environment for democratic transition, which was not new as a concept; and in a somewhat less positive regard, the compromises and concessions to numerous sides dictated by Moroccan political pluralism led – in the drafting of the amended Constitution – to a document of somewhat indistinct character. The King's authority, in particular, is not so limited as a contemporary parliamentary monarchy and he retains a distinct set of powers, particularly under the aegis of his role as 'Commander of the Faithful' (Amir al-Mu'minin). Nevertheless, there have been significant changes and this article examines the nature of these, their genesis and links to various political trends and parties. The uniqueness of the Moroccan model is demonstrated, though other Arab countries, notably Jordan, may follow a similar path.

Introduction

Various factors have converged to open up the possibility of constitutional reform in Morocco – ending a decade of hesitation in the face of recurrent calls for reform within political society. The constitutional amendments that were voted upon in 1996 heralded the way, along with the dawning of a new era for the country following the death of King Hasan II and accession of Muhammad VI as reflected in the amendments. Yet today a new political milieu has provided a realm of possibility that had not been forthcoming in the recent past.

One can distinguish between the three most instrumental and prominent factors driving the reform process as follows:

- The will of democratic forces and significant strata among the population, coupled with their desire to complete the process of reform initiated with the vote on constitutional amendments in 1996.
- The need for the regime to reform itself and project a democratic image in accordance with the King's own drive to dispense with some of the hereditary aspects and mechanisms of the suppressive era prior to his accession.
- The massive popular pressure for change, which burgeoned in 2011.

From the time when members of the Moroccan National Movement signed the 'Petition for Independence' on 11 January 1944, it was clear that a form of correspondence between nationalism and democracy had begun to emerge in the national consciousness. This was illustrated in the stress placed by the Petition on the necessity for an independent Morocco to enjoy elected democratic institutions. Additionally, both principal Moroccan political parties – the Independence Party (IP) and the National Union of Popular Forces (UNFP) (which later became the Socialist Union of Popular Forces (USFP)) – persistently emphasized the importance of constitutionalism from the moment of independence and during their participation in the first post-independence governments of IP leader Aḥmad Balafrej and that of UNFP leader Abdullah Ibrahim. However, with the support of the Moroccan Federation of Labour, headed by al-Maḥjūb bin al-Ṣiddīq; the Liberation Army (within the party), led by Muḥammad al-Faqīh al-Baṣrī; and the opposition current, the UNFP pushed the demand for constitutional change further when it stressed the necessity of electing a founding body in order to promulgate a constitution. This was rejected by the regime and thence dropped from the list of opposition demands in favour of imposing what is still being termed in the literature of the 'National Union' (for Popular Forces (UNFP)) and that of the Left: '*al-dustūr al-mamnūḥ*' (the grant constitution).

Following the promulgation of Morocco's first Constitution in 1962, six amendments were made to it, four of which were fundamental (in the years 1970, 1972, 1992 and 1996) and two of which were relatively minor: one with regard to the minimum age of succession for the Crown Prince in 1980 (where he was not to be considered as having reached the age of majority until sixteen) and another with regard to the time of submission of the official state budget for debate in Parliament. With the exception of the amendments of 1996, which were endorsed by the USFP headed by ʿAbdul Raḥmān al-Yūsfī, throughout the critical period between 1962 and the beginning of the 1990s – during the tenure of three prominent leaders: al-Mahdī bin Baraka, ʿAbdullah Ibrāhīm and ʿAbd al-Raḥīm Bū ʿUbayd – the Party abstained from voting on a constitution that it insisted had been 'granted'. It persisted with the claim even when it was participating in all parliamentary, municipal and provincial/village elections that had been arranged on the basis of the rules of the selfsame Constitution. The reason for the seemingly 'abrupt' change that then occurred in the position of the Party vis-à-vis the legitimacy of the text, which it had contested relentlessly for so long with utter persistence, is not difficult to discern. Trust between the Party and the regime had collapsed. At that point it was incumbent upon the Party to vote in favour of the Constitution (as amended in 1996) pending the formation of a government of 'consensual rotation' (of power), headed by ʿAbdul Raḥmān al-Yūsfī in March 1998, given that the Party had won one-third of the parliamentary seats in the 1997 elections.

In fact this shift in 1996 did *not* constitute a total surprise, as there were precursors to it in 1991 when the late ʿAbdul Raḥīm Bū ʿUbayd (original author of the amendment) along with former Secretary General of the IP, Mohamed Boucetta, submitted a constitutional memorandum to Hassan II, which was interpreted as though both parties were prepared to come to an agreement over a single constitutional formula that would enjoy consensus and break the principle of boycotting the vote on the Constitution or voting against it, which had become standard practice of the Party. There is no doubt that the King was keen to break this trend, which deprived the regime of consensus over the legitimacy of the Constitution. The constitutional memorandum paved the way for the formation of a 'democratic bloc' (including the IP, UNFP – later the USFP, the Party of Progress and Socialism (PPS) and the Organization of Democratic Popular Action (OADP) before the withdrawal of ʿAbdullah Ibrāhīm from it) just as it opened the way to constitutional amendments on 4 September 1992, which did not satisfy the parties of the bloc.

This is a glimpse at the history that clarifies the importance of the constitutional issue in the political discourse of the progressive movement in Morocco and its legacy of struggle. It also sheds some light on another aspect of development heralded by constitutional demands leading ultimately to a new constitutional formula, ratified by public referendum on 1 July 2011.

* * *

The consecration of the formula of 'consensual rotation' (of power) – which has produced three successive governments since 1998 headed, respectively, by ʿAbdul Raḥmān al-Yūsfī, Idrīs Jiṭṭū and ʿAbbās al-Fāsī and which permitted the members of the 'democratic block' to participate in the administration – was insufficient to mark the completion of constitutional reforms. It is true that emphasis on the issue of constitutional reforms has lessened in terms of magnitude and frequency, and has generated less heat than it did in the 1990s or beforehand. However, no suitable occasion has been missed to raise the issue during Party conference sessions, or during any meeting of the executive apparatus of one of the Leftist parties or in joint political communiqués. What made it imperative to reopen the subject is the fact that the actual 'consensual rotation' and representational experience post the parliamentary elections of 1997, 2002 and 2007 has been fraught with numerous difficulties and has uncovered points of imperfection in the constitutional structure that precipitated recurrent calls for constitutional reforms.

In the context of the inception of a series of Arab revolutionary movements and the birth of the February 20 Movement in Morocco, the circumstances presented an opportunity to take the demand for political discourse to the street, which was settling on the formula and slogan of a 'parliamentary monarchy' and generating an unprecedented level of popular pressure. This demand had been made previously, and prematurely as it transpired, initially at the time of the Third Conference of the 'Socialist Union' at the beginning of December 1978. Shortly afterwards the OADP (after the Socialist Democratic Party (PSD) split off from it) became a lone voice promoting and theorizing about parliamentary monarchy. However, in February 2011 the time was ripe for this demand to assume a popular resonance that compelled other parties from the Left and the Right to adopt it and to present their constitutional recommendations on the basis of it. Similarly, it led the constitutional amendment committee to uphold it in the draft Constitution and later to uphold the concept in the final form of the Constitution submitted to a referendum, still in terms of describing the monarchy as parliamentary rather than 'constitutional', 'democratic' or 'social'.

The amended Constitution met with a high level of popular support in the referendum of 1 July 2011 and enjoyed the approval of the most prominent and largest political parties in the country. It was regarded as a compromise text that took into consideration the suggestions of all parties without imposing itself on the people and the political society as a 'grant constitution'. Despite all of this, it was still possible for some parties and political groups to oppose it and boycott the vote on it, or to call for a vote against it and ardently criticize it – describing it as a 'grant constitution' and on the consideration that it represented a political setback and that it thwarted calls for change, or maybe to find in it veiled if not clear vindication of absolute monarchial rule. Among the critics were parties, political groups and protest movements such as the February 20 Movement, the (Democratic Socialist) Vanguard Party (Ḥizb al-Ṭalīʿah) and the Unified Socialist Party (PSU). Yet an objective assessment of this pattern of radical rejection of a Constitution that impairs the country's social and political balances demands correlation of this rejection with the legacy of the Moroccan democratic struggle on the consideration that it represents an early precursor to a new upcoming phase of constitutional reform, or one might say the completion of a phase that will ultimately arrive at a parliamentary monarchy.

* * *

Since the ratification of the first state Constitution in 1962, the political system in Morocco has been subject to a remarkable paradox embodied in the rigid intransigence of constitutional and legal texts, on the one hand, and flexibility – and sometimes toleration – in putting them into practice, on the other. And from within this paradox it was possible for many on the margins to find a way towards achieving a stable, organized and relatively consistent political life. Whoever reads the 1962 Moroccan Constitution and its amended versions over the period leading up to the most recently amended Constitution – that is over a period of approximately 50 years (1962–2011) – might not notice many Chapters where the provisions are dedicated to the recognition of many democratic and political rights such as various liberties, political pluralism, representation, oversight of government work, legal guarantees before the courts, equality in terms of rights and opportunities between sexes, etc. Indeed, there is little doubt that what draws attention are the number of different and unregulated powers that the King enjoys – especially those specified in Chapter 19, the chapter of all chapters in the Moroccan Constitution. It was this section that served as the basis for consideration of the mode of government in Morocco to be a type of 'absolute monarchy'.

In point of fact, it is not a simple matter for someone who knows the system in Morocco from within to assert with conviction that the system of governance prevailing in Morocco before the referendum on the new Constitution on 1 July 2011 was a system of absolute monarchy, except by choosing to deduce that from the constitutional texts or by reducing the entire Constitution to Chapter 19. Such a reductive textualist reading is likely not a correct way to understand the nature of the current political system, or else the plan of political possibilities would have checked in it, nor is it a correct way for one to anticipate the map of future political possibilities within the system as one does not find in the written text that which commends this or dictates this. Such a reading falls under the rubric of approaches that commit the error of *reductionism*, where a fixation on Chapter 19 prejudices a just reading of other chapters, especially those that specify and proclaim various rights. This leads to a mistaken impression and the failure to notice that the unwritten *implied* constitution is influential and more effective, in many instances, than the written one. This is a fact for which evidence is abundant in Morocco's political life since independence.

In the light of this principle, two related facts can be observed: first, that since independence, the extent of powers granted to the King did not prohibit Morocco from enjoying a stable, relatively consistent, political life in which the minimal extent of basic liberties was enjoyed. These included freedom of expression, freedom of association, freedom to organize demonstrations and form associations and parties. Also during this time electoral dates were fixed and women as well as workers, peasants and trades people gained a great deal of their rights, in part by affiliating to unions that were independent from the political power, etc. Second, the connection between the national movement and the King remained intact, producing conditions for mutual understandings that extended – in their givens and results – beyond the framework of *written* constitutional texts and existing institutional structure. In the scope of these agreements, that is, within the *implied* constitution, it was possible, for example, to begin implementing the policy of 'consensual rotation' (of power) that allowed parties of the Democratic bloc to form a government headed by then leader of the USFP, ʿAbdul Raḥmān al-Yūsfī, which made it possible to create a base for the implementation of the 'democratic methodology' that permitted the formation of the current government of ʿAbbās al-Fāsī.

Although it may have been preferable for this 'implied Constitution' to cover the gaps and points of weakness of the written Constitution, hope remained that this gap would be bridged completely through the writing of a modern Constitution through which authority would be redistributed equally and numerous powers of the King would come to belong to the government and the Parliament. When Muhammad VI came to power in July 1991, the new era was considered to be ripe and an appropriate phase for a constitutional revolution to bring about a parliamentary monarchy in place of the prevailing executive monarchy. The policies of Muhammad VI furthered this conviction, especially among those dedicated to the elimination of aspects of hereditary autocracy and repression and seeking justice for those adversely affected by the King's privileges. The King also made strident efforts to restore and improve the image of the monarchy in the popular consciousness by according it a social patina as an institution concerned with fair treatment of the poor and underprivileged or in his call for the adoption of a 'new concept of authority'. Even so these constitutional expectations had to wait for the revolutionary Arab changes to put them on the agenda – first as a matter for implementation, then as a facet of life, socially and politically – and attain general acceptance.

In the address of Muhammad VI on 9 March 2011, there came a profound, official response to these long-awaited constitutional expectations. Perhaps it counts as the second most important address in the history of the monarchy since the death of his grandfather, Muhammad V, who announced the independence of Morocco 56 years ago. It would not be an exaggeration to say that this address paved the way to re-establishing the monarchy in Morocco along contemporary lines as it is highly significant for the King to have submitted his powers – with the exception of his status as 'Commander of the Faithful' – to constitutional deliberations, political debate and amendment after they had been considered, for many decades, to be an absolute taboo not subject to consideration and well outside any public forum. Thus, it was a huge step for him to form a committee for constitutional amendment, most of whose members are not affiliated to the political authority, and to demand that it engage in *ijtihād* (independent reasoning) outside the framework of his instructions and with complete professional freedom.

In these contexts, what is most important is that the factor of the 'will of the King' is among the leading factors in empowering and promoting constitutional reforms, in addition to the factor of the democratic struggle of the people and its forces. Any objective analyst familiar with the political equation in Morocco will also have to concede that the will of the King for change has greatly facilitated the public will for change.

* * *

Just as the 2011 movements of Arab youth appeared as a surprise to all with respect to their revolutionary momentum, their power of determination, their calm composure in confronting the violence of apparatuses of repression, so did the Moroccan February 20 youth Movement appear when it first began and mobilized masses behind it and when it formulated its slogans with courage and faced down security officers in its protests and demonstrations. Since the very outset the Movement knew what it required and made sure to express its demands with a clear 'terminology of demand', such as calling for political reforms, anticorruption efforts and the establishment of a parliamentary monarchy. It did *not* begin with humble slogans before subsequently ending up with more radical and daring ones, such as what transpired in other Arab public spaces, but rather it did not depart from its initial demands and persisted with them, which saved the Movement therefore from falling into experimentalism, which is the enemy of every struggle movement in history. This was because its thinkers, supporters and youth leadership possessed a great deal of clarity in their heads over what they wanted.

Acknowledging a sense of surprise over events entails the admission of a generation gap in Morocco, as in all other Arab countries, which explains the absence of a minimal threshold of necessary contact or communication that would have permitted greater anticipation, more accurate assessment or at least a lessening of the shock for those among the elites or public who were caught off guard by what occurred. Those who were surprised by the youth movements and their protest and revolutionary power are many, including the government, along with its apparatuses and offices, political parties, the media, in addition to international forces and their embassies. Such may also be said for the Arab countries in which the revolution succeeded, as well as for those which are still in the 'throes of labour' or that have had a miscarriage. Yet, revolutions generally occur by surprise and discussions of their precursors and initial signs come later in time, after things have stabilized. Surely, the revolution of Eastern Europe provided just such examples? Thus, revolutions in history are akin to earthquakes and volcanoes as being exceptional occurrences which might be impossible to expect.

Similar to the epicentre of an earthquake from which emanate seismic waves, the epicentre of the Arab revolutions was in Tunisia and Egypt, immediately followed by aftershocks and repercussions throughout the majority of Arab societies. The after effects of what happened reached Morocco and violently jolted the monotonous political complacency. Thus, the February 20 Movement needs to be seen in this context of the awakening ignited by the Tunisian and Egyptian revolutions, by which the shackles obstructing progress have been broken or the tethers of hesitation about the future have been undone. This awakening is neither subject to dispute nor to the issue of a *fatwā* since the Movement was born of that momentous historic turning point witnessed by Arab social movements since the beginning of 2011. It transferred the struggle, for the first time in centuries, from the struggle of ancient, worn-out opposition groups and savage despotic systems into a struggle between rising societies and waning regimes. Those movements signify a decisive turning point and the emergence of a movement with actual and virtual energy that takes all political possibilities into account – whether being those of the political authority or any given party.

The vital and influential energies of those movements have been revealed in their conspicuous mobilizing capabilities and ability to mobilize wide sectors of the Moroccan youth in the battle for democracy, as illustrated by the protests called for and organized by them and the fact that other political parties were compelled to graft their activities onto and assimilate with the February 20 Movement. The virtual reach and power of the phenomenon is evident in the swift official response to calls for reform that the Movement prompted, and by the prescience demonstrated by the Movement and the authorities in grasping that a slow response or attempt to ignore it by the regime would only grant these movements a more conducive opportunity to expand and earn them a wider audience and more supporters. Both the ruling authority and parties have recognized this, especially after they had come to see the limits of their ability to contain the Movement or to adapt their positions to this alternative or that.

Perhaps the greatest asset of the February 20 Movement lay in its independence; which has definitely fostered its efficiency, influence and credibility to the extent that, at certain moments of the democratic movement, it constituted the centre of political decision-making with regard to the constitutional reforms. The Movement had no intimations of assuming other roles than the one with it initially began; that is, to awaken society and the nation while creating a social platform of timely democratic demands that had been stifled within the rigid frameworks of parties. Another factor in the independence of the February 20 Movement is its distinctness from any other party among political parties of Moroccan society, at the level of the tools, apparatuses, and the means of communication and mobilization. The Movement transcended the limits of the organized political party mindset and mentality that is fixated on obsolete instrumental givens, and it innovated highly original styles on the basis of modern communications resources to provide even greater opportunities for mobilization and mass action.

However, distinguishing between the February 20 Movement and all other parties and political institutions in Morocco and stressing its formation outside of the Moroccan political party scene, along with paying due respect to its distinctive mobilizing and regulatory performance, etc., is not at all to suggest that the Movement is completely *separate* from the party scene, or that it is entirely new to political life in Morocco. Even so, it is true that it has effected a decisive rupture with organizational party culture and its dilapidated traditions, such as cronyism, insularity, isolation from the social realm, and its complacent and supercilious discourse. It has also returned to politics its lost vitality and status as a matter of public affairs not as a profession engaged in by a small elite that performs the role of the society and the nation. Additionally, it freed politics from its seasonality (usually determined by the schedule of elections) and from the traditions of bargaining and exchange of symbolic gestures and messages between the opposition and political authority, making it actually *speak* after a long silence and rendering a stuttering discourse fluent. The February 20 Movement also emerged from the womb of a progressive democratic political culture in Morocco, which has spread over the past 30 years throughout the country, and in which parties, intellectuals and media have factored in its prevalence. Examples of this are to be found in the slogans, positions and statements of the Movement whose leading symbols are young; therefore, they all share similar features including youth to the extent that one could say, without exaggeration, that one is witnessing the rise of a new generation of politicians in Morocco that establishes its relation to what came before on the principle of 'continuity and rupture' simultaneously in the methods and instruments of work and the lexicons of mobilization it adopts.

As indicated, meanwhile, the inception of this Movement, in keeping with the broader revolutionary Arab protest awakening, was necessary in order to put the issue of constitutional reforms in Morocco on the political agenda and the schedule of political works and deliberations. Another decisive factor has been the official will – especially the royal will – and that of the action of the advocates of democratic choice in Morocco, whether among parties, elites or individuals, in opening the way to dialogue over these reforms and establishing a means for their execution. However, there was no doubt that the idea required a social carrier along with a popular force to exert pressure to be able to take the country and its political life out of monotonous complacency, hesitation and anxious questions raised about the future and to the point where Morocco can handle its destiny courageously and open up for discussion some most sensitive issues in the political system. It was the February 20 Movement that provided the social carrier and material force for this demand for change.

This is the essential background against which to understand constitutional reforms in Morocco and the forces that played the most influential roles in initiating the reform process. It would be a mistake to attribute what has occurred to one group in particular to the exclusion of others, even if it is necessary to concede discrepancies in the various capacities to influence among such. This is because reforms – along the lines of the constitutional formula produced and submitted to popular referendum – brought about the joint participation of various forces (the royal institutions, the democratic movement, the February 20 Movement). As for the share of each member of the partnership and its rights within it, as well as the relative sense of fairness and satisfaction with what it obtained from it, these are matters about which people differ, as discussed below. It is important to note here that what has been made public up to now about reforms is *not* a translation of the will and desires of any one group of political society, but rather is a product of the interaction of wills – some of which appeared to be incompatible – whereas others seemed clearly to bridge with others. It goes without saying that the inception of reform springing from mutual interaction and partnership is not an ordinary detail that may be disregarded or minimized. This is because one is unaccustomed in Arab political life to viewing the fruits of political struggles as anything but an act of charity and largess by the ruler or a victory of his opponents over him and an extraction from him, where there is no middle ground between the two sides. The political culture will remain – until other indication – impoverished of the concept of contractualism and consensual accord, which renders it impossible to comprehend political 'concessions' such as the Moroccan concession.

* * *

The demand for 'parliamentary monarchy' has entered into the sphere of popular parlance since February 2011, in the wake of the Egyptian revolution and after a protracted period of having remained a demand of political parties and their organizations on the weakly represented political Left and at the social base (the largest and most well established of which was the Socialist Union). The largest role is attributable to the February 20 Movement in sustaining and activating this demand and entering it into the sphere of general demands as a primary slogan to mobilize the masses for change in Morocco. It encouraged, through its momentum and initial impetus, many to break through hesitation over it and to make it a goal of the reformist demands of the Movement. This is the situation of some of the parties that had reduced the magnitude of their democratic demands after they participated in political authority when 'consensual rotation' (of power) was introduced and they began to fathom the 'red lines' in politics, or rather sought to determine these conceptually or demarcate them. It became itself an invitation to work along the lines of the demand it had initially carved out decades ago or adopted decisively during the years of the political dark ages when political expression was weighed in gold and taken into serious account.

When the demand for 'parliamentary democracy' imposed itself as a goal of reforms and a slogan for political and popular mobilization and a work agenda for the political parties' recommendations, one might reach the conclusion that the ceiling for demands and expectations among the opposition in Morocco did not reach this high threshold except as a result of the new emerging Arab revolutionary circumstances and the internal social movement which, along with their implications and ramifications, have given rise to a political historical possibility for the tangible realization of this goal. The royal address of 9 March 2011 and what it communicated of a desire to entrain pervasive constitutional reforms reinforced what was ostensibly the general belief that the time for 'parliamentary monarchy' in Morocco had become the 'matter of the day'. However, the start of consultations over constitutional amendments gradually revealed to the largest parties of the democratic movement the potential limits of the demands for change, the issue that was illustrated in their constitutional recommendations presented to committee charged with amendments.

Anyone who reads the recommendations submitted by the major and most representative political parties – such as the IP, USFP, the Justice and Development Party (JDP) and the Popular Movement (party) as well as the National Rally of Independence (NRI) – will notice certain contrasts with arrangements familiar to European democracies. This becomes apparent if the parties – albeit with some disparity between them – set about recommending amendments to the previous constitutional structure and the powers conferred on the King, the government and the Parliament, including recommendations affecting the system of parliamentary monarchy. The political engineering upon which these recommendations are based is not directly related to the system of parliamentary monarchy as understood in modern constitutional *fiqh* or the current reality of modern European monarchies, even though features of these parallel those familiar in the contemporary history of Morocco since independence.

These discrepancies did not come about as a result of an inability to grasp the import of a modern system of parliamentary monarchy by these parties since they have their constitutionalists who know much about the subject. Rather this comes about as a result of two disparate points of departure even if they intersect in results.

The first of these is the lack of desire on the part of some parties to entertain the possibility of genuine change to the structure of the political system in Morocco and thence disrupt the balances of power that were settled upon decades ago, which have enabled them to enjoy a pride of place, role and interests within that system. This applies to those political parties connected to and owing their inception, development and expansion to the ruling political authority, that itself had held them in reserve in the battle against the nationalist and progressive movements. The most sensitive issue for these parties – a matter which became clear in their constitutional recommendations – has to do with the extensive powers of the King under the previous Constitution, even though the royal address of 9 March 2011 did not place any severe limits on thinking about these powers.

The second point of departure is the realization of the parties of the nationalist movement (the IP and the Socialist Union) and the Islamist JDP that the scope for constitutional reform – even if wide and deep – will not take the country towards a parliamentary monarchy along the lines of the European pattern. The facts of the political situation in Morocco and the balances of its forces do not permit this. Rather, reinforcement of some of the powers of the King imposes itself as being a guarantee of political balance and social stability. The issue here, therefore, does not pertain to ensconcing his religious authority as 'commander of the faithful' (*amīr al-muʾminīn*) alone, but rather also to consecrating his political authority to rule as well.

In exchange for their defence of the demand for a parliamentary monarchy, capitalizing on the popular and political power of the February 20 Movement and the Justice and Charity Organization (JCO), the small Left-wing organizations have transformed this defence – over time – into the defence of a *principle* and not of a demand capable of immediate realization. As for the committee charged with formulating the amended Constitution, it was constrained by the thresholds imposed by the recommendations submitted to it by the parties. Moreover, it is unfair to attribute to the committee any shortcoming in producing an ideal constitutional text or one tailored to the forces with the most radical demands, as it was called upon to write a constitution that would involve all its formulations and thence its authority. For this reason it was incumbent upon the committee to find the appropriate means to reconcile an array of recommendations and to pinpoint the commonalities between them. Thus circumstances, the balance of powers, the clash of interests, and the multiplicity of political choices and alternatives produced a result commensurate with the middle ground or common denominator, which pleased some – and possibly the majority – but not all.

* * *

Many accepted the amended constitutional text with acclaim and support that was endorsed in a referendum on 1 July 2011. The supporters exerted the utmost effort – during the preliminary campaign for the referendum – to promote it across the widest possible popular base by elucidating its merits. They highlighted the advances it contained on issues that had long since been a source of contention and the gains for those of the major political parties in Morocco who did embrace it gladly (some, though not all, of which are participating in the current coalition government that is the 'ruling' parties and the opposition), in addition to a large number of unions and humanitarian, women's and youth organizations affiliated to these parties or close to them.

Meanwhile, outside this broad political spectrum there exists an even wider Moroccan society that transcends any party representation and which constitutes the traditional historical base of the monarchy: not only in rural areas – as is customarily asserted by opposition groups – but also in cities and within all classes of society: from owners of capital, to major land owners and prominent merchants and businessmen, to the middles class and onto the toiling producers. It is only natural therefore that this wide base participated in supporting the constitutional amendments for which the King himself had called and which ensured the stability of the country and delivered a positive result in the referendum.

In contrast to these supporters, others greeted the amended constitutional text with objection and criticism. Some called for boycotting the referendum on the proposed amendments and others for voting against it, while still others – albeit not a homogenous group – considered the constitutional amendments a disappointment to the hopes and demands of the people by only touching upon these in a cursory way. Thus, the amendments as they stand do not open the gates to real, genuine reform to the political system in Morocco. However, the problem of this last group of political society, which exercised its constitutional right to object and criticize with courage and principle, is that it lacked the political and social weight sufficient to carry forward its opposing stance and alter the general stance towards the Constitution. With the exception of the JCO, which was possessed of a relatively wide political base, all other Left-wing organizations sharing the same position (the (Democratic Socialist) Vanguard Party, PSU and Democratic Approach Party) do not enjoy a wide political base or a broad mass appeal capable of transforming the position of the opposition into an effective, influential and tangible force. And perhaps this factored in on the coming together of the February 20 Movement – which is not affiliated to any political current – as a social base capable of producing significant and concrete pressure.

What combines the two camps – both supporters and opponents of the amended Constitution – is that they both decisively concede – despite the variance and divergence of their arguments and terminologies – that the amendments undertaken to the Constitution did not lead to the birth of a system of parliamentary monarchy, cheered vociferously by demonstrators, and hailed in the discourse of politicians and in the works of writers and journalists. However, while those who accept the amendments consider such to be entirely normal given that the circumstances in the country cannot – for various reasons – offer anything other than this constitutional formula, opponents still see an opportunity for Morocco to transition to a parliamentary monarchy – and to a degree hitherto unprecedented in any period – which was squandered by the system and the parties who conceded to partial solutions. Advocates of the reforms see the Constitution as amenable to the recommendations of all parties concerned, and therefore a 'consensual' one, whereas opponents consider it to be a 'grant constitution' because it was endorsed by a committee appointed by the King (*intuitu personae*) and not by a founding body duly elected by the people and representative of their general will.

This dispute will continue in Moroccan political society. So long as the idea of reform is able to instigate political mobilization in Morocco and the surrounding Arab environment, it will not be possible to attain a shared vision and understanding on the matter between parties of different points of departure and divergent options. However, every observer of this tableau of fervent political debate about the Constitution will be conscious of two factors.

The first of these pertains to the nature of this constitutional text and its status in the dialectic of 'consensual' versus 'granted'. It is possible to assume that any constitution not promulgated by an elected body is a 'grant constitution'. However, the intended meaning of 'grant' – in the common parlance of the term in the constitutional context – pertains to constitutions decreed by kings, tailored to their desires and written by those whom they have tasked to this end, and which originally applied in the case of the previous Constitution of Morocco. However, the present amended Constitution diverges from this principle because it was written on the basis of recommendations and conceptions of various parties. Thus, it is an exaggeration to regard it as being 'granted', unless one intends to consider the IP, Socialist Union Party, JDP and Party for Progress and Socialism (PPS), as well as others, as being merely tools and mouthpieces for the ruling regime – a contention which is utterly unacceptable in this author's view, even if others wish to accept it. Consequently, those who termed the end product a 'consensual constitution' were correct, even though consensus was not comprehensive and inclusive of all parties.

The second factor concerns the extent to which a constitution can be relied upon that was promulgated by an elected founding body. We are sceptical that the current Constitution is more legitimate than either the 'grant constitution' or the 'consensual one'. However, the term 'more legitimate' does not necessarily mean more progressive or more balanced, since there is no guarantee for the advocates of a parliamentary monarchy that elections will produce an elected founding body that will share in this view. Furthermore, what balance of power in any society will permit the production of a modern, progressive founding body to be in the first place? And what assurance is there that the constitution promulgated by such a body will be better than this 'consensual constitution'? Or rather, who can guarantee that the constitution produced will not be even worse and take one back to a situation worse than what has gone before? It is needless to say then that this democratic principle should pay heed to a political fact that cannot be ignored: that the device of consensus/compromise is also an advanced instrument among mechanisms in the toolkit of democracy.

* * *

One could persist in extolling the advantages of the new consensual constitution in Morocco, as there is a great deal to commend it. One could discuss the virtues of consensus in societies where agreement, concurrence and unanimity are impossible. Consensus is after all a cherished aspiration in every society that suffers from a serious lack of the political values and their foundations, which cannot be reached except at their point of their actual entrance into the political age, meaning – in the modern context – entailing the ability to manage and regulate competition according to agreed upon norms and principles. It may also be said unreservedly that democracy does not always emerge in the context of a winner-take-all-type victory (in the modern connotation and not in the sense intended by Ibn Khaldun) that is established by the ballot and the rules of the majority–minority dialectic. However, it can emerge, and actually *has*, from the acceptance of consensus/compromise between two contending parties.

One could elaborate here and deploy the terminologies of political thought and theory – modern and contemporary – to contend with those who adopt the Darwinian connotation of democracy in which the strongest prevails, and those with the greatest number of votes in elections exercise majority dominance over the minority in the name of popular legitimacy. Here the argument of our school of democracy that prefers compromise and consent over pure majority rule is considered decisive. Resort to consensus-building and arbitration of differences have produced many benefits at the level of the formation of political authority in a number of countries in transition to democracy (and the most recent model experience is that of South Africa). One may also cite the modern Moroccan precursors – the most recent of which is the experience of 'consensual rotation' with all its faults and imperfections – to clarify some enlightening aspects of the process of consensus and compromise. However, this will be left aside in order to focus on a less edifying aspect of the Moroccan case, namely the negative side-effects of the spurious fabrication or concoction of a compromise between elements that do not accept compromise or consensus. This, in the author's view, is the situation and context in which the constitutional amendments have taken shape.

* * *

The text of the amended constitution, which was intended to be consensual, was supposed to garner a minimum level of agreement in an environment of extremely contradictory and contentious political groups, with respect to their orientations and contrasting schools of thought. The divisions are between Right and Left; between the secularists and the Islamists; between those calling for parliamentary monarchy and those for the King to retain an active executive role; between those who are hastening for change and those who consider such to be a long-term political process; and between those who are convinced of a universal paradigm for democracy and those who defend the concept of specificity according to particular objective conditions. They are those who believe that the moment is historic and exceptional and those who doubt that it might alone suffice to bring matters to fruition; as well as those who cling to the principle of obligation, and the pragmatic who adhere to the possible. It has not always proved possible for those formulating the text of the constitution to arrive at common ground and a lowest common denominator. This was not because the political forces participating – behind the scenes, in committee sessions tasked with formulating the text – abstained from following a practice of making mutual concessions, without which any consensus cannot be reached. Rather, this has been due to the huge differences between them that made reaching minimal standards of agreement extremely difficult without one party or another sensing that its opinion had not been taken into consideration.

This impasse had the greatest of impacts on the elaboration of solutions and formulas that are bereft of the connotation of *consensus* and which have occasionally represented little more than an arbitrary joining together or merging of what cannot be joined. Therefore, consensus, in this context, seemed to be an imprecise compensatory measure and a sort of recompense without accountability: a granting of rights that cancel each other out to the extent that some of the sections of the constitution appear as if pieced together like mosaics without any sort of uniformity or consistency to the text!

Many examples of this muddle can be culled from the constitutional amendments; however, it will suffice to mention just a few. The first such example is the balancing of two opposing demands (at once) – such that some aspects of the executive monarchy are maintained to satisfy the party calling for guarantees of stability and national unity, as opposed to transferring numerous powers to the government formed and stemming from the Parliament, as sought by another party with reservations about the concept of a parliamentary monarchy. This balancing act almost led the constitutional text into a 'schizoid' realm of double investiture in the executive authority. Still worse, it took the authority of the head of Parliament (i.e. the Premier) to the limits of absolute authority or that which exceeds the thresholds of the legislative authority. How else to explain the significance of him having the jurisdiction and authority to dissolve Parliament, when the exercise of such authority that had long been subject to efforts to restrict it and subject it to the authority of the people acting through elected representatives?

In a second example, attempts to satisfy diverse cultural and linguistic demands – no doubt a legitimate endeavour from the standpoint of cultural democracy – have strayed from an appropriate course. In the name of pluralism and recognition of the multiplicity of linguistic and cultural wellsprings and tributaries that enrich society, the demands of such-and-such a person are lumped together with those of so-and-so in a single basket, without paying heed to the effects this mishmash will have on the unity and integrity of the cultural entity. As a result, one finds oneself confronted by a mosaic (in the constitutional text) that cannot be justified, except as a desire to please everyone. Searching the amended Constitution to find the clearest statements defining the national identity, it is found they do so by referring one back to its Arab, Islamic, Berber (Amazigh), Saharan-Hassanic, Hebraic, Andalusian, Mediterranean and African influences, which does not add anything to the fact that Moroccans constitute a *single* people. Consequently, it is a definition unfamiliar to constitutions, the only function of which is to curry satisfaction. One might well ask what would be the case if the United States Constitution were textually to *specify* that the official languages are English, Spanish, Hindi, Chinese, etc., and that lineages of American identity are numerous, such as European (including British, French, German, Irish, Spanish, etc.), American (Mexican, Cuban, etc.), Indian, Chinese, Arab, Jewish and Slavic, etc. What would be the national opinion about such definitions? The same could be said for constitutions across the entire world as well.

The third example pertains to the hybridization of the relationship between religion and state as conceived in the amended Constitution – which speaks of contradictions underlying the definition of the state, to the effect that Morocco is an Islamic state, and then alternatively describing it as being a 'civil' state in which the people are the source of authority. This hybridization is indicative of the extreme consensualist inclinations and predilections that governed the constitutional formulation, which rejected acknowledging one view over the other and attempted to conjoin both disparate views. However, this conciliatory measure is entirely ill-suited to producing a coherent structure, if not actually to say conducive to fomenting a constant conflict when considering the matter in the long-term. It might have been sufficient in this regard simply to specify the functions of the King as the 'Commander of the Faithful' (*amīr al-muʾminīn* – according to the historical Islamic soubriquet), as a sufficiently substantive expression of the relationship between religion and the state, and thence obviate against any chance for disagreement in the matter between secularists and Islamists. The constitutional text – with its internal confusion and ambiguity in its two different languages, that is, the religious and the civil – does not leave room for Islamists to oppose secularists on terminology clearly indicating the 'civil' nature of the state, while at the same time it also precludes secularists from opposing Islamists given 'religious' terminology affirming the 'Islamic' character of the state.

These are only a few of many examples of the negative repercussions of compensatory mechanisms of compromise and (mutual) acquiesce, which is transformed into a hybridized consensus aimed at courting acquiescence among diverse parties.

Consensus is worth defending for its own sake as the only way to manage the struggle over politics or conflicting interests. As for whatever falls outside the sphere of politics – such as religion, identity and language – such matters are not amenable to being approached through political means because such means cannot possibly produce an acceptable entente. Even if compromise were to be achieved, it would ultimately be spurious and a mutual deception. Prudence dictates that matters of political contention be directed to the authority of the King, among which is the authority to arbitrate in matters that are not subject to political accord because these – in toto – are not among the concerns of politics, such as those previously mentioned.

* * *

Whoever, reads the text of the amended constitution comparatively will notice that it did take genuine steps towards the political engineering of a regime based – to a reasonable degree – on a 'balance of powers' between the essential institutions of the state. Also, the revised text succeeded to a limited extent in redistributing power by transferring certain levels and spheres of it to the government formed by the parliament, whereas these had been subsumed under jurisdiction of the authority of the King in previous constitutions.

And if criteria for evaluating the amended Constitution, in the view of many of who opposed it, ought to be found in the balance of reality, needs and demands and not in comparison with precedents – which is actually a worthy argument – then, in comparison with what came before, one can perceive the magnitude of the pervasive change that has been introduced into the constitutional structure in Morocco. The conclusions that can be drawn from such a comparison permit the evaluation of the new constitutional amendments in light of realities and needs in order to demonstrate the level of their responsiveness, whether negative or positive. It must be emphasized, however, that this type of assessment requires starting from a sound political base in order for it to be correct, since there is a tremendous difference between judging the Constitution according to the logic of possible reality and judging it according to the logic of principle obligation.

* * *

One registers these preliminary observations without delving into either of the comparative perspectives, and focuses instead on what appear to be the new facets of the amended constitution, taking into account at the same time, of course, the existence of shortcomings or deficiencies. The most important thing to demonstrate is that which has previously been termed the 'balanced and equitable distribution of political authority' in it. The clearest manifestation of this is the rectification of the defects on which the political system in Morocco was previously based. The consequences of consolidating powers in the hands of the King and restricting the latitude of the specialization and responsibility of the government, or rather turning the Council of Ministers (Cabinet) headed by the King into the primary platform for the executive power *in lieu* of the Parliament or *Majlis* – headed by the Premier – require careful examination. In addition to the absence of a constitutional base for the naming of a head of the government, along with the fragility of the official formula for making appointments, which yields an impression of 'double investiture' for government – in the King and the Parliament – the changes make it entirely plausible for the King to appoint a Premier, at the same time as they open the doors wide to questions over whether the government is answerable to the King or to the Parliament or both and to what extent?

One might summarize this new balance by describing it as a 'balance within the executive authority' – between the authoritative powers of the King and those of the government – and a 'balance within the legislative authority' between the powers of the King and those of the Parliament, with a shared 'partnership' – that cannot be described as being equal – in other powers, such as security, military and legislative powers, etc. If one wanted to sketch this novel relative balance vis-à-vis the actual powers of the King, one could depict them in gradation: from exclusive powers, to shared powers, to the independent powers enjoyed by the executive and legislative institution, according to the following series:

- Primary exclusive powers enjoyed by the King in accordance with specifications in Chapter III 'Of the Royalty' Article 41 of the amended Constitution, which are subsumed under the authority to issue royal proclamations/decrees (*ẓahāʾir* – referred to in the official French-language version of the *Bulletin Officiel* as '*Les dahirs*')[1] pertaining to religious affairs on account of his being the 'Commander of the Faithful'. From this standpoint he heads the 'Supreme Council of Scholars' (*ʿulamāʾ*) charged with issuing official *fatwās*, which none can be delegated to sign or has the right to sign in the stead of King. The authority to issue royal decrees (exclusive to the King) extends to other circumstances such as those specified in the following sections of the Constitution: Article 44 (pertaining to the Council of the Regency (Majlis al-Wiṣāyah)); Article 47 (in the first paragraph pertaining to the appointment of the Head of the Government and the sixth paragraph pertaining to the disbanding of the Government upon the resignation of its Head); Article 51 (pertaining to the right of the King to dissolve both Chambers of Parliament or either one of them in the case of eventualities specified in Articles 96, 97 and 98); Article 57 (pertaining to the approval of the King in the appointment of magistrates by the Supreme Council of the Judiciary); Article 59 (pertaining to the declaration by royal decree of a 'state of exception' after consultation with the Head of Government and the Heads of the two Chambers of Parliament); Article 130 (pertaining to the appointment of the Constitutional Court); and finally Article 174 (pertaining to proposing initiatives and recommendations to review the Constitution through popular referendum of the people).
- Shared powers between the King, the Government and the Parliament or so-called 'participatory governance'. Among these are the authority of the King to issue decrees that may be signed jointly with the Head of the Government in circumstances other than the aforementioned. However, this sharing of authority extends to virtually all areas with the exception of what falls under the heading of religious affairs, and is restricted to the King. Technically, therefore, the King shares executive powers with the Council of Ministers, whose jurisdiction is constrained and circumscribed by the dictates of Article 49, most of which are subject to the Parliament – in addition to being subject to a decision to dissolve the Chamber of Representatives (where Article 104 specifies that 'The Head of Government can dissolve the Chamber of Representatives, through a decision taken in the Council of Ministers, after consultation with the King, the Head of the Chamber and the Head of the Constitutional Court'), as well as in deliberations of the Supreme Security Council where it is possible for the

King to grant to the Head of Government powers to head convocations of the Parliament according to Article 54. Also, among these shared powers are those between the King and the Parliament such as their shared authority over the composition of the Constitutional Court, in accordance with Article 130, where the King appoints six members, the Chamber of Representatives elects three and the Council of Councillors elects three. A similar sharing of powers can also be seen in the discussion by Parliament of every agreement or accord submitted by the King before these are ratified.

- Independent powers of the Parliament and the Government, meaning those functions which the Constitution specifies as exclusive to both (with the exception of the authority to issue royal decrees), the scope of which has been expanded to an unprecedented degree in the amended Constitution. In this respect, the jurisdictions that the executive authority of the Government has come to enjoy and the influential executive powers that the Head of Government enjoys connote – for the first time in the history of the Moroccan political system – a genuine transition towards a balance of powers, as opposed to the pro-forma distribution of powers that has been propounded since the inception of the first Constitution following Independence (the Constitution of 1962). Along the same lines, the legislative latitude of the Parliament became considerably wider than what it was previously, thereby resolving the rivalry between the Council of Councillors (*majlis al-mustashārīn*) and the Chamber of Representatives to the benefit of the latter, just as its oversight authority and powers over government work are greater than what they were before.

The truth of the matter is that whoever scrutinizes the text of the new Constitution closely will realize that many of its articles and provisions answer to the demands and recommendations of the 'Democratic Bloc' announced publicly in 1996. This is with a substantial caveat that the Bloc was going out of its way to avoid mentioning the powers of the King, about which its leader at the time, ʿAbd al-Raḥmān al-Yūsufī, said: 'There is not a single recommendation that we have proposed that effectively constrains or modifies the jurisdiction of his Majesty the King', and that 'all we want is to reinforce the extant institutions – that is, the Parliament and the government. The powers of his Majesty the King are not subject to change by these (recommendations)'. In point of fact, these powers of the King have become the subject of discussion in the context of amending the current Constitution, along lines and to a degree perhaps not even anticipated by these parties themselves.

* * *

The picture of this new reality on the constitutional and political scene in Morocco is not complete unless one adds what the amended Constitution has consecrated with regard to rights and gains previously struggled for. The most important of these are those pertaining to public freedoms, human and democratic rights that are, unfortunately, almost insignificant when it comes to the discussion of democracy, the rule of law and institutional arrangements – at the forefront of which are the rights of the opposition. This discussion can be summarized under three main headings:

- Human rights and public freedoms (including women's rights). The preamble of the Constitution reiterates that the state 'reaffirms its determination to abide by universally recognized human rights', and 'is aware of the need of incorporating its work within the framework of the international organizations ... [and] fully adheres to the principles, rights and obligations arising from the charters of such organizations'. Chapter I, pertaining to General Provisions, outlines the basic principles in this regards thus: 'A one-party system is an illegitimate system' and citizenship is the basis of politics and representation where 'political parties may not be established on a religious-, linguistic-, ethnic- or regional basis ...' (Article 6), and 'Political parties and union organizations may not be dissolved or suspended by the public authorities except through a legal decision of the court' (Article 8). Chapter I also states that 'Associations of civil society and non-governmental organizations (NGOs) ... may not be dissolved or suspended by the public authorities except through a legal decision of the court' (Article 12).[2]

Chapter II in the constitutional text on these freedoms is dedicated to fundamental freedoms and rights, formerly mentioned in the previous Constitution, or which are spelled out with clarity for the first time, and among these is the transition from mere textual specification of the equality between men and women in their civil, political rights and freedoms to stressing that 'The State works to realize fairness/equality between men and women.' In addition, 'an authoritative body for fairness/equality and combating all forms of discrimination is hereby created, to this effect' (Article 19). Likewise the 'practice of torture, in any of its forms and by anyone, is a crime punishable by the law' (Article 22). Also, 'Arbitrary or secret arrest and forced disappearance are the most dangerous of crimes and expose those responsible to the severest of punishments' (Article 23). The Constitution also states that the 'domicile is inviolable' and 'private communication are confidential' (Article 24). Also, 'freedom of assembly, mass meetings, peaceful demonstration, and to establish associations and belong to syndicates and political affiliations are guaranteed'. These are in addition to the 'right to strike', however an 'organic law delimits the conditions and the modalities of its practice' (Article 29).

- Rights of the opposition. These are rights specified by modern democracies and encompassed by constitutional and legal guarantees that ensure their protection against monopolization of power and the decision-making processes – which might afflict any political system or government apparatus – that might stem from a parliamentary majority. The truth is that not all of the provisions in the amended Constitution pertaining to the rights of opposition are entirely new to Moroccan political and constitutional life. Some were familiar to the recent past: such as the freedom of expression, of opinion and of public gathering and the right to benefit from 'air time at the level of the official media, proportional to its representation' and from 'public finance, in conformity with the provisions of the law' (Chapter I, Article 10). This is in addition to the right to oversee the work of the government in Parliament and in its capacity to issue a vote of no confidence, over and above the 'inclusion of proposals of law on the agendas of both Chambers of Parliament' (Article 10). However, the amended Constitution specified other rights as well such as the right of the opposition in the Chamber of Representatives to participate in 'proposing candidates and to elect members of the Constitutional Court' (Article 10) and 'to head the committee charged with legislation of the Chamber of Representatives' (Article 10) over and above textual specification of the right of the opposition to 'the exercise of power in local, regional and national spheres, by way of democratic alternation [of power], within the framework of the provisions of this Constitution' (Article 10). All this is in addition to other rights specified in the Articles of Section 10 of the Constitution. It goes without saying that the enjoyment of these rights by the opposition gives new meaning to the body politic in the system – transitioning it from merely an opposing body into one that participates in power; that is, along lines in which it is not simply the holder of an opinion but rather is a group whose opinion is guaranteed *by* law the opportunity to *become* law or part of a law.

- The ascendency and adjudication of international legislation. The amended Constitution specified that the state 'is committed to subscribe to the principles, rights and obligations enunciated in' international 'charters and conventions' and 'affirms its commitment to abide by human rights such as they are universally recognized' (Preamble). And the text of the Constitution did not suffice in stating its endeavour 'to protect and to promote human rights and international humanitarian law … given their universal nature', but also pledged that the state is committed to

> comply and abide by international agreements ratified by it, within the scope of the provisions of the Constitution and of the laws of the Kingdom, and its immutable national identity, and that immediately upon issuance of these conventions, to accord them primacy over the national legislation of the country, and consequently to endeavor to render suitable the relevant provisions of national legislation.
>
> (Preamble)

The implication here is that respect for and commitment to abide by international law is conditional on its being in conformity with the articles of the Constitution, the laws of the country and its identity. And what might limit this commitment is acknowledged and understood, in light of the particularity of the sphere of personal status/civil affairs independent of positive civil law and the fact that other countries besides Morocco, including some in the West, do not always submit to the ascendency of international legislation over national legislation. The American position with regard to the International Criminal Court is a case in point.

* * *

For a time the constitution, as amended, was assumed to embody the concept of parliamentary monarchy as understood and demanded by those who constituted major segments of the social movement making demands in Morocco and, given the agreement of a wide sector of political society to this consecrated constitutional formula, it did not take long to obtain popular legitimacy by way of a referendum. However, the formulation thus endorsed is not parliamentary–monarchial in character, *and* it differs from the previous formula in that it extends the sphere of the balance of powers in a way conducive to the ruling regime to a degree unprecedented in modern and contemporary Moroccan history. This assessment is made in the realization that passing judgment on the amendments along these lines is not warranted except in keeping with three observations.

First, the amendments did not entirely dispose of the idea of a parliamentary monarchy once and for all, it only managed to delay it temporarily, as previously mentioned.

'Temporarily' is used in the sense that it remained on hold until the maturation of the inherent (internal) and subjective conditions that would provide the conditions of transition to a parliamentary monarchy. In effect, the concept has only been aborted today because these (suitable) conditions have not been realized yet to open the doors for its materialization, as many had hoped, as will be illuminated below.

Second, the constitutional amendments did not produce a deceptive formula with respect to the demand for parliamentary monarchy as some believed, but rather they were expressive of that concept in terms of the outcome of (the better represented) balances of social, political and cultural forces in Moroccan society. Similarly, they provided, from another standpoint, an advanced way station on the path towards a more radical review of the constitutional system in Morocco in the coming stage, which might be protracted or shortened in accordance with the level of cumulative political, social, and cultural experience in the country and its nature and orientation. A basic principle in the history of societies is that the law of development is always governed by accumulation (of experience); where sought-after ends need driving impulses, and where results proceed from precursors. Thus, a parliamentary monarchy cannot emerge without accumulating a history of requisite experience, where the moment that a balance of powers is attained represents a primary historic moment in terms of political authority.

Third, the constitutional amendments, produced through a consensus among numerous parties of the political society, were not forced on people as some of those who announced their opposition to them suggested. This is because they had be formulated with the consent of genuinely representative forces of significance, which are the Parliamentary forces most representative of society (with the caveat that one lacks a criterion by which to measure the magnitude of representation other than elections in which all participated, including forces opposed to the amendments – with the exception of the JCO and *Annahj Addimoqrati* (La Voie Démocratique) (i.e. the 'Democratic Voice/Current'). This is also because the amendments were subject to popular referendum in which they were accorded legitimacy. If any were capable of contesting the extremely high percentages of participation and voting in favour of the amended Constitution, then such would necessarily remain only theoretical due to the lack of supporting evidence to the contrary. Even if the probability for statistical error were taken into account, and possibly even weighted heavily, this would not change the fact that the people voted in favour of the amendments; and that the decision to boycott the elections taken by some did not have a significant effect in reality and it cannot be construed to connote a lack of participation.

Of these three observations, what is of concern here in particular is the first, which pertains to the future of the concept of parliamentary monarchy and the demand for it in Morocco after the faltering (on the way to its realization) in the latest experience of constitutional reform. The truth is that this faltering does not seem to be a stumbling block or a setback, except according to those whose expectations led them to consider it a matter on the agenda of today's democratic struggle, to be realized in the current emerging Arab revolutionary climate and expansion of the social movement initiated by the February 20 Movement. If not everyone in Moroccan political society shared the expectations of these groups – with the exception of a segment of those of the parties of the progressive nationalist movements which had actually called for parliamentary monarchy – it was because they were uncertain that parliamentary monarchy had become a foreseeable historical possibility. As for what they demanded so vehemently (and especially the 'Socialist Union'), this was not due to their opportunism or their courting of the youth element of the Arab street – as they were actually the first among those who had raised this banner over one-third of a century ago (at the Third Conference of the USFP in 1978). Rather, they did this from the standpoint of approaching this as a strategic goal of the democratic struggle that might require some time to materialize.

The concept of parliamentary monarchy shall remain a pressing one in the Moroccan democratic consciousness as being a strategic goal capable of material realization, if the requisite conditions are extant. As for these conditions, they cannot be reduced to those of the political sphere only – as is commonly assumed in thinking about the matter of politics – such as changing the balance of power in political society to the benefit of democratic forces or the victory of the movement of democratic struggle in exercising sufficient pressure to bring about a constitutional deal that would lead to the inception of parliamentary–monarchial system. These conditions are not merely political but also cultural, social and economic; and they are not in the offing as political conditions except at a time when Moroccan society and its vital forces take steps to bring about many of its social and cultural prerequisites. This is because no parliamentary monarchy can develop in a society that suffers from a huge deficiency in the culture of democracy in its social fabric – from the family to party to school to factory to administration to unions and civil society associations – and which also suffers from a heavy burden of inherited legacies in thoughts, mindsets, structures and institutions not conducive to such. A parliamentary monarchy will only come about at such time as Morocco adopts a pervasive democratic public culture and attains a vital, uncorrupt and transparent political society as well as a genuinely modern and independent civil society and contemporary political class which has thoroughly imbibed the values of responsibility and public welfare. 'Parliamentary monarchy' is not simply a phrase uttered in giving an opinion or in the banter of discussion, nor is it is a desire expressed by only one group in society, but rather it connotes a continuous construction of politics, society and culture. If modern monarchies have come to persist in some of the areas of the world – such as in Great Britain, the Netherlands, Denmark, Norway and Spain – underlying them all is an amalgamated political, social and cultural structure that both gave rise to and nurtured them. This matter is not political in this sense except as a strictly political consciousness (*waʿī siyāswī*) that separates politics from its attendant economic, social and cultural structures. Therefore, there must be another approach to this legitimate political demand, one that embodies a profound historical vision and which puts the list of things that ought to be done in the balance of history, development and accumulation (of requisite experience).

* * *

The future of the February 20 Movement is the prime question for consideration in the new constitutional scene, which came to light on 1 July 2011 – the date of the popular referendum on the amended Constitution. There is no doubt that the movement and the constitutional scene are coincident, wherein February 20 took pressure for demands to the farthest limits and it was joined by other political forces that assisted it or shared the burden. It was the February 20 Movement that outlined the political goal of the democratic movement by announcement of its demand for parliamentary monarchy. It was also the movement that brought about an end to the opposition to the constitutional amendment sessions – in terms of form, mechanism and content. Furthermore, it finds itself and its demands outside the sphere of official response and execution. In addition to the above, the February 20 Movement is the only social force that was sufficiently patient – in contrast to all the other forces of opposition – whose actual and hypothetical power was taken into consideration; and the mechanism of reform moved according to the rhythm of its vociferous calls. Naturally, when the situation is such, the question of its future is at the very heart of political questions today in Morocco.

Although fairness dictates acknowledgement that the effect of the opposition on the upshot of reform is extensive, and that it subsumes various political forces including the Islamist JCO, the left (Democratic Socialist) 'Vanguard Party', the PSU and *Annahj Addimoqrati*. However, these forces do not possess – with the exception of the JCO – the ability to rally and mobilize social forces sufficient to front an opposition too far removed from the February 20 Movement or without being affiliated to it. This is what explains why these forces have remained clinging to the framework of the February 20 Movement as one sufficiently wide to embrace the demands of the opposition. Rather the Islamist movement itself found it inevitable to enter into the framework of the February 20 opposition via solicitation of the youth movement despite the major differences between them in points of departure and thought.

Those who are rushing to mourn the passing of the February 20 Movement or to issue its death certificate after the positive popular referendum on the amended Constitution are mistaken. It is true that it has lost its bet in the battle to deliver a parliamentary–monarchial system – and the like of it is the same as that of many other movements that came into existence decades before it. This was due to an underestimation or miscalculation on its part with regard to the political givens and the balances of forces; and it will necessarily have to undertake a courageous political review of the past phase of its work. However, it is supposed – according to what one believes – that the matter of constitutional reforms is only one battle of many among those of democracy and that this is not the end of the road for it as a social, democratic movement. Furthermore, perhaps in the context of its résumé, there is more than one indication that its struggle on the front of constitutional reform is only one entry among many under the rubric of its democratic struggle. The reason is that it harboured demands wider in scope than simply constitutional reforms and even before this was on the political agenda with the address on 9 March 2011. Thus, there is no sense in restricting its experience only to the constitutional struggle and assessing it exclusively on that basis.

In light of these precursors, the February 20 Movement must be addressed in a language that combines – in a constructive dialectic – terms of criticism and of encouragement in order for it to complete the role it began so courageously and whereby it cleared a path towards the future. It is not appropriate to switch between one sort of language and the other or to substitute one in the place of the other as the worst of what might await the movement from politicians and intellectuals is that they should address it by adopting a despondent or defeatist language or a patronizing one. That is a critique that only sees an accumulation of errors in the experience of the Movement and does not touch upon sources of strength and hope and thence is doomed to go nowhere and can have only the most negative of consequences – either through being deprecating or given to despair. Likewise any critique intended to encourage the Movement to continue without frankness about its need to criticize and review its own experiences is apt to sink to the level of hypocrisy and hits a dead end in not encouraging it to take genuine stock of matters – especially when there are many who would like to nullify the Movement through injudicious and inaccurate criticisms. There are indeed many who are eager to pass a verdict of extinction by means of inviting the Movement to commit more mistakes. It is for one to say that both sides have allied despite many differences for the purpose of bringing the Movement down.

In terms of frank necessity, the dialectic of criticism and encouragement calls one to express two committed positions or two interconnected calls. The first is a call to the February 20 Movement to give pause for bold critical thinking about the upshot of its work and struggle over the last half-year of its experience, considering in this assessment a set of interpolated questions:

- The actual distance between its slogans and demands, on the one hand, and its actual capabilities to mobilize sufficient numbers of the masses to handle these demands and achieve them, on the other.
- The extent of the possibility – or rather the legitimacy – of replicating the experiences of the Arab protests that have raised the ceiling of their slogans and succeeded with them, and what – if any – are the analogous socio-political givens that might permit this in actuality.
- The extent of the success of the Movement or its faltering in safeguarding the independence of its decisions from various forms of influence under the themes of assistance, alliance, coordination and advice (in the previous period).
- The styles of address and mobilization adopted in the past and what might potentially be required in the future in the way of renovation appropriate to the type of changes that have come into play since the beginning of the summer of 2011.
- Programmes of democratic work that can be realized in the coming stage that respond to delayed political requirements and might achieve success with improved planning.
- The extent of what it might encounter in terms of spontaneous voluntary popular inclinations and long-range choices that might have a devastating impact on the work of the Movement and its future.

The Movement cannot dispense with undertaking such a critical review and rehabilitating its internal structure, and it is a review that will not be beneficial and productive except when the Movement stands shoulders this burden itself without deputizing any other to undertake the task.

The second is a call for the Movement to pay heed to a set of major tasks it anticipates to be awaiting it in the scope of its reformist democratic movement, and there are a number of themes in this context. These include: the intensification of the focus on the demand to combat economic, fiscal and administrative corruption and mobilizing in order to generate a public opinion that can exert pressure to these ends; to devote attention to providing a social safety net against corruption of political and representative life and misuse of political capital, especially on the eve of the election season in the Fall of 2011; and dedicating real space to the social question in the work of the democratic progressive movement – equal to or exceeding the dimensions of the political question – expanding the scope of relations of the February 20 Movement with progressive democratic forces for the aim of expanding its social and political base, protecting its independence and assuaging doubts about its bias towards one group of political and democratic society at the expense of another and, subsequently, for the sake of expanding the scope of the democratic alliance in Morocco.

These are some preliminary thoughts aimed at giving advice to the February 20 Movement from a position of one who holds it in high regard and not an opponent and who wishes to be frank and not patronizing. The author holds that this language is the appropriate one with which to address the Movement today instead of the two prevailing ones: the language of machinations and intrigue, and the language of patronization and sycophancy!

* * *

Are there any influences or effects deriving from the experience of constitutional reform in Morocco that might have relevance to other Arab regimes that have not yet embarked on a process of reform in response to their peoples and their expectations? What might these effects and results be at the level of a limited sector of these ruling regimes wherein the prevailing systems are monarchial ones or emirates? The importance of this question has three facets:

- First, the constitutional reform undertaken by the royal establishment in Morocco came in the context of a successful pre-emptive political approach in dealing with a moment of crisis and providing a rapid response to legitimate popular demands without the country or social stability paying a high price. It is a situation that appears to be a model one in an Arab context characterized by the obstinacy of some regimes in confronting the demands of their people, where some are pushed to taking the countries to the frontiers of the unknown.
- Second, the Arab monarchies have not witnessed – with the exceptions of the situations in Morocco and Jordan – a genuine political life (in Kuwait there is only a representative/parliamentary political life) and which have never known any form of real distribution of power. This is to say nothing of the tribal and dynastic nature for most of the political systems in these countries over and above what the problems that the monopolization of resources (in rentier economies) and the monopolization of political authority leads to in the societies which these forms of rule prevail.
- Third, the protest movement that has thus far been sparked – to disparate degrees in the societies of Arab monarchies – is distinct from its analogue in Arab 'republican' societies in not having taken its demands to the extent of demanding or raising the slogan of 'bringing down the regime'. Rather it has constrained its discourse to calling for reform, an end to corruption and guaranteed democratic rights and freedoms.

These three aspects of the questions raised above give insight into the importance of thinking about the future of Arab monarchies from the perspective of the need for them to reform their situations in light of the new political changes and in view of the emerging popular democratic demands that can no longer be shunned or opposed. Choosing the path of responsiveness and positive assimilation, along the lines of what has occurred in Morocco, is the shortest path open before these monarchies towards guaranteeing social stability and renewing the bases of their legitimacy after whatever shake-up has occurred in their traditional and prevailing legitimacy. Furthermore, such an option is also the least costly in fulfilling the overwhelmingly desire to see a contemporary political system under the aegis of these monarchies that will redistribute power and authority as well as resources according to the dictates of new principles. Perhaps, it also might be a last chance to benefit from the modest nature of the popular demands for reform before the protest movements in such countries reach a point of no return where they can no longer be contained.

Even so, before entertaining the question of what the effects and influences of the Moroccan precedent might be on other Arab monarchies, a number of facts, which cannot be ignored, must be taken into account.:

- First, there is the fact that there are disparities in the historical weight and pedigree of the Arab monarchies, where some of them such as Morocco trace their roots back over a millennium and where others only first saw the light of day a few decades ago. Neither historical pedigree nor deep-rooted lineage is a minor matter in politics, when a state is building legitimacy. The more that a state (identity) is built up, the more it makes gains as an entity in the view of its people. As for the monarchy as a form of political regime, its share of potential longevity and legitimacy are greater the more deeply it strikes its roots in history, and this is what distinguishes the two monarchial systems in Morocco and Oman.
- Second, there is the fact that among the various monarchies (including the emirates) there are disparities in political development and in cumulative modernist and reformist experience that cannot be denied. While constitutional life has been known to some of theses – such as Morocco and Jordan for over half a century – others do not recognize the need for a constitution at all. Some regulate political life through work according to the constraints of a representative system (Morocco, Jordan, Kuwait and Bahrain), where others have found advisory (*shūrā*) councils sufficient – in which most of their members are appointed. Still others have known political pluralism, representative parliamentary life and organized assemblies, whereas some countries have prohibited the legal existence of political parties, representative systems and civil society associations. One among the Arab monarchies has witnessed a preliminary form of democratic rotation of power (the experience of 'consensual rotation' in Morocco since 1998), where the rest have not known such. It may be supposed that this discrepancy is not an ordinary detail because it connotes the difference between monarchies that have known the rise of politics and others in which politics is completely or almost completely absent.
- Third is the fact that the monarchies that developed in an open political environment with popular and political-party participation learned how to give and take, adapt and respond; and there gradually developed in their cultures the values of equality, making concessions and consensus-building and compromise. There accumulated in such countries a reformist impulse, even if in an objective and compulsory fashion. This is not the case in other monarchies that grew up in a climate of monopolization of power or criminalization and prohibition of politics.
- Fourth, there is a difference between monarchies erected on group sentiment and solidarity of the tribe, clan and family, which have narrow socio-political bases wherein reproduction of authority is within these narrow frameworks, and other monarchies where connections of tribal-group sentiment have largely come to an end (as in Morocco), or where the strength of such has lessened to a significant degree (as in Jordan). In countries where the tribal and familial connections are lesser, the result has been the expansion of the scope of social participation in power and authority and the entrance of a number of forces into the political arena; indeed, the formation of the political sphere is *itself* a result of this.
- Fifth is the fact that there is a difference between monarchies in which a ruling family elite monopolizes resources and allocates shares from these to state and

society in accordance with criteria and principles of loyalty and proximity or distance from the centre of power and those monarchies that know a form of resource distribution and which especially know forms of oversight of public monies and aspects of spending, as facilitated through official institutions of fiscal oversight as well as parliamentary accountability and the pressure of a free press and public opinion.

- Sixth, there are Arab political societies that have achieved – over long decades – a considerable measure of political, representative and civil experience predicated on accumulated struggle in which democratic movements have succeeded in achieving gains and securing rights. These are in glaring contrast to societies that lack accumulated political experience (due to the absence of conditions requisite for political work in them) and which confront demands through economic and social placation efforts to divert or contain such.

It is clear then that any rapprochement between Arab monarchies and thinking about the future of reform and modernization in them will run into problems because of the discrepancies between them as monarchies and the discrepancies between the political societies that exist in them, which cannot be ignored. Given this, the propensity of other Arab regimes to learn from the Moroccan political reforms necessitates that these categorical specificities and differences between structures, experiments and accumulation (of political, civil and representative experience) be taken into account. It is only in this light that the following four tentative possibilities can be broached:

- The first possibility is that experimentation with reforms – of disparate degree and extent – will go forward in some of the Arab monarchies whose societies know some modicum of political vitality as a result of the pressure of the ongoing revolutionary moment and in light of the results of the Moroccan experience. The most likely Arab monarchy as a candidate to witness that would be Jordan; and it has in fact embarked on such a process at the level of constitutional reforms, the form of which will be determined by the degree of popular pressure in the country and the extent of the desire of the regime for reform. The monarchy in Bahrain and the emirate systems in Kuwait and the Sultanate of Oman are among those that might be compelled to undertake reforms to contain and assimilate the popular movement; however, these will be strictly partial and calculated as well as possibly only symbolic.
- The second possibility is that the assimilative/absorptive politics of some of the Arab monarchies will emerge only within the scope of the extant and well-trodden tradition that persists within them of buying off political demands through some socio-economic concessions such as gifts and grants and the raising of salaries. That is, they will deal with these political demands as though they are the demands of syndicates or unions! It is not farfetched that this might be coupled with some superficial, cosmetic improvements to the system of local and national 'representation' that does not exceed the scope of censorship or precipitate the inception of a genuine electoral life. The preponderance of this possibility is commensurate with the perpetuation of the stifling and stagnation of the social movements in these countries.
- The third possibility is that popular pressure will increase the longer the situation of protest persists in the Arab world and so long as its political and psychological effects continue to penetrate the countries ruled by monarchial regimes. This

situation might generate a new reality that compels these monarchies to undertake political reforms. Furthermore, this might not be improbable in Jordan and possibly Bahrain even if there is – so far as can be foreseen – less of a likelihood in other Arab monarchies and emirates.

- The fourth possibility is that international forces – and at the forefront of them the United States – will take the initiative in exercising pressure and undertaking measures forcefully to persuade some of the monarchial regimes or emirates to undertake some reforms capable of absorbing the widespread resentment that persists over the monopolization of authority and resources and with the intention of preserving the stability of these regimes from the danger of the surrounding cyclone.

These are strictly possibilities that share in common two facets: the moment of an intense Arab revolution and the fear of ruling elites for their ability to repel the pressure building in their societies such that they may explode at any minute under the influence of what is going on in the Arab environment around them. It is abundantly clear that the potential for the Moroccan precedent to prompt emulation by other Arab monarchies is constrained by two factors: the availability of resources capable of containing the challenge of internal demands (and this was not available to other regimes such as those in Tunisia and Egypt) and the absence of a political heritage and climate to enable agreement upon modest possibilities for voluntary self-change – with societies that are bereft of politics and its requisite components. Given these two obstacles, it should not be forgotten what the wealthy Arab monarchies enjoy in terms of protection and support from the major states of the West (inapplicable in the cases of the regimes in Libya, Syria and Yemen) and one example of that suffices: in the international and regional assimilation and absorption of the *intifada* in Bahrain and how all were kept from even discussing it!

Notes

1. See http://www.sgg.gov.ma/BO/bulletin/FR/2011/BO_5956_Fr.pdf (accessed on 10 July 2011).
2. All translations from the 2011 Moroccan Constitution are taken from the official Arabic original in conjunction with reference to the official French-language translation. For the Arabic-language text, see http://www.sgg.gov.ma/constitution_2011_Ar.pdf?cle=78 (accessed on 7 October 2011).

Political Islam in Morocco: negotiating the Kingdom's liberal space

Emanuela Dalmasso[a] and Francesco Cavatorta[b]

[a]Department of Political Science, University of Turin, Turin, Italy; [b]School of Law and Government, Dublin City University, Dublin, Ireland

The uprisings of the Arab Spring have highlighted the weakness of traditional opposition actors that have been unable to predict and lead the revolutions. This paper, focusing on the case of Morocco, examines how the discourses and practices of the regime shaped the complex field of Political Islam, contributing to two distinct but interlinked phenomena. On the one hand, they have managed to lead Islamists and liberal secularists to overcome many of their previous divisions to sustain common battles in the name of democracy and human rights. On the other hand, they have deepened rifts and divisions among Islamists themselves on the crucial issue of political reforms.

Introduction

While it is too early to provide an assessment of the reasons that led to the 2011 Arab Spring or to postulate how the different uprisings are going to conclude, there are already a number of interesting elements that emerge from current events (El-Din Haseeb 2011). Among them is the very notable absence in the demonstrations at the helm of the uprising of traditional opposition parties and mainstream civil society movements, including the Islamists. This is rather surprising if one considers the existence of a variety of opposition movements in most countries of the region. This is true also in the case of Morocco where the 'February 20th' movement that emerged at the start of the current anti-regime demonstrations is also not affiliated to any specific opposition movement. While the absence of a clear political and ideological characterization of the different uprisings is in the short-term beneficial to the potential success of the movements heading them, in the long-term it might constitute a problem in so far as the success of processes of democratization, based on past experiences, seems to be dependent on the existence of strong political parties or social movements transformed into parties. What is needed therefore is an examination of opposition dynamics prior to the uprising in order to explain why they seem to play a rather limited role in the current situation. This article focuses specifically on the multiple facets of Political Islam in Morocco and argues that an explanation for the weakness of organized and structured social and political movements is due not only to the traditional differences between liberal secularists and Islamists, but also to fundamental disagreements among Islamists as well. In addition, the article argues that the case of Morocco demonstrates quite clearly how the discourses and practices of authoritarian regimes matter significantly in shaping opposition strategies and have unintended consequences beyond their attempts at authoritarian upgrading (Heydemann 2007).

Opposition politics in the Arab world

The literature on opposition movements in the Arab world has focused traditionally on the role they perform in challenging the incumbent regimes. As Albrecht (2010, p. 3) argues, 'opposition and contentious collective activism has almost exclusively been addressed by looking at the potential overthrow of incumbent regimes.' Recently, however, more refined analyses of opposition politics in the Arab world have emerged. These studies examine the way in which opposition parties and movements become, willingly or unwillingly, pillars of the authoritarian regime that they so resent. It has been argued further that Arab regimes can manage vast sectors of the opposition more through direct co-optation than repression (Albrecht 2005). The acceptance of many within the opposition camp to be co-opted stems from belief that they might in some way influence the politics of the regime or from the material benefits they might derive in becoming a 'loyal' opponent. More significantly, however, co-optation is at times the direct outcome of divisions within the opposition itself (Cavatorta and Elananza 2008). Opposition movements in the Arab world tend to subscribe to radically opposed ideologies and views of what policies the country should follow. These profound divisions undermine the unity of the opposition, which is a crucial asset if ruling elites are to be faced down convincingly.

In the Arab world, the main dividing line over the last four decades has been that between Islamists and secular-leftists, and while there have been numerous examples of cross-ideological cooperation between these two sectors and a convergence towards a shared definition of democratic accountability (Abdelrahman 2009, Clark 2010), mutual suspicions still remain and make successful and lasting cooperation difficult. The debate about the role of the En-Nahda party in Tunisia in the construction of a post-Ben Ali political system is, for instance, highly contested in spite of the party's pro-democratic declarations and its participation in coalition-building with secular parties while in exile (Martinez-Fuentes 2011). Thus, when cooperation occurred, this was often ad hoc and limited in time and space, failing to generate a sustained and effective coalition against authoritarian rulers (Clark 2006).

In Morocco this was also the case. During the 1990s and early 2000s Political Islam and secular leftist groups found it extremely difficult to find common ground due to their profound ideological differences. However, we argue that, paradoxically, the rhetoric of democracy, accountability, human rights and development that the regime adopted so openly after the arrival of Mohammad VI in power has been instrumental in creating the possibility for both sectors of the opposition to move beyond ideology and confront each other on concrete political issues. This has led to two phenomena. On the one hand, sectors of Political Islam entered a dialogue and cooperation with secular-leftists due to a convergence of interests and opinions. On the other hand, there has been a deepening of already existing divisions within both the Islamist and secular/leftist camps, indicating that a neat separation between the two might not be a useful analytical tool to interpret opposition politics in Morocco, as it has become clear that the divisions are the product of the acceptance or refusal of the rules of the game dictated by the monarchy rather than absolute ideological positions.

In this game whose rules are set by the Monarch, the sacralization of the public space is a crucial element (Tozy 1999). Although the July 2011 Constitution no longer refers to the monarch as sacred, the religious legitimacy of the monarchy is still a crucial aspect of its overall legitimacy to rule and opposition parties have to accept such legitimacy if they want to be able to participate openly in the political game. This has profound repercussions for political movements wishing to remove the central policy-making role of the monarchy by denying it a religious sacred legitimacy. This means that opposition politics and therefore the discourse linked to it are better understood by looking at whether Islamist or secular groups are included in the official and accepted political sphere or outside of it, which depends on accepting the religious pre-eminence of the monarchy, a concept that is potentially highly problematic for both religious and secular parties.

Since the early 1990s, the Moroccan monarchy has accompanied the sacralization of the political and public space with a discourse based on the values of democracy and modernity, including notions of liberal human rights and sustainable economic development. According to most observers (Amar 2009, Vermeren 2009) the Moroccan regime adopted a strategy of 'upgrading authoritarianism' (Heydemann 2007) by introducing such notions in its official discourse. While this is certainly true, the very introduction of such a concept has had unintended consequences. Adopting a mainstream and internationally accepted notion of globalization that rests on the values of human rights, democracy and development in order to 'divide and conquer' the opposition and to bolster its own international standing, the monarchy unwittingly opened the door to a re-composition of the political field where old divisions disappeared. Many of the Islamist activists in Morocco seized on this opportunity to advance their causes and objectives, linking up at times with leftist elements and therefore reshaping the way in which opposition politics works. This was made possible because the nominally global values of human rights, democracy and development have been enriched with local experiences and understandings, allowing different political movements to use them against the incumbent (Browers 2006). At the local level, various actors have appropriated the dominant global values discourse not only from a discursive point of view, but also from a practical one, enriching it with more complex meanings. In Morocco as elsewhere in the Middle East and North Africa (MENA), faraway from passively reproducing a dogma, this appropriation takes the form of an interaction which will inevitably contribute to the global understanding and practices of the dominant discourse. Moreover, this has led to a new set of cooperative efforts between Islamists and leftists, although it has also created new rifts that still allow the Moroccan monarch to dictate politics even in face of mounting protests. It is in this vacuum and contested space that both violent radicalism and youth-driven social movements not connected with parties become the protagonists of Moroccan political life.

The Moroccan liberal space

On 1 October 2010, the TelQuel media group formally announced at a press conference that the Arabic language weekly *Nichane*, which had become the best-selling weekly magazine in the country, would cease publication. *Nichane* was formally closed because it lacked the financial resources to continue operating, but in reality the magazine was a victim of a concerted campaign of financial boycott on the part of the state and business interests close to the regime, which refused to continue to place adverts in the publication. This occurred because *Nichane* had become too independent and critical of many of the policies that the government and the monarchy were pursuing. As the press release of the TelQuel group indicates,

> since 2009, the determined struggle of the State against independent newspapers and magazines has accelerated significantly … the Moroccan authorities seem to be bent on following the Tunisian model [under Ben Ali], where only the newspapers that serve the interests of the regime are tolerated.[1]

The closure of *Nichane* and the repression of independent journalism are among the latest episodes in the authoritarian retrenchment that Morocco has experienced since the mid-2000s. While some would contend that the new Constitution approved by referendum in July 2011 is a potent signal that Morocco is still on course for democratization, a degree of scepticism is necessary in so far as the central role of the monarch in shaping and dictating policies has not been undermined (Dalmasso and Cavatorta 2011). Repression and co-optation simply take on new forms. In many ways this authoritarian retrenchment is in sharp contradiction to the enthusiasm and genuine hope for political change that had greeted the succession of Mohammed VI in 1999 and with the liberalizing policies he implemented, including ones that 'made Morocco a regional exception in terms of freedom of the press'.[2]

During his first few years in power, Mohammed VI showed with concrete actions and policies his intention seemingly to democratize the country and instil a 'human rights' culture in state institutions. His father had understood in the early 1990s that Morocco needed liberalizing political reforms and he had begun to undertake some of them, including the creation of a Human Rights Ministry, but most Moroccans and many analysts simply believed these changes to be a facade and placed much greater hope in the son. They were not to be disappointed and, as one former political prisoner and human rights activist declared in 2005, 'society is now allowed to breathe'.[3] The change in emphasis in favour of both democracy and human rights was not only rhetorical, as Mohammed VI took meaningful steps to support his declarations. He fired the powerful Minister of Interior, Driss Basri, encouraged the creation of a reconciliation commission to investigate past abuses, the first of its kind in the Muslim world, and passed legislation aimed at making it easier for civil society organizations to be set up and be involved in policy-making processes.

The enthusiasm that these initiatives generated should not be underestimated and they gave a certain momentum to all those political and civil activists who had suffered during Hassan II's repressive era, mobilizing previously hidden and new energies within society. Thus, under Mohammed VI there has been what Howe (2005) termed 'an explosion' in civil society activism, including organizations promoting and defending human rights. Such organizations were involved in the setting up of the Instance Equité et Réconciliation (IER), which bought a significant amount of legitimacy to the King both domestically and internationally as did the 2004 reform of the family code. Such initiatives were coupled with the implementation of policies aimed at rendering the electoral process and the state's institutions more democratic. The 2002 legislative elections were in this respect a turning point in Morocco, as they did not display the same level of 'interference' from the authorities as did previous consultations. In addition, there seemed to be the genuine intention to involve Parliament more significantly in policy-making rather than relying exclusively on the executive, which is appointed by the King (Denoeux and Desfosses 2007).

While a small number of activists always doubted Mohammad VI's liberalizing intentions, the majority of them bought into the vision that they were contributing to building democracy in Morocco in the context of a Western-inspired globalization structured around precisely the values of democracy and human rights with which they could easily be reconciled. The changes that Mohammed VI introduced are not the product of globalization and were not generated from the outside, but were made possible because there was a framework that the monarch could utilize to placate both domestic and external critics. The notions and selective meaning of democracy and human rights that were acceptable to the international community were used in the Moroccan context in order to allow the new monarch the space to navigate the system and renew the legitimacy of the throne. In this context, Mohammed VI did not introduce anything innovative in so far as he follows on the tentative gradualist approach to selective democratization that his father had inaugurated, but what changes with the new global democratic zeitgeist is that forms of protest and dissent that were always in existence in Morocco and used to be repressed are now legitimate because the monarchy refers to them as a legitimizing tool for its new course.

This new course is however meant to co-opt previously repressed actors rather than fundamentally reconfiguring power. During Hassan II's reign those political and social actors that demanded democracy, justice and respect for human rights were countered by the monarchy by using notions of tradition and cultural specificity, resorting basically to using Islamism against the broad left. Once the legitimizing discourse changes and shifts in favour of notions of democracy and human rights, Islamists are also largely forced to follow suit although they appropriate these values differently.

The rhetoric and actions emanating from the Palace seemed in fact to substantiate the support that the King enjoyed in political circles previously hostile to the monarchy because of its authoritarian rule such as the leadership of the Socialist Party, the Marxist left and sectors of Political Islam. Thus, there was the legitimate expectation that the reforms would continue and that Mohammad VI would be the one enabling the Moroccan transition to democracy by gradually modifying the role of the monarchy from an executive to simply a representative one. On 16 May 2003, however, the history of Morocco took a different course. Fourteen suicide bombers, belonging to a local radical Islamist group called al-Salafīyah al-Jihādīyah, attacked targets in central Casablanca, signalling the end of the Moroccan exception. Until then, Moroccan ruling elites prided themselves on being exceptional within the Arab world in so far as the country was not troubled by terrorism. The attacks shattered the belief that Morocco was immune to regional trends.

The response of the regime was particularly strong and a new spiral of human rights abuses began, targeting specifically manifestations of Political Islam. Initially, large sectors of the human rights community were not overly concerned with such abuses as other reforms beneficial to 'human rights' in general were being implemented, but the repressive turn soon extended from Islamists to other social actors such as *Diplomés Chômeurs*[4] or independent magazines and newspapers. In addition to this, no meaningful democratization of the political system took place. For instance, the 2007 legislative elections were far from being the historic event that the regime enthused about with foreign diplomats, as ordinary Moroccans simply did not bother turning out (Storm 2008). If anything, the monarch has reasserted his central and undisputed authority on Moroccan politics and the Constitutional reforms of 2011 have not changed this. Thus, after over ten years in power, it emerges that, according to numerous scholars and observers of Morocco, Mohammed VI's reign has been largely disappointing in terms of democratization and the promotion of human rights (Amar 2009, Vermeren

2009). What is more worrying from a normative point of view is that the regime seems to have become more authoritarian and intolerant of dissent during the past few years, effectively ending any hope that Morocco would be the first country in the Arab world to move from authoritarianism towards democracy.

The way in which King Mohammad VI handled the transfer of power from his father to himself and the subsequent policies he adopted are now understood through the notion of 'upgrading Arab authoritarianism' (Heydemann 2007). While there is probably some truth in this analysis, this should not overshadow two significant points. First, this reading is applied after the fact and this inevitably underestimates the way in which society and the political system were genuinely opened up by Mohammad VI (El-Ghissassi 2006). The framework of upgraded authoritarianism is indeed a very useful one to account for the survival of Arab leaders in power, but it might wrongly assume that this strategy was intentional from the beginning and entirely successful. Second, today's Morocco is not the Morocco of the 'years of lead'. This does not mean that it is not authoritarian and that there are no echoes of past practices as the disappearance of salafist prisoners at the hands of the security forces demonstrates (Human Rights Watch 2010), but there is nevertheless a liberal space that exists and within which a number of political movements and civil society actors operate.

Democracy, human rights and economic development through integration with the global economy constituted the rhetorical framework that the monarchy utilized to implement political, social and economic reforms since the late 1990s and this links Moroccan domestic developments to global trends. The rhetoric of democracy and human rights has far from disappeared in the public Moroccan discourse and in fact constitutes the point of reference of the monarchy, which argues that repressive measures are necessary to protect the achievements of the past decade in the face of hostile and anti-democratic forces. As Mohammad VI pointed out in the speech with which he launched the IER, there is a connection between adhering to a human rights doctrine and fighting terrorism. He explicitly argued that

> this [was] the way to consolidate positive citizenship and to promote democracy, patriotism and the dissemination of a culture of human rights and duties. [These values] are the strongest ramparts to protect our society from extremism and terrorism, which We are determined to fight with the firmness required of those who are in charge of protecting the stability and security [of the country] in the context of the rule of law.[5]

This liberal environment, however limited it might be, has mobilized the different 'souls' of Islamism, which have responded in different ways to the changes in the Kingdom and reacted differently to both the rhetoric and daily practice of democracy, human rights and economic development as conceived of by the monarchy. It is therefore important to analyse the way in which these religious actors have dealt with the new political arrangements in place and how they have at times appropriated and at times fought against the rhetoric and the political values that the King through the new international pro-democracy context brought to Morocco, building on their own understanding and experience of such notions.

Political Islam in Morocco

Contrary to what scholars such as Munson (1991) argued in the early 1990s, Islamism in Morocco has become a political force to be reckoned with, indicating that the

Kingdom, despite the religious legitimacy of the monarchy, did not constitute an exception in the region. Reviewing the different expressions of Political Islam in Morocco, Laskier (2003) argued that there were three clusters of Islamism in the country and to a certain extent his analysis is still valid today, although new Islamist actors have also appeared on the scene since then.

First, there is a legally recognized political formation, the Party for Justice and Development (PJD), which is a socially conservative party integrated since 1996 into the political and institutional system devised by the monarchy. The party is indeed allowed to participate in institutional politics precisely because it accepts the limits imposed by the monarchy on the political game and therefore the PJD explicitly recognizes the primacy of the monarchy in the country's institutional and constitutional set-up. The PJD, despite never having entered a governing coalition, is deemed to be integrated into the liberalized autocratic system because of its unwillingness to criticize the monarch and bows to Makhzen's pressure when necessary. The acceptance of the sacred nature of the monarch was the precondition for being able to operate openly in the political system and the PJD certainly can be considered loyal opposition (Zeghal 2005). For instance, upon request by the authorities, the party decided not to run candidates in all constituencies at the 2002 legislative elections precisely to avoid sweeping the board and embarrassing the King with a significant Islamist electoral victory (Willis 2004). As recently as the spring of 2011, the PJD refused to support the protest movements sweeping across Morocco precisely because they believe that constitutional reform should not be demanded on the streets but be the product of parties' lobbying and should be formally initiated by the King. This attitude has triggered the resignation from the party of three prominent members supportive of the demonstrators.[6]

Second, there is the very popular semi-legal Justice and Charity Association (al-ʿAdl) founded by the long-time dissident Sheikh Abd al-Salam Yassine. This association operates like a social movement providing services and assistance to the poorer sections of society and is preoccupied with Islamizing society from below by promoting a sort of Sufi-infused utopianism (Kristianasen 2007). The social services it provides however have a considerable political dimension and the association also has a '*cercle politique*' that functions like a political bureau. The *cercle* is charged with drawing up the political positions of the association on a number of national issues and it has been consistently critical of the way Morocco is run and therefore directly critical of the monarchy, whose legitimacy to rule it does not accept. This anti-monarchical stance prevents the association from gaining not only the legal permission to operate social services, but also, crucially, prevents them from becoming a political party. In fact, in order to compete in elections the association would have to accept the limits, role and legitimacy of the monarchy, which is a price the association refuses to pay because it would then undermine its status as uncompromising opposition. Sheikh Yassine himself has been and still is a very outspoken critic of the Crown, which is blamed for not tackling the social and economic ills of Moroccan society (poverty, corruption of moral values, deference to the West, social atomization). Islam is pointed out as the solution to all these difficulties and the social services, the cultural meetings and the political activities of the association are all infused with religious piety in order to demonstrate that there is a concrete alternative not only to the way in which Moroccan society operates, but also a spiritual dimension with which governance should be infused. This does not make the association a naïve and purely spiritual group or a mad lunatic fringe as often depicted in pro-regime media. Over time its leaders have been capable of demonstrating their political acumen on a number of issues by adopting very rational positions (Cavatorta 2007). As prominent member Nadia Yassine argued, 'we have a *cercle politique* that draws up concrete policy proposals, [which means] that we are not only mad naysayers ... we have concrete proposals [for the country]'.[7]

The third Islamist camp is composed of different salafist tendencies. One is the clandestine al-Salafīyah al-Jihādīyah (Salafi Jihad), a nebulous group devoted to overthrowing the government through violence. It is a minority strand and does not enjoy much popular support, but was responsible for the May 2003 Casablanca attacks. The movement a-Salafīyah a-Jihādīyah has virtually disappeared due to the mass arrests it experienced over the last few years. The security forces' crackdown on Islamist terrorism and the marginalization of al-Salafīyah al-Jihādīyah by all other political groups combined to dismantle its network. Most of the militants are in jail and the activities currently visible in the public space connected with the movement are those that the association Ennasir holds in order to highlight the plight of the prisoners and their families. Most of these prisoners have been arrested and tried in very controversial circumstances and Ennasir attempts to highlight how the Salafi prisoners' convictions have been unlawfully obtained by the state, which employed kangaroo courts and torture. In addition, Ennasir struggles to defend the rights of the families of the prisoners as spouses and children suffer from harassment and discrimination on the part of the authorities in a number of realms ranging from the schooling of children to welfare benefits. The association Ennasir, founded in November 2004, is a self-defined human rights organization. By contrast, we have also the return on the scene of daʿwah salafism, which 'concentrates on Islamizing its followers and isolating them from the political process rather than directly challenging the state' (Boubekeur 2008, p. 2). While this phenomenon seems to be growing considerably in Algeria, it does not seem to have become as popular yet in Morocco, although there is a history of it in the country. Today, the best-known representative of this type of Islamism is theologian Sheikh Maghraoui, whose religious association promotes a very strict and literal interpretation of Islam. The Sheikh has come under severe criticism in recent years for his position on the issue of under-age marriage and in a 2008 *fatwā* he stated that

> the marriage of nine-year-old girls is not forbidden because according to a *ḥadīth* (a saying attributed to the Prophet Muḥammad, and here, according to his *sunnah* or 'normative practice'), Muḥammad married 'Āʾishah when she was only seven-years-old[8] and he consummated his union when she was nine.[9]

These declarations have political undertones in so far as they seem to indicate that political and social relations should be based on immutable interpretations of sacred texts and sayings, nevertheless this type of Islamism encourages its followers to adopt a non-political stance by isolating themselves from official and institutional politics. In any case they have provoked a backlash against the association and the Sheikh with the authorities intervening to shut down some of their activities, although the Sheikh himself has a considerable power base in Marrakech and has been left alone by the authorities who have allowed him to leave for Saudi Arabia.[10]

Finally, there exists a cluster of Islamism connected to and supportive of the monarchy, which is often marginalized in studies of Moroccan politics, but that nevertheless is an important factor in the legitimization of current political arrangements. There are for instance brotherhoods and associations such as the Sufi Zaouiya Boutchichia, which has an important role in Morocco because it functions as the connection between sectors of the pious middle-class and the monarchy. The movement is very much aligned with the monarchy on political and social matters, which means that it can be mobilized to compete with opposition Islamism.

Thus, the field of Islamism in Morocco is both varied and complex with competing trends and approaches to politics and social engagement, which depend on the religious beliefs held and on the political outlooks of leaders and members. Given the variegated field of Islamism in Morocco, the introduction of the values of mainstream globalization embodied in notions of democracy, human rights, and economic liberal development has had a different impact on the Islamist activists, which have taken these values and reinterpreted them to suit their specific agenda. What is interesting to note is that in the process of engaging with such mainstream values, all these movements attempt to give them a '*ḥalāl* rubber stamp' to make them compatible with their religious and political beliefs. This has led to different types of concrete relations with other actors on the political and social scene that do not subscribe to religious values as guides for policy-making and activism. The next section analyses these relations.

Between religious ideology and pragmatism

Haynes (2010, p. 149) recently argued that 'despite the undoubted impact of western-dominated globalisation ... the impact on the MENA in terms of changing the context, terms of debate and preferences in favour of liberal-democracy is relatively limited.' This argument carries a degree of validity in so far as the values of liberal-democracy might not yet be as widespread as one would expect, but it is also important to note that not all the MENA countries are the same and in the case of Morocco some religious actors have appropriated the discourse and practice of Western-dominated globalization to turn it in fact to their advantage and at times against its very proponents both domestic and international. It is this discursive and practical appropriation filtered through local traditions and modes of understanding that we investigate to illustrate how religious actors in Morocco operate. In turn, these different understandings of what democracy, human rights and development are produce significant divergences between the different souls of Political Islam and this has consequences for the way in which coalition-building among nominally opposition groups takes place.

It is generally understood that one of the core values of liberal Western-dominated globalization is the respect of individual human rights. While in the past Islamist movements, much like other religiously inspired actors in Christianity or Judaism, countered this discourse by rejecting the very notion of individual rights to focus on the notion of the common good, which implied that some individual rights could be sacrificed to obtain it (Fuller 2004), this is no longer the case today for some Islamist actors. The position of the association Ennasir linked to the Salafi Jihad movement provides an example of a group that would not normally be associated with the promotion and defence of individual rights. However, it is precisely this Islamist association that has for the past few years been at the forefront of the struggle for human rights in Morocco when it comes to the right to a fair trial, the right not to be discriminated against because of specific political beliefs and the right to be treated respectfully while in custody. While the association is certainly not representative of the broader salafist trend and has been set up with a very specific and narrow mission, it is still important to highlight that its struggle rests on a classic liberal interpretation of human rights and has benefited, paradoxically, from the rhetorical engagement of the Moroccan authorities on this very theme.

The Moroccan monarchy and the Moroccan state have built their current reputation on the willingness to break with past abusive practices and the necessity to have proper rule of law and respect human rights. Despite the authoritarian retrenchment in evidence since late 2003, the rhetoric, as mentioned above, has not changed. This stance exposes the Moroccan authorities to the charge of hypocrisy given the way in which the rights of the members of a-Salafīyah a-Jihādīyah and the families of the members have been treated and the association Ennasir utilizes the very same rhetoric to point at the inconsistency of the regime discourse. This does not mean that members of Ennasir uncritically accept the notion of individual human rights as a gift from the West for which they are grateful. There is an elaboration of such a concept taking place in light of the indigenous experiences, both practical and discursive, which is used to frame the demands they make, but, crucially, the resonance of the notion of human rights is much greater and carries more influence both at home and abroad. A further twist is in the reaction that the cause of Ennasir has elicited from other human rights associations and from fellow Islamists in their refusal to get involved in its activities. This has meant that large-scale human rights abuses committed against Islamists, however unpalatable their political views might be, did not find unanimous condemnation in traditional human rights circles because, again, the elaboration of such notions depends on the wider ideological framework that different movements and even individuals might have.

Rather than being welcomed in the human rights camp, Ennasir activists found that the doors to traditional left-wing-dominated human rights groups were closed to them when they raised the issue of the salafist prisoners. As Abderrahim Mouhtad, President of Ennasir, admitted,

> before taking the decision of founding Ennasir, we knocked on all the doors of NGOs [non-governmental organizations] involved in human rights issues here in Morocco so that they might wish to take up the *salafist* prisoners' issue. Truly, I want to confirm that these NGOs did not want [to help] us.[11]

Islamist prisoners are no longer shy about telling their stories of abuse at the hands of the state publicly, as Storm (2009, p. 112) argues. She states that

> radical Islamists often have unfair trials, and are ill-treated while in prison, something that is becoming increasingly apparent as more and more Islamists begin to tell their stories of torture and abuse, not only to their families, but now also to human-rights organizations and the media.

Their plight is therefore quite public, which makes the decision not to help out all the more puzzling.

Thus, the decision of many human rights NGOs in Morocco not to defend the rights of the Salafīyah Jihādīyah prisoners occurred irrespective of the often private acknowledgment that many of those who had been unjustly arrested, tortured, tried and sentenced in unfair proceedings were not guilty of any violent act, but were being punished for their political ideas or for their family ties. For example, the president of Forum Marocain Verité et Justice, an organization that in the past had seen the coming together of both Islamist and leftist activists in defence of human rights, recently declared that 'the [human rights] violations committed after 1999 are not as serious [as the ones committed before then]'.[12] While this might be correct purely in terms of numbers, given that the salafist prisoners who suffered and still suffer in jails number between 2000 and 5000, the headcount should be irrelevant when it comes to judging abuse. However, this declaration sums up the view of many within secular civil society regarding the human rights regime that the monarchy has put in place: human rights do not necessarily apply to problematic Islamists.

There is however one important exception to this trend. The secular-leftist Association Marocaine des Droits Humains (AMDH) has from the beginning been very critical of the regime's treatment of the Salafi prisoners and of the abuses to which they were subjected. Such an engagement with this issue dates back to at least 2005 when members of the families of Islamist prisoners were allowed to tell their story during the AMDH series of open forums entitled '*Temoignages en toute liberté pour la vérité*'.[13] As President of the association Khadija Ryadi declared,

> given that international conventions are our framework of reference [for our activism], our positions, discourse and demands are always in line with those conventions. This applies to every issue, be it the rights of women or the rights of Islamists. We defend everybody, all those who are victims of violence and abuse on the part of the regime.[14]

This is quite an important point because it indicates that one of the key values of liberal globalization, no matter what the specific elaboration of it, has become the glue of movements that are normally on opposing ideological sides.

Naturally, it could be argued that the belief in a liberal notion of human rights on the part of Ennasir is simply instrumental, but while this might be the case, it should be disregarded as irrelevant because once a movement begins to express support for specific ideas it is then bound to them to a certain extent (Schwedler 2006). The position of Ennasir is striking also because the other Islamist groups, including the Party for Justice and Development and Yassine's a-ʿAdl movement, prefer to remain almost entirely silent on the issue of salafist prisoners. Their virtual silence can be explained by the ideological and political threat that Salafism poses to both movements and by the fear of increased repression against them if they do get involved.

The al-ʿAdl, while critical of the monarchy, does not support the use of violence as a means to achieve political change in Morocco because this is not only religiously proscribed, but ultimately self-defeating politically as the masses have to be brought to be participants of change rather than simply having change imposed on them through a violent overthrow of the present regime.[15] The PJD is integrated into the political system designed by the King and it therefore has to tow the line on this very sensitive issue as well. Thus, the Casablanca bombings had the effect of crystallizing a fragmentation of civil society that still today prevents the creation of a unanimous front on what human rights actually are and how they should be promoted or defended. The upshot is the absence of a serious challenge to the interpretation and implementation of human rights policies that the Makhzen now has the monopoly on.

This particular relationship between movements of different ideological hues is not the only one that has drawn on the notion of human rights as understood in the liberal tradition. The discursive and practical applications of the different religious groups regarding the nature of human rights run along multiple and variable lines. In this context it is worth examining for instance how socio-economic rights entered the Moroccan political scene. In the face of the aggressive economic liberalization that the monarchy implemented over the course of the last decade to integrate the country into the global economy according to neo-liberal principles (Cohen and Jaidi 2006), some religious actors have turned to the language of socio-economic rights to criticize such policies and the devastating social outcomes they have had. The position of the a-ʿAdl is in this respect quite strong, as the association provides a thorough critique of the neo-liberalism and its effects in Morocco not by resorting to trite anti-imperialist sloganeering, but by focusing on the absence of respect of the most basic socio-economic rights of ordinary Moroccans, which, according to the a-ʿAdl undermines the quest for democracy. In this context, the dramatic socio-economic data – ranging from youth unemployment to rates of literacy and from gross domestic product per capita to the number of Moroccans emigrating – that the *cercle politique* employs in its critique are not simply equated with failed economic policies, but, crucially, they are seen as concrete denials of democratic rights.[16] Thus, in many respects socio-economic rights have primacy over political and civil ones because only when there is just economic development and a fairer distribution of resources can there be democracy. This debate is very similar to that carried out in many other developing countries and even in developed ones, whereby globalization is not identified as being negative per se because the negative effects it has are the product of the greed and mismanagement of national economic elites and rulers. They are the ones who are held responsible for the poor state of the nation. In the Moroccan case, a-ʿAdl's 2007 document concludes that 'it is the Makhzen that has become the real obstacle to democracy and development.'

Accordingly, a-ʿAdl is very engaged in supporting all forms of struggles that take place in Moroccan workplaces where workers strive for better pay and conditions and to end exploitation. It is therefore obvious that they support the current anti-regime demonstrations. This emphasis on socio-economic rights is in line with the thinking and the activities of some secular leftist groups and this has generated a degree of cooperation and coordination with them. The political formation with which the al–ʿAdl is most closely cooperating, Annaji Addimouqrati (AD), is a leftist group that is highly engaged in what they call alternative or 'alter-globalisation' initiatives and in anti-regime political activities. This leftist group shares with the leadership of the al–ʿAdl their analysis of the ills of Morocco It also considers the negation of socio-economic rights as the most significant obstacle to democracy because it conceives of democratic governance not merely as procedures and mechanisms for elections, but, crucially, as the necessary condition for the distribution of wealth. Thus, democracy has a considerable substantive dimension. At the operational level, this analytical coincidence with the al–ʿAdl leads the two movements to support all sorts of demonstrations, strikes and struggles that have an economic dimension and are therefore active in providing material and political support to workers in different industries that strive to better their conditions, to the unemployed and to people living in slums who demand better living standards. One of the leaders of AD, Ali Afkir, pointed to a specific example of cooperation with the al-ʿAdl: '[we both] support the struggle of factory workers in a factory for the treatment of phosphates to have their independent union recognised.'[17]

There is also a political and institutional dimension to this cooperation between the two. At the ideological level, the AD is committed to a type of political pluralism that includes the right of all movements to be heard on the public stage, including the Islamists of the al-ʿAdl, even if they 'have profound disagreements with them on the issue of personal freedoms. Ali Afkir declared that 'as long as the debate is conducted democratically and with respect, all have the right to express their political points of view.'[18] The same degree of tolerance of difference characterizes the discourse of Omar Iharchane, member of the *cercle politique* of the al–ʿAdl, who argued that al-ʿAdl

> is ready to enter into discussions with every other political force in Morocco. Obviously we are aware of the fact that some political movements perceive us negatively and are afraid of us, but the fears are mutual and this is why debating with everyone is important.[19]

The two movements have indeed taken their cooperation beyond declarations of mutual tolerance and beyond concrete support for workers into the institutional arena, having run candidates on the same list for elections in the professional association of the engineers.

At the institutional level, the regime has also made much of the notion of democracy and democratization to frame the politics of Mohammad VI. On this issue as well Islamists have applied different perspectives and subscribe to opposing readings. The PJD perceives itself as 'building democracy' through participation in institutional politics, running candidates for Parliament and attempting to influence policy-making from within the system. In this respect they cooperate with established political parties that have been loyal to the monarchy since their creation and behave as 'responsible' members of the establishment. Institutional participation in Morocco depends on the acceptance of the predominant role of the monarchy and its legitimacy to shape policy and the PJD, as a religious party, accepts this because the monarch is legitimated to rule by the fact that he is the descendent of the Prophet. There is therefore a religious justification for their participation in addition to the practical one that they prefer to be inside institutions and trying to affect change rather than being outside and being unable to see any of their most preferred policies implemented. In this respect they behave much like the Socialist party (USFP), a one-time foe of the monarchy and now fully co-opted in the political system.

Contrary to the PJD, the other clusters of Islamism refuse participation because they see it as selling-out to a monarch that has no intention of creating a genuine democracy where elected representatives rule and the King is simply a figurehead. This is the position of the al-ʿAdl for instance as well as Ennasir with both movements very critical of the notion of democracy used by the monarchy and the parties involved in the political structures that the King has attempted to revitalize. In this respect a crucial demand of those outside the official political system is a thorough reform of the Constitution that would significantly reduce or eliminate the executive powers of the monarch, but even the constitutional changes of 2011 failed to deliver on this. Criticizing the monarchy however is not what the PJD does. In fact the party prefers to see some of its policies implemented by relying on the monarchy itself and therefore it 'lobbies' it on specific policies because the party is aware that only the King can make things happen. While this strengthens the party due to the objectives it achieves, there is no doubt that such a strategy reinforces the authoritarian and arbitrary nature of monarchical rule, as the PJD competes with other parties for royal favours. As mentioned, it is not surprising that in the current revolutionary climate in North Africa, the PJD has steadfastly refused to encourage its members to participate in the demonstrations regularly taking place in Morocco since early February 2011 while both al-ʿAdl and other leftist forces not represented in parliament support the demonstrations and have militants participating in them.

Conclusion

The complexity of Political Islam in Morocco and the different ways in which it appropriates and 'contaminates' the language and values of globalization introduced by the monarchy demonstrate that religious actors can and do adapt to new circumstances and are far from relying simply on anachronistic stances. Furthermore, the divergences that exist between Islamist groups influence potential coalition building among opposition groups and the old divide between liberal secularists and Islamists is no longer a valid guide to politics in Morocco.

A number of points emerge from this analysis. First of all, 'religious' ideology does not seem to be very important when it comes to interacting with movements of a secular persuasion. In fact, quite the contrary is true. Islamist movements, which should have core ideological points in common, find it easier to strike alliances with non-Islamist groups and associations rather than within the same Islamist camp. This indicates the significant tensions that exist within Political Islam in Morocco, illustrating the impossibility of treating Islamism as a unified actor. This does not mean that religious precepts are irrelevant because Islamist movements in Morocco rely on different scholars and ideologues to justify their position and all of them have specific religious references (Zeghal 2005), but it is the political situation and the concrete objectives that movements wish to achieve that shape to a considerable extent the manner in which they operate. This leads to a second significant point. All Islamist movements seem to find credible and committed partners in secular movements from which, in theory, they should be distant. The case of Morocco confirms that factors other than supposed ideological distance explain the nature of cross-ideological relationships.

In Morocco, it is the relationship with the monarchy that determines the relationship with other political and social movements because of the sacred nature of the monarchy itself. For Islamist movements, despite their rhetorical and at times concrete opposition to secularism, in so far as it is believed to destroy the fabric of society because of its perceived elimination of spirituality from social and political life, secular actors can constitute an important ally in a struggle for an enhanced role in Moroccan political life. For instance, during the electoral campaign for the new Constitution of July 2011 one can see that the Sufi Brotherhood Boutchychya was in the pro-monarchy 'yes' camp while the Sufi al-ʿAdl was in the 'no' camp. The same division applies to the salafists, with the ones following Maghraoui in the 'yes' camp and the ones in Ennasir on the opposite side. Conversely, traditional suspicions that many within the secular left have for Islamists are assuaged because there is a degree of convergence on shared objectives. Finally, the most interesting finding of this analysis is that the values of Western-inspired globalization such as human rights, democracy, and development are being used and appropriated by a range of religious actors to advance their own understanding of those values, based on their own political philosophies and indigenous experiences, leading at times to a significant departure from the mainstream internationally accepted conceptualization. This is an effective strategy to reposition themselves away from the label of 'medieval' and 'unmodern' political actors and it is a strategy that the Turkish AKP has successfully implemented (Dagi 2009). The rhetoric emanating from Islamist movements in Morocco today is substantially different from the one they employed in the 1980s and 1990s when 'Islam is the solution' seemed a sufficiently clear slogan for supporters and enemies alike to identify the political positions of Islamist groups. While attachment to the notions of democracy and human rights might still be instrumental, the daily exchanges and relationships they have with secular counterparts suggest a rather radical rethink of Islamism on the part of its proponents, which have taken advantage of the limited liberal space in Morocco to offer alternative visions of society based on universal values.

Acknowledgements

The authors are grateful to Dublin City University for its financial support through the 'Building Research Capacity' Grant in conducting research in Morocco. They thank all those Moroccans who gave their time. Francesco Cavatorta is also very grateful to Paul Aarts, Kawa Hassan, Reinoud Leenders, Salam Kawakibi and Juliette Verhoeven for very fruitful discussions on opposition dynamics in the Arab world in the context of the HIVOS Knowledge Programme based at the University of Amsterdam. Finally, the authors acknowledge the very useful comments received by two anonymous referees whose input greatly contributed to improve this paper. An earlier version of this paper was presented at the ECPR Joint Sessions, St. Gallen, Switzerland, 12–17 April 2011.

Notes

1. Groupe TelQuel, *Communiqué de presse*, Casablanca, 1 October 2010.
2. Interview with Ahmed Benchemsi, Editor at the time of *Tel Quel* magazine, 2010.
3. Interview with the authors, 2005.
4. *Diplomés Chômeurs* literally means 'unemployed graduates' and is a collection of different groups of students with university degrees who cannot find suitable employment despite their qualifications and organize protests against the government to highlight their plight and the poor economic policies adopted. *Diplomés Chômeurs* activities, such as marches or sit-ins, are very often broken up by the police with violence. For more on this issue, see Badimon Emperador (2007).
5. Mohammad VI, *Discours prononcé par SM le Roi à l'occasion de l'installation de l'Instance Equité et Réconciliation*, 7 January 2004. Available from: http://www.maroc.ma/NR/exeres/B272623A-227C-46D3-AC67-557BE9DCDF7A/.
6. For the details of the PJD's position on recent demonstrations and internal repercussions, see the magazine *Aujourd'hui le Maroc* at: http://www.aujourdhui.ma/instantanes-depeche81050.html [Accessed 10 March 2011].
7. Interview with the authors, 2008.
8. Editor's note: The matter of the age of ʿĀʾishah bint Abī Bakr at the time of the Prophet Muḥammad's marriage to her has been a subject of both debate and controversy inside and outside the Arab and Muslim worlds. Various narrations suggest different ages, where there tends to be some agreement that her age at the time of *betrothal* may have been nine, her age at the time of *consummation* of the marriage – according to the dictates of Islamic *fiqh* – would not have taken place before the start of her menses. Alternatively, while there *are* Muslim scholars who posit a young age, Islām Buḥayrā makes a strong case and has noted correctly that ancient scholars concurred that ʿAsmāʾ bint Abī Bakr was older than her younger sister ʿĀʾishah by ten years and that she was born 27 years before the *hijrah* (migration) to Medina, meaning that the age of ʿAsmāʾ at the time of the beginning of revelation in 610 CE would have been fourteen, whereas ʿĀʾishah would have been four – having been born in 606 CE, according to this calculation. ʿĀʾishah is known to have married/been *betrothed* to the Prophet in 620 CE (when she would have been fourteen and ʿAsmāʾ would have been 24); however, the ancient sources also mention that ʿĀʾishah's marriage was *consummated* 'after three years and some months' – at the end of the first year *after* the *hijrah* or at the beginning of the second in 624 CE, which, in other words, implies that she would have been 17 or 18 years of age at that time. Available at: http://www.youm7.com/News.asp?NewsID=35802 and http://www.forsonna.info/showthread.php?t=65083 [Accessed 5 September 2011]. Additionally, it bears mentioning that Islamic law and *fiqh* rely on recognized custom – *ʿurf* – where what is familiar and well-known or established in a given society is recognized as valid practice (in so far as such does not contravene Islamic law); and, on this basis, the matter of child marriage is highly a-typical in the Arab Muslim world.

9. For the statement, see http://www.middle-east-online.com/ENGLISH/?id=27880 [Accessed 22 October 2010].
10. For more on Dawa Salafism in Morocco, see http://www.lobservateur.info/Maroc/enfance-salafiste-les-brigands-de-linnocence.php [Accessed 11 March 2011].
11. Interview with the authors, 2008.
12. *Le Journal* (9–15 January 2010, p. 10).
13. See http://www.amdh.org.ma/html/act_pub.asp [Accessed 11 March 2011].
14. Interview with the authors, 2009.
15. Nadia Yassine, interview with the authors, 2008.
16. For the *Lettre ouverte à toute conscience resposnable*, published in December 2007 by the *cercle politique* of the al-ʿAdl, see http://www.hoggar.org/.
17. Interview with the authors, 2010.
18. Interview with the authors, 2010.
19. Interview with the authors, 2010.

References

Abdelrahman, M., 2009. With the Islamists? – sometimes. With the regime? – never! Cooperation between the Left and Islamists in Egypt. *British Journal of Middle Eastern Studies*, 36 (1), 37–54.

Albrecht, H., 2005. How can opposition support authoritarianism? Lessons from Egypt. *Democratization*, 12 (3), 378–397.

Albrecht, H., 2010. Introduction – Contentious politics, political opposition, and authoritarianism. *In*: A. Holger, ed. *Contentious politics in the Middle East. Political opposition under authoritarianism*. Gainesville: Florida University Press, 1–33.

Amar, A., 2009. *Mohammed VI, le grand malentendu, dix ans de règne dans l'ombre de Hassan II*. Paris: Calmann-Lévy.

Badimon Emperador, M., 2007. , *Diplomés Chômeurs* au Maroc: dynamiques de pérennisation d'une action collective plurielle. *L'Année du Maghreb*, 3, 297–311.

Boubekeur, A., 2008. Salafism and radical politics in post-conflict Algeria. *Carnegie Papers*, 11, 1–20.

Browers, M., 2006. *Democracy and civil society in Arab political thought*. Syracuse, NY: Syracuse University Press.

Cavatorta, F., 2007. Neither participation nor revolution. The strategy of the *Jamiat al-Adl wal-Ihsan. Mediterranean Politics*, 12 (3), 379–395.

Cavatorta, F. and Elananza, A., 2008. Political opposition in civil society. An analysis of the interactions of secular and religious associations in Algeria and Jordan. *Government and Opposition*, 43 (4), 561–578.

Clark, J., 2006. The conditions of Islamist moderation: unpacking cross-ideological cooperation in Jordan. *International Journal of Middle East Studies*, 38 (4), 539–560.

Clark, J., 2010. Threats, structures and resources: cross-ideological coalition building in Jordan. *Comparative Politics*, 43 (1), 101–120.

Cohen, S. and Jaidi, L., 2006. *Morocco. Globalisation and its consequences*. London: Routledge.

Dagi, I., 2009. Beyond the clash of civilisations: the rapprochement of Turksih Islamic elite with the west. *In*: W. Zank, ed. *Clash or cooperation of civilisations? Overlapping integration and identities*. Aldershot: Ashgate, 43–64.

Dalmasso, E. and Cavatorta, F., 2011. The never ending story: protests and constitutions in Morocco. Available from: http://www.jadaliyya.com/pages/index/2365/the-never-ending-story_protests-and-constitutions [Accessed 21 August 2011].

Denoeux, G. and Desfosses, H., 2007. Rethinking the Moroccan parliament: the Kingdom's legislative development Imperative. *Journal of North African Studies*, 12 (1), 79–108.

El-Din Haseeb, K., 2011. On the Arab democratic spring: lessons derived. *Contemporary Arab Affairs*, 4 (2), 113–122.

El-Ghissassi, H., 2006. *Régard sur le Maroc de Mohammed VI*. Neuilly-sur-Seine: Michel Falon.

Fuller, G., 2004. *The future of Political Islam*. London: Palgrave.

Haynes, J., 2010. Democratisation in the Middle east and North Africa: what is the effect of globalisation? *Totalitarian Movements and Political Religions*, 11 (2), 133–149.
Heydemann, S., 2007. *Upgrading authoritarianism in the Arab world*, Analysis Paper, Saban Centre for Middle East Policy, 13, 1–35.
Howe, M., 2005. *Morocco. The Islamist awakening and other challenges*. Oxford: Oxford University Press.
Human Rights Watch, 2010. *'Stop looking for your son.' Illegal detentions under the counter-terrorism law*, October. New York: Human Rights Watch.
Kristianasen, W., 2007. Can Morocco's Islamists check al-Qaida? *Le Monde Diplomatique*, Available from: http://mondediplo.com/2007/08/06morocco [Accessed 25 March 2010].
Laskier, M., 2003. A difficult inheritance: Moroccan society under King Mohammed VI. *Middle East Review of International Affairs*, 7 (3), 1–20.
Martinez-Fuentes, G., 2011. El Islam politico Tunecino. Conflicto y coopearcion electoral en los comicios presidenciales de 2004 y 2009. *Revista CIDOB d'Afers Internacionals*, 93/94, 89–109.
Munson, Jr, H., 1991. Morocco's fundamentalists. *Government and Opposition*, 26 (3), 331–344.
Schwedler, J., 2006. *Faith in moderation*. Cambridge: Cambridge University Press.
Storm, L., 2008. The parliamentary elections in Morocco, September 2007. *Electoral Studies*, 27 (2), 359–364.
Storm, L., 2009. The dilemma of the Islamists: human rights, democratization and the war on terror. *Middle East Policy*, 16 (1), 101–112.
Tozy, M., 1999. *Monarchie et Islam Politique au Maroc*. Paris: Presses de Sciences Po.
Vermeren, P., 2009. *Le Maroc de Mohammed VI, la transition inachevée*. Paris: La Découverte.
Willis, M., 2004. Morocco's Islamists and the legislative elections of 2002: the strange case of the party that did not want to win. *Mediterranean Politics*, 9 (1), 53–81.
Zeghal, M., 2005. *Les Islamistes Marocains. Le Défi à la Monarchie*. Paris: La Découverte.

Interviews

Abderrahim Mouhtad (President of Ennasir), Casablanca, 24 November 2008.
Ahmed Benchemsi (former Editor of *Tel Quel*), Casablanca, 4 February 2010.
Ali Afkir (founding leader of Annaji Addimouqrati), Casablanca, 9 January 2010.
Aziz Rabbah (MP of the PJD), Kenitra, 8 February 2010.
Khadija Ryadi (President of AMDH), Rabat, 22 July 2009.
Nadia Yassine (leading member of al-ʿAdl), Salé, 12 December 2008.
Omar Iharchane (member of the *cercle politique* al-ʿAdl), Casablanca, 12 January 2010.

Copts in Egypt and their demands: between inclusion and exclusion

Mai Mogib*

Faculty of Economics and Political Science, Cairo University, Cairo, Egypt

This work rests on the assumption that to be a Copt is not equivalent to belonging to a specific religious sect. The term Copt refers to all Egyptian Christians. The article is an attempt to analyse the relationship between inclusion and exclusion policies and the nature of the Mubarak regime, the better to explain the nature of economic, social and political factors that led to many conspicuous social and economic imbalances and thence alienation and the appearance of social movements opposed to the state. Taking the Copts as a case study the work demonstrates that demands attributed to and/or defined as those of the Copts specifically are not necessarily an expression of minority or religious concerns so much as general citizen demands. The evidence presented is derived from a major study of the opinion of Coptic citizens towards political and economic demands. The purpose is to determine whether they are considered social, political and economic demands based on citizenship or on religious grounds. The research adopted a set of hypotheses to be confirmed or refuted through compiling and analysing the results of an empirically administered questionnaire.

Introduction

This study endeavours to analyse and explain the relation between inclusion and exclusion policies on the one hand and the nature of the previously prevailing political system in Egypt on the other. This relation has been influenced by a number of external and internal factors, including the collapse of the Soviet Union and the emergence of many states configured on religious and ethnic bases and also the emergence of a uni-polar international system led by the United States. These external factors have affected this relation, especially in the context of the sweeping changes manifest in the era of globalization and universal calls for human rights.

As far as internal factors impacting this relation are concerned, this study explains the nature of the economic, social and political factors that led to many conspicuous social and economic imbalances, which resulted in alienation and the appearance of new social movements opposed to the state and its policies. The previous Egyptian regime was characterized by hybridization between liberalism and dictatorship. The regime adopted an open economic policy and a closed, rigid political orientation that prohibited the devolution of power. This led to divisions on all levels: religious (Muslim–Christian); gender; and socio-economic (rich–poor) – all of which affect

Egyptian citizens' social integration and push them towards their more primary and primitive affiliations *vis-à-vis* the state. This analysis falls within the various theoretical frameworks that discuss the nature of state–society relations and its particularities in Arab and Islamic societies.

Among these divisions, the study attempts to analyse the factors that affected societal and religious relations among Muslims and Christians in Egypt through the Copts as a case study to examine whether their demands – social, political or economic– are civil demands and/or whether they are addressed on a religious basis as a reaction to the state's incapacity to fulfil its obligations towards its citizens.

At the outset of this study, it should be noted that Coptism is not a religion. The term 'Copts' (*al-aqbāṭ*) denotes all Egyptians, or it did so *historically*. 'Coptism' or the state of being Coptic (*al-qubṭīyah*) is not to belong to a specific religious sect, but rather refers to Egyptians altogether. In this study, however, the designation Copts refers to all Christians in Egypt and the term 'Coptism' is used as a symbolic indication of Christianity.

There are thirteen Christian sects actively engaged in religious activities in Egypt: Orthodox Copts, Catholic Copts, Protestant Copts, Roman Catholics, Roman Orthodox, Armenian Catholic, Armenian Orthodox, Syrian Catholics, Syrian Orthodox, Latin Catholic, Maronite Catholic, Chaldean Catholic, and Anglican Protestants. This large multiplicity of sects does not *only* spring from creedal differences in regard to the nature of the Christ, but *also* rather from the proliferation of numerous and different nationalities and ancient peoples who belong to these sects.

Common assumptions and some clarifications

First, any focus on Egyptian Orthodox Copts to the exclusion of Protestant or Catholic Copts is predicated on the false assumption that the attitudes of the Catholic or Protestant churches on political or social levels are distinct from those of the Orthodox ones, and this is not true. The three churches differ on doctrinal matters, but this variation does not influence their political situations or positions. In terms of their political status all three sects are generally characterized as homogenous, so reference to 'Copts' is in the inclusive sense of the three churches and their respective communities regardless of sectarian affiliation.

Second, at the same time that 'Copts' belong to a category, they do not represent a single independent group or closed, homogeneous bloc. Those within this category vary in terms of their social standing and political engagement and are spread throughout society – vertically and horizontally; they can be found among the ranks of peasant farmers, professionals, those engaged in business and trades, and merchants. The only common characteristics that they share are their nationality – they are all Egyptian citizens – and their religious affiliation – they are all Christians. They have different interests, visions and biases and, accordingly, do not adopt one unified position towards public issues and especially the Coptic question itself. Factors, such as educational background, class affiliation, subjective perception, historical circumstances and political roles, are all crucial in determining the attitudes and preferences of 'Copts' within and across this group or categorical concept.

Third, before attempting to answer the research questions to be addressed here, it is important to distinguish between Copts as a religious group represented religiously by the Orthodox Church and Copts as a social group enmeshed in the Egyptian national fabric. Since Egyptian Copts differ in their political, social and sectarian affiliations, they cannot be dealt with as one cohesive group, though a long history of religious tensions and a degree of integration between the community and its official religious institutions have forced the religious leaders and clergy to play multiple roles in defending the interests of the Copts as well as representing them in the public sphere and before the state.

Fourth, the concepts and rubrics 'Coptic group', 'Coptic issue' or 'Coptic question' yield an impression that Copts have a socio-religious system parallel to that of the Egyptian Muslim majority, who – it should be noted – are also not homogeneous. Also, these concepts connote a reference to Copts as forming a religious group in the process of transforming into a political lobby under the ascendancy of religious affiliations (Chitham 1986, p. 42). Use of these rubrics here is not intended to affirm either impression.

Primary research hypotheses

For the purposes of this study a questionnaire was designed to identify the opinions of the Coptic citizen towards the social, economic and political demands associated with the Copts as a group. This was to determine the nature of these demands and discern if the Coptic citizen recognizes and conceives of these demands on a civil basis or on religious grounds, especially under the relatively strong influence of the religious institution compared to that of the state.

The research adopted a set of hypotheses to be confirmed or refuted through compiling and analysing the results of an empirically administered questionnaire.

- Hypothesis: There is a positive correlation between perception of political exclusion and the political demands of the religious group.
- Hypothesis: There is a positive correlation between perception of social exclusion and the social demands of the religious group.
- Hypothesis: There is a positive correlation between perception of economic exclusion and the economic demands of the religious group.

These hypotheses complement the main questions of the research: What is the relation between policies of inclusion and exclusion and the nature of the political system in Egypt? What are the intermediate variables that influence this relation and thus the common field between the state and the society in Egypt?

The research attempted to answer these questions through focusing on 'Copts' as a case study to measure the orientations of inclusive and exclusive policies *vis-à-vis* Copts as a religious group and determine their place on the scale of inclusion and exclusion so as to discover if their problems or demands are based and conceived on religious grounds or on civil ones.

There are economic indicators for determining 'exclusion', which comprise: income insufficient to meet the basic needs of the individual; exclusion from joining the labour market in general or work in the public or government sectors in a situation where there is exclusion on the part of the state; and being deprived of participation in production. Indicators of political exclusion measure the extent of participation of an individual or group in political decision making, the extent to which they are availed of their rights to vote in elections or to be members of political parties or run as candidates, as well as the ability to freely express opinions without restrictions attached to religion or gender. In regard to social exclusion, this is measured by indicators of the relative strength or weakness of the belonging of the individual or the group to society; the relation of the individual or group with 'the other' – in order to ascertain the strength of social bonding; and, lastly, any obstacles to obtaining social rights and services.

The questionnaire

The researcher designed a questionnaire to measure the:

- Coptic citizen's perception of economic exclusion;
- Coptic citizen's perception of political exclusion;
- Coptic citizen's perception of social exclusion;
- nature of the 'Coptic' demands (social, political, economic, institutional) and the opinion of the Coptic citizen towards each demand in addition to the weight of each demand.

The questionnaire was divided into two main parts, the first of which focused on measuring the Coptic citizen's perception of economic, social and political exclusion. The researcher converted the concepts and aforementioned indicators of exclusion or inclusion into questions/responses that could be measured easily. Thus, economic exclusion comprised indicators such as: exclusion from the governmental labour market; low income levels when compared to basic needs; and deprivation or exclusion from participation in production. Political exclusion comprised indicators including: individual or group participation in decision-making processes; voting rights; membership in political parties; the right to express opinions freely without constraints related to religion or gender. Lastly, measures of social exclusion (Hills *et al.*, 2002) included indicators such as the strength of the individual's or group's sense of belonging to his/her homeland; relations with 'the other'; social cohesion and obstacles in the way of enjoyment of social rights (Kabeer 2000).

These measures and indicators were distilled into questions that could be asked of the sample to discover, first, if Coptic citizens perceived themselves to be excluded because of religion or not; and, second, the relation between exclusion and 'Coptic' economic demands (as in the case of appointment to high governmental posts); social demands (in respect to the freedom of religious conversion); and political demands (as correlated to the right of political participation).

The questionnaire was consistent with the two research variables and the indicators of each variable. Questions (1)–(6) focused on economic exclusion and questions (7)–(11) focused on social exclusion, while questions (12)–(26) focused on political exclusion. Questions (27)–(47) aimed at discovering the opinions of Coptic citizens concerning 'Coptic' economic, social and political demands. For each of the aforementioned indicators equal weight was accorded so as to measure exclusion across the spectrum, where each indicator measures a certain phenomenological dimension according to a scale of equal weight and importance. The survey also collected general data about the sample, such as age, gender, profession, neighbourhood, job sector and educational level.

The questionnaire was divided into two main axes: an axis of *exclusion* (economic, social and political) to discover if Copts perceive themselves as excluded because of their religion (1)–(26); and a second axis focused on *inclusion* of Coptic demands and the opinion of the Coptic citizens towards those demands (27)–(47).

Table 1. The sample distribution according to job sectors.

Job sector	Number	%
Governmental	34	18.7
Public	22	12.1
Self-employed	29	15.9
Private	44	24.2
Number who do not work	53	29.1
Total	182	100

The researcher endeavoured to select the sample group from different regions and took into consideration the major parameters of the Coptic society, including educational background, job sector, age, etc. Thus, the sample did not depend on a framework that allowed all the sample attributes an equal opportunity for representation but was chosen in a way that guaranteed the presence of multiple variables, including age, gender, neighbourhood and educational background (Dattolo 2008).

The sample size consisted of 182 Egyptian (Christian) Copts from Cairo, Giza and Kaliubya governorates, from diverse educational, social and economic backgrounds (Table 1).

Geographical scope

The survey was taken in the region of greater Cairo (Cairo–Giza–Kaliubiya). Although there is a very sizeable Coptic presence in Upper Egypt, the researcher was unable to conduct her survey there due to the sensitivity of the topic, in and of itself, on the one hand and because most Upper Egyptian towns or cities are socially conservative and closed in comparison to those in the Cairo and Giza areas. It should be noted that the researcher did not obtain permission from state security forces to conduct the survey; although this is typically a crucial and necessary requirement before any survey may be conducted in Egypt. Permission, if requested, will often be denied and may lead to complications for the researcher.

In addition to the survey, the researcher conducted informal, unstructured interviews with a group of prominent Coptic persons in Egypt with different political orientations so as to know their views and opinions of various Coptic demands. Some of the figures were former ministers, members of parliament and opposition parties, human rights activists, and clergy. The researcher also managed to meet with some important Coptic elites in the United States to ascertain their opinions about the Coptic issue and the main problems the Copts had faced under the previous political system of the ousted Hosni Mubarak.

Statistical methods and findings

The researcher utilized the following statistical methods: frequencies, percentages, Pearson Correlation, and reached a number of conclusions.

Economic exclusion and inclusion of 'Coptic' economic demands

Economic exclusion indicators are: low income levels, access to posts in governmental or public sectors, and obstacles to working in those sectors. Concerning answers to the question 'Is your income satisfactory?', those who answered 'no' said that this is due to the high prices and then the increasing cost of living demands/inflation, which would seem to refute the hypothesis that economic exclusion is on a religious basis for this indicator.

Also, those who work for the public or governmental sectors tend to be those who are more than 50 years old and not from younger Copts. This is because appointment in such sectors in the past was open to all without any obstacles and salaries were not that low relative to prices and the cost of living.

Additionally, most of the respondents referred to nepotism and the necessity of having connections (known commonly as *wastah* in the Arab world) in order to obtain jobs in the governmental sector, which also tends to refute the research hypothesis that there is a positive correlation between economic exclusion and rising 'Coptic' economic demands.

Through correlating economic exclusion indicators and the inclusion of Coptic demands via Pearson's correlation, approximately 40.1% of the sample responded to the demand for appointment in high government posts by perpetuating a societal culture that endorses toleration. This means that 40.1% of the sample associated the relative accessibility of high government posts with the perpetuation of a societal culture that endorses toleration. This shows that 'Coptic' economic demands are not a reaction to intentional economic exclusion directed against Copts in Egypt because of their Christianity. The percentage even confirms the weakness of the societal relations that require an endorsement of a tolerant societal culture towards the other.

Through application of the SPSS statistical programme and Pearson's correlation, it was discovered that economic exclusion correlates negatively with the rise in economic demands of Copts (–0.139), which refutes the research hypothesis on this issue. Copts' demands to be appointed to high governmental posts do not derive from a religious basis, especially since most of the sample responses stressed the importance of the spread of a societal culture based on tolerance *instead* of a quota for Copts in public posts.

Social exclusion and inclusion of 'Coptic' social demands

Indicators of social exclusion included: social cohesion; the degree of a sense of belonging to homeland; the nature of relations with 'the other'; and obstacles to enjoying social rights. The quantitative analysis of the sample responses showed that around half the sample espouse a desire to emigrate – especially the young Copts, which reflects a social reality where deteriorating living conditions and the obstacles to finding a suitable job are major causes, while religious discrimination is not the main reason.

Concerning relations with 'the other', a high percentage of youth preferred dealing with other fellow Copts rather than with Muslims, which is indicative of eroded societal relations among Egyptians.

As for obstacles to enjoying social rights and services, respondents referred to such obstacles in the context of reporting poor living conditions, followed by corruption and then the general apathy among citizens.

Through application of the SPSS programme and Pearson's correlation, the relation between social exclusion and the rising social demands of Copts measured 0.321, which would tend to affirm the research hypothesis that social exclusion results in the rise of 'Coptic' social demands. The correlation between social exclusion and equality in media opportunities is 0.056; promulgation of a unified Personal Status Law

(0.149); freedom of religious conversion (0.094); deletion of religious affiliation from national ID cards (–0.025); modification of educational curriculums (0.054); and registration by Copts in al-Azhar university (–0.007). This implies that social demands are correlated to a religious identity because of many factors, such as the way Copts opt to isolate themselves socially due to their feelings of distinctness and privacy and the rising role of the Coptic Church in offering social services to its followers due to the diminishing role of the state in this sphere. Social demands are related to the Copts daily lives and some such demands, such as the promulgation of the unified Personal Status Law, are related to religious doctrine, which justifies the religious basis of such demands.

Political exclusion and inclusion of 'Coptic' political demands

Political exclusion included the following indicators: membership in political parties, voting rights, and freedom of expression. The sample responses strongly suggested that the respondents are not involved in politics and not enjoying their political rights because of political apathy and lack of a political culture rather than for religious reasons. Furthermore, the majority of the sample does not belong to any political parties because of political apathy in the first instance and weakness of political parties in general in the second instance, as well as the absence of a party that represents their priorities in the third.

The sample responses also suggested that the majority had not presented their opinions in the official media before in regard to any internal or external political issues. They justified this variously with some declining to do so because they feel their opinion has no value or because of the burdens of life's responsibilities, or because they do not trust official media.

The results of SPSS analysis and Pearson's correlation between political exclusion and Coptic demands identified a correlation of 0.009; a value that refutes the research hypothesis that political exclusion leads to the rise of political demands of the religious group. The relation between political exclusion and quota demands was –0.032; establishing a religious political party –0.123; amending Article 2 of the Egyptian Constitution 0.044; and promulgation of the Unified Law for Places of Worship 0.038 – all of which imply that the respondents do not perceive the exclusion of their political demands on a religious basis.

Analysis

To substantiate or refute the research hypotheses and to answer the main question posed requires necessarily an analysis of the nature of the dialectic relation between the state and society in Egypt.

Through analysing such a relation and the main factors that influence it socially, politically and economically, it is possible to discern the main objective and subjective obstacles impeding inclusion of the 'Coptic' demands in Egypt. This involves two levels of analysis:

- the *state* level – related to the history, nature and the form of the political system. Herein, the lack of system legitimacy, the spread of corruption and the absence of real pluralism are all reflected in the societal landscape and have led to the rise of narrow affiliations.

- the *society* level – that encompasses all human interactions in the social, political and economic fields.

Theoretical treatments of state–society relations discern five main steps or stages through which these may pass. First, there is state formation, encapsulated in Thomas Hobbes' emphasis on the importance of the national state as a tool to control society and to protect it from the 'war of all against all'. Second, there is the secular state that aims at abolishing differences and spreading societal homogeneity. Third, there is the state that recognizes diversity and thus encourages the revival or survival of different cultures and identities. Fourth, the retreating state that witnesses the rise of primordial and sectarian powers. Fifth, the concept of 'mutual empowerment', as described by Joel Migdal (1994, pp. 1–4), in his book *State Power and Social Forces*, where he builds his theory on the central hypothesis that the state is a part of society and any state – democratic or autocratic – cannot be isolated from society.

Away from the theoretical definitions and academic classifications that analyse state–society relations, however, in the case of Egypt – with the possible exception of the period of more radical interventions under Nasser – the state has not and does not meet the requirements that are politically and culturally necessary to transform society to play a role in the dynamics of the new social contract.

A three-dimensional approach that encompasses Regime–Church–Copts is crucial to analyse the place of Copts before and after the revolution, meaning the nature and orientation of the political system before the revolution that framed a certain relation with religious institutions in general and the Church in particular, reflected on the Coptic community which in turn the regime dealt with – in the past – as a single homogeneous bloc represented by the Pope on both a political and religious basis.

To analyse that three-faceted relation, five variables should be considered. First, the structure of the community within the state would appear to be significant. If Copts are regarded as the largest Christian sect, the religious leader could potentially be regarded as a rival to the state, so it will be difficult for the state to challenge the Church leadership, which forces the state to adopt a policy of *rapprochement* backed up by repression if necessary. Alternatively, if different sects of the same religion exist, it is less likely that the state will perceive them as a threat. Second, the structure of the Christian community as a whole in relation to the rest of society is also important. In states like Egypt where there is a clear majority–minority situation, Christians are inclined to perceive themselves as more vulnerable to changes within the majority community. However, the existence of other minority groups can offer the minority community some space to articulate its concerns.

Third, Church–state relations are affected by both regime policies towards the presence of the Christian community and perceptions held by Christians regarding the impact of these policies on their security. This relates to the role of religious institutions under authoritarian regimes, which suggest the existence of a common enemy that threatens the security and survival of both the state and the society.

Fourth, there is the security dilemma. The Church is faced with the dilemma whether to defend the communal rights of its followers at all costs or to exercise self-censorship given that the regime is the ultimate provider of its security. Correspondingly, if this guarantee of protection is not fulfilled, it is more likely that Church leaders will be outspoken on particular issues.

Fifth, there is the question of the power and activity of so-called 'Christian civil society' and its ability to bridge the gap between the demands of the community and the Church support of the authoritarian regime that violates the rights of its Christian citizens. Such civil groups play an important role in influencing state decisions concerning Christians, especially after the refusal of many Christian secular activists to acknowledge the Church's ascendancy in political representation on behalf of the community.

The case of Egypt

A number of observations should be made in regard to state and society in Egypt. The Egyptian state suffers political, social and economic weaknesses. This means that problems in these spheres must be weighted correctly and neither over- nor underestimated. In terms of this case study, one of the major problems confronting the researcher into Coptic demands and issues is the necessity of distinguishing between those that arise as part of the general problems of the Egyptian milieu – which affect the population fairly uniformly – and those which may arise as a result of, or in support of, the contention that exclusion against Copts is due to their religion. This has the effect of reproducing the concept of minority and emphasizing differences based on religion.

A second important issue in attempting to determine causal factors is that prevailing state–society relations in Egypt can be described as 'eroded'. The weak state–weak society dichotomy is a primary model for explaining the relation between state and society in Egypt (Richards 1991, pp. 1726–1727). There is a marked difference between this model and that of the strong state that complements its society and the 'fierce' state that is not able to confront its society and shares in its alienation and apathy (Ayubi 1989, p. 18). This does not mean rigidity, especially if the current relation between the two sides is characterized by fluidity and dynamism.

As a result, the phenomenon of the separation and relative disconnect between society and the state led to the appearance of 'un-politicized/a-political citizens' and thus non-politicized uprisings (movements or protests that call for their demands without being affiliated to any political trend or orientation) that took place as an outcome of exclusion policies and the absence of the supremacy of law. Here each citizen plays a role in the 'parallel state' which contains both factors of chaos and stability (Fahmy 2002, p. 255).

The state alone does not hold sole responsibility for a weak society, but society also is responsible for its own weakness. The experience of exclusion suffered by society created in Egypt a profound sense of depression and isolation that foments and endorses the rise of religion in all spheres of life. Thus the nature of society impels it to search for an alternative society with alternative visions and ideas to solve its problems, which threatens both stability of the state and the union of society.

Research questions and the case study

The study attempted to answer a group of questions that are related to the research problematic.

(1) Which factor most influences the other: the political or the religious factor?

The dividing line between religion and politics is not a straight, clear or fixed one (Moser 2001). It traces its course depending on the social, religious and historical givens confronted by any society. Egypt is not an exception to this, where the state is the institutional incarnation of the unity of its nation and the expression of the inherent sectarian and religious contradictions and the political mechanism evolved to handle those contradictions. Therefore, religious or sectarian crises are the crises of the Egyptian state wherein the interaction between the religious and political arenas occurs.

(2) Which takes precedence in defining 'the other' in Egypt: religion or politics?

It may be obvious that religion influences political interactions since even politics uses religion to serve its interests, especially in the case of a fragile or weak state. Protests and uprisings are the normal outcome of the weakness of the state and society.

Under Mubarak, religious interactions did influence political relations, to serve the political interests of the regime, and through deployment of the 'religious card' which deepened the sectarian problem – reflected not only in Islamic–Christian relations, but also in the relation between the state and its citizens, that had turned into a pro forma one devoid of any substantive political linkages.

(3) Is the minority concept applied to Copts?

A minority – according to Eriksen (1997, p. 25) – is a group that

> must be non-dominant in society and the polity. A group can be conceptualized as a minority when its values and world views are either not reflected at all, or insufficiently reflected both in the public sphere and in the constitution of societal norms which signifies marginalization and exclusion. Also a minority group is a group that has characteristics which differ from the rest of the population and it wants to preserve its own characteristics where its values do not conform to the norms of the majority.

The extent to which Copts may be considered a minority depends on the criteria used. Ericksen's definition may not be, or is partly, applicable to certain Egyptian Copts.[1] Copts, for example, are not considered members of a minority group as they do not commonly occupy poorer jobs, earn less income, live in less desirable areas, receive inferior education, exercise less political influence than is average and are not generally subjected to various social indignities. Certain dimensions of minority status, under Mubarak, were inconsequential, and it is only recently – with the insensitivity and dogmatic views of certain extremist Islamists – that the question of Copts as a religious minority or even as a 'minority' *per se*, has come to the fore. Traditionally, the Copts have not been disadvantaged in Egypt in the way that minorities in other cultures and societies may be.

Copts may be considered a 'minority' in Egypt based on the criteria of numbers or religious affiliation, but they are not a minority from the perspective of societal interactions. They are not segregated in a certain region or a geographical zone. They are distributed across all social strata and formations. Therefore, Copts are integrated and do not all face any limitations or obstacles purely on religious basis.

(4) How can the Church–state relation be characterized in Egypt?

As will be apparent, the relation between the state and the Coptic Church in Egypt is confusing, and thus so is the relation between the state and the Copts. The Church supported the Mubarak regime with the justification that he was the 'protector of Copts' against the rise of Islamists, even though the regime at the same time did not deal with Coptic problems seriously.

(5) Does 'Coptic' discourse factor in deepening social divisions based on religion?

Here, one should distinguish between two main themes: Church discourse that is apolitical and politicized discourse. Church discourse that is directed towards followers is not politicized and should not typically give rise to any problems so long as the social and political spheres do not face any problems. Throughout history the Coptic group declares itself as 'Coptic' without any limitations. But the problem appears when the discourse is politicized, which transforms the Coptic religious distinction to the political sphere that separates 'Coptic cultural privacy' away from the commons of the Egyptian culture.

According to the parameters of state–society relations analysis, the Egyptian state (and this includes under Mubarak) may be characterized as being weak at the political level but fierce at the security level. Society suffers divisions that impair its ability to confront the state. The common ground between the state and society – the political sphere – suffers from rigidity and regression. The state creates society's orientations without being able to influence its preferences. To the contrary, society is independent at the social and economic levels and largely removed from state interference. This separation created a situation of a lack of belonging and hostility.

Thus if state–society relations persist as they did under Mubarak, the excluded masses will eventually revolt not only against the state but also against the social structure itself. Such masses revolted on 25 January 2011, not on a religious basis, but due to marginalization and exclusion.

The revolution of 25 January 2011 witnessed an active participation of Copts outside official orientations of the Church and support for the previous regime. The separation between the institution of the Church and Copts at the political level, while manifest even before the revolution, deepened following the sectarian events that took place *after* the revolution in Imbaba, Mirinab and Maspiro. Thence the revolution factored in the formation of many Coptic organizations and unions outside and away from Church influence.

Concerning the place of Copts between the state and society, the 25 January revolution tended to support the contention that political problems were created by the previous regime and used to guarantee Church support against the potential ascendancy of Islamists. This created a societal crisis between Muslims and Christians and transformed the Church into the sole representative of Copts at the political level, which paved the way for an isolated religious group and deepened religious polarization.

The relation between Copts and the regime thus has three primary dimensions: the institution of the Church, Copts, and the regime, but specifically the nature of the political system – either before or after the revolution – was responsible for treating Copts as a single, closed and homogeneous bloc represented by the Coptic Church both politically and religiously. Factors, such as the charismatic character of Pope Shenouda III and worries over the Islamic alternative, further confused the relation despite the refusal of numerous Coptic secular activists and movements to be manipulated.

Indeed, the 25 January revolution proved the failure of the 'divide and rule' strategy adopted by the Mubarak regime. The Coptic churches were not threatened at any time throughout the eighteen days of the uprisings despite the absence of state security forces to protect them. Participation by Copts in the uprisings was testament to their sense of belonging and their ability to defy political isolation.

The diminishing role of the state in dealing with sectarian crises continued under the rule of the Supreme Council of the Armed Forces – SCAF. Instead, sectarian crises were treated informally through the mediation of clergy and figures from the political elite, while the actual or underlying causes of the tensions between Muslims and Christians were not addressed directly. Thus, the path to democracy in Egypt – in regard to the Coptic issue – suffered setbacks at all levels, politically, socially and culturally and the same demands that the Copts had made under Mubarak continued in addition to new ones related not to the preservation of the *rights* of the Coptic community, but to the preservation of its existence.

Overall, the rise of many specifically Coptic organizations *and* secular movements derived from the political separation between the Church and the Coptic community. The Church is no longer the political representative of Copts nor does it speak out on their behalf against the state.

The death of Pope Shenouda III in the transitional period through which Egypt is passing necessitates a new form of state–Church relations, especially with the new givens presented by the rise of political Islamist trends and the drafting of a new constitution, in addition to community pressures for more flexible rules on certain social issues, including second marriages.

A vision for the future

While the fieldwork and survey undertaken for this study concluded in 2008, well before the revolution, some predictions were possible on the basis of the findings about the way in which the policies of exclusion to which Egyptians have been subjected would influence state–society relations thereafter and thus societal relations with all their complications.

In keeping with Migdal's (1994) theoretical framework, in this study the Egyptian state is characterized as a weak one that fails to fulfil its tasks towards society. The state opposes the formation of social groupings or institutions that represent society interests and thence creates an atmosphere pervaded by an absence of trust between the state and society. It also endorses and cements vertical relations based on corruption and favouritism that, in turn, create a weak society and lead to political and social regression. This sort of situation defeats the idea of the common sphere between state and society and also negatively impacts Muslim–Christian relations, which provides fertile ground for the type of bureaucratic authoritarianism described by O'Donnell (1986), whereby a deadlock occurs between the state and society as the excluded masses (including Muslims and Christians) revolt against the weak state. That is what Egypt witnessed on 25 January, a revolution by society at large – not a particular sect – against the political regime that controlled the state.

But the continuation of the protest of the excluded masses, unfortunately still excluded, may not only damage the fledgling weak state that is just now emerging, but may also damage the societal structure itself, where Muslim–Christian relations may be subject to real danger as long as societal relations remain delicate.

The need for a comprehensive and inclusive Muslim–Christian dialogue that can provide creative solutions for frequent religious crises will not be met unless there is a genuinely democratic stable state based on effective institutions, influential civil organizations, active citizen participation, and political–social consistency, etc. If these requirements are not realized, narrow affiliations and social polarization will replace the state and exclusion and alienation will be exacerbated.

Inclusion requires an integrated project from all society members and formations in an objective framework to overcome all manifestations of social inequality and societal divisions that share in exclusion and social marginalization. These requirements cannot be activated except under a functioning constitution, influential civil society, and active citizenry irrespective of primordial affiliations to ensure a real awareness of a national Egyptian identity.

Conclusion

By interpolating the results of a survey of Egyptian Copts living in the greater Cairo region with the actions, involvement and participation of Copts in the 25 January revolution that led to the overthrow of Hosni Mubarak's regime, certain interesting observations can be made about the situation of Copts within society and within the dialectic between the Coptic Church and the weak state that predated the revolution. The survey suggested strongly that, while Copts could be considered a religious minority, in many ways they were not subject to some of the exclusionary practices and inequalities experienced by minorities in many other countries. Rather, Copts have historically occupied high positions within the Egyptian government and been integrated into society along vertical and horizontal axes. Significantly, the survey showed that Copts did not attribute socio-economic problems to their status as Copts. Instead, Copts reported concerns and woes that were relatively general and indistinct from those of the Muslim majority and which correlated with widespread dissatisfaction, alienation and exclusion experienced by underprivileged segments of the population suffered under the previous regime at large. Perhaps, most importantly, Copts in the study did not correlate their demands with nor blame their hardships on their religious status, but attributed these to objective factors and conditions.

In what would seem to be a confirmation of this trend, the events surrounding the 25 January revolution might well suggest that change is in the offing. The Coptic Church as an institution, historically mediated – to one degree or another – between the Egyptian state and Coptic society, and began to compensate for diminishing social services as the state proved less and less capable of fulfilling the terms of the presumed or at least implied social contract. Nevertheless, the Church also supported the Mubarak regime that was careful to maintain such support over the years by playing on fears of an Islamist threat. What was unprecedented is that Copts, by and large, took positions against the Mubarak regime in the 25 January revolution – against the official position of the Church – and they participated side by side with fellow Muslim Egyptians in addition to forming numerous groups of their own – often of a secular nature – and outside the sphere of the Church.

There is much to suggest that Copts view themselves as much a part of Egyptian society as Muslims, and the grounds for considering themselves as a 'minority' are not fixed. Coptic youths seem to have no reason to isolate or insulate themselves from larger society and believe that they ought to enjoy the full sets of rights and entitlements of citizenship on civil and not religious bases. Barring any serious Islamist threat, their difficulties, opportunities, hopes and aspirations may be little different from their fellow Muslim Egyptians with whom they seek to exist on an equal footing.

Acknowledgements

This article is drawn from a synopsis of the book published by the Centre for Arab Unity Studies of the same title – *Al-aqbāṭ wa Muṭālibuhum fī Miṣr bayn al-Taḍmīn wa al-Istiʿbād* (Beirut: Centre for Arab Unity Studies, 2012).

Note

1. Being a minority or a majority doesn't matter, it is all about power and how a group of people is using its power to treat the rest of the population, which took place recently in Egypt because of the inferior vision from some Islamists towards non Muslims.

   Eriksen's (1997, p. 25) definition of minority – as mentioned – refers to the fact that the group number is not the criterion to evaluate or describe a group as a minority. The group(s) power, weight in the decision-making process etc. count in describing a minority. In the case study, and according to the thesis structure, it is concluded that different sects were excluded for the sake of the authoritarian regime, all groups had no influence, so in this case – according to the number criterion – the groups or the elites that manipulate and monopolize power can be described as a minority. This means that the concept is a political one, and has various usages according to the context.

References

Ayubi, N., 1989. Government and the state in Egypt today. *In*: C. Trip and R. Owen, eds. *Egypt under Mubarak*. London: Routledge.

Chitham, E.J., 1986. *The Coptic community in Egypt: Spatial and social change*. University of Durham.

Dattolo, P., 2008. *Determining sample size: Balancing power, precision and practicality*. New York: Oxford University Press.

Eriksen, T.H., 1997. Ethnicity, race and nation. *In*: M. Guibernau and J. Rex, eds. *The ethnicity reader: Nationalism, multiculturalism and migration*. Cambridge: Polity Press, 161–177.

Fahmy, N.S., 2002. *The politics of Egypt: State–society relationship*. New York: Routledge/Curzon.

Hills, J., Le Grand, J., and Pichaud, D., eds., 2002. *Understanding social exclusion*. Oxford: Oxford University Press.

Kabeer, N., 2000. Social exclusion, poverty and discrimination: Towards an analytical framework. Available from: www.ids.ac.uk/ids/pvty/social-policy/spconfpaps.html [Accessed 2008].

Migdal, J.S., Ed., 1994. *State power and social forces: Domination and transformation in the Third World*. Cambridge University Press.

Moser, M.T., 2001. Revising the Constitution? The problem of religious freedom. *The Journal of Religious Ethics*, 16 (2), 324–245.

O'Donnell, G., 1986. *Bureaucratic authoritarianism: Argentina 1966–1973, in comparative perspective*. Berkeley: University of California Press.

Richards, A., 1991. The political economy of dilatory reform: Egypt in the 1980s. *World development*, 19 (12), 1726–1727.

Appendix 1: Questionnaire

This study aims at identifying the Coptic citizens' opinions regarding some issues, such as the Copts' political participation, appointment in governmental positions, the Unified Law for Places of worship, etc. Your opinion and views are valuable and will help to measure issues related to the place of Copts in Egypt objectively.

Data collected will be used for academic purposes

Thank you for your participation

First: primary personal data:

1- Age:

1– less than 20 ( )
2– 20–30 ( )
3– 30–40 ( )
4– 40–50 ( )
5– more than 50 ( )

2- Sex:

1– Male ( )
2– Female ( )

3- Profession:

1– Works ( )
2– Do not work ( )

4- Job Sector:

1– Governmental ( )
2– Public ( )
3– Private ( )
4– Free ( )

5- Neighbourhood:

6– Educational level:

1– Average education. ( )
2– Secondary education. ( )
3– Graduate. ( )
4– Postgraduate. ( )

Please answer the following questions by marking (✓) in front of the alternative that expresses your opinion:

Second: Perceiving exclusion:

- **Economic exclusion:**

1- Do you work in a post or profession in the government or the public sector?

1– Yes. (answer the following question)
2– No. (answer question 4)

2- Did you face any difficulties, to get that post?

1– Yes, I faced difficulties. (answer the following question)
2– No, I didn't find any problems.
3– There were some problems, but I got the job through my relations.

3- If you faced problems, this may be due to:

1- The high number of those who applied for the job.
2- Your weak capabilities compared to the applicants.

3- Your religious affiliation.
4- The job requires relations and nepotism to be accepted.
5- Other.

4- In the case where you haven't found work, what is the reason?

1- I didn't find a suitable job.
2- The low income levels.
3- I think I will face religious discrimination.
4- Because I have other income alternatives.

5- Do you think that your monthly income is enough to fulfil your basic needs?

1- Yes, I feel my income is enough.
2- No, my monthly income is not enough. (answer the following question)
3- My monthly income is relatively enough and I depend on other alternatives.

6- Why is your income insufficient?

1- The daily increasing demands.
2- There are those with the same capabilities, but earn a higher income because of my religious affiliation.
3- High prices.

- **Social Exclusion:**

7- Did you think to migrate and live abroad?

1- Yes. (answer the following question)
2- No.

8– Why do you want to migrate? (choose one answer)

1- To find a suitable job.
2- Because of the low income levels in Egypt.
3- To overcome deteriorating living conditions.
4- Because I have relatives abroad.
5- Because I suffer religious discrimination.

9- Did you apply for a governmental job and you were excluded because of your religious affiliation?

1- Yes, I applied and was excluded because of my religious affiliation.
2- Yes, I applied, but was not excluded because of my religious affiliation.
3- No, I did not apply.

10- Do you prefer socializing with those who share your religious affiliation?

1- Yes.
2- No.
3- I socialize with all regardless of religion.

11- In your opinion, what are the major obstacles against enjoying your social rights? (Arrange in order)

1- Corruption.
2- Deteriorating economic and living conditions.
3- Religious affiliation.

4- Citizen apathy.
5- Governmental red tape.

- **Political Exclusion:**

12- Do you have an electoral card?

1- Yes. (answer the following question)
2- No. (answer question 15)

13- Did you use your electoral card before?

1- Yes.
2- No. (answer the following question).

14- Why you didn't use your electoral card?

1- Because I feel my vote is useless.
2- I am sure the results are previously known.
3- Political apathy despite having an electoral card.

15- I don't have an electoral card because:

1- I don't have time to go through procedures to get the card.
2- I am not interested in politics.
3- I am worried to be involved in politics because of my religious affiliation.
4- I feel my vote does not count.

16- Are you a member of a political party?

1- Yes. (answer the following question)
2- No. (answer question 18)

17- I am a member of a political party because:

1- I have a political orientation and found the party that represents it.
2- I feel being a member of a political party a kind of social and political prestige.
3- Because the party is interested in the Coptic issue.

18- I am not a member of a political party because:

1- Weakness of political parties in Egypt in general.
2- I am not interested in politics.
3- I can't find the political party that expresses my interests and priorities.

19- If the law permits setting up parties on a religious basis, will you:

1- Become a party member.
2- Refuse to be a member because the party won't be effective.
3- Refuse the idea of political parties on a religious basis because this enhances sectarian divisions.

20- Did you nominate yourself before in any previous elections?

1- Yes. (answer the following question)
2- No. (answer question 22)

21- Did you face difficulties in nomination?

1- I faced procedural obstacles.
2- I didn't face obstacles.

22- Why didn't you nominate yourself before?

1- Because I am sure I won't win because of my religion.
2- Because I am not interested in politics in general.
3- Because my capabilities are low compared to others.
4- Other.

23- Do you feel your opinion is worthy in political decisions?

1- Yes.
2- No.
3- I don't express my opinion because of my religion.

24- Did you express your opinion before via official media channels?

1- Yes. (Answer the following question)
2- No. (Answer question 26)

25- What is the nature of the issues you expressed your opinion towards? (You can choose more than one answer)

1- Political issues outside Egypt.
2- Political issues inside Egypt.
3- Local economic issues.
4- General social issues.
5- Issues related to Copts.

26- Why didn't you express your opinion?

1- Because I have other priorities.
2- Because I feel my opinion is useless.
3- Because of my sensitive situation due to my religion.
4- Other.

Third: Demands Inclusion:

– Economic demands:

27- In your opinion, is there a Coptic absence from high governmental posts as ambassadors and ministers?

1- Yes, there is a full absence.
2- No, there is a partial absence in some fields.
3- Copts work in all governmental posts without discrimination.

28- How can discrimination against Copts in high governmental posts be limited?

1- Through issuing a law that determines a quota for Copts in high posts.
2- Through guaranteeing that those who apply will be chosen according to their qualifications.
3- Through a societal culture that is based on tolerance and accepting the other.

29- Do you think Copts representation in high posts will improve their place in Egypt?

1- Yes.
2- To some extent.
3- No.

- **Social demands: (Civil/ religious)**

30- What is your opinion concerning the orientations of the Coptic figures in the TV programmes shown in the State's official media?

1- Agree, they represent the opinion of the Coptic citizen.
2- Agree, despite that their opinions do not represent my opinion.
3- There is no representation for Copts in the state's media.
4- Other.

31- Do you think that the opinions of the Coptic thinkers are represented in national newspapers?

1- Yes, they represent their opinions without any limitations.
2- Yes, but there are some limitations.
3- There is no representation for the opinions of the Coptic thinkers.

32- Do you think that issuing the unified Personal Status Law for non-Muslims will help to solve marriage problems that Copts suffer?

1- Yes.
2- The law will complicate the matter.
3- No.

33- Do you think the demand of Copts' 'Second marriage' after divorce based on a court ruling is a legitimate marriage?

1- Yes, it is legitimate.
2- No, it is not legitimate.
3- I don't know.

34- Do you agree that the issue of Copts' marriage and divorce is a private religious matter the state shouldn't interfere in?

1- Yes.
2- No.
3- The state must interfere in case one of its citizens asked for its interference through the judiciary.

35- How can freedom of religious conversion be activated without influencing the state's stability?

1- Opening freedom of religious conversion without limitations
2- Putting limitations as resorting to litigation.
3- Refusing to officially recognize the new religion except after the passage of a certain period not less than 3 years.

36- Do you accept the deletion of a religion check in the national ID?

1- Yes, because efficiency will be the criterion rather than religion.
2- No, because the person's name refers to his/her religion.
3- Deleting or leaving the check does not guarantee equality.
4- Other.

37- Do you think amending educational curricula in schools is a step towards maintaining a healthy religious atmosphere?

1- Yes, I think this may help to spread the culture of tolerance.
2- No, I don't think it will make a difference.

38- Do you see a necessity in amending history curricula to include the 'Coptic age'?

1- Yes, the Coptic age must be included.
2- No, I don't find a necessity for that.
3- The Coptic age is mentioned in the history curricula, but not in detail as other historical ages.
4- Other.

39- Did you think before to apply in any of Al-Azhar faculties?

1- Yes, I did, but my religious affiliation was an obstacle.
2- No, because Al-Azhar is closed to non-Muslims.
3- I didn't think before because Al-Azhar faculties are available in other Egyptian universities.

– **Political demands:**

40- Do you think a quota for Copts in the parliament will guarantee their representation?

1- Yes, I think this will give power to Copts in the parliament according to their actual number in society.
2- Yes, I think the quota is important, but this won't change anything.
3- No, I don't believe in the quota idea.

41- Do you accept establishing a Coptic political party?

1- Yes, I accept because it will help Copts to fight their political isolation.
2- No, because this enhances religious divisions.
3- No, because this won't activate Copts' political participation.

42- Does the 2nd article in the constitution that says that Islamic legislation is the main source of legislation turn Egypt into a theocratic state?

1- Yes, because it transforms non-Muslims to second class citizens.
2- No, because the constitution is not applied or activated.
3- Other.

43- In your opinion, how can the state deal with article 2 in the constitution?

1- Delete.
2- Amend.
3- Leave it because it guarantees security and citizenship of Copts in Egypt.

44- Does the first article in the constitution that provides citizenship make a balance with article 2?

1- Yes, it makes a balance.
2- No, It doesn't.
3- No need for texts as long as they are not activated.

– **Institutional demands:**

45- Do you know what are the main themes and bases of the Unified Law for Places of Worship?

1- Yes, I know the text of the law.
2- No, I don't know the text.

46- Do you see the current situation of building churches is better than issuing one Unified Law for Places of Worship?

1- Yes, because building churches is related to the relation between the church and the state regardless of laws.
2- No, because the main reason behind sectarian confrontation is the absence of this law.
3- It's not a matter of laws, more important is activating the law and applying it.

47- Below is a group of demands that Copts see as important. Categorize such demands as very important, important, relatively important, not important.

	Very Important	Important	Relatively important	Not important
1- Appointment in high governmental posts.				
2- Equality in media opportunities.				
3- Issuing the unified Personal Status Law for non-Muslims.				
4- Freedom of religious conversion.				
5- Amending the 2nd article in the constitution.				
6- Issuing the Unified Law for Places of Worship.				
7- educational demands as amending history curricula in schools.				
8- Deleting the religion check in the national ID.				
9- Activating political participation.				

'Suleiman: Mubarak decided to step down #egypt #jan25 OH MY GOD': examining the use of social media in the 2011 Egyptian revolution

Genevieve Barrons

Department of Political Science, University of British Columbia, Vancouver, BC, Canada

For the last decade, a debate has raged over the place of social media within popular uprisings. The 2011 Egyptian revolution shed new light on this debate. However, while the use of social media by Egyptians received much focus, and activists themselves pointed towards it as the key to their success, social media did not constitute the revolution itself, nor did it instigate it. Focusing solely on social media diminishes the personal risks that Egyptians took when heading into the streets to face rubber bullets and tear gas, as well as more lethal weapons. Social media was neither the cause nor the catalyst of the revolution; rather it was a tool of coordination and communication.

Preface

In the vlog she posted on YouTube on 18 January 2011, 26-year-old Asmaa Mahfouz asked viewers to join her in the streets on 25 January (a date that was to become symbolic) to protest government corruption rather than 'sitting at home and following [her] on the news [and] Facebook' or self-immolating, as four Egyptians had already done (QueenofRomance83 2011, Iyadelbaghdadi 2011). Her video, which quickly went viral, exemplifies the role of social media in the 2011 Egyptian protests. She used these tools to encourage her fellow Egyptians to leave their computers at home and join her in the streets. The posting of the video itself did not constitute the main act of rebellion, but it did help to coordinate and instigate those acts.

Around the same time, after seeing the success of the Tunisian protests in bringing down that government, Wael Ghoneim, a 31-year-old Egyptian Google executive and the anonymous administrator of the Facebook group 'We Are All Khaled Said', set up an event for 25 January – a holiday that traditionally celebrates a police revolt against the British, and which had been the date of minor protests by the 'April 6 Youth Movement' for the previous two years. He told followers of his Facebook group that a protest would be held if 50,000 people agreed to attend (Kirkpatrick and Sanger 2011). Within three days, more than 100,000 people had signed up. Ghoneim, however, was still sceptical as to whether the protest would actually take place, as clicking 'attend' on a Facebook event and protesting on the streets require two radically different levels of commitment. Ultimately, it is estimated that on 25 January tens of thousands of people gathered in Cairo, with thousands of others protesting across Egypt (Kirkpatrick and Sanger 2011).

For the last decade a debate has raged over the place of social media within popular uprisings. By social media I mean 'a group of Internet-based applications that build on the ideological and technological foundations of Web 2.0, and that allow the creation and exchange of User Generated Content'.[1] Key examples include Facebook, Twitter and YouTube. Some scholars and journalists, including Frank Rich and Malcolm Gladwell, suggest that the emphasis on social media within popular uprisings has been misplaced – the product of a lack of understanding of the intricacies of the situation and a bias towards Western-created media. Others, including Larry Diamond and Clary Shirky, claim that while social media does not cause these uprisings, it can be a key catalyst and tool of coordination. They are, however, careful to say that uprisings tend to come at the end of a long process of incremental change.

The 2011 Egyptian revolution shed new light on this debate. Numerous articles were written on the role of social media in the uprising. As one activist tweeted, 'We use Facebook to schedule the protests, Twitter to coordinate, and YouTube to tell the world' (Howard 2011). However, while these mediums certainly were used as the activist suggested, they did not constitute the revolution itself, nor did they instigate it. Focusing solely on social media diminishes the personal risks that Egyptians took when heading into the streets to face rubber bullets and tear gas, as well as more lethal weapons. Social media was neither the cause nor the catalyst of the revolution; rather, it was a tool of coordination and communication.

This article will survey the two sides of the debate surrounding social media. It will then examine the particulars of social media within Egypt, and how that media was utilized during the 2011 uprising. Finally, it will explore some of the implications of the use of social media on the revolution.

The debate: the role of social media in popular uprisings

Popular uprisings as far back as 2001 and the fall of Filipino President Joseph Estrada – when citizens used text messaging to amass a crowd of over 1 million people in downtown Manila – have been labelled 'social media revolutions' (Shirky 2011, p. 2). Other popular examples include the 2006 Belorussian Denim Revolution, the 2007 Burmese Saffron Revolution, and the 2009 Moldovan Grape/Twitter Revolution (Shirky 2011, p. 2, Diamond 2010, p. 81). However, the term began to gain real currency in the aftermath of the June 2009 election in Iran. According to proponents of the power of social media, supporters of opposition presidential candidate Mir Hosein Musavi used Twitter, YouTube and Facebook to mobilize tens of thousands of Iranians to participate in a series of rallies that took place in Tehran, in what would eventually come to be known as the Green Revolution (Diamond 2010, p. 80). However, despite the massive outpouring of support for the protestors – both domestically and internationally – the Islamic Republic managed to remain in power through force. In the aftermath of the uprising, the very tools that activists had used to spread their messages were used to track down and detain them (Diamond 2010, p. 81). This apparent failure of social media – after so many early claims of success – focused attention on the forces behind these uprisings. Two very clear camps of academics and journalists emerged: the first opposed to the idea that social media was a force for democracy and liberation; the second continuing, albeit rather more cautiously, to claim that social media could be a tool in the coordination and execution of these uprisings.

The most outspoken opponent of the idea of social media revolutions is author and journalist Malcolm Gladwell. He points to the fact that revolutions occurred long before social media, as proof that these new technologies are not a necessary part of the equation (Gladwell 2010). He suggests that our reading of these revolutions is historically anachronistic, quoting historian Robert Darnton who suggests, 'the marvels of communication technology in the present have produced a false consciousness about the past – even a sense that communication had no history, or had nothing of importance to consider before the days of TV and Internet' (quoted in Gladwell 2010). Gladwell points to research which suggests that in many of these countries (e.g., Moldova; Morozov 2011), access to these technologies is actually fairly limited, and that social media receives undue attention due to lazy journalism or an inability to reach people on the ground (Gladwell 2010).[2] For example, in Iran, despite serious calls to nominate Twitter for a Nobel Peace Prize based on the role it played in the 2009 uprising, researchers have found that the vast majority of tweets hashtagged #iranelection were in English and coming from outside of the country (Gladwell 2010). Gladwell suggests that social media is unsuited to coordinating or executing social uprisings, for two main reasons. He claims the social media creates 'weak ties', and according to sociologist Doug McAdam, high-risk activism requires strong ties (Gladwell 2010). That is, people are not willing to risk their lives for the casual acquaintances they formed on the Internet. Social media can increase participation, but it does this by making participation easier (Gladwell 2010). For example, people are much more likely to sign a petition if they can do it from their computer, rather than having to mail a postcard or speak with a canvasser. Yet, even though they signed the petition, they are no more likely to join a protest around the issue. Gladwell claims: 'Facebook activism succeeds not by motivating people to make a real sacrifice but by motivating them to do the things that people do when they are not motivated enough to make a real sacrifice' (Gladwell 2010).

Additionally, Gladwell suggests that social media creates networks rather than hierarchies. Unlike hierarchical organizations, a single authority cannot control social media. Decisions are made by consensus and members of groups are loosely bound together (Gladwell 2010). This structure makes networks adaptable and resilient in low-risk situations. Social uprisings, however, are not low risk. According to Gladwell, they require clear goals and lines of authority. Peaceful protests in particular require a high level of discipline, as the actions of a single protestor can send the demonstrations wildly out of control and compromise the moral legitimacy of the entire movement (Gladwell 2010). Therefore, Gladwell argues, social media is unsuited to the high risks and demands of popular uprisings and revolutions.

On the other hand, proponents of social media claim that Gladwell and others fail to understand the role these forms of media can play, becoming instruments of coordination for groups that might not be able to do so otherwise. However, since the failure of the Iranian Green Revolution, almost no one suggests that social media is an unadulterated vehicle of democracy and liberation. Instead, as Diamond suggests, these technologies are merely tools 'open to both noble and nefarious purposes' (Diamond 2010, p. 71). Access to the Internet does not automatically lead to openness and democracy. As Belorussian academic Evgeny Morozov points out, social media can – and has been – used to track and arrest dissidents, already conveniently networked together. It can also be used by pro-government supporters to spread misinformation in an effort to confuse protestors (Morozov 2011). Repressive states and activists are involved in a constant race to outwit each other technologically.

Supporters of the theory of social media revolutions are careful to note that activism is not in any way the main purpose of social media. Indeed, it is this multipurposefulness that can make it such an effective tool against totalitarianism. Ethan Zuckerman, a senior researcher for Harvard's Berkman Center for Internet and Democracy, calls this the 'cute cat theory of digital activism' (Shirky 2011, p. 8). Tools designed specifically for political dissent can be shut down with very little political penalty, but tools designed with a broader purpose (e.g., sharing pictures of cute cats on the Internet), draw much wider public outcry when they are taken away (Shirky 2011, p. 8). This can lead to increased scrutiny of whatever it is that the government was trying to hide, a phenomena popularly called the Streisand effect (Shirky 2011, p. 10).[3] Additionally, social media and the Internet are increasingly tied to the economy, and shutting down the former can severely affect the latter (Shirky 2011, p. 11). Most countries simply cannot afford to go without the Internet for more than a week or two before the economic costs become too high. Using social media as a tool of coordination can in some ways insulate activists from government censorship.

While Gladwell may see weak ties as a drawback, Diamond and Shirky suggest that this lose formation can actually make coordination easier, especially in strict authoritarian countries, where meeting in person could be dangerous. It can reduce the cost of coordination, which may ultimately compensate for the disadvantages of undisciplined groups (Shirky 2011, p. 7), and allows for the dissemination of information and literature (Shirky 2011, p. 5). Through such coordination and dissemination, social media can produce a sense of shared awareness, eventually creating an 'imagined community' (Shirky 2011, p. 5). Social media can be used to form a sort of alternate media, as activists share images, videos, and stories of government abuses and corruption. In turn, as in the 2007 Saffron Revolution in Burma, this information can be shared with the world, creating awareness of what the government is doing, and ultimately putting pressure on it to stop.

While signing a petition online does not automatically equal the kind of commitment necessary to protest in the streets, it can lead to it. Shirky (2011) points out that the process of changing minds and forming opinions is twofold, involving both media and personal relationships. If you only read something online, you are unlikely to act on it. But if you read it online, discuss it with your family and your friends, this could lead to a considerably different outcome. Social media can empower small pockets of dissidents by connecting them with like-minded people and assuring them that they are not alone in their opinions. Thus, if you find out about a protest for a cause you already believe in, and can share it with friends over social media, this could create exactly the sort of strong ties necessary to take part in high-risk activism. Proponents of this theory are careful to note that this is not an instantaneous process. Indeed, they suggest that access to the Internet and social media can only facilitate a slow and incremental process of change.

In the aftermath of the 2011 revolution in Egypt, which successfully ended the 30-year presidency of Hosni Mubarak, the debate between these two camps has once again become front-page news. The string of uprisings throughout the Middle East and the relative speed at which the regimes of Mubarak and Tunisia's Zine El Abdine Ben ʿAli fell seem to go beyond even the best outcomes that Shirky or Diamond predicted. However, as with the Iranian uprising, there has been a tendency to overstate the role of social media – as if the use of social media itself constituted the revolution. This is not the case. The Egyptian Revolution was not a Twitter or Facebook or YouTube revolution. Rather, it was a revolution that used Twitter, Facebook, and YouTube to coordinate and communicate. Examining the specific use of this media will provide a better understanding of the exact role these tools played and ultimately how they affected the outcome of the uprising.

The situation in Egypt: social media prior to the January 2011 uprising

Prior to the protests and ensuing blackout, the Internet in Egypt was relatively uncensored (Cohen 2011). There was very little that could not be accessed, including Al Jazeera, the websites of opposition groups and social media. However, compared with the citizens of other nations in the Middle East, relatively few Egyptians had access to the Internet. Estimates ranged from about 20–30% of the population (i.e., 15–25 million people) (International Telecommunication Union 2011). Access was concentrated mostly in urban areas, and among the educated youth (Kirkpatrick and Sanger 2011). Due to the poor economic conditions in Egypt, many of these young people, despite holding university degrees, were unemployed (Friedman 2011). While the 2011 protests encompassed people from all walks of life – including labourers and peasants – social media remained primarily the province of the educated youth; the employed as well as the so-called 'educated unemployables'. It is worth noting that more than half of Egypt's total population is under 30 years of age (UNICEF 2011).

In the weeks leading up to the Egyptian revolution, Egyptians were closely following developments in Tunisia. The popular uprising in that country, which ended on 17 January with the resignation of Ben 'Ali, was an obvious and much commented on catalyst for the Egyptian revolution. Throughout the first half of January, a number of Egyptians, following the example of Tunisian Mohamed Bouazizi, set themselves on fire as a form of protest against the government. Behind the scenes and facilitated by social media, Tunisian and Egyptian activists maintained a line of communication, sharing best practices and ideas (Kirkpatrick and Sanger 2011).

Immediately prior to and during the first protests there was a massive surge (e.g., an increase of 68%) in Internet use (Roberts 2011). It can only be assumed that, in the wake of the first protests on 25 January, Egyptians were trying to figure out what was going on in their country. Tellingly, while traffic to Al Jazeera and Google also increased, the biggest surge was in the use of Facebook (Roberts 2011). This was perhaps because the international news media, including Al Jazeera, was not yet thoroughly covering the protests – and the domestic media was purposefully not covering it. Instead, Egyptians turned to friends and family to figure out what was happening.

This massive surge in Internet use came to a sudden and abrupt end on Friday, 28 January when, in the space of about twenty minutes, the government imposed a countrywide Internet blackout (Cohen 2011) (Figure 1). Up until that point there had been intermittent blackouts of Twitter and some mobile networks, but this was a total blackout (Raoof 2011). Only one provider, Noor – which hosts the Egyptian stock exchange and the National Bank of Egypt, among other high-profile clients (Elkin 2011) – stayed online for a few more hours. By Monday, 31 January its service was also shutdown. Thus, as many critics of social media revolutions have noted, throughout some of the biggest protests, Egyptians literally did not have access to any of these tools. Some attempts were made to get around the blackout, but for the most part – despite the widespread attention they received – they were fairly minor and mostly attempted by foreign journalists with satellite phones.

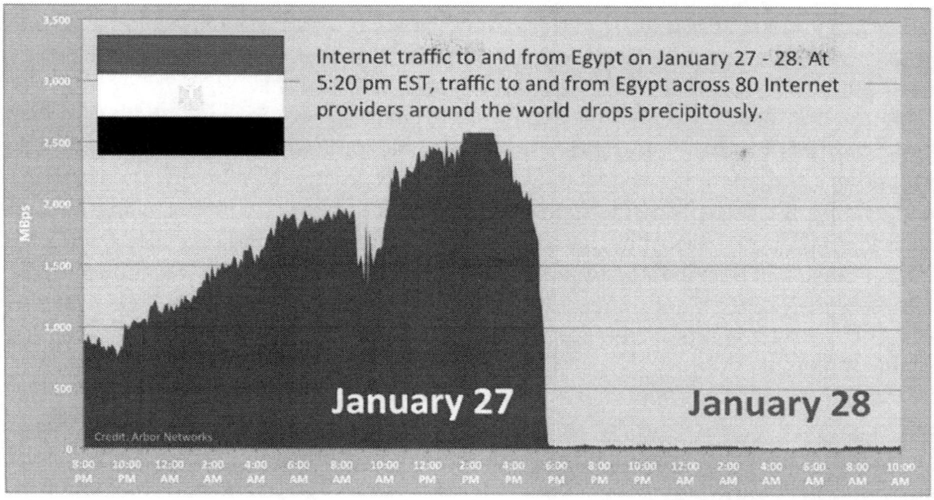

Figure 1. Internet traffic to and from Egypt, 27–28 January. The sudden drop off is due to the government's enforced blackout.

Still one should not discount social media. The protests were not spontaneous or accidental. Months of planning and waiting had gone into them.

Survey of the social media used in the 2011 uprising

Al Jazeera

Although Al Jazeera is not itself a form of social media, it used social media extensively throughout the revolution both to find and to share information. During the protests, 'Al Jazeera' became the most searched term on the Internet after 'Egypt' (The Peninsula 2011). In a 24-hour period, on Saturday, 28 January, the live stream was viewed for a total of 26 million minutes (The Peninsula 2011). It became the most tweeted link on the Internet (Hoffman 2011). The website experienced a 2500% increase in traffic, and 4 million views from 28 to 31 January (Hoffman 2011). Of these views, 1.6 million were from the United States, where Al Jazeera English is available on cable in only three cities. Interestingly, 70% of the total traffic came from social media networks, e.g., links that had been posted on Twitter or Facebook (Borthwick 2011).

It is worth noting that Al Jazeera was actively cultivating this following on Twitter. They created a promoted Twitter trend,[4] which helped to increase the already high awareness of the network (Ellis 2011). Thus, Al Jazeera's interest in the uprising was both journalistic and commercial, as they used the protests as an opportunity to put increased pressure on American cable networks to include their channel.

Observers suggest that Al Jazeera's impressive coverage was a result of both old and new technologies. They already had traditional media on the ground, which allowed them to connect better with key players and relay the intricacies of the situation (Ellis 2011). However, they also actively solicited help from Egyptians, tapping into a network of citizen journalists and bloggers that they had connected with prior to the start of the protests (Ellis 2011). During the protests, when the whole Internet was blocked, Egyptians turned to Al Jazeera for coverage of what was happening across the country. Of all the networks involved, it was Al Jazeera that was projected onto screens during the blackout in Tahrir Square and beyond (Ellis 2011).

In turn, they used a variety of social media to share these stories with both Egyptians and the world (Ellis 2011). In Egypt, during the blackout, Al Jazeera printed pamphlets with updates and alternative ways to access its news coverage. When its own reporters could not use the Internet to file reports, they began to phone in stories using Scribble Live and Audioboo – websites that allow users to post audio and text files from smart phones (Ellis 2011). At their headquarters in Qatar, staff used Storify to curate and keep track of citizen reports and other content. Much of their coverage was then released through Creative Commons, creating the opportunity for it to be shared as widely as possible (Ellis 2011).

Without this reliance on social media, it seems unlikely that Al Jazeera would have been able to reach nearly as many viewers – especially in the United States. This massive viewing audience was important in keeping the focus on what was happening in the Middle East and forcing various governments, including the Barack Obama administration, to take a stand on the issues. The coverage provided by Al Jazeera, in both English and Arabic, created a sense of shared awareness that stretched across cultures and continents. As they blatantly favoured the cause of the protestors, the stories they shared helped to combat the official narrative being espoused by the Mubarak regime. Al Jazeera, although not controlled by the protestors, became a key tool of communication between them, their fellow Egyptians and the world.

Facebook

Facebook is a social networking service that allows users to create a personal profile, add other users as friends and join common interest groups. As of January 2011, there were about 600 million active Facebook users worldwide. Approximately 5.5 million of these Facebook users are Egyptian (Social Bakers 2011). During the massive surge in Internet use on 26 January, 39% of that traffic was to Facebook, while only 27% was to news sites (Roberts 2011). Facebook was seven times more popular than either Google or Al Jazeera (Roberts 2011). In the two weeks prior to 25 January, 32,000 new Facebook groups and 14,000 new pages were created by Egyptian users (Sullivan 2011).

Two Facebook groups in particular have drawn attention for their role in the uprising: the 'April 6 Youth Movement' and 'We Are All Khaled Said' (Kirkpatrick and Sanger 2011). Both groups were formed in part from the remnants of the Egyptian Movement for Change (EMC), also known as Kefaya (Enough), which had been all but destroyed by a series of arrests in 2005 (Kirkpatrick and Sanger 2011). The April 6 Youth Movement was created in June 2008 to support workers in the town of El-Mahalla El-Kubra who were planning a strike. By January 2010, the group had over 100,000 members (Facebook 2011a). The group specifically describes itself as a collection of previously apolitical youth whose only goal is to have political freedom in Egypt (Facebook 2011b). They were careful to note that they were not aligned with any of the opposition groups in Egypt.

The other group, We Are All Khaled Said, attracted more coverage after its creator was revealed to be Wael Ghoneim, the Google executive who went missing for the duration of the protests. The group is named after a young Egyptian man who was killed in

Alexandria on 6 June 2010, after being arrested by Egyptian police – allegedly for having taken video footage of police corruption, which he planned to share on the Internet. Pictures of his badly beaten body were released onto the Internet and quickly went viral. Outrage over his death spurred Ghoneim to create the group, and by January 2011 the group had almost 1 million members.

On the discussion boards of both of these groups, weeks before the protests actually took place, plans were being laid. Users debated exactly what hashtag should be used on Twitter (they eventually settled on #egypt and #jan25). They discussed the intricacies of the Tunisian uprising, and collaborated with their fellow activists across the Middle East. In the wake of the Tunisian revolution, Tunisians advised Egyptians to 'put vinegar or onion under your scarf for tear gas' (Kirkpatrick and Sanger 2011). It appears that activists in these two countries had been in contact via social media for almost two years. They had 'brainstormed on the use of technology to evade surveillance, commiserated about torture and traded practical tips on how to stand up to rubber bullets and organize barricades' (Kirkpatrick and Sanger 2011). Additionally, they had both reached out to a Serbian Youth movement called Otopor, which had helped to topple Serbian dictator Slobodan Milosevic (Kirkpatrick and Sanger 2011). It seems unlikely that any of these relationships could have been established without the use of social media.

Western journalists also used Facebook extensively to share their reporting. Nicholas Kristof, a reporter for *The New York Times*, updated his status multiple times per day in order to tell readers what was happening on the ground.[5] His coverage was immediate and intense, different from the static nature of most news reports. Meg Garber at the Nieman Journalism Lab suggests that this style of reporting repositions the journalist and the reader, creating a much more intense reading experience. Every update was a reassurance that Kristof was okay:

> Kristof's Facebook reports … – like his Twitter feed fleshed out – 'treat the present moment' not only as their subject, but as their point: This is what I'm seeing now. No varnish – and very little artistry. And that makes them particularly compelling.
>
> (Garber 2011)

During the weeks of the protests, news of Egypt flooded many social media sites including Facebook. As a result, it became somewhat impossible for users to ignore what was happening. However, too much focus has been put on Facebook in some news coverage. As it is a Western form of media, its use by Egyptian protestors allowed some in the West to feel a sense of control over what was going on. Some reports focused almost exclusively on the role of Facebook, giving credit to it as the cause of the revolution. Ultimately, Facebook became a symbol of the revolution and a tool of collaboration, rather than a cause or even catalyst. It allowed protestors to form strategic relationships, both within Egypt and across the world. These Facebook groups, prior to the protests, became virtual headquarters, from which discussions could take place and plans could be formed. Facebook also allowed news of the protests to permeate the public consciousness in a way that traditional news media could not. Regardless of whether you were following the events in Egypt, undoubtedly some of your friends were doing so and their posts on the subject were likely to show up in your feed as well. This constant news coverage increased interest in the events and put pressure on Western governments to respond.

YouTube

YouTube is a video-sharing site that allows users to upload and view videos. Registration is not required to watch these videos. While the protests in Egypt did not take over YouTube in the same way they did Twitter or Facebook, a search for related content yields literally thousands of videos. Many of these videos were clearly taken on cell phone cameras by protestors. Some of them were featured on news sites like Al Jazeera and the Associated Press, both of which actively solicited related video footage from protestors (Matherne 2011).

There were several notable videos posted on YouTube. The most watched video related to the protests was posted on 27 January by an Egyptian named Tamer Shaaban. It was a video montage of the first two days of the protests. Shaaban is a member of the We Are All Khaled Said Facebook group. The video was viewed more than 2 million times. It used footage from a variety of Western and local news sources and was clearly aimed at an English-speaking audience. It can be assumed that Shaaban was trying – apparently rather successfully – to inform a Western-viewing audience of what was happening in Egypt and gain their sympathy. Prior to the protests, YouTube was instrumental in sharing footage of Khaled Said. There were numerous video montages that showed him before and after his torture and subsequent death. Undoubtedly, these videos helped increase outrage at the actions of the police and the regime. Another influential video was that posted by Asmaa Mahfouz. The original was watched over 100,000 times (QueenofRomance83 2011), and was reposted to YouTube multiple times with subtitles in a variety of languages (e.g. Iyadelbaghdadi 2011). This video, as mentioned in the introduction, helped to spark the initial protests on 25 January.

During the protests, *Wired Magazine*, a publication that focuses on the effect of technology on culture, the economy and politics, carried a story about a group of activists and filmmakers who camped out in Tahrir Square during the protests, collecting video from their fellow protestors. In total, they collected over 100 gigabytes of pictures and footage, which were released onto the Internet after the blackout was lifted (Elkin 2011). The footage corroborated the accusations that protestors made as to police brutality and their claims about the size of the protests. This collection and dissemination of media helped to counter any official narrative that the Mubarak regime was trying to spread. It showed those not present in Cairo what was happening in Tahrir Square.

All the videos posted on YouTube became a digital record of the events of the revolution. They allowed the protestors to share their side of the story, which quickly became the dominant narrative. YouTube, and all user-generated videos, were undoubtedly important tools of communication between the protestors and those watching what was going on from home, in Egypt, the Middle East and abroad.

Twitter

Twitter is a micro-blogging service that allows users to 'tweet' messages of 140 characters or fewer. Tweets are publically accessible. Users can subscribe to and be followed by others. Twitter allows for the broad sharing of messages through a process called re-tweeting, whereby one user reposts the message of another user. Particularly interesting tweets can be re-tweeted literally hundreds of times. Tweeters can also indicate the broad topic of their message by including a hashtag (e.g., #egypt or #jan25). These hashtags allow for quick searches and easy identification.

The sheer number of tweets with the hashtag #egypt increased substantially from the week of 16–23 January (122,319 tweets) to that of 24–30 January (1.3 million tweets). However, it is worth noting that only 0.24% of these Twitter users listed their location as Egypt. While the real number might be slightly higher, as some Twitter users may keep their location secret in order to protect their identities, the vast majority of tweets about Egypt were coming from outside of the country (O'Dell 2011). On 25 January – when Twitter was at least partially available in Egypt – approximately two-thirds of all tweets were in English (Nieman Journalism Lab 2011). Almost 70% of all tweets were re-tweets, suggesting that information was being shared and re-shared, rather than created or discussed. The most re-tweeted and also one of the most prolific tweeters was not a protestor but an Egyptian journalist in New York, Mona Eltahawy.

Interestingly, during the first few days of the protests, when even Al Jazeera was criticized by Egyptians for its limited coverage and state media was providing no coverage whatsoever, Egypt had already garnered substantial interest in the Twitter sphere. According to Harvard's Nieman Journalism Lab, by 25 January at 3 p.m. EST, two of the ten most popular links on Twitter were about Egypt. Tellingly, however, one of them was a link to an article noting that Twitter had been blocked in Egypt. The service would remain relatively inaccessible from within the country for the rest of the protests.

Some attempts were made to allow Egyptians access to Twitter, despite the government-enforced blackout. Journalists such as Eltahawy posted their email addresses and promised to tweet any updates that were sent to them (Eltahawy 2011). On 1 February, the third day of the blackout, Google and Twitter launched a voice-to-text service that allowed Egyptians to phone in their tweets from landlines and cell phones (Arthur 2011). However, these services never constituted a major portion of the Twitter sphere.

Twitter, despite the blackout, continued to be abuzz with Egypt. Some analysts suggested that the site was being used to share information; however, most of the tweets appear to have been in reaction. For example, the greatest number of tweets hashtagged #egypt happened on 11 February, immediately following the resignation of Hosni Mubarak. In the hour or so following the announcement by his prime minister, the number of tweets hashtagged #egypt reached fully 4% of the total number of tweets on Twitter.

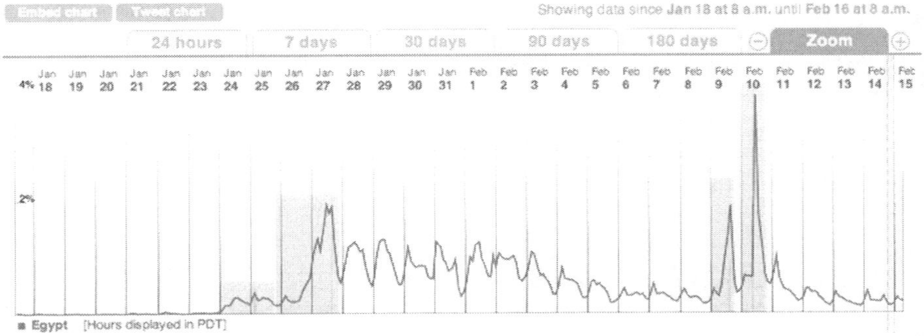

Figure 2. Presence of hashtag #egypt from 18 January to 15 February. The *x*-axis is time (PST); the *y*-axis is the percentage of total tweets.

Thus, Twitter is more of a measure of international interest in the protests than a tool of coordination. It was used by reporters, news services and a few protestors to share stories, but it did not in any substantial way appear to coordinate the protests. The majority of tweeters, and the most prolific tweeters, were looking in from outside the country. It brought early attention to the protests, but for the remainder of the revolution remained mostly reactive.

Evaluating the outcome, rethinking the debate

The blackout, which lasted from Friday, 28 January until the middle of the week after (service returned at different times for different providers), essentially eliminated the possibility of using social media within Egypt during the initial days of the protest. Opponents of social media, like *New York Times* columnist Frank Rich, have suggested that this proves the irrelevance of social media. If the protests relied on social media, he argues, surely they would not have been able to sustain themselves for that duration (Rich 2011). Certainly they would not have continued to grow and multiply throughout the last few days of January as they did. Alternately, others have suggested that there was a link between the blackout and the increasing size of the protests. Writing in *The New York Times*, Noam Cohen suggested that it reminded many young Egyptians, who might not otherwise have been politically motivated or interested in the protests, of the limits on their freedom (Cohen 2011). He argued that the sudden inaccessibility of Facebook and Twitter pushed them out into the streets; increasing the size of the protests and escalating the situation.

Both views misunderstand the role of social media. They frame social media as a cause of the revolution. As Noam Chomsky pointed out in a BBC television *Newsnight* interview, the roots of the revolution long predated the actual protests and even the early planning by activists through social media (BBC *Newsnight* 2011). Social media was a tool of coordination. By the start of the blackout, the protests were already well on their way. They no longer needed social media to continue because, as one activist noted, Egyptians could simply look out their window to know what was happening. Instead, social media had two main effects: first, it served initially as an online headquarters from which activists could coordinate and plan; and second, it allowed the protestors to control the narrative and kept the events in Egypt in the news and public consciousness.

Social media shaped the revolution in some very specific ways. Rich (2011) suggests that the events in Tunisia would have precipitated protests in Egypt, with or without social media, but it certainly accelerated the speed of those events. It gave the protestors a certain degree of control over the narrative, allowing them to combat whatever the Mubarak regime was saying. The constant flow of reports from journalists created a sense of urgency and immediacy that kept the protests in the public eye, and began to put pressure on Western governments. This pressure is clearly seen in the changing position of the Obama administration.

One of the most remarkable effects of social media was to facilitate what appears to have been a truly leaderless revolution. The traditional opposition parties and figures, including the Muslim Brotherhood and Mohamed ElBaradei, did not become involved in the protests until they were already well under way. No single figure emerged as the authority of the revolution. There has been some push for Wael Ghoneim to assume such a role, but this was largely towards the end of the protests, after his identity – up until that point unknown – was revealed. There has been some sense that the protestors intentionally remained non-hierarchical in order to protect themselves from the police. By focusing exclusively on two clear demands, they gave the Mubarak regime very little room to negotiate and removed their ability to detain central figures. However, while a protest may be able to survive without a leader, a government cannot. How the non-hierarchical nature of social media affects the creation of a new government has yet to be seen.

Chomsky argued that the regime has not changed, even though Mubarak has gone (BBC *Newsnight* 2011). There was certainly continuing discontent among the April 6 Youth Movement that called for more protests via Facebook. Whether the Egyptian government and society will undergo the substantive changes the protestors' desired has yet to be seen. If the old regime manages somehow to survive, those protestors who used social media may still have to worry about the double-edged nature of the technology. Thus far there have been no reports of social media being used to track down and detain activists, but the online record – literally thousands of posts on Facebook and tweets on Twitter – do create that possibility.

Ultimately, the full extent of the revolution will not become clear for many months and possibly years. The situation in Egypt has not stabilized enough to determine whether the protests resulted in real, sustainable change. As events continue to unfold, our perception of the role of social media will undoubtedly shift. However, at this point it is clear that social media played a major role in the coordination and communication of protests. It did not cause the revolution, but it did help to create the conditions that allowed for the success of the protests. Social media, however, continues to be an open rather than a deterministic tool. It does not ensure democracy or liberty. Regardless, the revolution in Egypt will – as it has already done in Libya, Yemen and Bahrain – continue to inspire activists across the world and encourage the use of social media by opposition groups. Whether this changes the way that governments seek to regulate and control social media has yet to be seen.

Acknowledgements

This paper would not have been possible without the advice and support of Professor Hani Faris.

Notes

1. I adopt the definition used by Kaplan and Haenlein (2009), p. 61.
2. Short messages on microblogging services such as Twitter are often tagged with a series of words written without any spaces and preceded by a hash symbol (#) in order to indicate a subject and allow other users to search more easily for news or discussion on a particular topic (e.g., #iranelection).
3. The Streisand effect is named after American singer Barbra Streisand whose attempts to suppress photographs of her home in 2003 led to widespread publicity of those same photographs.
4. Promoted twitter trends are paid advertisements. Trending topics are listed on the right-hand side of the Twitter website and on the sign-in page. The majority of twitter trends reflect the most popular hashtags and words used in tweets at a certain time and place. However, advertisers can also purchase 'Promoted Twitter Trends', which ultimately encourage users to tweet about that topic. When users click on the promoted trend they will see a search of what other users are saying about the topic at that time.
5. Facebook allows readers to post short messages for all their Facebook Friends to read. These messages are called status updates.

References

Arthur, C., 2011. Google and Twitter launch service enabling Egyptians to tweet by phone. *The Guardian*, 1 February. Available from: http://www.guardian.co.uk/technology/2011/feb/01/google-twitter-egypt/ [Accessed 5 April 2011].

BBC Newsnight, 2011. Noam Chomsky and Jeremy Paxman's interview in full. BBC. *Newsnight*, 8 March. Available from: http://news.bbc.co.uk/2/hi/programmes/*Newsnight*/9418922.stm/ [Accessed 5 April 2011].

Borthwick, J., 2011. *#Jan25: Sorry for the inconvenience, but we're building Egypt*, Borthwick, 12 February. Available from: http://www.Borthwick.com/weblog/2011/02/12/jan25-sorry-for-the-inconvenience-but-were-building-egypt/ [Accessed 5 April 2011].

Cohen, N., 2011. Egyptians were unplugged, and uncowed. *New York Times*, 20 February. Available from: http://www.nytimes.com/2011/02/21/business/media/21link.html/ [Accessed 5 April 2011].

Diamond, L., 2010. Liberation technology. *Journal of Democracy*, 21 (3), 69–83.

Diebert, R. and Rohozinski, F., 2010. Liberation vs. control: the future of cyberspace. *Journal of Democracy*, 21 (4), 43–57.

Elkin, M., 2011. Cairo geeks survive Tahrir Square assault. *Wired Magazine*, 2 February. Available from: http://www.wired.com/dangerroom/2011/02/cairos-band-of-geeks-survives-tahrir-square-assault/ [Accessed 5 April 2011].

Ellis, J., 2011. *#DemandAlJazeera: how Al Jazeera is using social media to cover Egypt – and distribute its content in the US*, Nieman Journalism Lab, 4 February. Available from: http://www.niemanlab.org/2011/02/demandaljazeera-how-al-jazeera-is-using-social-media-and-hopes-to-use-twitter-to-get-on-us-tv/ [Accessed 5 April 2011].

Eltahawy, M., 2011. Twitter. Available from: http://twitter.com/#!/monaeltahawy/ [Accessed 5 April 2011].

Facebook, 2011a. *شباب ابريل 6' [April 6 Youth Movement]*. Facebook. Available from: http://www.facebook.com/group.php?gid=9973986703/ [Accessed 14 September 2011].

Facebook, 2011b. *Info*. Facebook. Available from: http://www.facebook.com/group.php?gid=9973986703&v=info/ [Accessed 14 September 2011].

Friedman, T.L., 2011. China, Twitter and 20-year-olds vs. the pyramids. *New York Times*, 5 February. Available from: http://www.nytimes.com/2011/02/06/opinion/06friedman.html/ [Accessed 5 April 2011].

Garber, M., 2011. *Nick Kristof turns to Facebook to report from Egypt*. Nieman Journalism Lab, 30 January. Available from: http://www.niemanlab.org/2011/01/nick-kristof-turns-to-facebook-to-report-from-egypt/ [Accessed 14 September 2011].

Gladwell, M., 2010. Small change. *The New Yorker*, 4 October. Available from: http://www.newyorker.com/reporting/2010/10/04/101004fa_fact_gladwell/ [Accessed 5 April 2011].

Hoffman, P., 2011. *Al Jazeera attracts massive audience through Twitter*. Editors Weblog, 9 February. Available from: http://www.editorsweblog.org/web_20/2011/02/al_jazeera_attracts_massive_audience_thr.php/ [Accessed 5 April 2011].

Howard, P.N., 2011. *The Arab Uprising's cascading effects*, Miller-McCune, 23 February. Available from: http://www.miller-mccune.com/politics/the-cascading-effects-of-the-arab-spring-28575/ [Accessed 5 April 2011].

International Telecommunication Union, 2011. *Estimated Internet users per 100 inhabitants*. International Telecommunication Union. Available from: http://www.itu.int/ [Accessed 14 September 2011].

Iyadelbaghdadi, 2011. *Meet Asmaa Mahfouz and the Vlog that Helped Spark the Revolution*, performed by Iyadelbaghdadi on YouTube, 1 February. Available from: http://www.youtube.com/watch?v=SgjIgMdsEuk/ [Accessed 5 April 2011].

Kaplan, A.M. and Haenlein, M., 2009. Users of the world, unite! The challenges and opportunities of social media. *Business Horizons*. 53(1), 59–68.

Kirkpatrick, D.D. and Sanger, D.E., 2011. A Tunisian–Egyptian link that shook Arab history. *The New York Times*, 13 February. Available from: http://www.nytimes.com/2011/02/14/world/middleeast/14egypt-tunisia-protests.html?pagewanted=all [Accessed 15 December 2011].

Matherne, R., 2011. *Social media helps spread revolution in Egypt*. Six Estate. Available from: http://sixestate.com/social-media-spreads-revolution-in-egypt/ [Accessed 5 April 2011].

Morozov, E., 2011. *The net delusion: the dark side of Internet freedom*. New York, NY: PublicAffairs.
Nieman Journalism Lab, 2011. *January 2011 archives*. Nieman Journalism Lab. Available from: http://www.niemanlab.org/2011/01/ [Accessed 5 April 2011].
O'Dell, J., 2011. *How Egyptians used Twitter during the January crisis*. Mashable. Available from: http://mashable.com/2011/02/01/egypt-twitter-infographic/ [Accessed 5 April 2011].
QueenofRomance83, 2011. بنت محفوظ أسماء. [*bint mahfouz asma'*], performed by QueenofRomance83 on YouTube, 18 January. Available from: http://www.youtube.com/watch?v=ZhbKN9q319g/ [Accessed 5 April 2011].
Raoof, R., 2011. *Egypt: sequence of communication shutdown during 2011 uprise*. Egyptian Blog for Human Rights, 8 February. Available from: http://ebfhr.blogspot.com/2011/02/egypt-sequence-of-communication.html/ [Accessed 5 April 2011].
Rich, F., 2011. Wallflowers at the Revolution. *The New York Times*, 5 February. Available from: http://www.nytimes.com/2011/02/06/opinion/06rich.html/ [Accessed 5 April 2011].
Roberts, P., 2011. *Facebook owned 42% of Egyptian web traffic before blackout*. Threat Post, 31 January. Available from: https://threatpost.com/en_us/blogs/facebook-owned-42-egyptian-web-traffic-blackout-013111/ [Accessed 5 April 2011].
Shirky, C., 2011. The political power of social media. *Foreign Affairs*, 90 (1), 28–41.
Smith, C., 2011. *Graph visualizes Egypt's Internet blackout*, Huffington Post, 3 March. Available from: http://www.huffingtonpost.com/2011/01/28/this-is-what-egypts-cutoff-from-the-net-looks-like_n_815335.html/ [Accessed 5 April 2011].
Social Bakers, 2011. *Egypt Facebook statistics*. Social Bakers. Available from: http://www.socialbakers.com/facebook-statistics/egypt/ [Accessed 5 April 2011].
Sullivan, A.D., 2011. *Rich and Gladwell, wallflowers at history: Egypt*. The Atlantic, 14 February. Available from: http://www.theatlantic.com/daily-dish/archive/2011/02/rich-and-gladwell-wallflowers-at-history-egypt/175823/ [Accessed 5 April 2011].
The Peninsula, 2011. *Al Jazeera uses social media to avoid Egypt curbs*. The Peninsula, 30 January. Available from: http://www.thepeninsulaqatar.com/qatar/140845-al-jazeera-uses-social-media-to-avoid-egypt-curbs.html/ [Accessed 5 April 2011].
UNICEF, 2011. *Egypt*. UNICEF. Available from: http://www.unicef.org/infobycountry/egypt_statistics.html/ [Accessed 14 September 2011].

Egypt's Muslim Brotherhood and the January 25 Revolution: new political party, new circumstances

Mona Farag

Institute for Arab and Islamic Studies, University of Exeter, Exeter, UK

This paper highlights the Muslim Brotherhood's experience in Egyptian elections since the 1980s with an emphasis on their last attempts during the Hosni Mubarak era in 2010 and in light of their most recent showing in the 2011 elections. This summary reveals how past electoral activities and failures have positioned this organization the better to capitalize on the newfound democratic climate in a post-revolution Egypt and perform well during the 2011 parliamentary elections. Drawing on these and more recent sources, an attempt is also made to bring the features of today's Egypt's political field into clear focus in the wake of the January 25 revolution and the subsequent emergence of newly formed political parties on the Egyptian scene. The paper concludes with a broad assessment of the prospects for the political future of the Muslim Brotherhood in view of its showing in the initial phase of elections for the People's Assembly that took place in November 2011.

As the world watched the much publicized Egyptian legislative elections of November 2010 in an admixture of anticipation and trepidation, one vital question was on everyone's mind: would the Muslim Brotherhood (MB) repeat its successful performance of 2005 when the movement won 88 seats in the National Assembly, or would it even surpass that achievement? As it transpired, the 2010 elections were blatantly rigged (Stanton 2010) and concluded with the National Democratic Party (NDP) gaining almost all the seats and a minimal showing for the opposition Wafd party, while the MB lost all of the 88 seats it had won in the 2005 elections, thereby stripping the movement of any and all representation in the Egyptian government. Given the events that took place both before and during the elections, in particular the regime's tactics in eliminating any and all opposition elements that did not abide by its agenda, observers were left asking: what next for the most organized and effective opposition movement, and what would its elimination from the parliament portend for Egypt and its rotting facade of a democratic system?

Countless actions taken by the Egyptian government against the MB following its impressive win in the 2005 elections, including the erosion of the rights and freedoms of its people (such as significantly curbing freedom of speech and opinion by shutting down several television stations and newspapers), were among the many factors that led to the January 25 revolution. This revolution shook the world and drew away the blinds that had concealed from the international community the authoritarian nature of the regime. It also uncovered the oppression and suffering of the Egyptian masses, especially the country's youth, who were largely responsible for the initiation and success of this historical event.

To understand better the many potential opportunities and obstacles faced by the MB over the year preceding the revolution, specifically in the months leading up to the parliamentary elections in November 2010, one must review the organization's relationship with the regime that once was, and the changing dynamics of that relationship. Against this backdrop, the MB's post-revolutionary political and social standing will be examined in terms of how the movement is now viewed by Egyptians, as well as the concerns that the Western world harbours towards an Islamic political faction.

The Muslim Brotherhood and the state: a brief summary

What started in 1928 as a simple movement to engender an Islamic way of life and thinking, grew over the years to encompass a myriad of thoughts and beliefs that ranged from apolitical currents at the very beginning – intended to spread an awareness of Islamic teachings and jurisprudence through religious *madrasas* – to non-violent social movements with political undertones, devoted to providing the basic needs of the suffering masses, giving succour that should have been provided by the Egyptian state as part of its responsibilities (Dede 2008). Not only is the Egyptian MB the oldest religious movement in the Middle East, but also almost all of today's different religious movements trace their origins back to the MB and its inspiration (Shenker and Whitaker 2011). During the brief phases in which the MB has resorted to violence – namely during the period of British occupation, and around the time of the assassination attempts of Gamal Abdel Nasser and marked by the growing interest in the teachings of Sayyid Quṭb – groups like *al-takfir wa al-hijrah* rose up in response to the MB's 'failed' attempts at reforming Egypt's secular state into a religious one (BBC 2011). Other Islamist groups or sects were formed in reaction to the MB's failure to transform Egyptian society and government.[1] *Salafists* who decided to follow the fundamental teachings of Wahhabism reverted back to the private sphere, thereby excluding all political rhetoric from their Islamic teachings (*Al Masry Al Youm Online* 2011). Yet, with their strict interpretation of the faith, such *salafists* enjoyed considerable freedom in spreading their vision through media and other societal tools.

When looking at the MB's political activities, it seems that they constantly changed and adapted their vision to whatever political climate prevailed, and in particular the movement adapted to the regime's tactic of capitalizing on the MB's 'Islamizing' social presence and growing influence to make the government's 'democratic' agendas and plans appear more appealing to the masses. This resulted in the regime giving more political freedom to the MB to counteract the secular parties that espoused a more democratic vision, for fear that a popular secular party could threaten the governing NDP and its success (Abaza 2006, p. 18). This 'evolutionary' trait of the MB is clearly evident through its history of electoral activities from the 1980s to the present day. However, the regime has consistently used religion as a tool to achieve its political ends, by reassuring the Muslim majority in Egypt that the government relies on the tenets of Islam to guide its executive decisions. Meanwhile, through adaptation, the MB of today's Egypt has evolved into something completely different from the movement founded by its original leader Hasan al-Banna. The survival of the Society of Muslim Brothers, that endured four different eras of government rule, notwithstanding being forced to work underground and in secret as a banned organization, is testament to the strength of the Islamist phenomenon. Nevertheless, al-Banna's actions during the brief period of his leadership of the organization have been reflected in the organization's evolving relationship with the regimes of Nasser, Anwar Sadat, Hosni Mubarak and the post-revolution era. Al-Banna's 'accommodationist' style was evident in his changing views of electoral and parliamentarian politics, as well as his accommodation to the governing system.[2]

Through forming alliances with other parties, since it was officially banned as a political movement from 1954, the MB managed to win a considerable number of parliamentary seats, exploiting its presence and appeal at the grassroots level, as well as the active membership of many of the brothers in Egypt's professional syndicates. As the MB's political clout began to grow and exert more influence across Egypt's population during the 1990s, the regime in turn became more aware of the MB's threat to its own standing, stability and longevity in Egypt's political game.

During the 2000 elections, the MB continued to perform well, winning enough seats to retain a considerable political presence, but not so many as to incur the outright hostility of Egypt's authoritarian regime.[3] In 2005, however, the MB gained 20% of the 444 seats in the parliament, thereby creating a real threat to the NDP's political weight and popularity. As a result, from 2005 to 2010 the MB had to endure some of its worst years in terms of political oppression, as the regime systematically made life difficult for the MB's members, closing their businesses, revoking their licences, and continuously and freely arresting many members thanks to the emergency law[4] that allowed such action without recourse to the courts. In effect, this period was considered the worst era of military crackdown on the MB since the first days of Mubarak's elevation to the presidency (Michael and El Deeb 2010).

The 2010 elections and the beginning of the end for Mubarak?

The 2010 elections were described as one of the most flagrantly oppressive, undemocratic and fraudulent displays of authoritarian rule. At issue was not just the military's actions in rounding up MB candidates and supporters in the immediate run-up to the elections. Over the course of the five years leading up to the polls, many changes had been implemented which compounded the democratic deficit in Egypt. These included a constitutional amendment of Law 88 that had required judges to oversee the electoral process to ensure no violations took place (Anon. 2007). In 2007, that role of the judges was changed to include overseeing voter participation, but it stripped them of any jurisdiction to take action against violations witnessed (Hauslohner 2010). In 2010 several local organizations,[5] such as the Center for Trade Union and Workers' Services, approached the regime offering their services in monitoring the elections, but all were rejected, as the government insisted that it had the situation under control (Bradley 2010a). This could be seen as further evidence that the government had something to hide and was going to continue its long-standing tradition of bribing voters and vote-rigging. It is for that reason that the 2010 elections will likely be remembered by many as the worst display of alleged 'democracy' ever to take place. When it came to the poll, many voting stations were closed at the last minute – most of which were located in areas known for their MB affiliations – and the presence of the military was evident at every station that remained open (Stanton 2010). In the months leading up to the 2010 elections, over 1000 members of the MB – candidates included – were arrested (Bradley 2010b) in an attempt to deter the organization's many activities and derail the preparations that had been set in place. It was not that these actions by the regime and the military were new, given their wary attitude towards the MB. Rather, it was the sheer scale of the continuous bullying and overwhelming lack of transparency that was evident in all the oppressive acts that took place in 2010 that ensured the failure of the MB and any other party and enabled the NDP to remain victorious and in power.

Nonetheless and as is clear from the long history, summarized above, of the MB's relations with Egypt's governing regimes and ruling party systems, what saved the movement from extinction was its accommodationist style. This and its resilience ensured the continuation and growth of the MB rather than its complete obliteration as an organization and grassroots movement. Crucially, however, in light of recent events, that have forever changed the political climate in Egypt, it is also clear that the MB's history is only a reflection of the virility of the MB as a movement. That history cannot necessarily determine its future successes and failures – given that the MB is now entering new and uncharted political waters: a new dawn for all of Egypt, characterized by the ideological appeal of democracy and demands for transparency.

The January 25 revolution

The obvious vote-rigging and the absence of any democratic principles and governance in the 2010 elections were the 'straws that broke the camel's back' of a corrupt system of governance. The suppression of all opposing voices by the authoritarian regime was more than the Egyptian people could bear. In particular, it was the Egyptian youth that could no longer accept the status quo, the economic deterioration of their country, and the rising inflation and unemployment rates (Falk 2011). The younger generation of Egyptians had watched their parents suffer silently under the injustices of their government for years, and saw their grim future mirrored in their parents' dismal present, as more graduates entered the market with little hope of securing a job in Egypt's current economy. During the years immediately preceding the 2011 revolution, Egypt's economy saw gradual improvement in terms of certain statistical indicators, but none of these improvements generated a 'trickle-down' effect to benefit the masses. Corrupt practices and corruptive habits, where profits of all shapes and forms have been appropriated by the wealthy elite, only increased the plight of the lower- to middle-income families in the face of rising rates of inflation (Chams El Dine 2011).

The movement that started as a small protest initiated by a frenzy of internet activity, and which exploded into a full-fledged revolution in 2011, was a youth movement. Initially, the MB was aware that this protest was planned and chose not to take any part in it (PBS Frontline Series 2011a). But as the days passed and the situation in Tahrir Square grew more fractious, the movement no longer belonged to one faction or party – it took on a whole new spirit of nationalistic anger and indignation directed at a failed government, emanating from all classes, irrespective of educational background and from all walks of life in Cairo. Thus when the MB joined the people and the movement in Tahrir Square, they joined as Egyptians and not as a socio-religious movement with an agenda of its own. The goal of the revolution was clear: to regain the dignity and rights of the Egyptian people. According to ʿIsām al-ʿAryān, the MB was careful not to give a religious slant to the revolution whenever members of the MB were allowed to join in the protests, but they participated on their own accord and without pushing the MB's agenda or chanting any of its slogans (Chammah 2011). Nonetheless, their presence was felt as the days went by, especially when security issues became a serious concern. Amr Hamzawy, Research Director of the Carnegie Middle East Centre, noted that those who stood at the security checkpoints at Tahrir Square were Muslim Brothers, ensuring the safety of people. They were also responsible for providing tents, blankets and tea for people who chose to stay in the Square until Mubarak stepped down (PBS Frontline Series 2011b). The Muslim Brothers were taking an active role in the revolution, but only to provide their greatest asset: their organizational and mobilizing strengths.

The constitutional referendum

With the fall of the old regime and the stepping down of Mubarak, the MB changed tactics. Various possibilities opened up for the organization and for other activists, who wanted to take part in rebuilding their country's governing body, its political party or parties, and most importantly its constitution. Indeed, it could be argued that the MB was united with the secular clique until the objective of eradicating the old regime, and opening up the political ground to any and all, was reached.

As the old regime was dissolved, military rule in the shape of the Supreme Council of the Armed Forces (SCAF) stepped in to govern the country through its transitional period, inclusive of new parliamentary and presidential elections in 2011–2012. Despite the fact that Egypt has always had a strong military backbone to its ruling establishment, the military was seemingly not altogether comfortable in its new executive role (Nicoll and Johnstone 2011). As a result, the initial process of amending the constitution was rushed and undertaken in a matter of days by several prominent politicians and judges. Not unexpectedly, a representative of the largest organized movement outside of the NDP had to be present, so am MB member was invited to take part in this important milestone event.

The first democratic act to take place in Egypt's post-Mubarak era was the referendum on the amendments to the constitution. The majority of what might best be called secular society in Egypt, consisting of a large percentage of the Christian minority, together with members of the upper and middle classes, the educated and intellectuals, encouraged a 'no' vote to render the amendments null and void (Hellyer 2011). The main reason behind such an effort was that despite the amendments made to the constitution, it still contained many components that resonated from the much-hated Mubarak era. The majority of the MB, however, wanted to vote 'yes' to the amendments, not least for the purpose of preserving Article 2, which states that *sharīʿah* is the source of legislation for the state. In effect, the MB – as well as other Islamist factions – needed to ensure that the constitution passed. The results of the referendum were 77.3% 'yes' and 22.8% 'no' (Majdoub 2011). These results were greeted with a number of allegations and speculations that the MB had engaged in its own activities of vote-rigging, by convincing the sizeable ranks of illiterate members of the population in the vast rural regions of Egypt that it was their Islamic duty to vote for the amended constitution (Shehata 2011).[6] Irrespective of how the majority verdict came about, a democratic process had taken place in Egypt, and the people had spoken, given that it was the highest turnout of voters that Egypt has seen in a long time, if ever. However, this outcome begged the question: what next? Was the MB well on its way to winning the majority of Egyptians' loyalty and following? Or would the Egyptian people choose to stay away from an Islamist agenda?

The Muslim Brotherhood post-Mubarak: obstacles and opportunities

Since the referendum, whose result could be perceived by the MB as a small victory, the MB has been scrambling to take full advantage of the newfound freedom. However, the MB did not foresee two major hurdles in its path to becoming a fully legitimate socio-religious organization with a functional political party: the newly formed Freedom and Justice Party (FJP). The first hurdle was that from the day of the MB's inception as a political organization, it was built and grew into the giant that it is today by being a banned entity – by working underground and hiding from the limelight. As a result, it has always been a force of resistance to an oppressive ruling establishment, and that is how its organization functions: as an opposing force. Now, and for the first time in the history of the MB, it has been recognized as a legitimate organization and accorded equal opportunity with the rest of the parties that have been struggling under the weight of the corrupt NDP for the past few decades. This is not to mention the array of new parties that have emerged, teeming with secular ideals and slogans of democracy and human rights (El Deeb 2011). In addition, it could be argued that the MB had previously gained most of its followers by empathizing and sharing common ground with the oppressed masses against the corrupt regime. Now that the organization is fully 'legalized' and there is no overbearing entity to hate and unite against, it could be expected that the Egyptian people would realign their priorities and political affiliations to whatever they think suits them best.

The second hurdle, and one that the MB (especially the MB's old guard) had turned a blind eye towards, is the organization's young members and their secular agenda for the MB. The revolution's main characteristic was that it was largely a youth movement, spearheaded by young activists tired of the old haggard regime and wanting a new one more likely to serve the needs and demands of Egypt's poverty-stricken population. The MB's tactic during the revolution was to provide support to enable the formation of a cohesive bloc across Egyptian society to end the Mubarak era. What the MB old guard seems not to have fully anticipated was the effect on the younger brothers of mingling and connecting with other youth movements, which, for a time at least, resulted in both sides discovering a more secular common ground – a common ground that was devoid of an Islamist character (Sennott 2011). One telling incident of the rift that occurred between the older and younger generations in the MB was the MB Youth Conference held in March 2011. Hundreds of young Brothers assembled, against the orders of the MB's Supreme Guide, and demanded 'better representation of young Brothers in the group's highest power structures and the full independence of the Muslim Brotherhood's nascent Freedom and Justice Party from all proselytizing bodies' (El-Hennawy 2011a). As expected, none of those demands was acknowledged, which gave way to the formation of a new political party by the MB youth, completely breaking away and severing all ties to the Ikhwān (MB). According to Muḥammad Shams, co-founder of Ḥizb al-Tayyār al-Maṣry:

> The manifesto of Ḥizb al-Tayyār al-Maṣry [Egyptian Current Party] does not mention Islamic *sharīʿah* as its frame of reference; it only refers to the Arab Islamic civilization. We cannot refer to the Islamic *sharīʿah* because this is not an Islamist party, and it is not a party for the Muslim Brotherhood youth. Not all founders belong to the Muslim Brotherhood.
>
> (El-Hennawy 2011c)

The phenomenon of members of the MB, particularly young ones, breaking away and forming their own political parties with a more secular platform is certainly worthy of note. In fact, this is not the first time that such an event has taken place, as some members belonging to the middle generation did leave the fold of the MB in the 1990s to form the more moderate Al-Wasaṭ (Centrist) Party (Mikhail and Perry 2011).

The important point, however, is to understand why the younger generation chose, at such a critical moment in Egypt's democratic reformation, to step away from the shelter of the MB. What were the fundamental issues that they disagreed with when defending their views to the MB's elders residing in the senior guidance council? In addressing this question, it is worth recalling three specific factors that reflect the roots of the international community's fears and concerns about a rise to power of the MB in Egypt.

The first two factors are interconnected: the implementation of *sharīʿah* law as the main source of legislation and the fate of the Christian minority (comprising approximately 10% of the population). The long-term vision of the MB is the formation of an Islamic state: for Egyptians to live in peace and conform to the ideals of an Islamic society (Sennott 2011). For that vision to become a reality, *sharīʿah* law has to become the only source of legislation. This leads to the second factor, namely Christian minority rights in today's Egypt and, more specifically, their right to run for the position of the President of the Arab Republic of Egypt. The MB publicly stated in 2007 that it would never agree to a Christian or a woman as head of state (Levinson 2011). In effect, this leads to the third factor: the status of women in Egypt's political and social realm. Certainly the MB's organization is filled with female members, and several female candidates were actively backed by the MB in the elections of 2005 and 2010; however, to date there have been no female members in the Upper House Shūrā (Consultative) Council (Shehata 2011). This is no doubt reflective of the MB's contention that no woman is mentally and emotionally able to be president (Mahmoud 2011). With regard to the issue of women, the prevailing norm among the MB's old guard seems to be that a woman's natural place is in the home, to educate future generations to become active leaders of tomorrow (Abdel-Latif and Ottaway 2007, pp. 7–9). Once this task is completed, then women can enter the public sphere and actively engage their society toward the betterment and advancement of an Islamic state. In contrast, the younger generation in the MB seems to be more in tune with the secular current in Egypt that believes women's participation in all levels and spheres of life in Egypt today is vital for a democratic future. In any case, many parties are forming and joining the political game in Egypt, some of which had former ties to the MB, such as the New Renaissance party, formed by young former MB member Ibrāhīm al-Zaʿfarānī along with fifteen other members (El-Hennawy 2011d). Such activities indicate a measure of internal fragmentation within the giant organization that is the MB, thereby revealing the cracks in its ideology and ruling style.

Due to the many hurdles and changes that are occurring around them, the MB has been trying to give its political party, the FJP, a liberal edge. It selected Coptic Christian member Rafīq Ḥabīb as its third in command (Hope 2011a) and it undertook negotiations with several parties, liberal in nature, in an honest attempt to find common ground and form an alliance ahead of the parliamentary elections. Even though the political party is not allowed to represent or serve any religious faction, it is clear the MB's grand organization has been overseeing every step and plan set out for the FJP. Nathan Brown described this relationship as the MB acting as the 'helicopter parent' (Brown 2011) hovering close to its infant, the FJP, protecting it and dictating its future direction. A telling act of such parental behaviour was the permanent reassignment of three members of the Guidance Council – Muḥammad Mursī, Saʿd al-Katātnī, and

ʿIsām al-ʿAryān – to the FJP to run it (Brown 2011). In addition to this strict way of overseeing every move the FJP makes, the organization of the MB has written the party's platform and also approved its bylaws, which clearly state that 'the party is dedicated to peaceful and gradual reform along Islamic lines' which includes the 'reform of the individual, the family, the society, the government, and then institutions of the state' (Brown 2011).

The major concern in the case of Islamist rule or a dominant Islamist discourse in Egyptian politics, for Western observers and Israelis at least, is the peace treaty with Israel, and the fact that in the past the MB has expressed its desire to end it. Also, it is a well-known fact that the majority of Egyptians harbour an intense dislike, even hatred, towards the Israeli state, and would more than likely side with the MB regarding the termination of the treaty. Aware of the international community's concerns, the MB has gone through extensive efforts to try and quell their fears, by publicly stating time and again that they have no desire to win a majority of votes and were interested in gaining no more than 30% of the seats in parliament (Keath and Hendawi 2011). In addition, they have vowed not to elect an MB official to run for president as they professed no desire to become a ruling majority anytime in the near future (Kirkpatrick and Goodman 2011). However, their statements and promises tend to change, as is the case with this organization, as elements around them evolve and transpire.

Another rising concern in the eyes of the Western world is *salafist* activity (Lynch 2011). With the fall of the old regime, mechanisms for repressing political parties of a religious or socialist nature have come apart, resulting in the MB stepping into the political limelight at last. Along with their newfound freedom, the minority *salafist* movement and its associated groups have ridden on the MB's coat-tails and have been mobilizing their supporters to form their own political group and agenda (Dabbash and El-Waziry). This is despite the fact that they had long berated the MB for participating in a political system that encouraged ideologies other than the one true ideology of implementing the laws of Islam in its most fundamental of forms (Hendawi 2011a). As a result, the current political climate in Egypt resonates heavily a strict Islamic tendency, which is increasingly worrying the secular and socialist tides in Egypt, and has resulted in the West and Israel rethinking their political ties[7] with the largest Arab nation in the Middle East.

During the latter months of 2011 the *salafists* engaged in several public protests against the 'hedonistic' state, mainly targeting the Christian minority and the secularist population, while demanding the formation of a true Islamic nation, one that closely resembles the Saudi Arabian Wahhabi state. Effectively, by winning a plurality of seats in ten new assembly the MB has opened the way for *salafists* to latch onto that newfound power and authority, and push for their demands to be met, which eventually will include the complete 'Islamisation' of Egyptian society, with little or no regard for the Christian community. The MB is aware that the actions of the *salafists* – either negative or positive – directly impact the image and message of the MB's party. At the start of the campaign season in October 2011, the MB warned the *salafists* to 'tone down their harsh speech' (Sheffer 2011), fearing that such negative Islamist rhetoric would hurt their 'moderate' Islamist campaign and approach. As examined below, in the event both the FJP and the *salafists* made significant gains in the first round of elections in November 2011, all be it with the FJP in the dominant position. The trend toward the Islamists, including *salafists*, was repeated in subsequent rounds.

How popular are the Muslim Brotherhood or their religio-political ideologies? Early indicators

Among the many impressive talents and skills that the MB acquired over the years as a forbidden organization struggling beneath the heavy weight of an authoritarian regime was its media-centric tenacity. Now, with the dissolution of all governmental restrictions on media outlets, it has succeeded in appearing repeatedly on the front pages of various Arabic language newspapers, as well as making numerous appearances on television talk-shows, university debates and whatever forum to which it could gain access to assert its message. But does continuous exposure affirm its dominance or popularity? This might not be the case, at least according to many people in Egypt who insist that the MB is not as popular as the media coverage might imply. To assess the true popularity and dominance of the MB, a survey of the relevant statistics is instructive.

Egypt has the largest population of any state in the Middle East, numbering over 80 million people. In the past, voter turnout in Egypt was less than 20% (Hendawi 2011b). However, in March 2011, more than 14 million people made their way to the voting stations to exercise their rights as citizens, free from elements of corruption and fraud. The number of Egyptians registered to vote is estimated at 45 million of the 80 million total population; 29.6% are illiterate and come from poor neighbourhoods. Fifty-seven per cent of the population lives in rural areas; 21.6% live well below the poverty line (United Nations Development Programme (UNDP) 2010). Given the MB's extensive social networks that assisted those in need by providing medical care, food and monetary support (Korany 1998, pp. 59–63), it would make sense to assume that the needy have been instrumental in delivering such electoral gains as the MB made in elections to date. However, a survey conducted by the Pews Research Center (2011) indicated that the 'support for the MB is somewhat less intense among lower-income Egyptians (26% very favourable) than among those in middle- (41%) and higher- (43%) income categories'.

In the immediate aftermath of the 25 January revolution, a number of polls and surveys were conducted in Egypt by American research centres, among them the Pews Research Center, the International Republican Institute (IRI), and The Abu Dhabi Gallup Center. Opinions were canvassed on issues ranging from women's rights to the implementation of *sharīʿah* law and the peace treaty with Israel. For the purpose of providing an overall view of public opinion, people from almost all districts and governorates were represented, as were those from the lowest economic classes to the highest, and from educational levels spanning from illiterates to holders of doctorates. The Pews Research Center (2011) revealed the following through conducting 1000 interviews in Egypt:

> Most have a favourable opinion of the Muslim Brotherhood, and looking ahead to the elections, it has as much potential support as any of a number of political parties. … Three-in-four express a favorable opinion of the Muslim Brotherhood, and 37% have a very favorable opinion of this organization.

With regards to the primary objective that the MB lives and dies by, namely that *sharīʿah* is to be the main source of legislation, a full 62% of Egyptians believe that Egyptian law should strictly adhere to the word and teachings of the Qurʾān. That said, a number asserted that they feel that 'religious leaders are having a positive impact on the country, although the topic of religion clearly divides Egyptians' (Pew

Research Center 2011).[8] When asked about their loyalty or preference towards one political party over another, there was a spectrum of diverse responses, clearly indicating that there is a lack of consensus or majority preference amongst the Egyptian people regarding which party they felt could lead the country into its new democratic phase. Moreover, the survey revealed that:

> One-in-five express support for the New Wafd Party, while 17% would like to see the Muslim Brotherhood lead the government and about the same percentage (16%) favour the Al-Ghad Party; about one-in-ten express support for the Tajammuʿ Party [National Progressive Unionist Party] (11%) or the National Democratic Party (10%)
>
> (Pew Research Center 2011)

In a survey carried out by The Abu Dhabi Gallup Center *before* the revolution the conclusion was that 'Egypt tops the region in two things: Egyptians are the most likely to say Muslim progress requires democracy, and the most likely to say Muslim progress requires attachment to spiritual and moral values' (Mogahed 2011). This may explain why a subsequent Abu Dhabi Gallup Center poll, the results of which were published in June 2011, revealed that the majority of Egyptians 'envision a representative government where religious principles guide the democratic process, but with clerics limited to an advisory role … religion remains important to most Egyptians (96%), and 92% say they have confidence in religious institutions' (The Abu Dhabi Gallup Center 2011, p. 6). Muslim Egyptians are attached to their religion and values that are deeply entrenched within that religion, but at the same time they reject a model of government similar to that of Iran. The majority of Muslim Egyptians are in complete support of a democracy and fully reject the idea of a theocracy. At the same time, it is understandable that 'Egyptians may not think the MB should run the country, according to Gallup research, but 75% of Egyptians have a "somewhat favorable" or "favorable" opinion of the organization, according to the Pew Research Center' (The Abu Dhabi Gallup Center 2011, p. 18). Moreover, a survey of 2400 voters conducted by Al-Ahram Centre for Political and Strategic Studies (ACPSS) in September 2011 revealed that of the 62% who had made a decision, 39% would support the FJP, 20% would support the centrist Wafd Party and 6.8% would back Al-Nūr (a *salafist* platform) (Hope 2011c).

The Muslim Brotherhood and its political aspirations: FJP progress

With the dissolution of the once powerful and corrupt NDP of the old regime, the MB gained a very real prospect of gaining a large number of seats during the first post-revolution parliamentary elections. After surviving decades of oppression and building its intricate underground networks, the MB has emerged as the most organized collective in modern Egyptian politics. Yet there remains a lot of inconsistency in the messages conveyed by the movement to the public. The MB has insisted that it is not aiming to take over the government and transform it into a theocratic system of governing. Over the past year the MB has repeatedly tried to quell fears that it intends to garner the majority of parliamentary seats, and it claims instead to seek an atmosphere of 'partnership, not supremacy' in the Egyptian parliament. In April 2011, soon after the formation of its 'secular' FJP, however, the MB declared that it would contest 50% of the seats in parliament (Michael 2011). In addition, a prominent MB reformist by the name of ʿAbd al-Munʿim Abū al-Futūḥ declared in May 2011 that he would run in the next presidential election (El-Hennawy 2011b). This step was in clear defiance of the MB Senior Guide's strict orders against the inclusion of any representative of the organization or the political party in a presidential election. According to Abū al-Futūḥ's campaigners, he quickly accumulated 20,000 signatures of the necessary 30,000 signatures required to be eligible for the presidential race. True to its word, on 16 June 2011 the MB's consultative Shūrā Council decided to expel Abū al-Futūḥ for his defiant act of running for president (Saleh 2011). Following in Abū al-Futūḥ's footsteps, potential presidential candidate Ḥāzim Ṣalāḥ Abū Ismāʿīl had to leave the secretive fold of the Society in order to run for the position of Egypt's future president.

The organization's desire to acquire 50% of the parliamentary seats was quite an ambitious one, and also quite threatening to other parties running in the elections. In effect, it leaves very few seats for other parties such as the socialist parties, or the newly formed parties run by secular-minded, ex-Muslim Brothers. The fact of the matter is as follows: with a total of 444 seats to play for, if the MB successfully targeted 50% of the seats for the FJP, that would leave only 222 for former NDP members and loyalists and the remaining twenty-something parties to battle over. In pursuit of its objective of winning a majority in the People's Assembly elections, the MB chose to play it safe by forming an alliance with several other parties – many liberal and leftist in ideology – in June 2011, under the banner of the 'Democratic Alliance', to strengthen their position during the election process. Its coalition with the oldest political faction in Egypt, the Wafd Party (El Deeb 2011) was also intended to level the playing field. Meanwhile, the MB is adamant in portraying its party, the FJP, in a friendly liberal light, with its quota of female and Christian Copt members (Hope 2011b). Expectedly, some of the liberal, leftist parties were nonetheless wary of how the MB's party's strategy of forming alliances and pooling resources to ensure the greatest number of votes might play out. In October 2011, the FJP – as part of the Democratic Alliance – announced its lists of candidates in twenty of 27 governorates. According to one source, the names only included 'candidates running for the proportional-representation seats and not individual seats'.[9] This was problematic, as it affirmed that the MB was aiming for a much higher representation in the parliament – independent of the parties within the democratic alliance – than it purported to seek and was set to contest '90 per cent of the individual seats and 70 per cent of the party-list seats … [i.e.] nearly 77 per cent of the total seats in parliament' (Tadros 2011).

Many questions resulted: how was the MB planning to share these votes and seats with the parties with which it planned to ally? How would the diverse voices and ideologies be represented when the new Egypt finally gained a democratically elected parliament that would energize all civil society and attend to the well-being of a poverty stricken and economically weak nation? According to Brown (2011), the MB could be expected to move away from its 'insular attitude – one that served the movement well under harsh authoritarian conditions' and find its way into a democratic and open dialogue with the masses and Egypt's growing number of political parties. Also, Waḥīd ʿAbd al-Majīd, Deputy Director of the ACPSS and head of the Coordinating Committee of the Democratic Alliance, assured worried observers that 'the Brotherhood does not dominate the alliance. The joint candidacy lists consist of the finest candidates that shall lead Egypt to a better future' (Tarek 2011). One thing is for certain, with this alliance the Egyptian people's choices were reduced on election day, permitting them only to vote for parties that were pro-MB or those that could be perceived as anti-MB, or the MB's competition.

The People's Assembly elections first round (November 2011)

As the results of the first phase of parliamentary elections were revealed in early December, the world watched in dismay as the Islamists claimed 60% of the votes.[10] The weak liberal showing of 15% was seemingly an affirmation that the MB and Islamists were ultimately more successful in organizing and mobilizing support and votes. Many attribute the liberal parties' failure[11] in the first phase of elections to their continuous presence and focus on the protests that took place through November. With the overthrowing of the Mubarak regime, and with the SCAF as a representative of an 'interim government', the months leading up to the first phase of elections in November 2011 were punctuated with Friday protests that mainly focused on overthrowing the SCAF and ending its practice of military trials of civilian protesters and suppression of their activities. This dedication to ending military rule before entering democratic elections negatively impacted their campaigning efforts for the elections. In the meantime, the MB chose not to participate in the protests against SCAF, and was in full force campaigning and organizing for the 28 November elections. Despite the sweeping Islamist victory, and the seeming inevitability of the formation of an Islamic state, as of November 2011 it was still debatable whether the Islamist parties – both the FJP and the *salafist* Ḥizb al-Nūr party – would gain a clear two-thirds majority in the parliament, giving them enough power to make unilateral decisions that would impact all walks of life. As it transpired, the Islamists did attain a majority between them. That said, the parliamentary elections are only stage one of a long process to include the drawing up of a new constitution, and the subsequent referendum and legislative elections will determine just how 'Islamic' Egypt's new governing system will be.

The MB has yet to prove itself as a functioning political machine, working in transparency in the absence of an oppressive other, and able to tackle all issues that plague Egypt post-revolution. Also, the new parliament by itself does not enjoy significant powers in comparison with the executive. The MB's future actions will determine whether or not it will have the support and backing of the revolution's youth and the organization's remaining younger generation. Plus, the persisting rule of the SCAF and its unwillingness to show any signs of handing over power to a civilian government is an issue that both Islamists and secular forces need to deal with, as the 30 March constitutional amendments did not list any privileges or responsibilities that the new parliament would possess independent of the omnipresent SCAF.

Conclusion: it all comes down to the economy

According to the several surveys conducted, the clarity and detail of the economic plans tabled in the contending parties' platforms will be the deciding factor in the parties' success and not their ideological or religious character. The IRI Egypt Index revealed that 81% of Egyptians rated their economy as poor, and 'more than one-third of Egyptians (41%) said they have trouble feeding themselves and their family or providing for the most basic needs' (IRI 2011, pp. 1–2). In addition, it seems that one of the major reasons people supported and joined the January 25 revolution was because of poor economic conditions and unemployment, and not purely as a result of their obvious disenchantment and distrust of their corrupt authoritarian government.

Currently, the MB has a lot of issues that need to be dealt with, such as the lack of any viable and clear policy of any kind that is not sociologically specific; and they have yet to create a detailed and plausible economic policy to resuscitate and revive Egypt's declining economy, its diminishing foreign investment and aid, as well as its high unemployment rate. The MB's purely Islamic ideologies of justice and equality – as an alternative to the 30 years of corruption – might have been the attractive feature that drew the support of the Egyptian masses, but their as yet undefined economic plan and reforms are what will decide their fate and long-term prospects.

Notes

1. Most notably, the Islamic *jihadist* groups, such as the *al-takfir wa al-hijrah*, which resorted to the use of violence instead of following the MB's 'accommodationist' rhetoric and style.
2. Originally, al-Banna did not approve of party politics as it encouraged fragmentation and disunity, whereas an Islamic nation should partake in the action of *bay'ah* (complete support and show of loyalty for one source of rule and law). However, that did not stop him from joining electoral activities in an effort to appease the government's suspicions of him and his organization.
3. The MB, alongside its independent candidates, won 17 seats in the 2000 legislative elections.
4. Law No. 162 of 1958 has been a source of contention since its effect in 1967 (the Arab–Israeli War). This law allows for arrests, censorships and military crackdowns without presenting any probable cause.
5. International organizations are barred by the Egyptian government from acting as observers to any and all electoral proceedings.
6. It has also been pointed out that another reason why many Egyptians voted 'yes' could be due to their desire to move quickly, i.e. for the country to have its first real democratic elections and establish a sense of stability in Egypt.
7. Polls (see below) have indicated that the majority of Egyptians – including the *salafist* wave – encourage the annulment of the peace treaty with Israel. In addition, there have been several media reports regarding Egypt's interests in renewing its ties with Iran in the post-Mubarak era.
8. Eight out of ten Egyptians (81%) think religious leaders are having a good influence on the country.
9. The new electoral law decrees that in one-third of the seats which represent the smallest districts, candidates are to be directly elected, and the remaining two-thirds are to be determined by a proportional party-list competition (Tadros 2011).
10. The FJP won 40% of the seats, while the *salafist* party – Ḥizb al-Nūr – won 20% of the seats.
11. Members and supporters of almost every party that did not contain an Islamist agenda and which was not part of the democratic alliance participated in these protests.

References

Abaza, K., 2006. *Political Islam and regime survival in Egypt*. Policy Focus No. 51, January. Washington, DC: Washington Institute for Near East Policy. Available from: http://www.scribd.com/doc/20890623/Political-Islam-and-Regime-Survival-in-Egypt [Accessed 28 February 2012].

Abdel-Latif, Omayma and Ottaway, M., 2007. *Women in Islamist movements: toward an Islamist model of women's activism*. Carnegie Middle East Center No. 2, June. Available from: http://www.carnegieendowment.org/2007/07/10/women-in-islamist-movements-toward-islamist-model-of-women-s-activism/mvs [Accessed 28 February 2012].

Anon., 2007. *The citizen's guide to ballot on constitutional amendments in March 26, 2007*, on the official government website set up at the time. Available from: http://constitution.sis.gov.eg/en/enconst1.htm (FN No. 36, p. 14). *In*: *Elections in Egypt: state of permanent emergency incompatible with free and fair vote*. Human Rights Watch, December 2010. Available from: http://www.hrw.org/en/reports/2010/11/23/elections-egypt [Accessed 3 June 2011].

BBC, 2011. *Profile: Egypt's Muslim Brotherhood*. BBC, 9 February. Available from: http://www.bbc.co.uk/news/world-middle-east-12313405 [Accessed 12 February 2011].

Bradley, M., 2010a. Egypt rejects civilian observers over 'security' fears. *The National*, 26 November. Available from: http://www.thenational.ae/news/worldwide/middle-east/egypt-rejects-civilian-observers-over-security-fears?pageCount=0 [Accessed 26 November 2010].

Bradley, M., 2010b. Ruling party risks Egypt slipping through tight grip. *The National*, 28 November. Available from: http://www.thenational.ae/unassigned-content/polls/ruling-party-risks-egypt-slipping-through-tight-grip?pageCount=0 [Accessed 29 November 2010].

Brown, N.J., 2011. The Muslim Brotherhood as helicopter parent. *Foreign Policy*, 27 May. Available from: http://mideast.foreignpolicy.com/posts/2011/05/27/the_muslim_brotherhood_as_helicopter_parent [Accessed 3 June 2011].

Chammah, M., 2011. Listening to the Muslim Brotherhood. *Montréal Review*, April. Available from: http://www.themontrealreview.com/2009/Listening-to-the-Muslim-Brotherhood.php [Accessed 10 April 2011].

Chams El Dine, C., 2011. Egypt's 25th January: a revolution and its roots. *Montréal Review*, March. Available from: http://www.themontrealreview.com/2009/Egypt-25th-January-a-revolution-and-its-roots.php [Accessed 10 April 2011].

Dabbash, H. and El-Waziry, H., 2011. Brotherhood leader: media highlights mistakes to disparage group. *Al Masry Al Youm*, 28 May. Available from: http://www.almasryalyoum.com/en/node/454611 [Accessed 29 May 2011].

Dede, A.Y., 2008. *Islamism, state control over religion and social identity: Turkey and Egypt*. Thesis (PhD), Western Michigan University, Kalamazoo, MI.

El Deeb, S., 2011. *3 new political parties register in Egypt*. Associated Press, 15 June. Available from: http://en.news.maktoob.com/20090000803224/3_new_political_parties_register_in_Egypt/Article.htm [Accessed 15 June 2011].

El-Hennawy, N., 2011a. Brotherhood divided over Friday's protests. *Al Masry Al Youm Online*, 26 May. Available from: http://www.almasryalyoum.com/node/452783 [Accessed 28 February 2012].

El-Hennawy, N., 2011b. Brotherhood reformist launches campaign, reveals divisions. *Al Masry Al Youm Online*, 13 May. Available from: http://www.almasryalyoum.com/en/node/435125 [Accessed 13 May 2011].

El-Hennawy, N., 2011c. Defying leadership, Brotherhood youth form new party. *Al Masry Al Youm Online*, 21 June. Available from: http://www.almasryalyoum.com/en/node/470079 [Accessed 21 June 2011].

El-Hennawy, N., 2011d. Political freedom, competition drives rifts between Muslim Brotherhood factions. *Al Masry Al Youm Online*, 24 March. Available from: http://www.almasryalyoum.com/en/node/372967 [Accessed 20 April 2011].

Falk, R., 2011. *Egypt's Berlin Wall moment*, Al-Jazeera, 8 February. Available from: http://english.aljazeera.net/indepth/opinion/2011/02/201127952299253 77.html [Accessed 20 April 2011].

Hauslohner, A., 2010. Available from: http://www.time.com/time/world/article/0,8599,2033050,00.html?xid=rss-fullworld-yahoo [Accessed 30 November 2010]. *Egypt's elections and the impersonation of democracy*, Time.com, 27 November.

Hellyer, H.A., 2011. Partisanship can still sink Egypt's national project. *The National*, 23 March. Available from: http://www.thenational.ae/thenationalconversation/comment/partisanship-can-still-sink-egypts-national-project?pageCount=0 [Accessed 24 March 2011].

Hendawi, H., 2011a. *Islamists look for gains in Egypt's freer politics*. Associated Press, 5 April. Available from: http://news.yahoo.com/s/ap/20110405/ap_on_re_mi_ea/ml_egypt_rising_islamists [Accessed 10 April 2011].

Hendawi, H., 2011b. *Mubarak's fall sparks Islamists' rise in politics*. Associated Press, 28 February. Available from: http://en.news.maktoob.com/20090000603048/Mubarak_sfallsparksIslamists_riseinpolitics/Article.htm [Accessed 3 March 2011].

Hope, B., 2011a. A Coptic Christian's reasons for backing the Muslim Brotherhood. *The National*, 22 June. Available from: http://www.thenational.ae/news/worldwide/middle-east/a-coptic-christians-reasons-for-backing-the-muslim-brotherhood?pageCount=0 [Accessed 22 June 2011].

Hope, B., 2011b. Egypt recognises new Muslim Brotherhood political party. *The National*, 8 June. Available from: http://www.thenational.ae/news/worldwide/middle-east/egypt-recognises-new-muslim-brotherhood-political-party?pageCount=0 [Accessed 11 June 2011].

Hope, B., 2011c. Egyptian election campaigns kick off. *The National*, 3 November. Available from: http://www.thenational.ae/news/worldwide/middle-east/egyptian-election-campaigns-kick-off?pageCount=0 [Accessed 3 November 2011].

Keath, L. and Hendawi, H., 2011. *Egypt: Muslim Brotherhood plans political party*. Associated Press, 15 February. Available from: http://news.yahoo.com/s/ap/20110215/ap_on_re_mi_ea/ml_egypt [Accessed 20 February 2011].

Kirkpatrick, D.D. and Goodman, J.D., 2011. Muslim Brotherhood in Egypt to be political party. *New York Times*, 15 February. Available from: http://www.nytimes.com/2011/02/16/world/middleeast/16brotherhood.html?_r=1 [Accessed 13 April 2011].

Korany, B., 1998. Restricted democratization from above. *In*: B. Korany, R. Brynen and P. Noble, eds. *Political liberalization and democratization in the Arab World*, Vol. 2: *Comparative Experiences*. London: Lynne Rienner, 39–70.

Levinson, C., 2011. Brothers' in Egypt present two faces. *Wall Street Journal*, 15 February. Available from: http://online.wsj.com/article/SB10001424052748704629004576135882819143872.html [Accessed 21 February 2011].

Lynch, M., 2011. Uncertainty and optimism in Egypt. *Foreign Policy*, 12 June. Available from: http://lynch.foreignpolicy.com/posts/2011/06/12/tense_times_in_egypt [Accessed 28 February 2012].

Mahmoud, H., 2011. Muslim Brotherhood's 'Freedom and Justice' papers soon to be submitted. *IkhwanWeb*, 8 April. Available from: http://www.ikhwanweb.com/article.php?id=28362 [Accessed 20 April 2011].

Majdoub, T., 2011. *Egyptians say 'yes' to military's post-Mubarak plans*. Yahoo News, 20 March. Available from: http://www.bayoubuzz.com/africa/203957-egyptians-say-yes-to-military-s-post-mubarak-plans-(afp) [Accessed 28 February 2012].

Al Masry Al Youm Online, 2011. Salafis to run in Egypt's upcoming parliament race. *Al Masry Al Youm Online*, 14 April. http://www.almasryalyoum.com/en/node/387264 [Accessed 28 February 2012].

Michael, M., 2011. *Egypt's Muslim Brotherhood eyes big political role*. Reuters, 1 May. Available from: http://en.news.maktoob.com/20090000718556/Egypt_s_Muslim_Brotherhood_eyes_big_political_role/Article.htm [Accessed 2 May 2011].

Michael, M. and El Deeb, S., 2010. *Egypt picks parliament after roundup of opposition*, Associated Press, 27 November. Available from: http://news.yahoo.com/s/ap/20101128/ap_on_re_mi_ea/ml_egypt_elections [Accessed 30 November 2010].

Mikhail, S. and Perry, T., 2011. *New party shows deep political change in new Egypt*. Reuters, 19 February. Available from: http://jasminhim.posterous.com/new-party-shows-deep-political-change-in-new [Accessed 28 February 2012].

Mogahed, D., 2011. *What Egyptian women (and men) want*, 10 March. Abu Dhabi Gallup Center. Available from: http://www.foreignpolicy.com/articles/2011/03/10/what_egyptian_women_and_men_want?page=full [Accessed 10 April 2011].

Nicoll, A. and Johnstone, S., 2011. Egyptians choose order over further political upheaval. *Strategic Comments (The International Institute for Strategic Studies)*, 17 (March). Available from: http://www.iiss.org/publications/strategic-comments/past-issues/volume-17-2011/march/egyptians-choose-order-over-further-political-upheaval/ [Accessed 30 April 2011].

PBS Frontline Series, 2011a. *Interview with Heba Morayef*. PBS Frontline Series, 22 February. Available from: http://www.pbs.org/wgbh/pages/frontline/revolution-in-cairo/interviews/heba-morayef.html [Accessed 23 March 2011].

PBS Frontline Series, 2011b. *Interview with Amr Hamzawy*. PBS Frontline Series, 22 February. Available from: http://www.pbs.org/wgbh/pages/frontline/revolution-in-cairo/interviews/amr-hamzawy.html [Accessed 23 March 2011].

Pew Research Center, 2011. *U.S. wins no friends, end of treaty with Israel sought*. 25 April. Pew Research Center. Available from: http://pewglobal.org/2011/04/25/egyptians-embrace-revolt-leaders-religious-parties-and-military-as-well/ [Accessed 30 April 2011].

Saleh, Y., 2011. *Egypt's Muslim Brotherhood expels presidential hopeful*. Reuters, 21 June. Available from: http://www.reuters.com/article/2011/06/21/us-egypt-muslim-brotherhood-idUSTRE75K61L20110621 [Accessed 22 June 2011].

Sennott, C.M., 2011. Inside the Muslim Brotherhood: Parts 1 & 2: How should the world engage with this political player? *Global Post*, 22 February. Available from: http://www.globalpost.com/dispatch/egypt/110222/inside-muslim-brotherhood-part-2 [Accessed 2 March 2011].

Sheffer, S., 2011. Muslim Brotherhood tells Salafi leaders to tone down harsh speech. *Bikya Masr*, 2 November. Available from: http://bikyamasr.com/47161/muslim-brotherhood-tells-salafi-leaders-to-tone-down-harsh-speech/ [Accessed 3 November 2011].

Shehata, S., 2011. Islamism in Egypt: legitimate concerns? *Ahram Online*, 20 April. Available from: http://english.ahram.org.eg/NewsContent/4/0/10405/Opinion/Islamism-in-Egypt-legitimate-concerns.aspx [Accessed 20 April 2011].

Shenker, J. and Whitaker, B., 2011. The Muslim Brotherhood uncovered. *The Guardian*, 8 February. Available from: http://www.guardian.co.uk/world/2011/feb/08/egypt-muslim-brotherhood-uncovered [Accessed 9 February 2011].

Stanton, C., 2010. Brotherhood win no seats in first round of Egypt vote. *The National*, 8 February. Available from: http://www.thenational.ae/news/worldwide/middle-east/brotherhood-win-no-seats-in-first-round-of-egypt-vote [Accessed 30 December 2010].

Tadros, S., 2011. The Muslim Brotherhood's shrewd election tactics. *NationalReview.com*, 31 October. Available from: http://www.nationalreview.com/corner/281746/muslim-brotherhoods-shrewd-election-tactics-samuel-tadros [Accessed 2 November 2011].

Tarek, S., 2011. Muslim Brotherhood party addresses the poor in first popular conference. *Al Ahram English*, 29 October. Available from: http://english.ahram.org.eg/NewsContent/1/64/25384/Egypt/Politics-/Muslim-Brotherhood-party-addresses-the-poor-in-fir.aspx [Accessed 2 November 2011].

The Abu Dhabi Gallup Center, 2011. *Egypt: from Tahrir to transition: Egyptians on their assets and challenges and what leaders should do about it*. June. Available from: http://www.abudhabigallupcenter.com/147896/Egypt-Tahrir-Transition.aspx [Accessed 28 February 2012].

The International Republican Institute (IRI), 2011. *IRI Egypt Index: summary*. 5 June. IRI. Available from: http://media.washingtonpost.com/wp-srv/world/documents/IRI_Egypt_Index_April_14-27_2011.pdf [Accessed 28 February 2012].

United Nations Development Programme (UNDP), 2010. *Egypt Human Development Report 2010*. Available from: http://www.undp.org.eg/Portals/0/NHDR%202010%20english.pdf [Accessed 28 February 2012].

Repercussions of the Arab movements for democracy on the Saudi street

Mohammed Iben Sunitan

Head of the National SAS Center for Public Opinion and Research

Introduction

This paper posits a reading of the repercussions of the current movements on the Arab street, on the Saudi street in particular, and offers a brief account of the Saudi opposition since the establishment of the state. It constitutes an analysis and not a treatment of this historical moment in light of the legacy of political sociology; if it does contribute some proposals in passing – dictated by the occasion – it is where the Arab revolutions for the sake of democracy evince the fall of the Berlin Wall and that, as such, they ought to yield results tantamount in importance. Yet, this is in the realization that we are unable to make an early assessment of the results and expectations that the Arab revolutions have projected onto the region, as there are manifold complexities and zigzagging convolutions and they have yet to come to rest. There is no 'political Richter scale' to measure the outpouring of people; however, we would affirm that the popular Arab political catalyst and driving force has been unleashed.

It has begun to sink into the consciousness of all Saudis, as is the case with all Arab peoples, that the people (*al–shaʿb*) can change their reality even if they fear, with manifest trepidation, the consequences of attempting to change this reality. They are at a crossroads: the Yemeni, Libyan and Syrian models, on the one hand, and the Tunisian and Egyptian ones, on the other.

A historical overview of the opposition in Saudi Arabia

Since its inception, Saudi Arabia and its political leadership has confronted opposition – an opposition vacillating between armed opposition and military coup and an opposition centred on remonstrative protest and the drawing up of petitions. During the reign of King ʿAbd al–ʿAzız there occurred the armed clash at al-Sablah in 1929 when the Bedouin tribes known as the Ikhwan, whom the King had utilized to unify the Kingdom (at the most minimal or no cost), rose up and were crushed. This single event almost threatened to abort the attempt at unity and all its gains. There would be other incidents such as the attempted coup by officer al–Shamrānī within the fledging military institution; then the movement at the College of Internal Security Forces; and later the movement of the Air Force Officers. In addition were the movements of the free emirs followed by nationalists, Ba'athists, communists, and then those protesting the introduction of television and girls' schools, as well as the occupation of the precincts of the *masjid al–ḥaram* in Mecca under the leadership of Juhayman al–ʿUtaybī – a latter-day descendent of the Ikhwān – in a bloody battle in shadow of the *kaʿbah*, the precursors and consequences of which resembled those at al-Sablah. Those who participated in both events hailed from Bedouin tribes who saw that the state owed its existence to their military struggle for its security and the strength of their numbers. Yet despite this they were marginalized politically, developmentally and economically and the highest administrative levels of state were devoid of 'sagacious, capable and well qualified persons among them', as I have clarified in my *Saudi Elites* (2005). These events were subsequently followed by the protests over the presence of foreign forces in Saudi Arabia in the Gulf Wars beginning in 1990.

During the reign of King Saʿūd previous to that, the state witnessed an economic downturn that led to a deficit that precluded the payment of salaries to employees for more than nine months, and dissatisfaction rippled through the various strata of society. There appeared an opposition represented by an educated cadre in the armed forces and a civilian one, as well as Saudi workers at ARAMCO who were disgruntled as a result of the exploitation by the Americans within the company and the deprivation of Arab Saudi workers of their right to work. As for the opposition of intellectuals, there crystallized in their formation a secret revolutionary democratic organization called The National Reform Front which announced a number of goals (Iben Sunitan 2005, p. 35). This occurred simultaneously with the establishment of two newspapers in the Eastern Province: *al–Fajr al–Jadīd* (*The New Dawn*) and *Akhbār al–Ẓahrān* (*The Dhahran News*). The government arrested the members of the Front and closed the newspapers.

In the same period, 60 years ago, the Organization of School Students was set up in al–Qaṣīm; and while it might seem strange, their primary demand was the disbanding of the *amr bi–l–maʿrūf wa nahī ʿan al–munkar* (vice squad/moral disciplinarian) groups who had engaged in skirmishes with the students in Buraydah. Also, among their demands were educational reform and the establishment of universities.

In 1956 King Saʿūd undertook a visit to the Eastern Province, and the opposition met him with slogans defying imperialism and demanding the closure and evacuation of the American base. The result was the promulgation of a royal decree criminalizing protests and punishing those involved in such with prison terms, not to exceed three years.

Demands have continued and in the last five years there has been more than one communiqué and petition in addition to articles all demanding reform and affirming the necessity of it.

In the Saudi political experience with all the opposition movements it has become clear that the Saudi political leadership has succeeded in burying them all alive, and it is that which has empowered and enabled it. Perhaps an implication of this empowerment is to concede an absolute minimum to those making demands, most importantly the extremists among the *salafists*. However, if the movement of Juhayman al–ʿUtaybī was quashed, the adoption of its demands by extremists constituted an aggravating factor both within and in confrontation with the outside, among the most important consequences of which were the events of 11 September 2001.

The matter of reform in Saudi Arabia is in the category of forbidden subjects, yet whenever an internal or external crisis occurs, the dossier of promised reform initiatives is brought out and touted to assuage tensions, only for matters to return to the previous status quo once the crisis has passed.

During the reign of King ʿAbd al–ʿAzīz, as a result of the revolt at al-Sablah, a roster (*diwān*) of fighters was set up in order to embrace and assimilate former attackers. When Faisal succeeded King Saʿūd, he promised political reforms for the transfer of power which have yet to see the light of day. During the Second Gulf War, King Fahd promulgated regulatory systemizations for governance and the regions, but that changed nothing within the status quo.

Second: the opposition after 9/11

After the events of 11 September 2001 and the appearance of many petitions and demands for far-ranging reforms, the government undertook to establish the King ʿAbd al–ʿAzīz Center for National Dialogue on the grounds that this represented an effective political policy to achieve reform. The Center embarked on a tour of the cities of the Kingdom announcing its goal of reform and asserting that it would translate the ideas of citizens into tangible reality. At the conclusion of every meeting the end result would be the sending of a telegram of thanks and acknowledgement to the King followed by newspaper coverage of the meeting, whose records would then be filed in the archives. If reform occurs, it consists of little more than raising the salaries of employees of the state, the benefit of which is swiftly offset by a corresponding rise in prices, leading only to increased pressures on the lives of non-governmental employees. If there were initiatives for growth and development, and there have been a number of these, their execution has been restricted to a limited number of family corporations or to the well-known names and influential personalities within the state – a matter which has rendered the miniscule size of the middle class a uniquely Saudi phenomenon, despite the fact that it spends billions of Saudi riyals annually.

In this context, we may recollect the elections for the municipal councils, which are actually fair elections but are in effect for *show*, as the influence of these councils is even less than the influence of the most junior employee of the municipality itself, even if the council is supposed to legislate, oversee and carry out decisions. We also might mention the participation of women in the Chamber of Commerce who do not meet with the men in a single session, except via telephone, along with the realization that the voice of a woman in Saudi Arabia is still considered to be provocative.

If these millions spent on dialogues, political propaganda and foreign relations with the outside were channelled appropriately, they could – at a minimum – effect developmental reforms that might assuage the social mood, even if temporarily. However, all that the National Dialogue initiative has achieved is to split off the Saudi people and fragment them into various currents and trends from the *jihadist–salafist* ones to those that see obedience to the sultan as mandatory, even if he whips your back and takes your money. There are also scattered informed opinions and ideas, which *salafists* describe as trends or currents, and subdivide into ‘modern’ and ‘liberal’. These divisions in society raise a cry at night to the extent that one imagines that a march of millions will materialize with the rising of the sun; however, just before the dawn, everyone runs humbly to obey and carry out orders. The furthest limits of bravery of the most audacious are to be found in the penning of articles in which the author spends more time editing and scrutinizing than he does writing for fear of the editor-in-chief, whom he fears more than any member of the political leadership. Therefore, he uses his wicked cunning to get the article through to publication and this alone is really his only ultimate aim and highest hope.

Theorizing in political writings is rare in the extreme. Political writings have appeared in stories that are termed ‘fiction’, but which are, entirely, commentaries on that which is not said where the taboos practised clandestinely are greater by far than those in open societies. Similarly, they deal with issues such as women driving cars, lifting their veils in market places, or travelling on aeroplanes without a male guardian from among their unmarriageable relations. In this, the *salafist* and political intellectual trends can be summed up in their mutual disdain for one another, where the weapon of each against the other is the ruling political authority. The ruling Saudi political authority frees the hand of the *salafists* to accuse the intellectuals of unbelief and charge them with heretical sin; while, on the other hand, it opens up the newspapers for intellectuals to attack the *salafists* and accuse them of zealotry and extremism. As for the final arbiter of all – to adjudicate in all their cases, it is the ruling political authority. Therefore, if a *salafist* goes to the ruling authority to complain about an intellectual and cast aspersions and doubts on his religiosity, he finds that the intellectual has preceded him in this and accused him, before the sultan, of holding back the development of the country and causing problems with Western states. All the cards of the game are, in fact, in the hands of the strongest player, which is the ruling political authority to whom authority has been delegated as the *walī al-amr*. As a poet might say, ‘O my heart do not grieve and be at rest for there is a long night before you.’

As for the other segment which the National Dialogue managed to split off, it is that of Shīʿite intellectuals who engaged – despite their cultural and activist endeavours – to constrain their reform initiatives to the freedom of worship according to the *madhab* (sect) and practice of its rituals, with the exception of some demands pertaining to the rights of citizenship represented in themes such as ‘a perspective on the present state of the nation and its future’ and ‘partners in the nation’.

These currents, with all their ideologies, are entirely removed from the dictates of the present stage gripping the region, due to their distance from the national reform initiative and their agreement to shared national, economic, political and developmental commonalities.

Debate between the various sides does not arrive at what is correct but rather can be labelled fanaticism against the culture of ‘the other’, and in this situation one might evoke the Ottoman–Safavid conflict. The major question for all is: Why should recourse to *madhab* constitute the requisite means of expression instead of civil rights and shared national commonalities about which all should rally around?

Saudi Arabia is in need of social engineering in governance and administration of social diversity; and perhaps most important is emphasizing and reinforcing the principle of citizenship through just distribution of resources and power as well as effective participation at the highest and mid-levels of state. This is for the reason that every society that lacks social justice is destined for discord, disunity and factionalism, whereas successful administration of a plural society promotes and reinforces national identity and the political legitimacy of the state.

Third: Saudi leadership

The Saudi leadership has stood against all the Arab revolutions out of a fear of contagion and that Saudis will absorb the culture of demonstrations and protests. If Arab countries of the Middle East from the region of the Tigris and Euphrates to the strait of the Bāb al-Mandeb in Yemen are transformed into new regimes according to the democratic concepts of the youth and the demands to which the regimes of inherited/dynastic rule find it difficult to adjust – especially as among these are the 2010 revolution in Egypt that evoked in the states of the Gulf memories of the events of the previous Egyptian revolution of 1952 and their effects on the entire region – this will pose a serious conundrum for the rulership. The Saudi leadership realizes the magnitude of the repercussions of these revolutions that shatter their composure, but it is unable to do anything as it is divided between a (rightist extremist) camp that sees that reforms only whet the appetites of the Saudi people for a gradual transition towards a constitutional monarchy, which is a violation of precedent, and a moderate middle camp – at the head of which is the King – that sees that reforms perpetuate the royal family in power and which looks on the people with new eyes in the wake of the Arab revolutions. There are other internal matters that have led to a dead end in thinking about how to administer society in accordance with changes to life in the Arab world.

We have not yet put our hands on a project of state, but rather there is a project of the ruling family that sways according to the ebb and flow of the Saudi street, and in the channels of information and web blogs that observe and are finely attuned to external/foreign reactions more than internal/domestic ones.

The Saudi leadership stood by Yemeni President ‘Ali ‘Abdullah al-Ṣāleḥ at the exclusion of all the other Arab heads of state besieged by revolutions – aligning with him for political reasons, among which was his position against the Ḥūthīs, who had spilled over the border with Saudi Arabia. The political considerations operative in this context deserve note:

- The region of Ṣaʿdah is inhabited simultaneously by Yemeni–Saudi tribes, the people of which are brothers and cousins as well as fellow clan and tribe members who overlap in both habitation and geography, which facilitates crossing the border, infiltration and escape and makes controlling them difficult.
- The Ḥūthīs have raised the sectarian banner and this is what provides Islam with a firm toehold in Yemen, and in a strategic region of Saudi Arabia, in particular.
- The matter of the border issue between the two countries, which has been settled by agreement just recently, is critical given that Saudi Arabia is afraid that this agreement might be annulled by an incumbent new regime, especially given that extremist Yemeni demands and claims that penetrate deep into Saudi territory as far as the region Ṭāʾif.
- In the absence of the ‘Ali ‘Abdullah Ṣāleḥ‘s regime, al–Qāʿidah will gain strength in Yemen whereas Saudi Arabia from the standpoint of its security has, up till now, been able to repel the cross-border incursions of al–Qāʿidah effectively.

The Arab revolutions have eliminated some terrifying bugbears, which Arab regimes used to employ every now and then to considerable effect, such as the threats of tribalism, sectarianism, political Islam, al–Qāʿidah, terrorism, and other internal and external challenges. These all melted away and dissolved in revolution and patriotism when the entire nation became like a single entity, a single individual, a single tribe and a single sect – transforming the demands of citizens that they no longer be regarded as subjects and residents, but as citizens and decision-makers.

Fourth: Saudi elites

Saudi Arabia lacks effective elites, whether in the ranks of the masses or in the Saudi leadership itself, with the exception of the *salafist* religious current and whoever supports it *among the political leadership* to shore up its centre against the other group – be it the ruling family, on the one hand, or to contain the general popular *salafist* trend, on the other. There is no civil society, nor are there political parties or an influential bloc, just as there are no intellectual trends or trade-based affiliations. Furthermore, there is no role worthy of mention for the sheikhs of tribes, despite the tribal character of the state. There are, however, writers of articles in newspapers whose influence does not even reach the classrooms of university students, despite the fact that most of the writers are university professors.

Fifth: the youth

The Arab revolutions engendered a political consciousness for reform in the Saudi youth. They possess latent youthful energies and resourceful innovativeness and vision; and such can be perceived through internet websites; however, they lack symbols or a civil society capable of developing this consciousness and linking it decisively to presenting demands to society and the ruling family.

There is no yardstick for measuring the repercussions of the Arab revolutions on Saudi society, as the mapping of public opinion in Saudi Arabia is deprived of a free press, civil society, polling and public opinion research centres, as well as censuses such as those of the Kuwait model. The source of information is the apex of the pyramid, and there is no feedback that ascends from the bottom to the top of the pyramid, but rather the anticipated feedback is that of the security bureaucracy and apparatus in all their various specializations, and most of them detain the good and let the bad go free.

The masses follow and do not lead – watching and waiting to be the *tenth* and *not* the first. Every individual in society wants someone else to stand up for him and is not even willing to make the sacrifice of lending his voice, where he makes every sort of calculation (the calculations of a miserly accountant); however, change will not be handed to him on a golden platter. Freedom has its price and democracy its costs, and gain is according to the extent of the hazard confronted.

There are those among the youth, and they are few, who have begun to sense the importance for the youth to be a part of the political process and not remain marginalized, like the other members of society who are satisfied to remain on the sidelines. Is this political dissolution or a reality of society?

Saudi citizens have imbibed, like their other brethren in the Gulf, the culture of the political lexicon which is connected to a wide array of civil society concerns: democracy; human rights; the free citizen; constitutions; laws; the democratic transfer of power; the independence of branches of authority; the just distribution of resources; political pluralism; anti-corruption efforts, regionalism and tribalism; breaking up gangs monopolizing resources, contracts and high offices; business councils; the freedom of the press and public forums; the freedom of thought and expression; the freedom to raise one's voice; the absence of censorship and surveillance of internet sites; respect for human being and reinforcement of the principles of citizenship; the expansion of local government; perpetual growth; reinforcement of the authority of the judiciary and its independence; reinforcement of institutions of oversight; the right of people to health insurance and free education; and the freedom of sect and religious creed – and that people should not be compelled to belong to a single *madhab*. All these precepts have become requisite topics of discussion in youth society, sitting rooms and clubs.

We have to know that the contemporary Arab revolutions are not propelled by intellectuals, thinkers, civil society, civil institutions, the army, the outside or any of the traditional influences. The true motivator is to be found in the regimes themselves wallowing in corruption and immersed in autocracy and the underestimation and under-appreciation of their peoples to a degree that they can no longer bear, and hence people who had stifled and suppressed their accumulated reactions exploded forth naturally like a volcano at the opportune time.

In any case, nothing assures us of our safety from the events transpiring in the region; and we cannot take solace in the apparent peace and calm imparted by the map of widely dispersed security forces. However, up until now there has been nothing to give a modicum of hope that regimes in the Gulf, among which Saudi Arabia is the largest, have comprehended their peoples and their needs. Although they do recognize what is happening around them, they are still in a coma, shocked by the magnitude and gravity of the realities and current events. There is no lifeboat to rescue the Kingdom from surrounding events in the Arab world and no one knows what the future holds or can control, except when the people of the nation are satisfied and real reforms are being sought to the furthest possible extent. Who among us would have expected what happened to Zine El Abidine and Hosni Mubarak so quickly, easily and at such little cost?

Conclusion

I see that it is incumbent upon the intellectual, cultural and religious elites in Saudi Arabia gradually to begin undertaking reforms along the following lines:

- The election of half the Consultative Council – Majlis al–Shūrā (i.e., as opposed to appointment of its members).
- Enabling the Consultative Council to oversee revenues of the state and their expenditure as well as the preparation of the budget.
- Restricting the share of royal family members in sovereign governmental positions to ministries only, without assigning them public positions, including the administration of regions and without combining power and money, which is a strategy followed by King ʿAbd al–ʿAzīz, along with allocating for the Consultative Council – Majlis al–Shūrā – whatever share it requires.
- Establishing a Judicial Council – Majlis al–Qaḍāʾ – elected by judges and prominent senior *ʿulamā* of various *madhabs* (sects) that will be charged with responsibility for: appointing and removing judges; promulgating a law for the judiciary and its regulations, which neither the King nor the government has the authority to overturn or overrule; and to allocate its budget from the government.
- Separating courts of public prosecution from the Ministry of Internal Affairs and affiliating them to the proposed Judicial Council – Majlis al–Qaḍāʾ – and providing *habeas corpus*, entailing the prohibition of arresting someone or imprisoning him except through due process of the law and a court ruling issued against him by the Court of Justice.
- Defining a new national pact that creates a new relation based on Saudis being citizens instead of residents and partners instead of subjects.

- Narrowing disparities in income between social classes and regions, maintaining a balance in development and the distribution of resources throughout the entire kingdom. Along these lines, as it has been said: if you see a society divided into an 'A' and a 'B', then wait for the revolution.
- That the highest and mid-levels of administration be a public right for all those who are capable and qualified among citizens, regardless of their class, *madhab* or region; where preference is accorded to those who are best qualified and most competent, capable and worthy to manage a diverse society.
- That citizens should be free in their religious choices and social traditions and customs, without the domination of one *madhab* over another or the customs and traditions of one region over another, and that religious freedom be only restricted to rituals of worship only.

An outcry of voices must be raised for society in the Gulf to avoid the catastrophic results of the events in Syria, Libya and Yemen because not every ruler in power is a Zine El Abidine or a Hosni Mubarak and not every army is like that of Tunisia or Egypt. Offering advice, or making demands and opposition, is only in the interest of ruling families who are the cornerstones of society and part of our social fabric; and we do not seek except what is best for them and for us if there is sound thinking and reasoning, judicious opinion or penetrating insight, or even, simply, fear for their position in power.

If ruling families in the Gulf desire safety from the volcano of Arab revolutions, then the guidance of rational thinking and sound reasoning and their enlightened ideas will be the like of lighthouses, life preservers and lifeboats assuring security for us and them since we are part of them as they are part of us.

Reference

Iben Sunitan, M., 2005. *Al-Nukhab al–Saʿūdīyah: Dirāsah fī al–Taḥawwulāt wa al–Ikhfāqāt*, 2nd ed. PhD Theses Series No. 48. Beirut, Centre for Arab Unity Studies.

Repercussions of the Arab movements for democracy in Bahrain

Ali Mohammed Fakhro

Bahraini thinker and politician

Foreword

History confirms that the countries of the Arab Gulf all throughout the past century have been influenced by the various political events of the Arab Mashriq (East) and have interacted with cultural and conceptual changes of the Arab world at large.

After the eruption of the two successful revolutions in Tunisia and Egypt their after effects reached many countries of both the Arab Mashriq and the Maghreb, and despite disparities raised the following question: Would Arab Gulf societies be affected by this revolutionary propagation? The answer came quickly – first in Bahrain, then in the Eastern Province of Saudi Arabia, and subsequently in and around Muscat and, to a limited extent, in Kuwait. This paper will be restricted to Bahrain.

The reasons why Bahrain has been affected by propagation of the revolutionary wave

Bahrain was affected much more than other Gulf states by events and this is due to a number of reasons, the most important of which are as follows:

- The existence of related constitutional, legal, and life conditions and problematics. While these have shown the need for dialogue, the search for reasonable solutions has long remained suspended, waiting to be put forward in times of political unrest. Specific examples include:

  - Contention over the legitimacy and core articles of the 2002 'grant' Constitution when compared with the 'contractual' Constitution of 1973.
  - The electoral laws that the opposition sees as prejudicial against more just representation of Shīʿite voters.
  - The powers and authority of the elected legislative assembly (*majlis*) as well as the question of its independence and relation to appointed Shūrā (Consultative) Council.
  - What is termed by the opposition as 'political naturalization' (i.e. gaining political citizenship).
  - The issue of ownership and the impact on prices of competitive bidding over very sizeable off-shore underwater maritime properties and the prospect of their reclamation (from the sea) that have a negative impact on residential policies. This is with the existence of long waiting lists for housing, realizing that the wait may take twenty years before individuals can obtain a modest house or a limited loan.

- Financial and administrative corruption.
- The existence of active public political associations with members in Parliament and major social and media activities. The existence of organized unions with an historical pedigree, some of which are connected to the political associations, in addition to highly diverse civil, professional, rights and women's institutions with political connections.
- The existence of a politically militant street since the 1950s capable of mass, wide-scale and committed political mobilization.
- Coincidentally, the occasion of 14 February 2011 marked the passing of ten years of work on the National Pact along with an inclination by the King and the political forces to evaluate the democratic experience after the Pact and to initiate a social dialogue for the development of this experiment for the purpose of attaining to higher levels of democracy. When it happened that the 14 February anniversary fell in the midst of the major Arab events, it was only natural that the precepts, goals and means deployed – depending largely on social media and carried out by the youth in Egypt, Tunisia and elsewhere, who were not organized into political parties – would have an effect on Bahrainis, especially on peers of the same age group.
- It is possible to add two additional factors. First, the initiative of King Hamad bin Isa Āl Khalīfah in contacting some of the political leaderships in order to confirm that he, personally, is considering undertaking an evaluative review of the post-National Pact experience and subsequently of developing the democratic process. Second is the case of 300 or more people incarcerated and awaiting trial for a number of months and belonging politically to two associations that have dissociated from the Wefaq movement (i.e. the Islamic National Accord Association) – the mother association – that have refused to integrate into parliamentary life, along with their belief in the necessity of militarizing the street on numerous occasions.

These are some of the reasons that have made Bahrain more receptive to the impact of emotional and portentous events in the Arab world.

The vacillation between security concerns and political ones

Many had the impression, from the decision made by demonstrators to descend onto the streets on 14 February, that the demonstrations would be peaceful in the extreme: it was understood that demonstrators would not be throwing stones, setting fire to cars or raising non-Bahraini flags. It can be said without equivocation that the demonstrations were peaceful and orderly on the first day and possibly that they could be considered a type of exercise in free speech of the sort guaranteed by the Constitution and the National Pact. However, the killing of a demonstrator on the first day and another on the second, during the funeral procession of the first, altered the situation radically. Blood had been spilled and the death of the two martyrs added to the momentum of events. The situation was sufficiently precarious for the King to appear personally on Bahraini television and to convey his regret for what had happened, announcing that there would be an investigative committee. Similarly, the Interior Minister, Lieutenant-General Shaykh Rashid bin Abdullah Āl Khalīfah, offered his apologies for what had occurred and ordered an immediate investigation.

These were two pacifying steps, stemming from a high sense of responsibility among the leadership at the political and moral levels. Yet, it was only about eighteen hours after these two pioneering steps that demonstrators were attacked at the Pearl Roundabout (*dawwār al–lu'lu'*) in the early dawn hours, and the death of four protestors was announced. This development was a shock and threatened to incite sectarian strife. In order to calm things down, the King ordered the withdrawal of the armed forces and permitted the peaceful protest to proceed at Pearl Roundabout.

The return of the demonstrators to the roundabout

The deceased protestors would inspire a thousand others among the living to speak in their names, and thousands of Bahrainis would remain on Pearl Roundabout over the following three weeks, as well as wandering about the streets in clamorous protests. In this confused atmosphere the protestors at the Roundabout, along with the political associations rushing to seize the moment, committed what can be considered errors and mistakes. Among the most significant of these were the following:

- The inclination in some of the daily addresses towards stereotypical defamation of some of the major personalities of the rulership.
- Raising the threshold of their demands to unreasonable limits, such as the bringing down of the regime (*isqāt al–niẓām*), i.e. bringing down the ruling family, despite the fact that such a demand would nullify the essential historic bright points in the post-independence experience of Bahrain and demolish the social and constitutional contracts between society and the ruling family. Such a call would also negate the import of the referendum conducted by a commission of the United Nations at the beginning of the 1970s that confirmed the Arab character of Bahrain and the satisfaction of most with the rule of the Āl Khalīfah family; and the like of the 1973 Constitution or that of 2002; and the 2000 National Work Pact that specified succession to rule by inheritance among the Āl Khalīfah family.
- The engaging by some – and here lay great disaster – in demanding the replacement of the current system of royal rule with a republican system. This represented a direct clash with the rulership, the crossing of a red line and an incentive to violence.
- Closing the street extending from Pearl Roundabout to the financial port of Bahrain – a street of the utmost importance as it constitutes the primary artery into the commercial district in the centre of the capital. Here, freedom of expression transitioned into freedom of action of a sort that cannot possibly lead to anything except hostile infringement upon the interests and rights of others. This is what happened and led Bahraini businessmen and merchants to complain publicly over what they considered to be a threat to their interests and livelihood.
- Futile actions reached a peak when a decision was taken to demonstrate in the district of al–Rifāʿ in front of the King's palace. Despite the warnings of many against such an action as being insanely futile with no value, a number of demonstrators did go to al–Rifāʿ where there were horrifying clashes with locals and security forces.
- There was the conviction of many among the Sunni leadership that what was happening was in disregard of them or, rather, was against their interests; and,

moreover, tens of thousands gathered in front of al–Fātiḥ Mosque to affirm that the Sunni street had its own demands and political positions particular to it.

If we add to this the social cleavages, the degree of complexity is clear as is the possibility of it becoming a social crisis of the first order. Here the demonstrators at the roundabouts and the rulership found themselves confronting a new scenario; and the ruling authorities reached the conviction that the balance had tipped and that it was time to deal decisively with the situation.

Thus, the Peninsula Shield Force entered Bahrain on 16 March and the country became the theatre of a regional struggle. The implementation of a national security law was announced (i.e. a state of emergency was declared), and the roundabouts were cleared of demonstrators by force – their presence vanished completely. Bahrain descended into an inferno of sectarian and social schism the like of which was previously unknown throughout its history, just as it transitioned to security solutions instead of political ones. As for the many who had the courage to make complaints as a result of their being tortured or having their dignity trampled upon – and among whom were many women – they were arrested and large numbers were brought before military tribunals where sentences of execution or life imprisonment were handed down. Officials engaged in sorting people at inspection checkpoints according to their names, which indicated their sect and the regions of their residence, etc.

Could things have possibly turned out better than they did?

Was it possible to have avoided all this? The answer would seem to be 'yes', if the following had been observed:

- No escalation in the use of force in the first days of the demonstrations, which would have prevented the peaceful movement from having been 'baptized with blood'.
- No resort to the use of erroneous slogans of the sort previously mentioned.
- Restriction of the sit-ins to the roundabouts only, thus avoiding adverse impacts on the daily lives and interests of people.
- Not involving or obstructing the main government hospital—al-Sulaymaniyah Hospital—in the political conflict, where the appropriate domain for peaceful demonstrations are the roundabouts and streets to which these should be confined so as not to jeopardize or confound the lives of citizens.
- Lack of delay on the part of political associations into entering the promised dialogue that Crown Prince Salman bin Hamad bin Isa Āl Khalīfah had advocated with the blessing of the King. The Crown Prince had put forward important points as a schedule of work for the dialogue; and here it must be stated that the fear of the political associations of losing the Bahraini street in the present and the future made them lose their balance and led them to prefer the tactical advantage over the strategic.
- Not dissipating or escalating demands, but constraining them to only the demand for reasonable constitutional amendments and political reforms to render the Representative Parliament (*majlis*) into an effective and independent institution able to achieve numerous vital reforms.
- Work with greater seriousness and more in-depth understanding to effect a balanced mutual understanding between the demands of the demonstrators at

Pearl Roundabout and those of al–Fātiḥ Mosque; this was to be done for the sake of rendering the dialogue between a diverse and understanding society and ruling authority disposed towards accepting many reform solutions.

- A different approach by the various sides to what happened previously, during the period of the national security/state-of-emergency law, with vigilant preservation of the dignity of people and basic humanity and absolute rejection of sentiments of hatred and blind malevolence and infantile defiance in what would have permitted the triumph of civil solutions over security and military ones. Exercising extremely humane sensitivity in the spirit and letter of human rights law in dealing with any accused person as well as not permitting some of those agitating to incite civil strife that would consume all.

All parties made mistakes and errors, and they lost a historic opportunity to transition towards the future through democratic outcomes.

The future is the priority

Now that the national security law/state of emergency has been lifted and the King has put forward the two slogans of rebuilding the national body (literally, rebuilding the national flesh) and returning to the table of unconditional dialogue *(al–ḥiwār ghayr mashrūṭah*), the political associations and others among the official and unofficial actors in the arena of politics and religion need to benefit from the lessons of this experience. They have to do so at the beginning of a course thousands of miles long, when only a few months ago it was a much shorter distance.

Bahrain now needs to ascend to what transcends sectarianism, tribalism and nepotism as well as abuses of the media and the madness of agitators, opportunists and those with narrow vested interests in addition to regional sectarian and political disputatiousness. This must be in conjunction with the victory of unifying patriotism and religious solidarity, mutual historical co-existence and the principles of democracy in order to become an oasis of life and peace for all its peoples within the larger context of their Arabness, Islam and the Arab world. This historic challenge must be confronted and met; and in Bahrain there are many intelligent and rational people.

Conclusion

There were high hopes that all would learn from the bitter lessons of February and March 2011 as well as from the pain and grief of the period of the state of emergency. However, it appears that the social schism now is greater, deeper and much more complicated than was anticipated by many. Bahrain has not ceased to experience an unhealthy political atmosphere; and at times it is living on the edge. The reason may be due to one or more of the following influential factors:

- The persistence of a number of external actors in making Bahrain a theatre for a war of nerves between divisive regional forces split along sectarian, political and security lines. Naturally, there are external forces that are acting according to their own agendas.
- The national dialogue called for by the King has faltered due to extreme differences of opinion about his leadership, his agenda, the relative degree to which he represents Bahrainis, and the extent of the ceiling he puts on demands or which he allows. The result of this was the withdrawal of the largest political bloc in the

country – the Wefaq group – a few days after the beginning of the dialogue and the issuing of critical communiqués – from one side or the other – and allegations of bias in the leadership of the conference. Naturally, all this led to the dashing of hopes that were tied to the effectiveness and seriousness of the dialogue.

- Lack of decisiveness in dealing with the case files that had been accumulating as a result of the events; and among these were the issue of those who were fired in the public and private sectors, whose number reached 3000 male and female citizens, as well as the issue of keeping numerous prominent persons of the political leadership incarcerated – a matter which inflames the sentiments of their followers. In addition, there is the matter of those who were brought before and sentenced in military tribunals and the necessity of referring these cases back to civilian courts. Lastly, there is also the issue of cases of murder/wrongful death due to the events and the extent of wilful wrongful intent and illegal violations or violations of human rights. Hope is now pinned to the results of the investigations being undertaken by the fact-finding commission that the King ordered to be set up with the aim of finding those responsible for the errors and infractions committed during events. People hope that the report of this commission will be the first step on the path to justice during the transitional period that must be taken in order for people to be assuaged and for justice to take its course and to bring those deserving of punishment to it.
- The persistence of an atmosphere of stultifying media campaigns replete with calumnies and slander as employed by numerous official and local media outlets. This is one of the most significant obstacles confronting rational, unbiased and forthright dialogue at the level of the general Bahraini body politic. In this context the external is mixed with the internal and the agitating individual with the ignorant group imbibed with politics.
- The lack of a solution for the parliamentary vacuum that came about as a result of the resignation of eighteen members of Parliament affiliated with the Wefaq group, and that was in the failure to find a solution for its root causes and its surrounding circumstances. Dealing with the resignation of 45% of the members of Parliament for political reasons as though such is an ordinary occurrence that does not call for more than supplementary elections – when everyone knows that a large number of voters will boycott these – is a way of dealing with the problem that will harm the image and legitimacy of the democratic parliamentary system in Bahrain.

The climax of the political travails and tribulations in Bahrain would be if the King were to order the re-instatement of those who were fired; however, days pass without a large number of them returning. He advocated a comprehensive national dialogue but it was derailed by this side or that. Despite the King's emphasis on national unity in every addresses and the integrity of the social fabric, the social schism is increasing continuously.

Is there hope for escape from this catastrophe? Yes, and that would be through a new and serious effort by the King. Just as the historic initiative of the year 2000 succeeded in bringing together all the social components of society around the unifying, progressive democratic National Pact, what is necessary and possible is to take practical balanced steps to redress the mistakes that were committed and to reactivate the Pact and review it when necessary. And in all of that to let political rationality hold sway and arbitrate, the axis of which turns on social justice and democratic policy.

Palestinian youth and the Arab Spring. Learning to think critically: a case study

Nadia Naser-Najjab

Department of Philosophy and Cultural Studies, Birzeit University, Birzeit, Palestinian Territories

The subject of this paper is a case study based on evidence gathered informally through delivery of a course at Birzeit University entitled 'Modern and Contemporary European Civilization' and from end-of-semester evaluations that asked students to reflect on the impact of the course on their lives. The author is, naturally, aware of the limitation of the methodology used in this study, and does not claim that its findings can be generalized authoritatively to a wider group of people in the Arab world. What is clear, however, if one considers reviews of internet blogs and media programme debates, is that extrapolations from this evidence have wider reference, revealing commonalities and similarities between Palestinians living in the Occupied Territories and Arab youth involved in the Arab Spring on the subject of political reform. The discussions engaged in by my students actually parallel the debates generated by traditionalists and secularists in post-revolution Egypt and Tunisia. These debates revolve around what it means to live in a civil, democratic state that grants social justice and freedoms, and crucially, at present led by scholars and politicians, address the possibility of reconciling the concept of modernity with Islam and the legislative framework of Islamic law (*sharīʿah*). It could be argued that the data collected are specific to this one case study, since Palestinians living under Israeli occupation form a unique group in the Arab world and probably are more concerned with basic issues of daily life and more sensitive to Western concepts of modernity. The significance of this data is, however, that gathered during the Arab Spring, they were based on reactions to material covered in a class which related to issues raised by the Arab revolutions, such as democracy, liberalism and revolution. Furthermore, these tentative findings suggest that more research is needed into issues such as the role of education, gender, tolerance and the reconciliation of Islam with modernity – areas of interest which are of particular importance at a time when Islamic groups are winning elections and debates on concepts of authority, democracy and liberalism occupy the foreground of media programmes in countries such as Egypt and Tunisia.

The course 'Modern and Contemporary European Civilization' uses texts by Renaissance and Enlightenment thinkers to discuss the concepts of democracy, social contract, political rights, justice, conformity, social norms and individual freedom. It encourages students[1] to question a priori assumptions, to think innovatively and to be more open to other perspectives. Using class discussions and student responses to an end-of-semester evaluation[2] about the impact of the course on their views and lives, I examine whether the course precipitated shifts in students' thinking and how students conceptualize the concept of liberal democracy in light of the Arab revolutions. In addition, I use student discussions and the current debates in Egypt and Tunisia to examine the concept of modernity[3] in relation to Islam and the state. I argue that the concepts of modernity and liberal democracy are contentious in the Arab world. Traditionalists, and even modern Islamic thinkers, struggle with the concept of a modern state because they argue that Islamic law must be a reference point for guiding state formation and governance. This is similar to my students' opinion of theories on the modern, secular state articulated by Western philosophers.

Broadcast on Arab channels, public debates examine the meaning of concepts such as democracy, freedom, social justice and pluralism in relation to regimes and religion (see below). According to Arkoun's (2006) outline of the central issue of such debates:

> In all contemporary societies, developed and underdeveloped, the most recurrent debate is the competition, or radical opposition, between the religious and the secular model in building the best polity assuring the safest and the most beneficial governance for its citizens.
>
> (p. 260)

However, much like debates observed in Egyptian and Tunisian youth, my students neither reject Western ideas outright nor accept fully, modern Islamic thought. For example, students reject the views of modern Islamic thinkers such as Nasr Hamid Abu Zayd and Jamal al-Banna, especially their contemporary reinterpretation of the Qurʾān using the concept of *ijtihād*, or independent enquiry and interpretation of *sharīʿah*. Students accuse such thinkers of preaching heresy and label them as disbelievers and atheists. Instead, students and activists tend to engage in an unacknowledged reinterpretation of Islam that occurs as needed to enact social change and develop the state so that it remains relevant to the lives of its citizens, especially during the revolutions.

Impact of the Arab Spring on Palestinian youth: authority and ideologies

The fact that youth ignited the Arab Spring was a surprise to Arab nations, especially to its thinkers and politicians. Traditionally, political parties have been the main players in political activities and in mobilizing the street. However, in the current political revolutions, the youth are the main source of leadership and mobilizing because they have refused the authority of the political parties and called for political and social change. While such change responds to modernity to a certain extent, it does not do so fully.

Palestinians' political aspirations are in line with the Arab Spring's calls for freedom, dignity and justice; they want to achieve these goals by dismantling the Israeli occupation. While in a recent poll conducted in the West Bank and the Gaza Strip on Palestinian youth, the majority of youth consider employment as their top priority, with personal freedom as number four, following covering educational expenses and corruption in Palestinian institutions. The majority of youth, 72%, are willing to demonstrate against the occupation and 57% are willing to be active in a new *intifāḍah*. However, only 18% in the West Bank and 21% in Gaza would be active in demonstrations against the Palestinian governments (Arab World for Research & Development (AWRAD) 2012). Palestinians are currently dealing with the aftermath of the second Intifada and the heavy-handed Israeli practices of social control that were implemented after the uprising; Israel constructed the wall, built settlements in the West Bank and changed the course of roads, all of which resulted in the partition of Palestinian land and the disintegration of social life. The success of the Egyptian and Tunisian revolutions inspired a sense of power and agency in youth in other Arab countries, and encouraged them to revolt. In contrast, Palestinian youth seemed to experience feelings of powerlessness and despair because they were facing a double challenge: the Israeli occupation and the internal divisions between Fatah and Hamas, which has led to the establishment of two separate authorities in the West Bank and the Gaza Strip (Roy 2004).

In spite of these feelings, Palestinian youth were inspired by the Arab revolutions to take action. They took to the streets on 15 March and called for an end to the split between Fatah and Hamas. Some voices also called for democratization of the Palestinian Liberation Organization (PLO). President Abbas immediately announced his willingness to go to Gaza to reconcile a four-year rivalry. On 27 April Fatah and Hamas signed an agreement to form a unity government. In the meantime, both parties are working on forming an interim government, with youth groups anxiously awaiting the results. Moreover, there has been an increase in Palestinian voices calling for peaceful popular resistance against the occupation to gain international support. For example, when the Israeli state confiscated over 60% of the land in the Palestinian village of Bilʿīn for building Israeli settlements and the separation wall, the people of Bilʿīn began calling for and organizing non-violent resistance in 2005. Over the years, the village has garnered widespread local and international support for its campaign. At Bilʿīn's sixth annual conference, participants called on Palestinian political parties and civil society to end the occupation by engaging in non-violent resistance (Bilin Village 2011). In addition, Palestinians created a Facebook page calling for a third Intifada through peaceful demonstrations and invited other Arab countries to join in solidarity and march to the borders on 15 March 2011 (Morrow and al-Omrani 2011).

Unlike Tunisian and Egyptian youth, however, Palestinian youth are not an integral part of the process of change. Sabri Saidam, former Palestinian Minister of Communications and Technology, told a *Haaretz* journalist that:

> there is no Palestinian Wael Ghonim [the young Google marketing executive who became a symbol of the Egyptian revolution]. … It's the issue of getting bored of the fact that they see leaders who existed for dozens of years. They don't want any leaders.
>
> (Mozgovaya 2011)

In these Arab countries, youth initiated the revolt and did so outside the system of established political parties. Arab youth refused the authority of current leaders and ideologies and instead called for the establishment of basic human rights such as freedom, justice and dignity. Palestinian youth, however, are still under the influence of political parties. When President Abbas announced his willingness to reconcile internal divisions, the main political parties concerned started negotiating and meeting, while the youth who called for that change waited on the sidelines. This is contrary to the situations in Egypt and Tunisia where youth representatives are a central part of the post-revolutionary process of change, although, perhaps, not directly in decision-making but in monitoring the political developments and being ready to revolt again.

Although it is still too early to speculate the outcome of the Arab Spring, signs of modernity can be read in the demands raised during the revolution, such as freedom of speech. However, the exact demands are still not clear. In some Arab countries, people are deeply divided by either religion or tribal affiliations. For example, in post-revolution Egypt, violence between Muslims and Christians erupted for a short time. Internal fighting in Libya and Yemen is also taking place during the revolution. In light of such violence and division, I believe that the concepts of liberal democracy and liberalism, especially as manifested in the principles of social and religious freedom, are still distorted and contentious in the Arab consciousness. Decades of one-party rule and dictatorship seem to have had a negative influence on people and their attitudes and might prolong the implementation of a modern state with elements of liberalism (Khalidi 2011). It will take time for people to accept the fact that democracy is an antidote to the suppression of minorities under the rule of the majority.

As a matter of fact, many Arabs in the light of the popular uprising are sceptical about the views of Western countries, especially the United States. This is because Arabs think that some Western leaders who praise the revolution originally supported the Arab dictators. The United States is accused of employing a double standard on issues of freedom and social justice in their full support of Israel. Many Arabs think that Western governments, while they preach concepts of modernity, are selective in practising them. Therefore, when Western governments offer financial support in the post-revolution period, Arabs believe that the West will impose a political agenda that ultimately aligns with and supports Western interests (*The Nation* 2011). In the case of Palestine, youth tend to associate Israel with the West and decades of Israeli occupation have had a negative influence on their perceptions of the West, modernity and Western thinkers. In class, this negativity is expressed as opposition to and dismissal of modern European thinkers, an attitude that mirrors the Arab position on the role of the West in the Arab Spring.

Philosophy class discussions: idols versus rationality

The reaction of the students to theories discussed in the 'Modern and Contemporary European Civilization' class varied. The reaction of the students to these theories revealed their divergent attitudes to supporting modernity in relation to politics, but being much more cautious about its acceptance in relation to social norms. My students, for instance, enjoyed John Locke's *Two Treatises of Government* (1689), but were frustrated with John Stuart Mill's *On Liberty* (1859). Locke promotes the idea of the social contract, in which the governed endow the government with legitimacy and authority as long as the government fulfils its duties and guarantees citizens the right to declare war if the government fails to do so. Mill, however, argues that government's role should be limited and that individual freedoms of speech and action should remain unchecked as long as the exercise of those freedoms does not cause others harm. Students tended to agree with Locke's idea of the social contract and the legitimacy of authority derived from consenting individuals; this idea also corresponds with demands and goals voiced in the Arab Spring. Most students also supported Locke's idea that the government has an obligation to treat people as equals and to respect the right to declare war on the government if it fails to fulfil its duties. Mill's text, however, inspired intense and heated discussions. Students accepted Mill's idea that individuals should be able to act as they choose, but only when those actions do not run counter to clear-cut Islamic beliefs such as consuming alcohol or denying the existence of God. They are much more likely to apply Mill's ideas to personal and social issues such as the right of women to drive that are not clearly spelled out in Islam.

One student said, 'Mill is the thinker that disturbed me the most.' When I asked why, she explained, 'I will never allow alcohol in our society.' I responded that some Palestinians are Christians and that their religion permits alcohol. She proceeded, 'They should leave then.' I responded to her strong statement by reminding the class that Palestinian Christians have always been an integral part of the Palestinian struggle and that we should not exclude them just because we disagree with them. Although there was no further response or comment by any of the students at the time, the majority of the students later reported in the evaluation that learning to consider other perspectives was an important benefit derived from the course.

Discussions on assumptions and idols of the mind as articulated by Francis Bacon in *Novum Organon* (1620) revealed that students have a hard time questioning their own assumptions. Bacon discusses how idols of the mind – biases that predispose one's mind to certain assumptions and hinder scientific knowledge – lead to prejudiced opinions. In class discussions on assumptions, for example, students said they assumed that genies existed and had the power to affect their lives, especially because they are mentioned in the Qurʾān. Students believed in their existence to the extent that they adopted certain behaviours and practices to avoid any potential harm caused by genies. Three students told me that in their villages they had to cook for the genie to appease him and arranged with sheiks for *ʿaṭwah* (the tribal method for resolving disputes and achieving truce) between people and genies. One student also told me a story about how a sheik used the Qurʾān to cure a relative who was being haunted by a genie. Another thought that a nice genie used to come and clean the house for the family when they were away. Students giggled but did not challenge her story. In such discussions, no student questioned the plausibility of the stories or doubted the existence of genies. My colleagues in the department told me they had had similar class discussions with their students. In the evaluation, the majority of the students thought that the course did not cause them to question or change their assumptions or ideas. Most of the students thought that assumptions are hard to challenge, but that the course helped them understand certain concepts such as how to respect others' views without necessarily adopting them.

Dr Salam Fayyad, Palestinian Prime Minister, has highlighted the lack of analytical thinking skills and the presence of conservatism among Palestinian college students. In his speech honouring distinguished students in high schools and colleges, Fayyad emphasized the need to improve students' analytical skills and to end some conservative practices such as refusing to shake hands with the other sex (Quds 2011) because he believes that such practices are not part of our religion or culture. Just like the Enlightenment thinker Immanuel Kant, Fayyad wants to encourage the growth of creative and productive personalities and the use of reason to cope with social, cultural and human changes. The next day, Hamas leaders critiqued Fayyad and accused him of calling for the relaxation of ethical principles. Fayyad's appeal is important and required changing the deep-rooted assumptions accumulated since childhood. The majority of the students have reported that they find it hard to challenge assumptions adopted during childhood. One student wrote, 'it is difficult to change any of the assumptions that I was brought up with. Such change requires teaching in early childhood life and schools'. In addition, the majority of the students thought that René Descartes' method of acquiring and producing knowledge by challenging all childhood assumptions and re-examining all ideas is not possible. They believe that they do not have to question most of their major ideas because their beliefs serve them well. The majority reported that a circular Cartesian enquiry that questions the existence of God, as Descartes suggests in the *Meditations on First Philosophy* (1641), is not logical or necessary because the existence of God is an irrefutable fact.

Students responded in a similar fashion to Kant's argument on using reason and having the courage to reject the authority of others and to think independently in *Answering the Question: What is Enlightenment?* (1784). In class, I used the example of broadcast programmes that feature clergymen who answer questions from the audience on daily life practices such as whether, according to Islam, it is better to sleep on your right or left side to discuss the issue of legitimate authority. Students defended the need for clergymen to guide them because they assumed that the latter were more knowledgeable about religious issues. Overall, I noted that students seem to depend on others for their knowledge. For example, before we started on Karl Marx and Friedrich Engels's *The Communist Manifesto* (1848), I asked students what they knew about Marx and the majority of them said that all they knew was that he was an atheist. Most students rejected Marx and his theory because they have second-hand information about certain aspects of communism, such as its negative stance on religion. The problem is not only the lack of knowledge, but also the lack of motivation to know. Here is a discussion between student and me when I announced that we would discuss Marx and Engels in the next class.

Student: Skip Marx.
Me: Why?
Student: I do not like Marx.
Me: Do you disagree with him?
Student: Yes.
Me: So if I have a Marxist guest in the next class, will you be able to challenge his or her beliefs on Marx?
Student (with embarrassment): No.

When students learn about *The Communist Manifesto*, the class discussion tends to become a debate about the advantages and disadvantages of socialism. Students support the notion of social justice and the equal distribution of resources, but they still think that communism is wrong; they believe that public ownership and state control over the means of production undermines the incentive to work hard and be creative. This is when they agree with Mill's argument that competition leads to progress. They also argue that Islam already calls for such social justice. As a matter of fact, I asked my students whether they changed their opinion on Marx after the readings and discussions. The majority told me that they were surprised that Marx called for social justice and complained that the information they previously had was from textbooks which spoon-fed information and did not encourage critical thinking. The school curricula are also limited to certain resources on certain topics.

Their reactions betray the paradox at the heart of both their own ambivalent attitudes to modernity and those found elsewhere where in the Arab world, even in the revolutionary claims of the Arab Spring. Students are critical of the 'feeding' teaching method used in secondary schools and the university. They complain that teachers try to impose their opinions on students and do not allow them to express their views freely. And yet their own acceptance, with apparent equanimity, of the fact that their childhood educational conditioning has provided them with an infallible set of beliefs, undermines the very major premise of their complaint against its pedagogical method. This confusion involved in believing in modernity, while also restricting its expression, is clarified in Azzam's (2001) analysis of Sheikh Rashid Ghannouchi's[4] views on teaching philosophy to Muslim students:

> Ghannouchi proposed that instead of teaching students two separate subjects, the first called *al-falsafah al-gharbīyah* (Western philosophy) and the other *al-firaq al-islāmīyah* (Islamic sects), one subject that teaches all ideas, both Islamic and non-Islamic, should be taught but from an Islamic perspective.
>
> (p. 37)

Ghannouchi fears that teaching Western philosophy to the youth will undermine their Islamic beliefs and may encourage them to adopt foreign ideas that will ultimately estrange students from their culture. His argument is similar to my students' attitude toward philosophy. Instead of seeing Western philosophy as a source of new ideas and ways of thinking, most students believe it is just another subject such as chemistry with information to be learned. Students believe that Islam has the answers to all questions raised and that Western theories are not suitable for Arab cultures. Unlike Ghannouchi, however, who does support the teaching of Western philosophy, albeit from an Islamic perspective, some students believe that Western philosophy should not be taught at all because it is irrelevant to their lives. In fact, students routinely label philosophy professors at Birzeit University as atheists, and some even name and publicly shame those professors on Facebook. It is worth mentioning that such cases include professors who use texts by modern Islamic scholars to teach courses on Arab and Islamic thought.

Complexity of modernity

As noted above, class discussions reflect divergent attitudes and views towards modern European theories. In response to my end-of-semester evaluation, students thought that the course educated them about European philosophers and theories, and had a positive impact on their lives by helping them to be more open to other perspectives. However, such openness is limited to social issues that do not clearly conflict with Islamic beliefs. Students are generally supportive of political modernity in the Arab world, even though it is influenced by Western thinkers such as Locke; but they are less likely to apply the concepts of personal and social freedom as articulated by Mill to their cultural and religious lives, which are deeply rooted in their upbringing and early childhood education.

Most students believe not only that Islam already grants basic human rights and promotes justice, but also that Islam is self-evident and therefore unquestionable. Consequently, they do not support tolerance of actions and free speech that clearly conflict with Islamic beliefs such as the consumption of alcohol, but they do support it in relation to social and personal issues that do not clearly conflict with religion, such as the right of access to education for women. In fact, at Birzeit University a greater number of women earn degrees than men in the humanities, business, technology, engineering and graduate programmes. In 2011, 1116 women earned degrees as compared with 714 men. In addition, the law and science departments have a greater number of female graduates.

This tendency was reflected in the fact that class discussions on liberalism tended to be more relaxed when I gave examples using 'safe' issues that related to students' social and personal concerns. For example, students responded positively and with an open mind to issues such as the right of education for women, the appropriate marriage

age for women, the right of women to choose their future husbands and the immorality of honour killings. Similarly, students supported the right to freedom of action for individuals such as the right of women to drive.

Examples that conflict with religion, however, such as the freedom to consume alcohol are rejected. In class, I often use Mill's argument to challenge students' rejection of practices such as drinking alcohol and say that they should not expect a non-Islamic state to respect the rights of Muslims such as establishing and praying in mosques if they are not prepared to accept the practices and beliefs of non-Islamic actors in predominantly Islamic states. In response, students tend to start discussing how to accommodate practices that are contrary to Islam, which is in essence the practice of *ijtihād*. One student, for example, suggested that Islamic countries should allow people to drink alcohol in restricted areas where Muslims are not allowed to enter.

Similarly, Arab nations are practising reform and *ijtihād* on social and personal issues on which there is no definitive answer to be found in the Qurʾān. However, they are doing so without acknowledging that such issues are compatible with modernity and that activists in modern Western states have engaged in similar struggles to defend and fight for these rights. For example, women have been active participants in the revolutions and have even led demonstrations and protests. When Yemeni President Ali Abdullah Saleh criticized women protestors for mixing with men in demonstrations, both men and women took to the street in protest against his statement. Activists called for a demonstration on 17 April 2011 and called it the 'honor and dignity' demonstration as a response to Saleh's charge that women were violating *sharīʿah* two days earlier. Yemeni women are looking forward to gaining rights and enacting reforms to ensure equality.

The complexity of modernity and liberalism is also reflected in a recent survey conducted in Palestine on liberalism (Stiftung, Freedom Forum Palestine 2010). The survey found that while 88% of Palestinians believe in equal rights for both Muslims and Christians, 71% would not vote for a Christian Palestinian president. Moreover, 82% of Palestinians prefer a religious state to a secular one. In another recent public opinion poll conducted in the West Bank and Gaza, the majority of Palestinians believe that *sharīʿah* should be either the only legislation or an integral part of the legislative framework. Palestinians supported the use of *sharīʿah* even though the majority of respondents did not support polygamy, an accepted practice in *sharīʿah*, in the same poll (Jerusalem Media and Communication Center 2008). Such contradictions point to the confusion about the meaning of liberalism and human rights. This shows how the concept of modernity is conditional for those students and that they accept or reject ideas in reference to Islamic teaching. As Esposito (2011) explains:

> Polls confirm that majorities of Muslims want key democratic components like self-determination, the rule of law, free speech, and a free press and see these rights as compatible with their faith. Muslims say they admire freedom and an open political system, but many do not believe they must choose between Islam and democracy, and instead they believe that the two can coexist.
>
> (p. 267)

I argue that the concepts of liberalism and the modern state among Palestinian youth do not exactly mirror such concepts in the West and that Islam is always considered a reference point for any change. This corresponds with the situation in Egypt and Tunisia in the post-revolution debates. For example, in the aftermath of the Egyptian revolution, the Muslim Brotherhood expressed their support for democracy, but stated that electing a Coptic president is illogical. This points to the difficulty in coming to terms with the concept of a modern state that grants equal rights to all citizens, including the right to run for president. Similarly, in Tunisia, Rashid Ghannouchi[5], upon his return from exile, said in an interview that he wants to contribute to 'democratic reform' in Tunisia (*The Telegraph* 2011). However, he wants to embrace modernity according to Islamic guidelines (Azzam 2001) because he believes that the practice of *ijtihād*, which ensures reforms and compatibility with social developments, ensures that Islam remains relevant to the modern world. The practice of *ijtihād*, according to Ghannouchi, is active in developed and civilized nations. However, this is not a straightforward matter because traditional Muslim scholars often criticize modern scholars who use *ijtihād* to call for a modern, secular state. In class discussions, for example, students rejected the ideas of modern Islamic scholars and enlightened thinkers, such as Nasr Hamid Abu Zayd and Jamal al-Banna, and labelled them as disbelievers. Students charge that Muslims in support of secular and modern states or political systems are Westernized and in support of Western agendas.

Arab modernity and the contradiction of Western democracy

During class discussions students were sceptical about the West's claim to modernity and enlightenment, and it is the basis for this scepticism – their perception of the way Western nations' political actions betray the intellectual principles upon which it is claimed they are based – that provides a key reason for the students' ambivalence towards modernity itself, the intellectual method upon which it rests. They cited contradictory examples such as the West's double standard in foreign policy with regard to the Palestinian cause. In addition, they are not convinced that US support for the Arab Spring is genuine because of its unconditional support for Israel. The United States' passive response to Israeli aggression against Palestinians has created a sceptical attitude towards any US intervention.

Students argue that Western powers preach democratic ideas and human rights, but support the Israeli occupation and do not speak out against the violation of human rights of Palestinians. They also argue that the West and Israel are far from being democratic or humanistic and give examples of human rights violations against Palestinians, such as the confiscation of land, the killing of civilians and the sieges on Gaza, all of which are underwritten by the United States. The majority of Arab people are also aware of the double standard in the Western position, especially that of the United States. Thus, students and many prominent Arab thinkers are critical of the foreign policies of Western powers and do not see any good intentions in their interventions. For example, students consider the NATO intervention in Libya in favour of the revolution as a form of occupation. Students also contrast the United States' unconditional support for authoritarian regimes with its cautious support of the Arab Spring and cite this contrast as evidence of the United States' opportunistic nature and its tendency to prioritize its own national interests, even when providing financial aid to other nations. Many Arabs think that the funds promised by the International Monetary Fund (IMF) and The World Bank and the billions pledged during the G8 summit to support Arab democracies will increase dependency on the West. Overall, Arabs tend to perceive the West as a hard-to-trust occupier and colonizer.

Of course, although many Arabs may be sceptical of the West's political agendas and reject its intervention in the Arab world, they do welcome and engage with Western culture, provided that it does not contradict religious beliefs such as wearing immodest dress. Therefore, I argue that the concept of modernity is rather complex, and although some Arabs are critical of the Western concept of modernity and want to preserve their authenticity, they are willing to adopt some aspects of modernity. I noticed, for example, that Yemeni youth are influenced by rap music and incorporate its stylistic elements into nationalistic songs and slogans. This may be explained by the fact that rap music in the United States is a form of protest or statement of revolt. Palestinians are also mixing their popular traditional dance (*Dabkeh*) with Western music and styles. Palestinians tend to appreciate such fusions and refer to them as Contemporary *Dabkeh*. The Palestine Popular Art Center (2011) even recruits international choreographers to train *Dabkeh* dance groups. In sum, while Arab nations accept the West's technology, education training, art and pop culture, they are less accepting of its political and economic ideologies and ideas.

But such acceptance of aspects of Western culture does not alter the fundamental distrust of the West as a whole. In class discussions many students believe that the West is hypocritical because its democratic values are only applied to its own cultures and to Israel and because it prioritizes its own interests. This belief is at the heart of my students' reaction to Western philosophy. The majority of students support political modernity, and while they think that Western philosophy does not suit our culture and customs, they agree that some theories are useful and should be considered, such as those of Locke. The majority of students believe that Islam grants social justice but that there is a problem in that *sharīʿah* is not implemented in the right way. I found, while discussing such issues with them, the students were not able to explain, however, the 'right way' of implementing *sharīʿah* and implied that the 'right way' was an unreachable ideal. This dilemma is manifested in the Muslim Brotherhood's statement that it supports a pluralistic state with Islam as a central guiding force: the Muslim Brotherhood 'envisions the establishment of a democratic, civil state that draws on universal measures of freedom and justice, with central Islamic values serving all Egyptians regardless of colour, creed, political trend or religion' (Taleb 2011). The statement, which echoes Ghannouchi's perspective on Tunisian politics, points to a profound discomfort with the concept of a truly democratic, civic state that privileges no religion because Islam is so deeply tied into every aspect of political, social and cultural life. Political actors such as the Muslim Brotherhood simply cannot imagine the existence of a secular state that would nevertheless ensure the continued influence of Islamic thought in every aspect of life.

Conclusion

Students' class discussions in my course 'Modern and Contemporary European Civilization' reflect both the struggle of Palestinian youth to reconcile modernity with Islam and tradition, and also a certain confusion in their concept of modernity itself and the consequences of its underlying intellectual assumptions. These class debates are remarkably parallel to those that are occurring in the post-revolution Arab states of Egypt and Tunisia and to those which occurred during the Arab Spring period.

Firstly, the analysis of class discussions and student-written evaluative responses to the course shows that students are confused by the concept of liberal democracy, particularly on the question of the tolerance of differing views which it necessitates. Some events in post-revolution Egypt and Tunisia reveal a similar confusion. For example, media coverage of many public figures such as actors and actresses being blacklisted for not supporting the Arab Spring betray the fact that the revolutionary activists calling for freedom do not understand the inferences of the platform they are advocating, being perfectly willing to practise the tyranny of the majority over opposing viewpoints, in process of its implementation.

Then there is the dilemma of the fact that full acceptance of modernity as a way of life involves tolerance of social practices on a basis that can only be called secular. Students accepted certain aspects of Western modernity, especially democracy, which parallels the Arab Spring process. I argue that in general, however, the majority of Palestinian students are vigilant about Western modernity; they deal with modernity as a concept that plays out differently in the political and social realms. My study suggests that such views might be shared with those of the youth in the Arab world. Political modernity is supported and accepted, even if it is based on Western theory. Social modernity, however, is a more complex issue. Some aspects are already achieved, such as women's right to education and, therefore, it is not unusual to see masses of women not only participating in protests, but also leading and chanting slogans, even in a traditional tribal country such as Yemen. Arab women will continue to demand more rights as active participants in making social change. But practices that contradict Islam, such as the consumption of alcohol, are not tolerated, indicating that students do not contemplate any fundamental freedom of choice in personal behaviour, or indeed, in some cases, in the question of state ideology.

The fact that modernity is associated with the West makes it a controversial concept for Palestinian students. They accept the West's technologies, science and even pop culture, but are not willing to allow any encroachment on their cultural identity and heritage, a reservation that can also be observed in the Arab Spring debates, as Arab activists try to make changes and move towards modernity, the outcome of which process might well result in a synthesis between Islam and modernity. It is this preservation of cultural identity and the central position held in any formulation of it by Islam that makes the issue of the reconciliation of Islam and modernity such an insistent and precarious issue for Palestinian youth, in particular. The increasingly close imbrication of Islam and Palestinian identity in the quest for national self-definition and liberation, due to Western support for Israel's brutal and illegal occupation of Palestinian territory, and the failure of the originally secular Palestinian Liberation Organization (PLO) to achieve any resolution of this situation, has meant that modernity itself, associated as it is with the West, finds it difficult to claim legitimacy with a growing constituency among the Palestinians on the West Bank and Gaza. How far this attitude is reflected in the youth involved with the Arab Spring is only now in process of discovery, as elections take place.

However, amongst the majority Islamic constituency, Palestinian views are not standing still, but are unconsciously reinterpreting *sharīʿah*, especially in terms of increasing educational opportunity and political independence for women, though less so in matters domestic. Similar developments can be found in Arab countries. In Yemen, for example, President Ali Abdullah Saleh failed to intimidate women even though he criticized their participation in demonstrations on Islamic grounds. This social change for women occurred alongside the Arab Spring's demands for social justice, freedom of speech and equality. The Arab Spring gave people, and youth in particular, a sense of self-efficacy and belief in their own ability to change their situation. This is even evident in Saudi Arabia, where women have challenged authority and driven cars in 2011. The event was publicized and covered in the media as television outlets interviewed women. A Saudi princess even recently stated publicly that every country should expect a revolution if freedoms and reforms are not introduced. She even criticized the role of the moral police in Saudi Arabia and their bad performance with women (Ormsby 2011).

Modernity is a key issue in the contemporary Arab world, in terms both of its intrinsic meaning and practice and in that of its reconciliation with Islam. Definitely it forms part of the consciousness of Palestinian students who are the focus of this study. This might well result in change that will eventually bring about contemporary modern states, albeit not necessarily in the West's meaning of the term. If this is to happen, however, education will be the crucial ingredient in the development, by producing a change in the way of thinking of the people. Modernity is a process and measures will be needed to create a generation who reason and form opinions independently and who question authority. To be sure that the next generation of Palestinians, in particular, engages in critical thinking and analysis, the pedagogy and curricula employed in schools will need a radical overhaul. Students have to be trained to engage in critical analysis and creative thinking, instead of learning by rote. They need to be encouraged not only to consider other viewpoints as an academic exercise, but also to accept challenges to their own views. They have to be taught to debate so that the opinions they themselves hold are not seen as fact, but as a point of reference. Training for scientific enquiry needs to be part of the curriculum and funds made available for research and development in this area. Lastly, universities should encourage research and train students in different types of research method.

It is still too early to speculate on the outcome of the Arab Spring. The current internal strife in some Arab states such as Yemen, Libya and Syria shows that coexistence in a diverse society is a precondition for these states to attain modernity. There was an upsurge of romantic euphoria during the Arab Spring; the next generation will need to be prepared to accept multicultural identities by implementing a comprehensive strategy for developing critical and rational personalities.

In light of class discussions and post-revolutionary discourse in the Arab countries, I argue that Palestinian educators and policy-makers should develop strategies for teaching critical-thinking skills in schools. In addition, textbooks should incorporate materials that encourage learning how to do research and analysis instead of feeding information as facts to be memorized. Universities should also use curricula that challenge dogmatic thinking and assumptions through constructive dialogues and debates based on evidence-based research.

Notes

1. Students are from a range of socioeconomic backgrounds from cities, villages and refugee camps.
2. I asked students in the fall semester of 2010 and the fall and the spring semesters of 2011 to complete an evaluation which would be used for research purposes. A total of 140 students responded. I have taught this course every semester since 2007, each intake numbering approximately 150 students.
3. I discussed modernity with my students, in light of the course themes raised in our study of selected texts in modern European thought. We focused on what I believe constitute the key issues in any introduction to modernity: the orientation of thought towards secularism and the issue of reason versus faith; the political concepts of equality; democracy and the rule of law based on consensus and separation of powers; the organization of the social and intellectual life of society based on the principles of liberalism and tolerance; and the paradigm of scientific and empirical methods of thinking.
4. Ghannouchi is a prominent Islamist–reformist Tunisian leader who calls for democracy and political pluralism.

5. He is leader of the Islamist Nahḍah Party which got the largest votes in the post-revolution elections.

References

Arab World for Research & Development (AWRAD), 2012. *Results of a Specialized Opinion Poll among Palestinian Youth: Youth Activism – Political Efficacy – Political Orientation – Elections – Negotiations – Arab Spring – Needs and Priorities*, February. Ramallah: AWRAD. Available from: http://www.miftah.org/Doc/Polls/AWRAD010212En.pdf [Accessed 21 February 2012].

Arkoun, M., 2006. *Islam: reform or subvert?* London: Saqi.

Azzam, T., 2001. *Rachid Ghannouchi: a democrat within Islamism*. New York, NY: Oxford University Press.

Bilin Village, 2011. *Closing statement of the 6th Bilin Conference on Popular Resistance*, [online]. Available from: http://www.bilin-village.org/english/conferences/conference2011/Closing-Statement-of-the-6th-Bilin-Conference-on-Popular-Resistance [Accessed 23 June 2011].

Esposito, J.L., 2011. *Islam: the straight path*. 4th ed. New York, NY: Oxford University Press.

Jerusalem Media and Communication Center, 2008. *Palestinian's opinions towards woman's rights, Poll No. 66 Part 2*, Available from: http://www.jmcc.org/documentsandmaps.aspx?id=433 [Accessed 25 March 2010].

Khalidi, R., 2011. The Arab Spring. *The Nation* [online]. Available from: http://www.thenation.com/article/158991/arab-spring [Accessed 20 June 2011].

Morrow, A. and al-Omrani, K.M., 2011. Activists preparing for Third Intifada. *The Electronic Intifada*, [online]. Available from: http://electronicintifada.net/content/activists-preparing-third-intifada/9937 [Accessed 12 June 2011].

Mozgovaya, N., 2011. Gaza, the most Facebook-friendly place on Earth. *Haaretz* [online]. Available from: http://www.haaretz.com/print-edition/features/gaza-the-most-facebook-friendly-place-on-earth-1.365970 [Accessed 8 June 2011].

Ormsby, A., 2011. Saudi princess says no one immune from Arab Spring. *Reuters* [online]. Available from: http://uk.reuters.com/article/2011/06/29/uk-gulf-britain-princess-idUKTRE75S83Q20110629 [Accessed 2 July 2011].

Popular Art Center, 2011. NGO profiles. *WebGaza*. Available from: http://www.webgaza.net/palestine/ngo_profiles/Popular_Art_Centre.htm [Accessed 10 June 2011].

Quds, A., 2011. *Ministry of Higher Education honoring distinguished students in high schools, colleges and universities*. Available from: <http://www.alquds.com/news/article/view/id/194242 [Accessed 19 June 2011].

Roy, S., 2004. The Palestinian–Israeli conflict and Palestinian socioeconomic decline: a place denied. *International Journal of Politics, Culture, and Society*, 17 (3), 365–403.

Stiftung, F.N., Freedom Forum Palestine, 2010. *A survey on public perceptions towards liberal values in Palestine*. Available from: http://imeu.net/engine2/uploads/fnffinaleng08_2_pdf [Accessed 2 June 2011].

Taleb, H.A., 2011. A revolution all of Egypt must share. *Ahram Online*, Available from: http://english.ahram.org.eg/NewsContentPrint/4/0/6428/Opinion/0/A-revolution-all-of-Egypt-must-share.aspx [Accessed 2 June 2011].

The Telegraph, 2011. *Exiled Tunisian Islamist leader Rachid Ghannouchi returns home* [online]. Available from: http://www.telegraph.co.uk/news/worldnews/africaandindianocean/tunisia/8292216/Exiled-Tunisian-Islamist-leader-Rachid-Ghanouchi-returns-home.html [Accessed 20 July 2011].

The Nation, 2011. Editorial: Will the Arab states go the way the West wants? *The Nation*, 1 June. Available from: http://www.nationmultimedia.com/2011/06/01/opinion/Will-the-Arab-Spring-go-the-way-the-West-wants-30156677.html [Accessed 1 June 2011].

The 'end of pan-Arabism' revisited: reflections on the Arab Spring

Youssef Mohamed Sawani

Professor of Political Science, University of Tripoli, Libya

This article draws on implications of the Arab Spring so as to elucidate the dynamics that characterize its revolutions. The analysis builds upon the results of major public opinion surveys conducted in the Arab world, both immediately before and after the Arab Spring, in order to facilitate the identification of developments that shape the relationship between Arabism and Islamism in the context of mass media, the demographic 'youth bulge' and Arab ongoing intellectual debates. The argument advanced here is that the Arab Spring consolidates the view that Arabism and Islamism have maintained their position and hold on public opinion and prevailing attitudes as the primary and inseparable trends of Arab thought. The interaction and shifting relative weights of both trends provide the context for the identity, conceptual outlook and reciprocal framework of contemporary Arabs; and the Arab Spring seems only to confirm the two trends as constituting the essential point of reference and departure for Arabs. Within this context and scope of analysis this article traces the emergence of a 'historical mass' for change that, coupled with an indelibly engrained link between the two trends is opening up a new conceptual sphere and public space for the emergence of a new Arabism. Such development is also supported by the role of mass media and the thoughtful intellectual contributions that have been advancing a new Arab paradigm which further refutes the 'End of Arabism' thesis.

Introduction

In 2011 the Arab region defied all those exceptionalist theorists who attributed the lack of democracy in the region to its fundamentally Arab–Islamic culture. The 'Arab Spring' revolutions, which began on a relatively small scale in Tunisia, only to spread rapidly to other Arab countries as distant as Bahrain and Yemen, gave notice that the appetite for democratization was not only present, but also may have reactivated engines of change beyond reverse. Though many commentators have focused on issues related to the role of the middle class and youth as the driving forces of change, it is, however, more important to trace in the uprisings the inception of what may be termed the 'historical mass' required for the realization of the changes called for in this Arab Spring.[1]

A full appreciation of this underlying driver will also reveal further flaws in the 'End of Arabism' thesis that explains the region in terms of a dualism or dichotomy between Arabism and Islamism or the 'religious' versus the 'secular' (Ajami 2012b). Apart from obscuring the genuine nature of these concepts, such approaches ignore realities and insist on projecting the interaction of trends and orientations in the region through the application of some Western or European conceptualizations without questioning their relevance. This is particularly true as far as the relationship between Arabism and Islamism, the two major indigenous trends in the Arab world, are concerned.

To understand the nature and magnitude of recent developments in the Arab world, it is crucial to investigate the fluid and changing environment in which Islamism and Arabism have always featured as integral parts of the region's belief-systems and attitudinal orientations.[2] Interaction between these fundamental elements has and will determine the content and trajectory of the Arab Spring, which will most likely be translated into political programmes. This is particularly true in so far as issues of democracy, justice, and an equitable distribution of wealth and resources are related to integration or any possible form of cooperation across the region.

The almost total absence from the theatre of contemporary demonstrations of slogans similar to those chanted by the 1950s' and 1960s' generations is noteworthy. However, this may be explained by the fact that new phenomena are being witnessed that share two primary distinguishing characteristics: (1) an age demographic weighted towards the young, whose enculturation takes new forms; and (2) a level of mass popular participation in the events of the Arab Spring which is genuine. The argument advanced here is that the Arabism of the recent uprisings *is* significant and present in more than *name* only, but the pan-Arab ideas and ideals of the 1950s and 1960s are not necessarily adopted in the exact same manner by today's youth. Like their counterparts everywhere else in the world, young Arabs are more absorbed in their phones and very different means of social interaction than they are in the sort of overt political ideologies that once predominated. Present-day youth seem to exhibit a different form of attachment to ideals and relate more to practicalities than to general principles and to material concerns more than big ideas.

However, this in no way implies that ideas or ideals do not constitute a part of the mindset of youth. Rather than abandoning these, it appears that they regard such ideals as best served if basic rights and democracy are in place first. In this sense, the issue appears to be more one of arranging priorities, indicating a shift in the relative weight accorded to big ideas and immediate practical concerns. It is important to register, for example, that in Egypt action in support of Gaza and the Palestinian cause was more common among the more globally oriented students at the American University of Cairo (AUC) than those at Cairo or al-Azhar universities. Differently stated, the youth were most concerned with things often correlated to economic demands and everyday life concerns. This highlights the centrality of social and economic issues that have long been overshadowed by the big or grandiose themes of Arab nationalists who opted for social change first and postponed democracy.

The youth have new perspectives on almost every issue related to the manifold contextual levels in which they act and interact. These perspectives are influenced by the content to which they are exposed through new media and information sources that have the backing of huge technological advances and vast financial resources. The new media have also facilitated the widespread use of a standardized form of Arabic. Given that over 60% of Arabs are in their youth, their exposure to this kind of media is likely to have profound implications over time. Yet, as some will argue, the youth of the Arab Spring are aware of and well immersed in Arabism at many levels. According to Bazzi (2012), 'A new generation of revolutionaries has fostered a revitalized sense of pan-Arab identity united around demands for broad political and social rights.'

However, this debate is not complete without differentiating between revolutions and mass uprisings, and recognizing the distinction between, on the one hand, top-down coups of the mid-twentieth century that brought the military to politics and their particular brand of Arab nationalism, and the revolts of the Arab Spring, on the other hand, which have been completely popular and from the bottom-up. It is also important to remember that the changes wrought in the first instance were initially popular and seem to have echoed and resonated with popular feelings and sentiments at grassroots' levels. The crucial point here is that the new level of involvement of the mass has the potential to change the form and content of Arab politics and play a decisive role in redefining Arab nationalism (Bazzi 2012).

It is striking, however, that the social and economic demands voiced in the public squares of the Arab Spring were *not* framed or phrased in slogans such as the equitable distribution of wealth or social justice of the style envisioned in the ideologies or political programmes common in the region before. The central characteristic of the Arab Spring is the reconfiguration and reconceptualization of popular yearnings and aspirations. It may be safe to claim that for the first time in its contemporary history the Arab world has witnessed the success of large-scale mass uprisings in ousting regimes. The people, who were hitherto represented and given voice through elites and vanguards, are now coming back into the picture. The theatre of political action and movement is now more grassroots than it was before.

A recent study based on a survey of Arab public opinion conducted by the Doha-based Center for Research and Policy Studies confirms that the Arab Spring revolutions put public opinion in its proper place as the most influential of all determinants of policies in the region (Arab Center for Research and Policy Studies 2012a, p. 21). This opens the doors for the emergence of an inclusive and democratic movement that highlights and values the role of the individual and the mass simultaneously. Another important feature is a change of paradigm in the popular struggle for dignity. Gone are the days when that struggle had to express itself solely in terms of liberation from colonialism or the fight against Zionism. However, it is almost impossible to admit a separation between old and new struggles. Even though the Arab Spring revolutions are primarily politically driven, they are also economic. Hence, realization of freedom of the people from all forms of tyranny and dictatorship becomes a priority that precedes any other objective. It appears clear that people have realized that national independence has not been complete (Arab Center for Research and Policy Studies 2012a).

Inseparable twins: Arabism and Islamism

Arab thought has always known two major trends: the Arab nationalist trend that sought the realization of a pan-Arab nation-state as the prerequisite for liberation and modernization; and the Islamist revivalist trend that sought a revival of a glorious Islamic past. Though the pan-Arabist trend exercised an ideological hegemony and played a significant role in the developments the Arab world experienced, the Islamist trend was not entirely on the periphery of politics and political domination as far as some parts of the region are concerned. The contemporary history of the region has been a testimony to the interaction of these two trends. Their relationship has had its ups and downs and was once characterized as an Arab Cold War.[3]

Taking into consideration that Arabism and Islam in the Arab Maghreb have been almost *synonymous*, Islam has always been at the centre of public life and imagination among the Arabs, the vast majority of whom are Muslims. This suggests that Islam has maintained its position in determining the political behaviour of the Arabs, and it is obvious that many secular policies had to be justified in Islamic terms to cater for the Islamic values and beliefs at the popular level.

The two trends have been interacting in a process in which the relative weight of each of them is changing. This process of change is directly connected to the changes that political, economic and social aspects of life are undergoing. This has been particularly evident at the level of Arab failures to realize development goals and the failure of many attempts in countries characterized by rentier economies or the limitations of the particularistic state.

It is clear from the examination of the content of slogans and the discourse of people in city squares or the theatres of combat of the Arab Spring that something of a unified psyche was generated, transcending any divisions between Arabism and Islam. The public squares and events of the Arab Spring have played the role of a 'melting pot' that gave rise to a new historical Arab mass. This mass transcends long held ideological divides.

However, Arabism and Islamism are ideals, aspirations or beliefs that significantly shape the content and direction of the societal value system and determine the behaviour of individuals and groups in addition to being the two basic components for the historical mass required for change. The Arab Spring provides evidence that these two ideals have interacted to produce the cultural and political grassroots movement with a potential to lead Arab society in directions more relevant to its long-professed goals of freedom and dignity than the top-down state-level projects of pan-Arabism of the twentieth century. Here religion and nationalism are melded together in a modern Arabism. The public opinion survey of the Arab Research Centre referred to above provides empirical evidence at a very critical juncture as it was conducted in 2011 and after the Arab Spring revolutions. The survey was conducted in Saudi Arabia, Yemen, Iraq, Palestine (West Bank and Gaza), Lebanon, Sudan, Egypt, Tunisia, Algeria, Morocco and Mauritania. Together these countries account for more than 80% of all Arabs, and the survey sample totalled 16,193 respondents.

The survey corroborates a widespread belief in the existence of a united Arab nation bound together by many factors, where 71% of respondents maintain such a belief. Feelings of a common identity are reflected in that 81% of the sample identified common threats to the 'National Security of Arab Homeland'.[4] Not only did they accept such a concept without question, but also 81% of the respondents were able to determine threats to this pan-Arab security. Moreover, 73% identified Israel and the United States as top threats to this 'Arab Homeland National Security'. This is further consolidated in that 84% still see the Palestinian issue as a pan-Arab one, while 79% opposed the treaties between Israel and Egypt, Jordan and the Palestine Liberation Organisation (PLO), in contrast to 67% who thought that intra-Arab cooperation suffers from a lack of will power, with about 75% in favour of adopting integration formulas of a nature that would support unification (Arab Center for Research and Policy Studies 2012b, p. 4).

While it may be adventurous to conclude that the debate is settled (Bashour 2012), as the Arab Spring would seem to demonstrate, one can identify elements of a new breed of Arabism in the making (Korany 2011). The challenge before Arab nationalist and Islamist trends, however, is that of countering opposing movements that provide more specific ideologies and hence are more cohesive. One may consider, for instance, Saudi-backed Salafists now in operation in Egypt, Tunisia and Libya, the movements of which are cohesive because they provide a very simplistic ideology, which appeals to a certain level of education or class. Nevertheless, if one, along with the advocates of such platforms, entertained, for the sake of argument, that the Islamist trend is now dominant, will this mean abandoning the long-held view that Arab society is a mosaic including minorities and other fragmentary identities? Can such a world-view be applied to an Islamist-dominated Arab world?[5]

Arab public opinion surveys conducted just before and after the Arab Spring erupted provide ample evidence that refutes both the 'End of Arabism' prognosis and the dominance of any one-sided view. The results of the survey conducted by the Doha-based Arab Center confirm the findings of another survey that was conducted by the Jordanian Centre for Strategic Studies on behalf of the Beirut-based Centre for Arab Unity Studies. This other survey was conducted in two phases: the first between late 2009 and early 2010; and the second during September and November 2010.

While the results of the Doha Arab Center survey clearly demonstrate the ascendancy of pan-Arab beliefs after the Arab Spring took hold, the other survey, which polled in Algeria, Morocco, Jordan, Palestine (West Banks and Gaza), Lebanon, Saudi Arabia, Yemen, Sudan, Egypt and Syria, revealed similar inclinations. It is indicative that 82% of those who took part in the survey confirmed that they considered Arab peoples closer to them than any other group. Europe, for example, was seen as having ties to the Arabs by only 7% of respondents, and non-Arab Muslim nations by only 4%. It also is important to note that 87% of the sample shared in an identification of common pan-Arab factors that included identity, language, religion, a shared history and geography, shared interests, common challenges, and shared customs and traditions. For these shared and common factors, 70% of the respondents supported Arab economic, legal, monetary, and other forms of political integration and/or cooperation (Centre for Arab Unity Studies 2012).

Given these findings, one should not fall once again in the trap of the 'End of pan-Arabism' thesis and see the Arab Spring only in light of a false dichotomy of Arabism/Islamism. The gains attained thus far by Islamist political parties in the Tunisian and Egyptian elections should not be projected as solely a victory of 'Islamists' and, hence, be utilized to herald the End of Arabism. There are indeed inherent dangers in espousal of this dichotomy. An obvious risk is to create an illusion that the Arabs are only of a 'single mind' and are therefore naturally not democratic. To suggest that Arabs have no experience of democracy or that they cannot deal with it is not tenable. They have, in point of fact, been dealing with the subject and related issues in highly perspicacious fashion from the end of the nineteenth century onwards and contemporary Arab political thought focused on democracy, in particular after 1967 (Sawani 2003).

Apart from the fact that the Arab Spring was in no way the work of Islamist movements, to project it as simply a victory for Islamist parties and leaders is akin to linking pan-Arabism entirely to personalities whose death meant the subsequent death of their ideas or the ideology they might have pursued.

Arab politics: from absent peoples to historical mass

Arab intellectuals and political leaders of Islamist orientations are aware that Arabism and Islamism alike were victims of dictatorial and authoritarian Arab regimes (Ganoushi 2012). Arabism, in fact, faced an onslaught intended to erode its popular appeal by the very regimes that were paying lip service to the project. Talal Salman argues that it is unjust to indict Arabism for all the horrific deeds of tyrannical regimes. Arabism, he stresses, was the primary victim of these regimes that pretended an Arabism to camouflage their actual animosity to Arabism itself (Salman 2011).

Authoritarian regimes exploited the appeal to pan-Arabism to excuse their failures in respect of economic development and disguise their desire to avoid democratic change.

Their undemocratic practices and centralized politics employed oppressive security and suppression of the populace while simultaneously reducing, to a minimum, cross-border movements of people and ideas. Both Arab Nationalist and Islamist intellectuals and movements were subject to repressive state policies and propaganda, while the regimes adopted a 'divide and rule' approach towards the twin trends. A case in point was the late Anwar Sadat, who practised a policy of co-opting the Islamists in the early 1970s in order to undermine leftist and Nasserite elements.

Developments in many Arab countries underlined the dangers associated with this policy on identity, national integration and social cohesion. Regimes and political movements alike resorted to practices and ideologies that revived and consolidated divisions at all levels. Such practices and the manipulation of ethnic, religious, sectarian and tribal loyalties further undermined nation building and unity at all levels (Yaakoub 2011, p. 40). The way Gaddafi pursued his Arab agenda is a clear example, as too the tactics he employed latterly to counter the revolution against his erratic dictatorship. He went to previously unimaginable lengths to instigate and antagonize tribal and regional identities in Libya for the purpose of fomenting civil war. His approach was that of labelling the rebels mere 'terrorist Islamist fundamentalists', 'jihadists', 'al-Qa'idah activists', 'agents of imperialism or Arab regimes' or 'secessionists' who sought tribal or local gains and the liquidation of others (Al-Hroub 2011).[6]

The Arab Spring provides the occasion but also some empirical evidence to suggest that previously held views are no longer valid. The Arab Spring was not the work of any particular political or ideological orientation, none of which can claim ownership of this people's project. The Arab Spring is not a moment of victory for either the pan-Arab or the Islamist trend. It is the work of ordinary Arabs who are and remain mostly Muslims. It is their moment of assertion and identification with the global and long-awaited moment of democracy.

Mohammed Ali Atassi has delved to the roots of this issue, suggesting that 'the only way to overcome the obstacles that stand in the way of future political development is to break down the awful polarity represented by the implicit choice between tyranny and religious extremism'. Further, he observes the composition of the historical mass that holds the key to change when describing the scene in Tahrir Square, where 'Islamists and secularists, men and women, old and young were emphasizing the most fundamental principle of democracy more eloquently than any outspoken rhetoric' (Atassi 2011, p. 33).

Therefore, the historical mass has taken the initiative and is expressing its historical mission in realizing change and accomplishing the long-desired but unattained objectives of Arabism. More important, however, is that this mass addresses the abiding issue of Arabism/Islamism duality and eradicates it. Television coverage, social media reports and video footage attest to the inclusive nature of the crowds in the spaces that incubated the Arab Spring events. People from all walks of life irrespective of class or gender were the actors in all public venues. Tahrir Square, as a prime example, witnessed the presence of veiled and unveiled women, Muslim and Coptic prayers, and was very representative of all segments of the Egyptian population.

Religious slogans were seldom chanted by people in places like Tahrir Square and people were careful to carry banners and chant slogans that promoted and emphasized the ideals of 'democracy', 'citizenship' and 'brotherhood'. Given that such expressions continued throughout the course of events, it is only appropriate to conclude that these events and the people who brought them about were entirely disconnected from the implications of the false dichotomy of Arabism and Islamism (Atassi 2011, pp. 33–34).

The Arab Spring and a new Arab order

Burhan Ghalioun has made the remarkable observation that the Arabs of today are 'a complex social phenomenon and reality that the western concept of nation may not express and encompass' (Ghalioun 1993, p. 93). By implication, political unity need not be restricted to the level of the traditional nation-state and nor is it the automatic outcome of nationhood. Since in the Arab world the forces of unity along with the forces of fragmentation are all at work in a dialectical relationship, political unity may not necessarily result. Therefore *social* integration within each Arab state is more important for Arabism than any role the factors of nationalism may be able to play in realizing some form of Arab unity.

The history of the region suggests that no longer is Arabism a static desire isolated from and immune to changing circumstances. The lessons of experience indicate that Arab cooperation or integration needs to be based on factors other than the affectionate reproduction of a preconceived glorious notion of Arab history. It is not an embodiment of Arab identity or the mere unification of a politically fragmented nation. Arabism needs to be seen in future terms. It is a requirement for development. Therefore, the new Arabism is future oriented and not occupied with nostalgia for the past.

There are many indications that this new version is developing into a new paradigm of pan-Arabism that significantly differs from the romantic Arab nationalism of the 1950s and 1960s. The survey on Arab attitudes towards Arab unity referred to previously provides significant evidence that this new Arabism is strongly rooted in economic, legal and institutional forms of integration. The survey indicates that desired forms of pan-Arab cooperation and/or integration are related to the issues that may be seen as the roots and causes of the Arab Spring revolutions, i.e. concerned with economic issues in the first instance.

The survey results show that 70% are in favour of free cross-border labour movement, 79% in favour of free capital movement, 76% in favour of a pan-Arab monetary union, 68% in favour of common Arab school curricula, and 72% call for an elected pan-Arab parliament. In contrast, only 55% were in favour of complete Arab political unification, and only 14% were in favour of the status quo (Centre for Arab Unity Studies, 2012, pp. 19–31).

But despite the agreement that traditional Arabism has failed, and perhaps has ended, the popular expressions of the Arab Spring harbour no illusions. There are now more reasons to admit the birth of a new Arabism and see more elements of an arrival at maturity regarding the rationales for a 'new Arab order'. While not neglecting the role of media and foreign non-governmental organizations (NGOs) in spinning them, the fact that demonstrators in Arab Spring countries have chanted the same slogans and voiced almost entirely identical desires is a live testimony that pan-Arab identity has re-emerged again.

This is not, of course, to say that Arabs now will be politically united or that each Arab state will favour trading with fellow Arab states rather than, say, the Chinese, but to suggest that the Arab Spring creates a new context that brings into focus the centrality of common challenges (Gause 2011, pp. 7–8). Expressions of this phenomenon are evident in the regeneration of nationalist legends, symbols and ideals and this is a clear indication that Arabism may not simply wither away.[7]

Crowds were keen on categorically rejecting any hint of foreign interference in the Arab uprisings. Even in Libya while Gaddafi's killing machine was inflicting huge losses, Libyans were adamant in their rejection of the presence of any foreign sources or 'boots on the ground' on Libya's soil. Moreover, it is interesting to register the open expressions, albeit latterly, of anti-Zionist and pro-Palestinian sentiments amongst crowds protesting in Tunisia and Egypt accusing the dictators of betraying the Arab cause and being servants of or agents for Israel (Zurayk 2011, p. 124). In Libya, not only was Gaddafi accused of similar indictments, but also people went so far as to make accusations questioning his Arab roots. This is interesting since, as mentioned above, in the survey of the Arab Research Center, Israel was identified as the primary threat to collective Arab security.

Arab media and the new Arabism

As the foregoing discussions indicate, this new Arab Spring not only confirms the existence of a wider meta-state Arabism, but also highlights the influential role of pan-Arab media. A new Arabism has been the product of geopolitical factors with unifying effect. According to Yassine Temlali:

> One of these factors is undoubtedly the massive popular rejection of the foreign military presence in the Middle East, but long before these two uprisings [Tunisia and Egypt], the (satellite) TV channels had already helped to create a transnational milieu for Arab media and politics in which the same debates were raging. Their coverage … helped to shape a new, anti-imperialist unity of opinion among Arabs. (Temlali 2011, p. 48)

Transnational Arab media was instrumental in focusing the minds of its audience on the commonality of challenges and opportunities. Transnational media is affecting audience and shaping views through a process that has four complementary components. These include: an intensity of a shared experience and issue; the uniformity of language; direct exposure and engagement; and a cultural–emotive sensationalism (Rinnawi 2010, p. 268). Most of the methods and techniques deployed are based on developments in behavioural sciences exemplified in the work carried out at Stanford University in California and utilized by its Hoover Institute that has identified a key component of the so-called 'colour revolution' strategies as the use of a framing process that involves the creation and employment of slogans.

At another level of interaction and effect, the debates, news coverage and platforms they offer on air to ordinary Arabs, and their competition to attract audiences also proved instrumental in strengthening 'the unity of Arabic … modern Standard Arabic is now entering its golden age. Never before has the language been so unified' (Temlali 2011, p. 49). In addition to the factors behind the new development already noted, analysts highlight the significant role of modern-day communications technology – especially the Internet and satellite television.

These modern-day essentials 'are fueling the rise of a new common Arab consciousness every bit as real as the "imagined communities"' (Pintak 2012). Lawrence Pintak makes use of the imagined community concept advanced by Benedict Anderson in his classic work on nationalism (Anderson 2006). In his analysis, which also utilizes concepts from Hans Kohn, Ernest Gellner, James Piscatori and others, Pintak concludes that:

> this new electronically-enhanced 'imagined' Arab *watan* (nation) is bound together by many of the classic touchstones of nationalism theory: language, media and *ethnie* … television is helping to craft a new Arab consciousness that … superseded national borders and religious divisions … the result is an increasingly cohesive Arab consciousness. (Pintak 2012)

Empirical studies further support this assessment. Of particular significance are those conducted amongst Arab diasporas in Europe. These communities of the Arab diaspora living in the West are, *according to modernization theory*, more prone to be disenchanted with ideas such as pan-Arabism and ideology. However, the studies suggest that 'an essential implication of transnational media is the strengthening of ties and relationships to their Arab world on real and virtual levels' (Rinnawi 2010, pp. 267–268).

Khalil Rinnawi argues that this amounts to the creation of a discourse that lends support to the emergence of a kind of Arabism along the lines of the Andersonian model. Since actual linkage to the real community is not possible there emerges a virtual nationalism or 'McArabism'. Rinnawi notes that 'this MC Arabism extends beyond the traditional boundaries of the nation-state … and includes the Arabs in the Diaspora' (Rinnawi 2010, pp. 267–268). Any examination of the networks and modes of interaction of Arabs in diasporas indicates distinguishing behaviours among Arabs living outside the Arab world, such as immediately looking for other Arabs, Arab food markets and mosques. Right away after moving into a new location they locate these and integrate with each other.

This Arab consciousness may also be attributed to the effects of the now greatly facilitated dialogues that take place amongst Arab youth in particular. They are playing a vital role by utilizing:

> blogs [that] finally, may contribute to the rebuilding of transnational Arab identity by creating 'warm' relationships among otherwise distant Arab youth … bringing in new voices … and challenging the norms and expectations governing Arab public political discourse. (Lynch 2012a)

It is still too early to determine the extent to which these trends and attitudes depart from or conform to Arab–Islamic norms or to what extent they may be merely echoes of Westernization. Clearly some analysts see in these developments and indications the emergence of a new Arabism, McArabism, Virtual Arabism, Arab Public Sphere, a New Arab Street, Popular Arabism, etc.[8] The Arab Spring accordingly entails 'tracing the outlines of a new, pan-Arab unity of sentiment, based less on ethnic or racial considerations than on a broadly political stance: rejection of foreign domination, aspiration to freedom, belief in the possibility of change' (Temlali 2011, pp. 48–49).

Temlali does not hesitate in anticipating:

> another kind of Arabism [is] about to emerge into the light. If it is strongly anti-imperialist, this will not be solely because of the military powers occupation of Iraq, but also because of their ongoing support for the autocratic regimes in the Middle East and North Africa. (pp. 48–49)

This content of new Arabism finds its foundation in the nature of the uprisings and the reasons behind its success. These include, according to Adib Nehme, a 'demand for a modern, secular state with a model of governance based on dignity, justice, respect for human rights and the importance of rotation of power.' The presence of such ideas reminds us of the ideas underlying the first Arab Renaissance – the Nahdah. From this perspective, 'current events should be considered as the beginning of a movement which will result in a second Arab Renaissance during the era of globalization' (Nehme 2011, p. 103).

The paradigm of 'New Arabism'

Arabism has passed through three major stages since its early inception as a movement and conceptual and ideological trend directed against the Ottoman Empire. In its early stage Arabism was an expression of a desire for an independent Arab identity, entity or existence. Therefore, the primary objectives were the liberation of the Arabs first from the hegemony of the Turks, and later this crystallized in the struggle for freedom from European colonialism. The second major stage reflected a preoccupation with social change and development. Now, Arab states are independent and the objective was not the realization of freedoms and liberties for their citizens – this goal was to be postponed until social change and some degree of development and economic justice were attained.

This choice of priorities was based on the shallow belief that the attainment of such goals was on the horizon and that it would not be long before democracy and empowerment of the people politically would be achieved. However, such thinking proved erroneous and Arabism had to learn the painful lesson that democracy may not be compromised or postponed without risking the erosion of any social achievements that proved impossible to sustain without the protection of democracy. Arabism learnt this lesson the hard way. It took the Arab defeat in the 1967 'Six-Day' War with Israel and the death of Nasser to realize the need to reconsider the issue and revisit democracy. Therefore, Arab nationalist thought embarked on a process of revision in which democracy and human rights became essential components of a new paradigm of Arabism (Sawani 2003, pp. 206–227).

Arab thought has been obliged by circumstances and the frustrations it has encountered to rethink its concepts and ideas and hence restructure its problematique. Political Islam has proven a very decisive factor in making Arab intellectuals realize how important it is to think anew about the concept of Arabism. Such a fresh approach and new thinking was deemed a necessity that had to base its concepts on reality and not nostalgia.

In this new breed of Arab nationalist thought, Arabism is no longer seen as a reproduction of the past. Rather, it is conceived as a future project to be dictated by needs more than by identity and history. Arab unity is no longer seen as the contradiction of the state system. It is believed that such unity may not be accomplished through the destruction of the state system but through a democratic choice of these states whereby they maintain their existence and do not wither away.

The new paradigm calls for transcendence, assimilation and accommodation. This reflects the desire to transform the conflicting ideological theses into a productive disagreement from which can emerge a new paradigm of Arab thought. Ideology in the Arab world still does have a role to play. Nonetheless, it is clear that any new paradigm, if it is to gain approval, should not be based on the hegemony of any pan-Arab or pan-Islamist concept that does away with all differences and particularities. This in turn means that the new paradigm faces a fundamental challenge. The challenge is that of building on its ability to continue the process of renewal and bypassing or overcoming the contradictions.[9]

The new paradigm still has a long way to go in order to be rid of all theoretical, epistemological and ideological deficiencies. Priority must be given to eradicating animosities and building bridges. If Islamism appears to be the mainstream trend of the present-day Arab Spring, its advocacy should not evade understanding the dialectics of its relationship with other currents or trends and the implications of the change in the relevant weight of each component. Once these lessons are properly understood, Islamists may transcend the temptations of politics of the moment and what may turn out to be a short-lived victory.

One quite clear conclusion that may be drawn from the commonalities in events leading up to, during and after the Arab Spring is that of the evolution of a new popular paradigm. This popular paradigm stands to offer answers to deficiencies that hitherto had plagued Arabism. Contrary to this historical experience, it seems that there has emerged awareness that some form of cooperation or integration is indispensible.

According to the survey on Arab public opinion towards Arab unity, it is evident that Arabs today are more convinced of the necessity of greater Arab integration and cooperation. The fact that a great deal of interest in furthering pan-Arab links is readily available amongst ordinary Arabs strongly suggests the prevalence of a new Arabism. This new Arabism is certainly not just sentimental but is a reflection of the complexities of today's Arab concerns leading to bridging the gaps and revitalizing national economies in a very competitive globalized world (Samad and Mohamadieh 2011, p. 116).

The spillover effect was clearly evident in the events of the Arab Spring right from its initial start in Tunisia. The fact that people in the squares of Tunisia, Cairo and other cities were shouting similar slogans calling for dignity and freedom further enforces the links and echoes the reassertion of the regional dimension of a common sense of belonging (Samad and Mohamadieh 2011, p. 118). These events and their commonalities are indicative of the interaction of all elements of the Arab–Islamic historical mass driving change and may be seen as an early indication of the emergence of this line of strategic thinking (Arab Center for Research 2012a, pp. 21–26).

Therefore, the Palestinian issue will always figure prominently and it is certainly linked to any possible realization of Arab aspirations even in the narrowest economic sense (Arab Center for Research 2012a, pp. 21–26). This is closely connected to the challenge issues of a societal nature pose without any ideological camouflage and will in turn lead, by default, to yet more validation and affirmation of an Arab regional vision for integration and cooperation that will be further cemented by the desire for a just and lasting peace in the Middle East.

New Arab nationalist thought, new Arabism

As alluded to above, the Centre for Arab Unity Studies in Beirut has been at the forefront of structured activities dedicated and devoted to the renewal of Arab nationalist thought. The Centre was set up in 1975 by a group of Arab nationalists who were aware of the need to renew Arabism and Arab nationalism and remedy its deficiencies through research and studies devoted to such related issues. Therefore, the Centre's contribution is indicative of the long-term emergence of a new breed of Arab nationalism.

In its endeavour to nourish and consolidate the view that supports Arabism that best suits the needs and the challenges faced by contemporary Arabs, the Centre has been engaged in intellectual activities for more than 35 years.[10] The efforts of the Centre towards building a historical mass that can play the role of an engine for change in the region focused on realizing the recommendations of the research project on 'Future Prospects for the Arab Region' that the Centre completed by the end of 1987. It is important to note that the project anticipated, amongst others, a future scenario of 'Unionist or Federal Arab Unity' (Ma'n Bashour, 2012).

The achievement of this was deemed dependent on the evolution of a new pan-Arab movement that has a 'civilization project'. This project rests on six elements inextricably linked to each other, which include: Arab unity, democracy, independent development, social justice, national and Arab independence, and civilizational renewal (Centre for Arab Unity Studies 2010). In order to realize such objectives a dialogue between the pan-Arabist and other progressive forces, including Islamists committed to democracy, was deemed indispensible. Therefore, a seminar was held in Cairo in September 1979 with the participation of some 50 intellectuals representing both these broad trends (Centre for Arab Unity Studies 1987a). Specifically, this was an occasion for pan-Arabist and Islamist trends to reach common understandings and positions on many issues including the relationship between Arabism and Islam. The endeavour was vital in effecting their approaches and provided the rationale for the establishment of the 'Nationalist Islamist Conference' (Centre for Arab Unity Studies 1995).

The conference that was established in 1994 has proved successful in bridging the gaps that hitherto intervened between Arab nationalists and Arab Islamists. The ad hoc organization also adopted a political and intellectual programme (National Islamic Conference 1999). One of the direct results of the work of the new association of the representatives of the two trends was the discussion of a civilizational project. This discussion was very animated with the participation of all trends of Arab thought, and as was obvious in a large gathering of participants in a conference devoted to the issue held in Fez in 2001 (Center for Arab Unity Studies 2001). Apart from the strongly felt participation of Islamists in the conference, Islamists were very active in the subsequent steps up until the project was concluded and the first edition of its cumulative proceedings and conclusions was published in 2010 (Centre for Arab Unity Studies 2010).

This reflects the ongoing dialogue between Arabist and Islamist trends in Arab thought and political movements. It is important to register here that this dialogue has been based on a realization of the organic relationship between Arab nationalism and Islam. It is also important to note that such dialogue *preceded* the Iranian Revolution of 1979 and, therefore, may not be interpreted as an attempt by Arab nationalists to respond to a new phenomenon at the time and not necessarily to indigenous needs and challenges.

A review of the literature resulting from these activities attests to the emergence of a common position. In this common position a commitment of Islamists to the values and objectives of the new Arab–Islamic project is clearly in evidence. Also apparent was that the realization of a project of pan-Arabism requires a historical mass which can only exist and perform its historical role in realizing the desired change if it is based on the inclusion of all forces loyal to these values.

Arab nationalists have initiated the idea and the project and seem determined, in both heart and mind, on *inclusion*. It is now, however, incumbent on Islamists, the rising star of the post-Arab Spring elections, to display an adherence to what they have committed themselves to in the process. This is in addition to demonstrating that they have not been politically opportunistic by putting into action the commitments they had previously made now they have the opportunity to adopt at will their political programmes.

According to Khair El-Din Haseeb, the man behind much of the development of the concept and its practical details, the historical mass faces a serious risk if the orientations and positions of the Islamist trend are to be judged exclusively on concepts and slogans dominant in the past. Certainly there is a need to understand the intellectual and political developments that characterized this trend over the last 25 years and that they do not represent a completely unified or uniform mass. There exist differences in ideas and positions as we are indeed bound to witness in political programmes.

Haseeb argues that judging the Islamists merely on intentions and casting doubt on the credibility of their pronounced ideas is harmful. Any judgment will have to wait until the Islamists are well ensconced in political power (Haseeb 2011). The lessons drawn from the experience of Islamists in Kuwait, Jordan, Lebanon, and even Egypt and Tunisia supports Haseeb's view as far as democracy is concerned, as Islamists have so far honoured the results of elections and seem bound by the democratic principle. However, Haseeb warns that any overestimation of the results of elections in Tunisia and Egypt may lead to a euphoria and, hence, endanger objective perception. Any intention or temptation to hijack the electorate will hinder the process of the evolution of the historical mass to which Islamists have been and remain an integral part, if not by choice then out of necessity.

This is important to realize, particularly since the 'victory' Islamists achieved in the elections is by no means final and may prove to be short lived. Therefore, Haseeb advises Islamists to avoid any such temptations and not repeat the mistakes of Arab nationalist or leftist governments. Any attempt to monopolize politics will prove to be fatal to Islamists and hinder the realization of the new Arab renaissance project (Haseeb 2011).

Conclusions: Arabism – challenges and prospects

It follows from the discussion and analysis presented so far that the historical mass driving change faces today the challenge of yet many societal problems. The last decades have increased the level and intensity of communications between Arab states to unprecedented levels, which in turn strengthens the idea of Arabism. However, problems are evident in the fields of politics, economy and development. These problems and the challenges associated with their resolution have many commonalities that are shared by all Arab countries. Their most obvious manifestations are apparent in the problems the contemporary Arab faces and the difficulties he encounters while trying to attain some of his aspirations.

Consequently, ideologies and visions of an Arab order exclusively based on one particular trend or of a single stripe may no longer have or be capable of maintaining a hold over the region. Therefore, Arab politics may eventually be freed from absolutism and the damaging secular/religious dichotomy, which in turn may herald the birth of a post-Spring Arab politics built on the interaction of 'right and left-of-center national alliances, religious and secular, none of which appears, at least in the near future, to be able to dominate the entire political theater' (al-Rahim 2012).

The developments in the region in the last decade and the popular Arab Spring impelled the Egyptian writer–philosopher Hasan Hanafi to a degree of euphoria declaring that 'finally Arab unity … is an objective reality' (quoted in Lynch 2012b). Marc Lynch is supportive of this prognosis and affirms that 'this unified narrative of change, and the rise of a new, popular pan-Arabism directed against regimes, is perhaps the greatest revelation of the uprisings' (Lynch 2012b).

This view and determination is echoed in places that were long considered far from any affiliation to Arabism. An Editorial in the Saudi daily *Al-Riyadh*, while affirming the birth of a modern Arabism, states that:

> the freedom slogan marking the new Arab mobility will create a different philosophy. There is not any other alternative that may distort Arabism towards any other trend. Even the Islamic religion, the role of which many attempted to conceal or turn into a

terror tool against Muslims and other religions, and organized groups will find that its integration with the new movement liberates them from single-sided thought and desires to monopolize the other trend. (*Al-Riyadh Daily* 2011)

The Arab Spring may be still at its infancy stage and will have to accomplish a great deal. The challenges are enormous but it is evident that a historical mass for change will not take the 'Arab Spring' into adolescence unless it is successful in understanding the indigenous nature of the phenomenon or otherwise risk a fruitless winter. An inseparable link between Arabism and Islam has only one outcome, a new Arabism. A new Arabism that 'had been written off, but here, in full bloom, was what certainly looked like an awakening' (Ajami 2012a, p. 56). The Arab Spring and the centrality of democracy to its objectives is clearly in evidence in the ability of the Arab peoples to master their own destiny and take back the initiative, which for decades was monopolized as the sole preserve of the military and ideological elements. This shift is evidently indispensable to consolidating the foundations of any potential form of Arab integration or cooperation. The Arab Spring reflects a pan-Arab revolutionary spirit – to the dismay of those who proclaimed that Arabism was dead.

Notes

1. Ali Kawari, coordinator of the project for democracy studies in Arab countries, which has an annual meeting at St Catherine's College, Oxford, employs a modified concept of the historical mass for democratic change. Based on the contributions of Gramisci, Haseeb and others, Kawari defines the mass as composed of trends and political forces seeking and working together towards a transition to democratic regimes. The mass is 'an alliance for realizing the people's party for drafting and applying a democratic constitution' (al-Kuwari and al-Māḍī 2010, p. 40).
2. The Arab Spring is the subject of a growing body of literature and analyses. Examples are numerous, but of particular relevance, see Kneissl (2011), Al-Zubaidi (2011) and Phillips (2012).
3. This section draws heavily on Sawani (1996).
4. The 'Arab homeland' is a concept utilized in traditional Arab nationalist thought and its exponents to refer to the unity of the Arabs in a conscious rejection of terms such as 'the Arab World' that might imply fragmentation.
5. Numerous publications have appeared in Arabic on these issues; recent examples are Belkeziz (2001, 2011).
6. Translations of quoted material are by the author.
7. On the relationship between Arabism and economic interests, see Al-Yūsif (2011).
8. For an analysis of the role of the Internet and blogs in the Arab world, see Frierich Ebert Stiftung (2012) and Rinnawi (2006).
9. For a critique of the old paradigm and the substance of the new emerging paradigm, see the excellent treatment of Belkeziz (2010), esp. pp. 115–179.
10. Two important publications register this effort: the *Proceedings of the Seminar on Arab Nationalism and Islam* (Centre for Arab Unity Studies 1981) held prior to the Iranian revolution; and *Proceedings of the Seminar on contemporary Islamist movements in the Arab homeland* (Centre for Arab Unity Studies 1987b).

References

Ajami, Fouad, 2012a. The Arab Spring at one: a year of living dangerously. *Foreign Affairs*, 91 (2), 56.

Ajami, Fouad, 2012b. *The end of pan-Arabism*. Available from: http://www.foreignaffairs.com/articles/30269/fouad-ajami/the-end-of-pan-arabism [Accessed 21 May 2012].

Anderson, B., 2006. *Imagined communities: reflections on the origin and spread of nationalism*. London: Verso.

Arab Center for Research and Policy Studies, 2012a. *Geostrategic balances and interactions and the Arab revolutions*. March. Doha: Arab Center for Research and Policy Studies. Available from: http://www.dohainstitute.org/file/pdfViewer/12364757-aa51-4c5f-be8a-d5d3df803708.pdf [Accessed 21 May 2012].

Arab Center for Research and Policy Studies, 2012b. *The Arab Index 2011: an Executive Summary*. March. Doha: Arab Center for Research and Policy Studies. Available from: http://www.dohainstitute.org [Accessed 21 May 2012].

Atassi, Mohammed Ali, 2011. What the people want … revolutions for democracy. *In*: Layla Al-Zubaidi, ed. *People's power: the Arab world in revolt*. Heinrich Böll Stiftung, p. 33. Available from: http://www.ps.boell.org/downloads/02_Perspectives_ME_2011_The_Arab_World_in_Revolt.pdf.

Bashour, Ma'n, 2012. Ra'yun fī ta'āmul al-qawmīyīn ma'a ṣu'ūd al-islāmīyīn. *Al-Mustaqbal al-'Arabi*, no. 388 (May), 171–175.

Bazzi, Mohamed, 2012. The death of the Qaddafi generation: the era of Arab strongmen comes to an end. *Foreign Affairs*. Available from: http://www.foreignaffairs.com/articles/136603/mohamad-bazzi/the-death-of-the-qaddafi-generation [Accessed 21 May 2012].

Belkeziz, Abdelilah, 2001. *Riyāḥ al-taghyīr fī waṭan al-'Arabī*, November. Beirut: Centre for Arab Unity Studies.

Belkeziz, Abdelilah, 2010. *Naqd al-Khiṭāb al-Qawmī*. Beirut: Centre for Arab Unity Studies.

Belkeziz, Abdelilah, ed., 2011. *Al-Rabī' al-'Arabī ilā ayn?: ufuq jadīd li-taghyīr al-dīmūqrāṭī*. Beirut: Centre for Arab Unity Studies.

Center for Arab Unity Studies, 1981. *Al-Qawmīyah al-'Arabīyah wa al-Islām* [Proceedings of the Seminar on: Arab Nationalism and Islam]. Beirut: Centre for Arab Unity Studies.

Center for Arab Unity Studies, 1987a. *Al-Ḥiwār al-Qawmī al-Dīnī* [Proceedings of the Seminar on: The nationalist–religious dialogue]. Beirut: Centre for Arab Unity Studies.

Center for Arab Unity Studies, 1987b. *Al-Ḥarakah al-Islāmīyah al-Mu'āṣirah fī al-waṭan al-'Arabī* [Proceedings of the Seminar on Contemporary Islamist movements in the Arab homeland]. Beirut: Centre for Arab Unity Studies.

Center for Arab Unity Studies 2001, *Naḥwa Mashrū' Ḥaḍārī Nahḍawī 'Arabī* [Proceedings of the Seminar on Towards an Arab Civilisational Renaissance Project]. Beirut: Centre for Arab Unity Studies.

Centre for Arab Unity Studies, 1995. *Al-Mu'tamar al Qawmi al-Islami* [The National Islamic Conference]. Beirut: Centre for Arab Unity Studies.

Centre for Arab Unity Studies, 2010. *Al-Mashrū' al-Nahḍawī al-'Arabī* [The Arab Renaissance Initiative: the call for the future]. Beirut: Centre for Arab Unity Studies.

Centre for Arab Unity Studies, 2012. Arab public opinion towards Arab unity. Unpublished report. Beirut: Centre for Arab Unity Studies.

Frierich Ebert Stiftung, 2012. *The Internet in the Arab world: playground for political liberalization*. Available from: http://www.fes.de/IPG/arc_05_set/set_03_05d.htm [Accessed 21 May 2012].

Ganoushi, Rashid, 2012. Unpublished speech given at the Seminar on Revolution and Democratic Transition in the Arab World, organized by Centre for Arab Unity Studies, Tunis, Tunisia, 7 February 2012.

Gause, F.G., 2011. Why Middle East studies missed the Arab Spring. *Foreign Affairs*, July/August, 7–8.

Ghalioun, Burhan, 1993. *Al-Miḥnah al-'Arabīyah wa al-Dawlah ḍidd Al-Ummah*. Beirut: Centre for Arab Unity Studies.

Al-Hroub, Khalid, 2011. Al-Thawrāt al-'Arabīyah wa al-Niẓām al-'Arabī: al-tafkīk wa i'ādat al-tarkīb. *Shu'ūn 'Arabīyah*, 146 (Summer), 21.

Haseeb, Khair El-Din, 2011. Interview with the author, Beirut, 7 December 2011.

Kneissl, K., 2011. *Elements for a scientific analysis of the Arab Revolutions in spring 2011*. Available from: http://epub.oeaw.ac.at/;internal&action=hilite.action&Parameter=elements%20of%20scientific%20analysis%20of%20the%20arab%20revolutions&arp=0x00290d58/.

Korany, Bahgat, 2011. The Arab Spring, the new pan-Arabism and the challenges of transition. *In*: Bahgat Korany and Rehab El-Mahdi, eds. *The Arab Spring: revolution in Egypt and Beyond*. Cairo: American University of Cairo, 300–310.

al-Kuwari, 'Ali and 'Abd al-Fatāḥ al-Māḍī, 2011s. 'Ali 'Abd al-Fatāḥ al-Māḍī al-Kuwari, ed. *Naḥwa Kutlah Tārīkhīyah Dīmūqrāṭīyah fī al-Buldān al-'Arabīyah (Mashrū' Dirāsāt Dīmūqrāṭīyah fī al-Buldān al-'Arabīyah)*. Beirut: Centre for Arab Unity Studies.

Lynch, M., 2012a. *Blogging the new Arab public.* Available from: http://www. arabmediasociety.com/index.phparticle=10&p=1 [Accessed 21 May 2012].

Lynch, M., 2012b. *The big think behind the Arab Spring: do the Middle East's revolutions have a unifying ideology?* Available from: http://www.foreignpolicy.com/articles/2011/11/28/ the_big_think [Accessed 21 May 2012].

Ma'n Bashour, 2012. Ra'yun fī ta'āmul al-qawmīyīn ma'a su'ūd al-islāmīyīn. *Al-Mustaqbal al-'Arabi*, 388 (May), 171–175.

National Islamic Conference, 1999. *Al-Mu'tamar al Qawmi al-Islami fī Suṭūr* [The National Islamic Conference: a definition]. Beirut: National Islamic Conference.

Nehme, Adib, 2011. Wither the political and social movements in Arab countries: can we expect a new Arab renaissance? *In*: Layla Al-Zubaidi, ed. *People's power: the Arab world in revolt.* Heinrich Böll Stiftung, p. 103. Available from: http://www.ps.boell.org/downloads/02_Perspectives_ME_2011_The_Arab_World_in_Revolt.pdf.

Phillips, C., 2012. *Arabism after the Arab Spring.* Available from: http://cjophillips.wordpress. com/2011/07/31/arabism-after-the-arab-spring [Accessed 5 May 2012].

Pintak, L., 2012. *Architects of a new Arab consciousness.* Available from: http://dartcenter.org/ content/new-mission-for-arab-media [Accessed 5 May 2012].

Al-Rahim, Ahmed, 2012. *Whither political Islam and the 'Arab Spring'.* Available from: http:// www.iasc-culture.org/publications_article_2011_Fall_al-Rahim.php [Accessed 21 May 2012].

Rinnawi, Khalil, 2006. *Instant nationalism: McArabism, al-Jazeera and transnational media in the Arab world.* Baltimore, MD: University Press of America.

Rinnawi, Khalil, 2010. Arab diaspora in Germany. *In*: A. Alonso and P.J. Oiarzabal, eds. *Diasporas in the new media age: identity, politics, and community.* Reno, NV: University of Nevada Press, p. 268.

Al-Riyadh Daily, 2011. Editorial. *Al-Riyadh Daily*, 1 March. Available from: http://www. alriyadh.com/2011/03/01/article609383.htm/.

Salman, Talal, 2011. Editorial: The revolution fights Arabism with Islam. *Al-Safir (Beirut)*, 16 November. Available from: http://www.assafir.com/article.aspx?EditionId=2004&Chann elId=47472&ArticleId=1466 [Accessed 21 May 2012].

Samad, Ziad Abdel and Mohamadieh, Kinda, 2011. The revolutions of the Arab Spring: socio-economic questions at the heart of successful ways forward. *In*: Layla Al-Zubaidi, ed. *People's power: the Arab world in revolt.* Heinrich Böll Stiftung, p. 116. Available from: http://www.ps.boell.org/downloads/02_Perspectives_ME_2011_The_Arab_World_in_Revolt.pdf.

Sawani, Youssef, 2003. *Al-Qawmīyah wa al-waḥdah fī al-Fikr al-Siyāsī al-'Arabī.* Beirut: Centre for Arab Unity Studies.

Sawani, Youssef Mohamed, 1996, Arab political thought on Arab nationalism and unity: the 1980s and the dialectic of old and new paradigms. Uunpublished PhD dissertation, University of Kent, Canterbury.

Temlali, Yassine, 2011. 'The Arab Spring' rebirth or final throes of pan-Arabism? *In*: Layla Al-Zubaidi, ed. *People's power: the Arab world in revolt.* Heinrich Böll Stiftung, pp. 48–49. Available from: http://www.ps.boell.org/downloads/02_Perspectives_ME_2011_The_Arab_World_in_Revolt.pdf.

Yaakoub, Hussein, 2011. Revolutions for democracy. *In*: Layla Al-Zubaidi, ed. *People's power: the Arab world in revolt.* Heinrich Böll Stiftung, p. 40. Available from: http://www.ps.boell. org/downloads/02_Perspectives_ME_2011_The_Arab_World_in_Revolt.pdf.

Al-Yūsif, Yūsif Khalīfah, 2011. *Majlis al-Ta'āwun al-Khalījī fī Muthalath al-wirāthah wa al-Nafṭ wa al-Quwwā al-Ajnabīyah.* Beirut: Centre for Arab Unity Studies.

Al-Zubaidi, Layla, ed., 2011. *People's power: the Arab world in revolt. Perspectives* Special Issue. Heinrich Böll Stiftung. Available from: http://www.lb.boell.org/web/52-579.html/.

Zurayk, Rami, 2011. Feeding the Arab uprising. *In*: Layla Al-Zubaidi, ed. *People's power: the Arab world in revolt.* Heinrich Böll Stiftung, p. 124. Available from: http://www.ps.boell. org/downloads/02_Perspectives_ME_2011_The_Arab_World_in_Revolt.pdf.

Index

Note: references to Tables and Figures appear in bold type

a-ʿAdl 210–11
active population 35
actors of social movements 22–7
AD 211–12
Algeria 13, 101–2, 114, 121
Al Jazeera 25, 243–4
Al-Riyadh 307–8
Amazigh 142–4
Association Marocaine des Driots Humains (AMDH) 210
American hegemony 27
anxiety over understanding 52–3
Arab autocracy 58
Arab consciousness 116
Arab Fund for Economic and Social Development 34
Arab future 109–11
Arab League 10, 14
Arab media 118, 302–3
Arab modernity 290–1
Arab monarchies: Morocco, and 196–8
Arab Monetary Fund 34
Arab players: role of 14
Arab politics 299–300
Arab public opinion 297
Arab regimes: attitudes 2
Arab rentier economy 47–8
Arab revolutions: co-optation of 74
Arab Spring: terminology 1
Arab youth 21
Arabism and Islamism 297–9
arenas of struggle 67
audiovisual communication 63–4
authoritarian regimes 20–2
Axis of Evil 72
axis of moderation 28

Bacon, Francis 286
bad growth 34; shifting to virtuous growth 43–7
Bahrain 8–9, 106, 113, 120–1, 276–81; avoidance of violence 279–80; demonstrations 8; effect of revolutionary wave 276–7; future developments 280; reconciliation committee 9; repercussions of Arab movements 276; return of demonstrators to roundabout 278–9; unhealthy political atmosphere 280–1; vacillation between security and political concern 277–8
barrier of fear 1–2, 4
beating heart of the revolution 81
Belkeziz, Abdelilah 52
body of the revolution 81
brain drain 36–8; curbing 45–6
brutality of negotiations 82
budget deficits 44

catalogue of failures 95–6
Challand, Benoit 23
chaos: central tendency towards 73; hierarchy of 78–80
China: economic interests 120
Chinese experiment 161
Chomsky, Noam 248–9
civil state 27
climate change 19–20
combined dynamic model of work mechanisms of creative destruction **88**
communication revolution 80–3
communication technology 99–100
Comte-Sponville, Andre 53
conflict revolution 61
conflicting axes 75
contagion 100
Copts 217–37; analysis of research 223–5; common assumptions 218–19; deepening social divisions 227–8; demands inclusion 234–7; economic exclusion 221–2; exclusion 217–37; future developments 228–91; geographical scope of survey 221; inclusion 217–37; minority concept 226; Mubarak regime, and 229; perceiving exclusion 231–4; political demands 223; political exclusion 223; primary personal data 231; primary research hypothesis 219–

20; questionnaire 220; research findings 221; research questions 225–8; sample distribution **221**; social demands 222–3; social exclusion 222–3; statistical methods 221
counter-revolution 83
corruption 19; curbing 45
creative destruction 71–91; American 72; authoritarian justifications 76–8; autocratic approach 76; polarization projects 75–6
cultural power 18
current account deficits 44
currents of chaos 80
cyber-mobilization 81
cyberspace 24

decisive factors 15
democracy; battle over and within 58–63; cost of transitioning to 63–8; establishment of 115; rejection of 94; transition to 55; Tunisia 5
democratic choice 54
democratic question: complexity of 56–7
democratic transformation: five tasks 57
demographic factors 18–20
despots: collapse of 94–5
determinism 52
developing non-violent outrage 82
development aid 37
dialogue 59–60
dignity 28
direct military intervention: failure of 74
domino effect 28
dynamic waves of the revolution **82**

economic and social developments: failure 96–8
economic indicators 18–20
economic returns 47–8
economic support: need for 120
Economist Intelligence Unit 20 economic returns 47–8
education 98–9
Egypt 5–6, 116; Arab vacuum, and 99; church-state relation 226–7; Copts 217–37; economic policy 217; free elections 6; religion and politics 225–6; security forces 5; state-society relations 225; the other 226; transitional period 6
electronic chaos 81
electronic contestation 80
emigration 36–8
end of Arabism 295–310
Engels, Friedrich 287
Ennasir 207, 209
Economic and Social Commission for Western Asia (ESCWA) 36
ethnicity 28–9
EU: double standarads 119
external variables: economic growth rate, and 36
external trade: deficiencies 41–3

Facebook 238, 239, 241–2, 244–5
factors for uprisings 4
fatalism 52
Fayyad, Dr Salam 286–7
February 20th movement 175, 178, 179–80, 193–6, 200
foreign investment 38–9
foreign powers: role of 2
foreign trade deficits 41–3
Foucault, Michel 50–1
Free Syrian Army 11
future developments 3

Ghannouchi, Rashid 288
Gladwell, Malcolm 240–1
globalization 85–7; lobbies for 74
Gulf Cooperation Council 6, 113
Gulf Marshall Plan 76

Hanafi, Hasan 307
high-risk political activism 24–5
historical bloc 118
historical perspective 92–4
history of protest 18
human rights: Morocco 189–90, 203–4, 208–9
human rights associations 23

illiteracy: suppressing 47
International Monetary Fund (IMF) 33–4, 44
Indonesia 13; per capita GDP 38
inequality 19
informal sector: integrating 46
information: loss of monopoly 94
inheritance of political rule 77
international community: double standards 15
International Finance Corporation 41
international legislation: Morocco, and 191
international players: role of 14
Internet: Egypt, in 242–3
intifada 51
invaders 86
investments: diversification 45–6; high concentration 38–9
Iran 13
Iraq 104
Islamic fronts and currents 117
Islamists 201
Israel: creation 92–3, negative position 119

joint investments 75

Jordan 12–13, 101, 113, 121; constitutional amendments 12; population 12
journalism 65–6
Justice and Charity association 206

knowledge 98–9
Kuwait 13

labels 17–18
labour movement 26
law of rules 20
Lebanon 13, 114
Libya 104–6, 120, 153–8; Arab-Islamic identity 157; army 157; constitutional system 156; democratic rotation of power 156; democratic system 155; foreign intervention 154–5; funds 157; hopes and fears 153–8; intervention of foreign forces 157; just socio-economic system 156; National Transitional Council 8,154; political pluralism 155; role in new Arab order 157; representation system 156; separation of powers 156; violence 7
listening 60
Locke, John 285

Machiavelli 59
markets: speculative nature 44–5
Marx, Karl 50–1, 287
Mauritania 13, 114
media 2–3, 63–8; role of 13
military:stance of 5
military elite 28
Mill, John Stuart 285
Mohammed Ali Atassi 300
monarchies 106–8
Moroccan liberal space 202–5
Morocco 11, 107, 114, 121, 173–99; absolute monarchy 177; Arab monarchies, and 196–8; balance of powers 187–8; consensual rotation 125; consensus 184–5; constitutional amendments 11, 173–99; criticism of constitutional amendment 183; democratic bloc 175, 189; democratic transition 173–99; diverse cultural and linguistic demands 186; divided political groups 185; February 20th Movement 175, 178, 179–80, 193–6; generation gap 178; grant constitution 176; human rights 189–90; implied constitution 177; independent powers of parliament and government 189; influence on other regimes 196–8; international legislation, and 191; king, powers of 188; left-wing organizations 182; nationalist movement 182; nature of constitutional text 184; opposition, rights of 190–1; paradox of political system 176; parliamentary monarchy 191–3; parliamentary monarchy, demand for 181–2; participatory governance 188; Petition for Independence 174; religion and state 186; will of the king 178; youth, mobilization of 179
multiplicity/ pluralism 54–8
Muslim Brotherhood 252–67; constitutional referendum 256; economy, and 262–7; Egyptian elections, and 252–67; elections of 2010 254–5; FJP progress 261–2; January 25 revolution 255–6; obstacles 257–9; opportunities 257; People's Assembly elections 263; political aspirations 261–2; popularity 260–1; post-Mubarak 257–9; state, and 253–4

Nasser, Jamal Abdul 93
national innovation: absence of systems to support 39–41
national liberation 92
NATO: Libya, and 7, 15
neo-liberal creed 44
neoliberal individualism 23
new Arab nationalist thought 305–7
new Arab order 301–2
new Arabism: paradigm 303–5
new loyalty 53
new political subjectivity 17–32
NGOs 23
Nichane 202–3
non-violent revolt 4

Oman 11–12, 106, 113
online petition 241
opposition politics in the Arab world 201–2
Orientalist terms 17
outside intervention 115

Palestinian Authority 101
Palestinian youth 282–94; Arab modernity, and 290–1; complexity of modernity 288–90; idols versus rationality 285–8; impact of Arab Spring 283–5; liberal democracy, concept of 291; modernity, and 292–3; philosophy class discussions 285–8; public debates 283
pan-Arab media 33
pan-Arabism 295–310
Party for Justice and Development 206
patrilinear family structures 23–4
planing to counter ridicule 82
political demonstrations 79
political imagination 51
political institutions 23
political Islam in Morocco 200–16
political system: failure 95

post-Gaddafi Libya 123–52; Amazigh 142–4; centrality of transitional phase 130–4; challenges 144–8; challenges of modernization 127–8; civil society 141–2; constraints of future 124; Febuary 17th Coalitions 136–7; future developments 148–9; influx of international powers 123–4; Islamist groups 137–9; liberal currents 140; local councils 136; nationalist currents 140; National Transitional Council 134–6; non-Islamist currents 140; oil 127–8; opportunities 144–8; perpetual dynamics 128–30; religion and politics 124–5; secularist currents 140; topography of institutionalized forces 134; tribalism and political authority 125–7
poverty indicators 35–6
pragmatism 208–12
private-public partnership 46
private sector:accountability 45
private sector: social responsibility 45

Qadhafi, Colonel 153

Ramadan, Tareq 25
rating agencies 44–5
Rawls, John 61
reflexive individualism 18
reflexive Islamism 26–7
regional Arab regimes: positions of 118
regional players: role of 14
religious ideology 208–12, 213
rentier economies 43
research and development 98–9; low level 39–41
revolution: nature of 73; use of term 114–15
revolution of democracies 74–5; use of term 114–15
rule of law 20
rural areas 47
Russia: economic interests 120

sacralization of public space 202
Salafi Jihad 207
salaries, stagtation of 35
Saudi Arabia 13, 106–7, 121: opposition 268–70; opposition after 9/11 270–1; reform proposals 274–5
Saudi elites 273
Saudi-Iranian strategic skirmishing 86
Saudi leadership 271–2
Saudi street 268–75
Saudi youth 273–4
savage capitalism 78
scenarios of construction 83–5
science and technology: fragmentation of systems 39–40
sectarianism 28–9
secular/ religious dichotomy 307
slogans 117
social cohesion 4–5
social means of communication 117–18
social media 13, 99–100; meaning 239
social media in Egyptian revolution 238–51; outcome 248–9
socio-economic factors 18–20, 33–49
social protests 79
spectacle 51
state apparatus: complexity 21
state of exception 21–2
Sudan 13, 101
Sultan Qaboos 11–12
Syria 9–11, 102–4, 113–14, 121, 159–72; compound crises 166; demands for structural reform 162; deprivation 164; destructive confleict 169; divided population 9; farmers 165; food distribution 163; foreign military intervention, danger of 171–2; impasse 10; Islamist opposition 169; Israeli occupation, and 164; new historic bloc 170; ongoing struggle 159; participants in uprisings 168–9; political sphere 160–3; possible solutions 170; regime, reaction of 166; sectarianism 169; security solution 167–8; social distribution 160; social insurrection 165; social structure 160–1; social trends 163–4; torture of children 167; violence 9–11; youth, demands of 162–3
Syrian Observatory of Human Rights 21–2

tax system: reviewing 47
television 64–5
the future of the past 55
thought: influence 54
tourism 36
trade balance 41–3
traditional phenomena 62
trafficking in protection 75
transition: challlenges 108–9
tribalism 28–9
Triple F crisis 19
Tunisia 5, 107, 116, 117; component factors 5; democracy 5
Twitter 239, 240, 241–2, 246–8
the United Arab Emirates (UAE) 13

unemployment 19, 35
United Nations Educational, Scientific and Cultural Organisation (UNESCO) 40–1
upgrading Arab authoritarianism 205
US: double standards 119

violence 58–9

War on Terror 72
Washington consensus 44
Western democracy: contradiction of 290–1
Western imperialism 25
Western media 33
World Bank 34

Yemen 6–7, 100–1, 113; Friday of Anger 6; Friday of No Return 6

youth: mindset of 296; new political subjectivity 22–6
youth revolutions 117
YouTube 238, 239, 241–2, 246